THE

NIXON

EFFECT

*How Richard Nixon's Presidency
Fundamentally Changed American Politics*

Douglas E. Schoen

Encounter Books
New York • London

First American edition published in 2016 by Encounter Books,
an activity of Encounter for Culture and Education, Inc.,
a nonprofit, tax-exempt corporation.
Encounter Books website address: www.encounterbooks.com

Manufactured in the United States and printed on
acid-free paper. The paper used in this publication meets
the minimum requirements of ANSI/NISO Z39.48–1992
(R 1997) (*Permanence of Paper*).

FIRST AMERICAN EDITION

LIBRARY OF CONGRESS CATALOGING-IN-PUBLICATION DATA
Schoen, Douglas E., 1953–
The Nixon Effect : How Richard Nixon's Presidency Fundamentally Changed American
Politics / Douglas E. Schoen.
pages cm
Includes index.
ISBN 978-1-59403-799-3 (hardcover: alk. paper)—ISBN 978-1-59403-800-6 (e-book)
1. Nixon, Richard M., 1913–1994—influence. 2. United States—politics and
government—1969–1974. 3. United States—politics and government—1989– I. Title.
E856.S285 2015
973.924092—dc23

2015010956

Contents

Walking in Nixon's Shadow

I believe the second half of the 20th century will be known as the age of Nixon. Why was he the most durable public figure of our time? Not because he gave the most eloquent speeches, but because he provided the most effective leadership. Not because he won every battle, but because he always embodied the deepest feelings of the people he led.

—BOB DOLE, AT RICHARD NIXON'S FUNERAL, APRIL 27, 1994[1]

[Nixon] was the inventor of the wedge issue, and his effort to Republicanize the South post-Lyndon Johnson because of civil rights helped redefine the parties. When there was no [longer] a conservative bloc within the Democratic Party, that pushed the Democrats to the left and the Republicans to the right.

—JOHN DEAN[2]

[Nixon] may never be fully understood by the historians and biographers who attempt to put a label on him. Even with his resignation, however, it is indisputable that he was and will likely always be one of America's most significant presidents, one whose actions had among the most far-ranging consequences of any man to occupy the Oval Office.

—PETER ROFF, *U.S. NEWS & WORLD REPORT*[3]

For forty years, Richard Nixon has been held up as the symbol of all that is corrupt and wrong about American politics. Despite his substantial accomplishments, Nixon became reviled across the political spectrum. Elected in reaction to the upheavals of the 1960s, he was always hated by the Left on the basis of being the dark and sinister figure who squelched the glorious social experiment of the counterculture. The Right never liked or trusted him either, preferring ideologically purer politicians. After Watergate, the Middle Americans of his silent majority abandoned him, and the elite media has always portrayed his presidency through the lens of its inglorious end, which became a mythic (and self-congratulatory) episode in American newspapering.

Beneath the hatred, however, lies a different reality. The shadow of Watergate obscures one of the most consequential and even salutary

American presidencies of the twentieth century. In my view, historians have yet to grasp the full scale and implications of Nixon's legacy, especially the broadly positive influence of his policies, his impact on the ideological formation of the two major parties, and his formative influence on modern politics and campaign strategy. Nixon's influence is so overarching that I have no hesitation in declaring him to be the most important American politician of the postwar era—for *both* parties.

Why Nixon? some readers may ask. If our focus is on presidential achievement, why not Ronald Reagan or Lyndon Johnson, both of whom, from different ideological poles, effected profound changes for the United States? If our focus is instead turned to the degree of influence on our politics, why not Barack Obama, with the divisions he has fostered with his health care law; or George W. Bush, with his Iraq War and War on Terror; or even Bill Clinton, with his sex scandal and impeachment struggle? Indeed, our three most recent presidents have been participants in—and, their detractors would say, purveyors of—a political climate that for two decades has grown increasingly polarized. Yet, as I will show, all of these politicians inherited, in some form or another, the divisions that Nixon identified, exploited, and to some extent perpetuated. In most of the key battles of not just the Obama, Bush, and Clinton years but even of those going further back, Nixon's footprints can be clearly seen. In cultural politics, too, Nixon's impact on American life remains profound: he is the spiritual father of the now well-known Red-and-Blue division that continues to shadow our electoral map.

It is the argument of this book, then, that Richard Nixon is the central figure behind the identification, articulation, and exploitation of America's contemporary political divisions—between urbanites and city dwellers, liberals and conservatives, patriots and critics, and hawks and doves. But it is also the argument of this book that Nixon is the central figure in laying the template for transcending these divisions politically and electorally, and that the presidents who have followed him have failed to unite the electorate when they forgot Nixon's lessons—when, as I put it, they didn't listen to Nixon.

Nixon was both divider and uniter—he united by dividing, in fact. In his case, that meant separating the electorate into a vast and electorally unbeatable silent majority, on one side, and a much smaller but impassioned political base, known variously as "the counterculture," "the peaceniks," and "the liberals," on the other. Nixon presided in explosive times, when tempers in American politics ran hot, and when the nation seemed at times about to split at the seams—and yet, in running for reelection in 1972, he marshaled his silent majority into the greatest landslide in American history, winning forty-nine states, 61 percent of the popular vote, and 515 electoral votes. If that's what we see as "division," the United States today could use more of it.

Before proceeding further, it's important to articulate how profoundly at odds this argument is with the conventional views of Nixon held in August 1974, when he resigned the presidency in disgrace and was written off as a political force. To be sure, that judgment modulated as the years passed and as Nixon, as I show in my chapter on his post-presidency, proved, once again, the depth of his political insights. Over the last forty years, Nixon has been acknowledged as a master statesman for opening US relations with Beijing, and for pioneering détente with the Soviet Union. On the fortieth anniversary of Nixon's resignation, in 2014, pundits across the spectrum acknowledged his tremendous political acumen and achievements in foreign policy. Even liberal critics conceded that he was a man of great intellectual gifts.

At the same time, however, Nixon's fundamental image has not changed all that much. Nixon is widely portrayed as a racist, for example—and to be sure, he does himself no favors in that regard on the White House tapes. He is seen on racial issues as a backward politician, one whose Southern strategy helped set the stage for more subtle but potent racial appeals to the electorate that have continued to the present day. "The worst thing Richard Nixon ever did was tell racists they had a point and welcome them into the party of Lincoln," wrote *Washington Post* columnist Richard Cohen. "The best thing he ever did for the Democratic Party is give its racists a place to go."[4]

Yet the truth is far more complex, as I will show.

Similarly, Nixon is seen as a warmonger—the man who dropped an untold tonnage of bombs on North Vietnam in his desperate attempt to win the unwinnable Vietnam War. His invasion of Cambodia was not only illegal and immoral, critics say, but it also set off the last great wave of US domestic antiwar protests, which culminated in the tragedies at Kent State and Jackson State. And his Christmas bombings of 1972 were widely decried as bloodthirsty. "To send B-52s against populous areas such as Haiphong or Hanoi could have only one purpose: terror," wrote Anthony Lewis. "It was the response of a man so overwhelmed by his sense of inadequacy and frustration that he had to strike out, punish, destroy."[5] The truth here, too, is more complex.

And finally, Nixon is still remembered by many as our criminal president, the only one ever to resign the nation's highest office. John Dean, who served as Nixon's White House counsel, helped engineer the Watergate cover-up, and then served as a witness for the prosecution, has written several books about the Nixon years. His most recent, in 2014, ironically titled *The Nixon Defense*, exhaustively chronicled the cover-up in day-by-day detail. The book "will remind people of why Nixon deserves so unflattering a historical reputation, despite the opening to China and détente with the Soviet Union," wrote historian Robert Dallek. "It should also serve as a renewed cautionary tale about elevating politicians with questionable character to high office."[6]

"I think we should celebrate August 9 as a day of national liberation every year," Democratic strategist Frank Mankiewicz said. "Every country celebrates the day the government got rid of its tyrants. We should too."[7]

Nixon's negative image is enduring across age groups. Those old enough to have lived through Nixon's presidency tend to have hardened views of his misdeeds, while those born after his tenure are even less inclined to give him a fair shake, more or less accepting the verdict of history.

I should make clear that I carry no brief as a defender of Nixon on the Watergate affair. It's clear to me from extensive reading of the Watergate literature that Nixon was willing to do things that few if any presidents would have seriously considered—ordering burglaries of private citizens' medical files and break-ins to safes that contained sensitive documents, and using the Central Intelligence Agency to obstruct a criminal investigation by the FBI, among other things. I believe that the House of Representatives' decision to vote impeachment articles against the president in August 1974 was justified, and that President Nixon's subsequent decision to resign the office, rather than face that ordeal, was the right one. He had lost the capacity to lead and squandered his moral and legal authority. Watergate will always shadow his reputation and legacy.

But to see Watergate as the *primary* Nixonian legacy, especially in light of the scandals that have followed, is to miss the range of Nixon's achievements. A close examination of the Nixon record reveals that few presidents achieved as much on a substantive, and enduring, level as he did. This most controversial and detested of American politicians created a new American governing coalition—one predicted by the writer and political commentator Kevin Phillips in his seminal book *The Emerging Republican Majority*—that became the dominant force in presidential elections for a generation. And no candidate owned that new majority more than Nixon: his forty-nine-state landslide in 1972 is the greatest wipeout in American history.[8] No politician can achieve that degree of consensus without great political skill and a deep attunement to the wishes of the electorate.

What were those wishes? Put most broadly, Americans of Nixon's time wanted a general continuation of the domestic liberal consensus that had prevailed since FDR: They were looking for maintenance and even some expansion of the New Deal social programs, especially those geared toward the middle class. They wanted progress in racial relations and equality, but without the fevered confrontational style of the 1960s—and certainly without the rising crime and sense of menace that had started to permeate American life. Americans wanted law and order and a return to some form of social stability. All of these things Nixon strove to provide, in policies or in rhetoric, or in both. He saw himself, in fact, as a "Disraeli conservative," a leader who could offer a "strong foreign policy, strong adherence to basic values that the nation believes in, combined with reform, reform that will work, not reform that destroys."[9]

Nixon's domestic-policy approach has often been characterized as canny and shrewd, even Machiavellian—but I think that misses the mark. To be sure, Nixon was a pragmatist, and as a president whose chief passion was foreign policy, he did regard domestic policy more flexibly than he regarded the great issues of statesmanship. Yet, at the same time, his approach also represented a more coherent, visionary program than either ideologically committed liberals or staunch conservatives could offer. His program was, in the end, a response to the moods and needs of the American people at this time. It was a philosophy of responsiveness that Republicans today have for the most part abandoned.

On foreign policy, too, Americans of Nixon's era wanted an approach that reflected a proud but pragmatic people's approach to the world: They were interested in self-defense and self-interest, a strong defense of our ideals and values, and the flexibility to make accommodations where necessary and possible in a dangerous world. What Nixon gave them, in bringing the Vietnam War to an end, in ending the military draft, and especially—and most historically—in forging new relations with Communist China and less hostile relations with the Soviet Union, was the embodiment of this complex and necessarily imperfect approach. Nixon is best remembered today for his foreign policy achievements, and for good reason, as I'll examine in detail in chapter 2.

Nixon's impact, then, is enduring, and the lessons of his presidency remain transcendent, despite the impact of his bad acts. That's the message of this book.

There were many ironies to Richard Nixon's career. He was the red-baiting young politician who helped bring down Alger Hiss, who called Senator Helen Gahagan Douglas "pink right down to her underwear,"[10] and who mixed it up with Nikita Khrushchev in the famous Kitchen Debate—yet he was also the American president who went to Beijing and forged a new American relationship with China.

He was the candidate, and president, who skillfully played on the political fears of whites and the working class with his Southern strategy and identification of the silent majority—yet he was also the president whose record on civil rights completely outstripped Jack Kennedy's and that stands as a worthy successor to that of Lyndon Johnson.

In this book, I'll examine one of the least known Nixon paradoxes: it was Nixon, a nonideological thinker, for the most part, who more than anyone else pushed the two parties further out to their ideological poles, but it was also Nixon who devised ingenious political strategies for navigating between them. The man who continues to stir up so much passion today was a consummate centrist, a pragmatic politician who nevertheless understood how to play on ideological loyalties with the skill of a maestro. Where major ideological realignments developed all around him—and often as a result of, or in response to, him—Nixon himself was nimble and adaptable. Smarter than his adversaries and supporters, he managed to confound both.

Nixon did all of this despite the fact that not just Democrats but also Republicans rejected, or claimed to reject, his political approach. In addition to being hated by liberals and Democrats, Nixon was also distrusted by Republican conservatives for his moderate domestic policies and *realpolitik* foreign policy. At the same time, the Right emulated his approach to cultural issues and New Democrats like President Bill Clinton explicitly built on his "triangulation" approach. He was the most successful politician of his era and unquestionably the smartest political operator the Republican Party ever had. In the end, Watergate gave both parties license to disown him—but neither party would be able to escape him.

Shaping Party Ideology and Identity

More than any other politician, Richard Nixon has shaped the ideological identities of the two parties today.

He has done this on the Republican side in two ways: first, by providing the party with conceptual formulations and concrete political strategies that have shaped its positioning ever since, and second by inadvertently prompting a conservative upheaval in the Republican Party through his centrist, even liberal, policies.

Nixon's impact on the ideological positioning of the GOP cannot be understood without understanding the context of the 1964 election, when President Lyndon Johnson crushed the Republican contender, Barry Goldwater, by what was then the largest margin in history and the Democrats won their largest majority in Congress since Roosevelt. At that time, Republicans held only seventeen of the nation's fifteen governorships. The Goldwater campaign was regarded as an historic presidential debacle, causing some to wonder about the future of the Republican Party. Yet the Democratic Party was also deeply in flux, mostly due to the Vietnam War. In spite of Johnson's powerful 1964 victory, his popularity waned as the war dragged on. He faced steep opposition from within his own party, embodied by such figures as the antiwar activist Allard Lowenstein and Senator Eugene McCarthy.[11] In 1968, the Democratic Party suffered a traumatic collapse symbolized by the street violence that took place outside the Democratic National Convention in Chicago.

Thus, the two major parties were both in turmoil in 1968. The Republicans, suffering as a result of their rightward turn in 1964, were struggling for a new identity. The Democrats were divided and leaderless. It was a perfect storm for the ideological realignment that was to come. And here is where Nixon entered the picture. (Or reentered it: Nixon had, of course, run as the Republican nominee for president in 1960, losing the narrowest election in history, and before that he served eight years as Dwight Eisenhower's vice president.)

The remarkable thing about Nixon's influence in pushing the GOP to the right is that Nixon himself was hardly an ideological conservative. He had a troubled relationship with the intellectuals who had forged the conservative movement, as well as with conservative Southern politicians. *National Review* refused to endorse Nixon for president in 1960; when the magazine decided to back him in 1968, it did so mostly for pragmatic reasons. Yet after Nixon, the Republican Party was primed for a conservative revolution. How did this happen?

Perhaps Nixon's most enduring influence on the GOP today is his formulation of conservative populism—a force that first took shape in his 1968 campaign and that, nearly half a century later, is still the vital engine powering the American Right, from the Tea Party to talk radio. Nixon put conservative populism on the map by pioneering a new target of populist opposition: not big business and the rich per se—the usual targets of FDR and other Democrats—but rather the intelligentsia, whether in the media, the academy, or the professions. Nixon portrayed these groups as privileged, out-of-touch mandarins no longer fit for governance.

Like all populist appeals, this one had a class-based element—but Nixon's class arguments were based on culture and values, not economics. Nixon helped show Republicans that they could borrow a traditionally Democratic strategy and make it work for them. And his timing was exquisite—the late 1960s, when the promises of liberalism's "best and brightest" lay in shards, from Watts, to the War on Poverty, to South Vietnam. Nixon's identification with ordinary Americans—he called them the "silent majority"—inspired conservatives and rallied them to his side, at least for a time.

To be sure, Nixon made race a political hot button in ways that continue to influence the GOP. He did this, most importantly, through his Southern strategy in 1968, in which the Republican candidate sought to sweep Southern states by playing on the resentments of white voters—some of them were threatened by the civil rights movement and explicitly antiblack in their views, and others were angered by the aggressive agenda of the Johnson administration and how it signaled Washington's increasing willingness to impose mandates on states in the most explosive areas of social life. Though he never made this an explicit pitch, Nixon's message unquestionably had racial undertones: he tapped into white fears, not only of black advancement but also of black crime and black militancy, and he forged a formidable voting bloc out of white anger at increasing black demands. Nixon sought to walk a tightrope, where he would stress racial moderation and his own civil rights record while also appealing to Southern whites drawn to Alabama segregationist governor and presidential candidate George Wallace. In effect, Nixon ran in 1968 (and 1972) as if all of white America were Southern—and it worked.

Here again, Nixon campaigned from the Right but governed from the center. Though he pushed racial buttons with his Southern strategy, he went on, as president, to effect remarkable and substantive gains for the civil rights agenda. But his political rhetoric and the tenor of the times conspired to present him as racially unsympathetic.

On race, then, the Nixon legacy has left the Republicans with unwanted baggage: the party has made major efforts to renounce the Southern strategy in the years since 1968, but it has had little luck in breaking free of the Nixonian identification. In a hotly contentious 2011 essay, Sam Tanenhaus branded the GOP "the party of white people."[12] Tanenhaus's characterization is unfair and historically dubious, but his opinion is widely shared among commentators and millions of minority voters. On race then, too, Nixon continues to shape the GOP reality—in this case, much to the party's chagrin. This legacy must be doubly frustrating to conservatives, since Nixon was never truly one of them.

By his own admission, Nixon said that "political positions have always come to me because I was there.... It all depends on what the times call for."[13] Except for his support for law and order, Nixon infuriated conservatives with left-leaning policies on everything from education, the environment, welfare, and affirmative action, to wage and price controls and monetary policy. In 1971, Patrick Buchanan, who had worked in the Nixon White House, wrote that conservatives were "the niggers of the Nixon administration."[14] *National Review* publisher William Rusher called the magazine's earlier endorsement of Nixon "the blunder of 1968"[15] and urged readers not to vote for Nixon in 1972. Many conservative Cold Warriors were appalled by Nixon's outreach to Moscow and Beijing. They saw his reaching out to Chinese totalitarians as shameful and his policies as an abdication of American anti-Communism and leadership on issues of democracy, liberty, and human rights.

As the seventies dragged on after Nixon's presidency, his ill-considered economic policies helped create stagflation—unemployment plus high inflation, a combination once thought impossible. A tax revolt began around the country. In California, businessman Howard Jarvis sparked Proposition 13, the landmark property tax reform that kicked off the modern tax-reform movement. A split developed and widened between mainstream Republicans and movement conservatives that continues to play out four decades later, though it has mostly been resolved in favor of the conservatives. Ever since President Reagan rode the conservative ascendancy to the White House in 1980, the GOP has been staunchly antitax and antiregulation. Moderates—especially domestic moderates, of the kind Nixon himself was—have become nearly extinct in GOP ranks.

Nixon also influenced the Democratic Party's future direction. Domestically, he did this by co-opting liberal domestic policies, thereby taking the center away and forcing the Democrats either to support his policies or to move further left. The most relevant example today is Nixon's attempt to mandate universal health insurance in 1971. Nixon's proposal is now regarded as the (more liberal) precursor to the health care plans put forth by presidents Clinton and Obama, the latter of which, the Affordable Care Act, became law in 2010.[16]

One key reason the Nixon health care legislation failed was the opposition of key liberals, including Senator Ted Kennedy of Massachusetts. Kennedy and his cohorts held out for an even-more-liberal health care proposal, and they helped kill Nixon's legislation. Their reaction illustrates how Nixon had boxed in liberals and progressives. Having offered such a liberal, generous program, Nixon gave Democrats room to maneuver only further to his left—well to the left of mainstream Americans. The other option was to vote with him and hand a Republican president a major political victory. For the most part, the Democrats chose to move further left, and their decision had disastrous results for the party. Kennedy later called it his biggest political regret.

Or consider how Nixon incorporated a liberal concern—the environment—into policy choices that pleased not only many mainstream Democrats but also the centrist Independents who made up a good portion of his silent majority. Nixon saw the momentum of the environmental movement in the early 1970s, and he knew that the man he assumed would be his 1972 challenger, Massachusetts Senator Edmund Muskie, had been an early champion of environmental protection. So he moved to preempt the Democrats on that issue by pushing popular and ambitious environmental-protection legislation, especially on air and water pollution.[17] Nixon's advocacy of environmental issues turned out to be a shrewdly moderate and appealing pitch to the middle class constituency whose support he relied upon. Nixon positioned himself, again, as a sensible centrist between those who rejected all environmental appeals as statist interference with business and those, on the other side, who wanted more radical ecological measures.

A similar dynamic occurred with Nixon's Vietnam War policies, which turned almost all Democrats into doves. Nixon made Democrats appear weak on national security and foreign policy by pursuing policies that were, again, essentially centrist: He emphasized a tough approach to peace—withdrawing our troops while simultaneously bombing aggressively in an attempt to force the enemy to the negotiating table. Americans supported this policy. To oppose it seemed defeatist or unpatriotic. The image of Democrats as guilt-ridden apologists, weak on national security and defense, took shape in the Nixon years and has held, more or less, ever since.[18] And, of course, Nixon's brilliant overtures to China and Russia both served America's national-security interests—by exploiting divisions between the two Communist powers and, at home, by blunting the antiwar Left's energy and bringing calm to the American domestic scene.

Nixon's perceived political cynicism also pushed Democrats leftward, inaugurating an era of Democratic efforts to reform the political process—leading to things from open primaries and campaign finance reform to an all-out embrace of identity-group politics. These efforts first took concrete form at the 1972 Democratic Convention, in which the party set up a commission to reform how it chose delegates. The commission eventually decided to impose a quota system so that blacks, women, and young people could be selected as delegates "in reasonable relationship to the group's presence in the population of the state."[19] The commission's chairman was Senator George McGovern of South Dakota, who would go on to become the party's 1972 nominee, with the most diverse set of delegates—including minorities, women, grassroots activists, and the young—in American history. What the Democrats did, in effect, was to empower activists at the grassroots level, maximizing local participation but creating unwinnable candidacies at the national level—such as with presidential nominees George McGovern and Walter Mondale and Governor Michael Dukakis. Except for President Jimmy Carter's narrow win in 1976, the Democrats, from 1972 until 1992, suffered one presidential blowout defeat after another, an unprecedented run of failure for a national party.

Even Nixon's demise in the Watergate scandal proved hugely influential on the opposing party: it ushered in a new generation of Democratic congressional leaders—the Watergate Babies—who were less traditional and considerably more liberal than their predecessors. That orientation has more or less held ever since. Though the Democratic party moved toward the center in the Clinton years, in 2008, it nominated Barack Obama, who couldn't have won without the key changes made to the primary system and whose coalition represented the maturation and fulfillment of the McGovern candidacy.

The Great Polarizer

More than any other politician, Richard Nixon planted the seeds of the polarization and partisan warfare that characterize our politics today. This is partly because, as just described, Nixon pushed both parties out to their ideological poles—a result not likely to produce political bipartisanship. Not only can the Nixonian dynamics be glimpsed between the two parties; they also can be glimpsed *within* the parties themselves, even forty years after he left office. Consider the state of the respective parties' current leadership.

Former House speaker John Boehner represents the contemporary Republican mainstream; by 2015 standards, he is a Republican moderate, or at least a Republican pragmatist, of the kind Nixon himself was. On the far right is Senator Ted Cruz, champion of the Tea Party and hero of conservative intellectuals. Cruz's leadership and rhetoric played a crucial role in the fall-2013 government shutdown, as he inspired his Tea Party caucus not to give in and make a deal with the Democrats. Cruz resembles no one as much as he does Barry Goldwater—the leader of the right wing during Nixon's time, a right wing that Nixon both neutralized and exploited for political advantage.

On the Democratic side, similar tensions prevail. Bill and Hillary Clinton remain the standard bearers of post-Nixon Democratic centrism; they are "small-*l*" liberals who learned from history that, for contemporary liberalism to survive, it needs to stay close to the concerns of the American middle class on both domestic policy and on matters of national defense. Further to the left are President Obama, House Minority Leader Nancy Pelosi, and most other congressional Democrats. Like Ted Kennedy in the early 1970s, they see themselves as progressives, and their political goals remain to institute an expansionist social welfare state and a pullback from American military commitments abroad.

Moreover, relations *between* the parties have deteriorated steadily since the end of the Nixon era, in no small part due to the scorched-earth political tactics that he and his team unleashed.

One of Nixon's longtime political adversaries, Democratic senator Adlai Stevenson, described what he called "Nixonland" as "a land of slander and scare; the land of sly innuendo, the poison pen, the anonymous phone call and hustling, pushing, shoving; the land of smash and grab and anything to win."[20] Nixon's approach to politics—being obsessed with leaks, at war with the media, determined to cripple political foes—was something like war, in that opponents were not just seen as misguided or wrong but, in fact, as evil and dangerous. It's an approach that has become the operative outlook of both parties today. (The obsessive secrecy of the Obama administration is a vivid example.)

Its genuine criminality aside, the lasting legacy of Watergate is less noted: it is the key event in shaping today's intense partisan polarization. Our Red-and-Blue political map—the outline of mutually incompatible Americas that don't understand one another and have mostly stopped listening to the other side—was forged in the Nixon White House.

As a young lawyer, the former secretary of state and presidential candidate Hillary Clinton served on the Watergate Committee investigating the impeachment charges against Nixon. Congress eventually voted to bring those charges, but before it could proceed, Nixon resigned from office. Twenty-four years later, some saw a Watergate redux—"payback," some called it—when conservatives in Congress marshaled enough votes to impeach President Clinton. Clinton was only the second Democratic president to win the election since Nixon, and the first Democratic president to win two terms since FDR. It was impossible to watch the Clinton impeachment drama unfold and not consider the lingering political bitterness that Watergate created.

The George W. Bush years were even more contentious. Bush's wars reawakened the split between Republican hawks and Democratic doves that had first surfaced in the Nixon years. Like Nixon, Bush possessed a seemingly limitless capacity to derange Democrats with fury and political resentment. The result was a party pushed further and further left until, by 2008, it nominated Barack Obama, its most liberal candidate since Franklin Roosevelt. During Obama's presidency, the polar split between the parties has grown even wider. Obama became the first president ever to pass major domestic legislation without a single vote from the opposition party, and he presided over the first downgrade of US credit in history when, in the face of a debt default, he was unable to make a deal with Republicans until the very last moment.

In short, polarization—between the two parties, between competing visions of the country, and between Red and Blue America—is a lasting legacy of the Nixon years. Even as we begin to look beyond Obama, the same Nixonian dynamics between parties seem likely to shape the playing field.

Those dynamics are often cultural as well as political, as Americans well know—and more than any other politician, Richard Nixon articulated the fundamental division in the ongoing American culture war: that between "elites" and ordinary Americans. It would not be an overstatement to declare that Nixon is the father of the culture war.

Nixon coined the term the "silent majority" to refer to the ordinary, hardworking, tax-paying Americans, or as he described them the "forgotten Americans—the non-shouters, the non-demonstrators,"[21] who felt under siege by the political and social tumults of the late 1960s. He first identified this group in a November 3, 1969, speech on the Vietnam War. Where his attacks on the media and intellectuals had redefined populism's targets, his recognition of the silent majority redefined populism's heroes—not as the proletarians or impoverished farmers of an earlier era but as the ordinary middle-class Americans, some in cities, some in suburbs, who were trying to live decent lives and who were contemptuous of political agitators.

Nixon's identification of the silent majority had a long and deeply personal pedigree. While attending Whittier College in the 1930s, Nixon was already fighting his own culture war. He started an alternative student organization, the Orthogonians, or "straight shooters" (a made-up term using *ortho*, the Latin prefix for "straight") to counter the elitist Franklins (the liberals), who didn't accept him for membership (because, he suspected, of his humble origins). From this episode flows much that would come later: his instinctive suspicion, as a young congressman, of Alger Hiss, upon the former FDR aide being called before the House Un-American Activities Committee and denying having been a Communist; his instinctive sense that Whittaker Chambers, the *Time* magazine editor and former Communist, was telling the truth about Hiss's Communist past; his resentment and jealousy of John F. Kennedy and the whole Kennedy crowd; his distrust of the Ivy League media and professoriate; and his powerful identification with modest Middle Americans and all Orthogonians, people like his father—even though he had almost as little in common with these people as did most of his political rivals. But these were the identifications, and they have endured.

The Master Campaigner and Strategist

More than any other politician, Richard Nixon designed the political strategy, communications, and tactics—including the television ads and message management—that national politicians are still using to get through to voters and win elections.

Nixon's explosive television ads—like his 1968 commercials that bluntly raised the issue of crime, his skillful repackaging of his image, and his disciplined message management forged the modern campaign-strategy model for the presidency. The Nixon political strategists and communication team pioneered a shrewd, fearless, and just-short-of-incendiary style of political communication.

The team included twenty-six-year-old wunderkind Roger Ailes, the media consultant who had helped make talk show host Mike Douglas into a "national icon of square chic."[22] Ailes and his team recreated the Nixon brand via television—the very medium that had sunk Nixon's presidential hopes against Kennedy in 1960. They achieved this by using staged campaign events to put Nixon in the most flattering light and play up a sympathetic image: the "New Nixon," as the slogan had it, was a common man at peace with himself, not the haunted, nervous character of the 1960 presidential debates against Kennedy or the suspicious-seeming figure dubbed "Tricky Dick" by his political enemies. The New Nixon was determined to bring America's polarized electorate back together behind shared goals. Ailes and his team produced a series of pioneering, made-for-TV "town halls," in which Nixon took questions from mostly friendly audiences and got his message out to millions around the country. The town halls, although seemingly spontaneous, were actually tightly choreographed; *New York Times* reporter James Reston called them "masterpieces of contrived candor."[23]

The town halls' influence on political communications strategies and tactics remains foundational to this day. Staged political events have become so routine that the authenticity of any seemingly spontaneous incident is immediately questioned. (The presidential "town hall" debate, a staple of the debate season during recent election cycles, often provokes accusations on both sides about questions being "planted" by attendees who may be secretly working for one of the campaigns.)

The Nixon communication team's true genius, though, was for televised campaign ads, in which they made heavy use of attacks on Democrats. The 1968 Nixon campaign broke new ground for negative campaigning, elevating the art of political attack to a new level. Nixon's ads often featured ominous voice-overs and music set against images of the unrest around the country, a subject with which Americans had become all too familiar. In the most memorable ad, directed by filmmaker Eugene Jones, a montage of still photographs showing scenes of unrest was accompanied by angry, disturbing music. The ads tapped into Americans' sense that the country was plunging into chaos.[24] Even viewed today, the ads retain their power and sophistication.

Nixon's 1972 reelection campaign was not as confrontational as the first, as is befitting to an incumbent, but it was equally as shrewd. Nixon used his ad campaign to portray himself as a successful world leader and to depict his Democratic opponent, George McGovern, as a dangerous radical. Pro-Nixon ads touted Nixon's accomplishments and also tried to humanize the president, showing him dancing with his daughter at her wedding and playing piano with Duke Ellington. These folksy touches would soon become prerequisites in political campaigning, mastered most notably by Ronald Reagan and Bill Clinton and to some extent by George W. Bush. Yet, the anti-McGovern ads continued to build on the 1968 imagery, playing on voters' fears of McGovern's dovish tendencies: one ad showed the image of a hand sweeping away toy soldiers, planes, and warships, depicting the opponent's plans for scaling back American military power. Another ad suggested that, under McGovern, nearly half of Americans would be on welfare.

Part of the effectiveness of this messaging owed to the Nixon team's skilled writers, especially Pat Buchanan and William Safire, who excelled at different things. Safire was urbane and witty—he coined Vice President Spiro Agnew's phrase "nattering nabobs of negativism" to describe the liberal press—while Buchanan's eloquence was for pugnacity and aggression. As a team they were the perfect combination to capture the sense of alienation and resentment of Nixon's silent majority.

And, in an early sign of the "dirty tricks" for which the Nixonites would become infamous, Nixon's team staged incidents at campaign rallies, in which protesters attempted to shout down the president and were then removed by police, to the cheering of crowds. In a typical incident, Nixon was speaking at a campaign event when a handful of antiwar veterans started chanting, "Stop the bombing, stop the war!" Unflustered, he paused, then turned to look into the cameras.

"I have a message for the television screens," Nixon said. "Let's show, besides the six over here"—pointing to the demonstrators—"the thousands over here." He gestured to the large crowd, which included schoolchildren, who now began shouting, "Four more years!" Police carted away the protesters; it later turned out that they had been mysteriously invited to the event by someone in the Nixon campaign.[25]

These incidents reinforced Nixon's critique of a country that was badly off the rails and in need of a return to law and order. By raising social, cultural, and even, very subtly, racial issues, Nixon tapped into a deep groundswell of conservative attitudes in an American electorate exhausted by 1960s political unrest, radicalism, and rising crime.

The Nixon tactics and style have been emulated ever since—perhaps most famously in the 1988 Willie Horton ad by the George Bush campaign, which used the story of a convicted murderer let out on furlough, only to then commit armed robbery and rape, to eviscerate Democratic candidate Michael Dukakis and portray him as a soft-on-crime liberal. In 2004, George W. Bush used the image of his presidential rival, John Kerry, windsurfing to depict him as privileged and—subtly—unmanly, a risky steward of the nation's security.

Similarly, Nixon's influence can be seen in every candidate who seeks to remake him or herself. Whether it be Mitt Romney trying to prove that he's a regular guy or Al Gore trying to show that he has a sense of humor, they each channel the New Nixon in the hopes of convincing the American electorate that its prevailing image of them as a candidate is wrong. Yet no one has ever been more successful than Richard Nixon himself in pulling off that feat.

A Record, an Influence, a Legacy

The picture that emerges from all of this is of a man derided and disliked—often hated—yet as accomplished as any American politician of the twentieth century, as measured not only by his political impact and influence but also by his substantive achievements in office. Though I freely acknowledge that mine is a minority view, I see Nixon on par with Franklin Roosevelt: he helped to bring an end to the Vietnam War on terms the United States could still have prevailed under; he developed a foreign policy framework that, along with the leadership of Ronald Reagan a decade later, helped to spell the end of the Cold War; and domestically, he institutionalized New Deal policies more extensively than Dwight Eisenhower. Nixon's record on civil rights and desegregation is stellar, and he was the first president to take a leadership role on the environment.

The majority of the chapters in this book focus on how Nixon's presidency influenced and shaped American politics. But before we try to understand why his influence has been so far-reaching, we must first reckon with his substantive record. Thus, in the first section, "The Nixon Record," chapter 1 begins with a survey of Nixon's domestic policy record—in which I argue that he was not only a pragmatic centrist but also perhaps America's last liberal president. In chapter 2, I look at the politician's foreign policy achievements, which have cast a long shadow—mostly positive—over American statesmen to the present day.

Section 2, "The Nixon Influence," dives into the American political history of the last forty-five years, looking at it through the lens of the Nixon record and its effect on both major parties. In two chapters devoted to each party, I argue that it is Nixon who is the presiding influence on the shape both parties have taken since the late 1960s—often in ways little noted or poorly understood. The section's final two chapters bring matters up to the present day, examining first how Bill Clinton, through his wielding of triangulation and middle-class appeals, became Richard Nixon's truest political heir, and then how George W. Bush and Barack Obama, from different ideological directions, forgot Nixon's lessons—especially in foreign policy—and pursued base-oriented presidencies, both of which would be marked by historic levels of ideological polarization and voter disgust.

In section 3, "The Nixon Legacy," the book's final section, I examine Nixon's place in history from two perspectives: The first involves an in-depth analysis of the Watergate scandal and its analogues in subsequent decades—especially the Iran-Contra scandal, the Iraq War, and the Obama administration's IRS scandal. Taking on Nixon's influence from another perspective, I then look at how Nixon's postpresidency deserves to better remembered as a template for influential statesmanship in retirement—not to mention, on its own terms, as a personal story of grit and resilience.

This book is being published as Americans gear up for what promises to be, in 2016, another crucial and highly contested presidential election. While commentary and analysis will not be in short supply, Americans would do well to step back and consider the deep roots of our current political divisions—and that examination relies heavily on understanding Richard Nixon's impact, the forces he set in motion (for good and ill), and the strategies he used. This book aims to make clear how we must understand our thirty-seventh president to understand American politics today.

SECTION I

THE
NIXON
RECORD

– CHAPTER 1 –

The Domestic Policy Pragmatist

Nixon remains the only modern president whose personality, rhetoric, and image can be used with impunity to dismiss or ignore his concrete achievements, especially in the area of expanding civil rights enforcement in particular, and domestic reform in general.

—JOAN HOFF[1]

Since [Nixon assumed office] . . . the great symbol of racial subjugation, the dual school system of the South, virtually intact two years ago, has quietly and finally been dismantled. All in all, a record of good fortune and much genuine achievement. And yet how little the administration seems to be credited with what it has achieved.

—DANIEL PATRICK MOYNIHAN[2]

The 2,027 days Nixon spent in office have been remembered most for Watergate, next for foreign policy, and least for domestic reform. I think this order should be reversed.

—JOAN HOFF[3]

Richard Nixon is many things to many people, but a little more than forty years after his crushing 1972 reelection victory, he is also something few would have imagined: America's last liberal. That may sound like a stretch, a misunderstanding of Nixon's presidency and his policies. But if we look back over the last forty-five-odd years, Nixon's credentials have put him starkly at odds with today's Republican Party. Though Nixon, and other Republicans in the 1970s, would never have expressed it in this way, our thirty-seventh president was a pro–big government, pro–public spending, and pro–safety net president.

To some extent his domestic liberalism resulted less from deep-seated convictions than from political pragmatism. Because the truth about Nixon is that he was never terribly interested in domestic policy. He once said: "I've always thought this country could run itself domestically without a President. . . . You need a President for foreign policy."[4] To be sure, this perspective sometimes got Nixon into trouble domestically: as I go on to briefly outline, Nixon's economic policies were scattershot, inconsistent, and not terribly successful by any measure. He lacked a firm foundation in economics, and it showed in his policies. Yet, in other crucial domestic areas—especially civil rights and the environment— he achieved remarkable successes unmatched by any of his successors (and some of his immediate predecessors). In further areas—especially health care and social welfare—he proposed bold, innovative reforms that, while not becoming law, helped to shape the reforms adopted decades later.

What's striking about all of these areas is how much Nixon's record plays against the conventional image of him. Nixon's image today, on racial and civil issues, for instance, is almost wholly negative. It's an image that he himself did much to create, especially on the White House tapes, in which he is heard saying things about blacks that had they been heard publicly, would have destroyed him politically. And yet Nixon's record on racial issues is remarkable for its substantive achievements. Few Americans know that the president's school desegregation legacy dwarfs that of his Democratic predecessors. When Nixon ran for president in 1968, nearly 70 percent of black children in the South attended all-black schools. By the time he left office in 1974, just 8 percent did.[5] Daniel Patrick Moynihan, a former Nixon White House aide, lamented "how little the administration seems to be credited with what it has achieved."[6]

On issues of social welfare, Nixon was emphatically not a Barry Goldwater conservative. He attempted to institute one of the most far-reaching plans of social welfare ever in the United States: the Family Assistance Plan. The plan was designed to expand welfare benefits and job-training programs, but more importantly, to provide *all* Americans with a guaranteed annual income. He pushed for a national health care plan to require employers to buy health insurance for their employees and to subsidize those who couldn't afford it. Nixon's version of national health care was far more liberal than Bill Clinton's or Barack Obama's— and it in fact failed because of Democratic opposition, not lack of support from Nixon's own party. (Ted Kennedy later said that opposing Nixon's health care plan was one of his biggest political regrets.)

Nixon was the nation's first—and, some would say, its only— "environmental president." He was not only a fervent supporter of the Clean Air Act, the first federal law designed to control air pollution on the national level, he also gave us the Environmental Protection Agency in 1970. The creation of the EPA was part of a broader environmental agenda embodied in the Natural Environmental Policy Act of 1969, which some refer to as the "natural environment's Magna Carta." NEPA set forth unprecedented ecological goals and targets and required the use of environmental impact statements—documents that describe anticipated environmental effects, positive and negative, of proposed policies.[7] With NEPA, Nixon instituted a systematic national environmental policy, which would include the Clean Air Act of 1970 and the Clean Water Act of 1972. These decisions clearly represented a significant expansion of a government mandate to oversee areas of economic and civic life that were previously lightly regulated. The Nixon environmental regulatory framework would face fierce opposition were it being debated today.

Finally, Nixon also ended the military draft. Ending the nation's system of military conscription single-handedly weakened the main impetus of the antiwar movement, dramatically calmed down social tensions, and ultimately put the US military on a much stronger footing. If a Democratic president had done that, there would be monuments to him in every state in the country. Yet for Nixon, this major reform is somehow regarded as an afterthought.

As I previously suggested, Nixon himself had much to do with his negative image. Yet he serves as perhaps the most dramatic example of how one must separate private behavior—and tape-recorded conversations—from actual policy. What made Nixon so divisive domestically was that while his *governance* was mostly centrist, and sometimes flat-out liberal, his *politics* were much more confrontational. The dichotomy is best illustrated in a pair of quotations attributed to Attorney General John Mitchell: In one instance, Mitchell told reporters, "This country is going so far to the Right you won't recognize it."[8] Another time, Mitchell warned people: "You will be better advised to watch what we do instead of what we say."[9]

Indeed, however rough, even callous, Nixon and his men could sound in their public rhetoric, the administration's policy record was one of innovation and substantive achievement. Mitchell's "watch what we do" comment, in fact, was made, fittingly, to a group of disappointed activists for civil rights—and no area illustrates the Nixonian tension between words and deeds more dramatically.

Civil Rights

Nixon's enduring image as a political villain, his appeal to the silent majority of mostly middle-class Americans, and especially his notorious Southern strategy—all of which I'll discuss at length in later chapters—have contributed to a widespread view that his record on racial matters is poor. Nothing could be further from the truth. Whatever the complexities of Nixon's racial *politics*, his *policies* achieved far more than those of his great rival, John F. Kennedy, who dragged his feet on civil rights until near the end of his time in office. Nixon's record on race today would qualify him, again, as a liberal.

"The time may have come when the issue of race could benefit from a period of 'benign neglect,'" wrote Daniel Patrick Moynihan, Nixon's counselor for urban affairs, in a memo that would become as infamous as it was misunderstood. "The subject has been too much talked about. The forum has been too much taken over to hysterics, paranoids, and boodlers on all sides. We need a period in which Negro progress continues and racial rhetoric fades."[10] What Moynihan was urging was not a retreat from government concern for minority advancement but less public attention to the highlighting of disputes between the races. Critics have often portrayed Moynihan's statement literally, as a proposal to "neglect" blacks, and Nixon's Watergate image and his own comments about race in the Oval Office tapes fed that impression. In some areas, Nixon gave them fuel for their conclusions.

Consider the tortured subject of busing, on which Nixon struggled to define a clear public position. Nixon was on the record opposing the forced busing of school children for the purpose of integration. At the same time, he tried to make clear his civil rights record, which had been strong throughout his career. As vice president under Dwight Eisenhower, Nixon helped lead support for the 1957 Civil Rights Act—for which Martin Luther King Jr. wrote to thank him. Nixon opposed segregation. In a 1968 interview on *Face the Nation*, presidential candidate Nixon said that "no funds should be given to a district which practices segregation."[11]

Some brief background: When the 1964 Civil Rights Act was drafted, Vice President Hubert Humphrey proposed amendments banning the act from ever being interpreted as one that required forced busing.

Humphrey wanted to outlaw segregation, but he opposed forcing integration according to race. Republican Senator Jacob Javits expressed similar views. However, by 1966, the Office of Education in the Department of Health, Education, and Welfare (HEW) had mandated that the success of desegregation efforts could be measured by numbers—that is, by how many children had been integrated. In certain areas, the only way to satisfy those targets was through busing.

The integration of schools was upheld by the Supreme Court's 1968 ruling in *Green v. County School Board of New Kent County*, which ordered an immediate end to de jure segregation.[12] The busing views were further bolstered in the Court's 1971 ruling in *Swann v. Charlotte-Mecklenburg Board of Education*, which ordered the school district to desegregate, allowing it to redraw districts, if necessary, and also to use busing. These two rulings effectively brought an end to de jure segregation—that is, segregation by explicit arrangement—in the South though they did not address de facto segregation, which was common in the North and West, not so much as a matter of law but as a result of residential patterns. Now several lower courts began to mandate busing as a means to eliminate de facto segregation as well.[13] Backlash to busing grew across the country, especially in suburban districts in the North and West.

Nixon did not see busing—forced integration—as a solution to racial inequality, let alone as a way to foster harmonious relations between whites and blacks. In addition, he objected to it on the grounds of community control. After the *Swann* ruling upheld the constitutionality of busing, Nixon asked Congress to pass a moratorium on new court-ordered busing rulings—which would not affect those already in place. The moratorium made it through the House but not the Senate. Throughout the first half of the 1970s, busing continued to be a hugely divisive issue socially and politically, sparking parent protests, sporadic violence, and even the firebombing of school buses in Pontiac, Michigan. By 1974, reflecting the new public mood, the court had ruled, in *Milliken v. Bradley*, that federal courts could not bus between school districts unless they could prove that these districts were deliberately drawn up so as to create segregation.[14]

Liberals at the *New York Times* and elsewhere blamed Nixon for his resistance to busing, but they somehow missed the astounding success he was having desegregating American schools, which was busing's main goal. When Nixon entered the White House, the desegregation of Southern schools was proceeding at a snail's pace. The fact that he had reduced the percentage of black children attending all-black schools from 70 percent to 8 percent by the time he left office in 1974[15] makes the record crystal clear: Richard Nixon desegregated more schools than all other presidents combined.

He accomplished this historic feat in no small part by applying Republican, conservative principles of governance, especially federalism—the philosophy that grants maximum autonomy to the states. Where desegregation was concerned, Nixon deferred to federalist principles as long as the states' efforts were consistent with federal mandates on civil rights. As the speechwriter and author Ray Price put it: "Nixon's aim was to use the minimum coercion necessary to achieve the essential national goal, to encourage local initiative, to respect diversity, and, to the extent possible, to treat the entire nation equally—blacks equally with whites, the South equally with the North."[16]

George Shultz, who served as Nixon's secretary of labor before heading up the Office of Management and Budget and later working as Ronald Reagan's secretary of state, told the story of how Nixon worked to enforce the mandate of *Brown v. Board of Ed* in a powerful *New York Times* op-ed in 2003. In the article, Shultz described how Nixon supported this legislation—which had been flouted for nearly twenty years—by asking him and Vice President Agnew to form biracial committees in the seven affected Southern states. The idea was that white and black representatives would work together to manage the process of desegregation with minimal interference from Washington—as long as the committees understood that they had to reach some kind of workable solution, or risk federal intervention. In many instances, the whites and blacks who served together got to know and respect one another to an extent few had foreseen. As the committees got closer to bringing their plans to fruition, Shultz knew that it was time to bring the president in. As Shultz told the story:

> When the time was right, I let President Nixon know that we were ready for him. We walked across the hall into the Oval Office, where the president gathered his guests around his desk. "We live in a great democracy where authority and responsibility are shared," I remember

him saying. "Just as decisions are made here in this office, decisions are made throughout the states and communities of our country. You are the leaders in those communities and you have to step up to your responsibilities." They left the Oval Office inspired.[17]

Reflecting on the gathering, Nixon said, "One of the most encouraging experiences that I have had since taking office was to hear each one of these leaders from the Southern states speak honestly about the problems, not glossing over the fact that there were very grave problems. As a result of these advisory committees being set up, we are going to find that in many districts the transition will be orderly and peaceful, whereas otherwise it could have been the other way."[18]

One of the black members of the fifteen-member Mississippi State Advisory Committee who sat in the president's office that day was so encouraged by the meeting that he told the president: "The day before yesterday I was in jail for going to the wrong beach. Today, Mr. President, I am meeting you. If that's possible anything can happen."[19] His optimism proved warranted. "In the end, the school openings were peaceful," Shultz wrote. "To the amazement of almost everyone."[20]

"There has been more change in the structure of American public school education in the last month than in the past 100 years," Moynihan wrote when he was Nixon's counselor. His verdict on Nixon's civil rights record remains true: "How little the administration seems to be credited with what it has achieved."[21]

Writing many years later, the *New York Times*'s Tom Wicker, hardly a champion of the president, stated: "There's no doubt about it—the Nixon administration accomplished more in 1970 to desegregate Southern school systems than had been done in the 16 previous years, or probably since. There's no doubt either that it was Richard Nixon personally who conceived, orchestrated and led the administration's desegregation effort. Halting and uncertain before he finally asserted strong control, that effort resulted in probably the outstanding domestic achievement of his administration."[22]

And desegregation was not the only area in which Nixon worked for the advancement of African Americans. How many remember today that Nixon was a champion of affirmative action? "Incredible but true," is how *Fortune* magazine described it in 1994 when Nixon died, "it was

the Nixonites that gave us employment quotas."[23] Though many credit
John F. Kennedy or Lyndon Johnson with initiating affirmative action,
it was Nixon who first sanctioned formal goals and time frames to break
barriers to minority employment (to be sure, the merits of these policies
depend on one's political views).

Nixon's administration also put together the Philadelphia Plan,
a forceful federal-level initiative to guarantee fair hiring practices in
construction jobs, with definitive "goals and timetables" for minority
inclusion. The administration would not impose quotas, Nixon himself
said, "but would require federal contractors to show 'affirmative action'
to meet the goals of increasing minority employment."[24] The plan took
its name from the city in which the first test case was run. Secretary
of Labor Arthur Fletcher said: "The craft unions and the construction
industry are among the most egregious offenders against equal opportunity laws...openly hostile toward letting blacks into their closed circle."[25]

The Philadelphia Plan was part of a broader agenda of supporting
what Nixon called "black capitalism." It came at a time, several years
after Dr. King's death, when the traditional civil rights paradigm seemed
to have broken down amid a changed legal and political climate. Some
problems had actually been solved; others remained. But the old-line
civil rights leadership seemed unable to grasp the new realities, and
the urban violence of the late sixties had exposed the limitations of its
approach—while prompting a backlash from whites. Nixon saw support
for black business efforts not only as a logical next step in black advancement but as a way to defuse racial tensions.

As Nixon speechwriter Ray Price put it, the rioting and other inner-
city violence posed the danger of "hardening attitudes into a simple
formula of 'it's us against them.'" Price lambasted liberal Democrats,
"who, faced with a riot, beat their breasts in a chorus of collective mea
culpas," along with white conservatives, "who don't recognize the cultural gulf between the ghetto and suburbia."[26]

Nixon's approach sought to bring Republican values of entrepreneur-
ialism to the black community, while also—so Nixon hoped, anyway—
reaching out to blacks and demonstrating to them that Republicans
also sought their advancement and wanted their support. As a result,
the Office of Minority Business Enterprise (OMBE), championed
by Republicans, put liberal Democrats on the defensive. Instead of a

constant drumbeat for government assistance or legislation, here was a different emphasis for black advancement: free enterprise and the American way. Eventually, some liberal politicians endorsed the OMBE. Black capitalism, said Graham T. Molitor, a pollster for liberal Governor Nelson A. Rockefeller of New York, was "a stroke of political genius."[27]

A good portion of the liberal establishment showed its myopia, however, in harping on the Nixon plan's limitations. The *New York Times* argued that the plan ignored institutional discrimination in home sales and wages and failed to fully account for the social, economic, and political concerns of blacks. But Nixon continued, undaunted.

In 1972, after presidential candidate George Wallace once again proved strong in Southern primaries, Nixon showed his newfound confidence in exerting a civil rights agenda—without losing his majority support among whites and even most conservatives. Nixon proposed the Equal Educational Opportunities Act of 1972, affirming that no state or locality could discriminate in education based on race, color, or national origin, while also making it clear that busing would be regarded only as a last resort.[28]

Writing thirty years later, in 2002, Patrick Buchanan summarized the administration's civil rights achievements in the following list. According to him, the administration:

* raised the civil rights enforcement budget 800 percent;
* doubled the budget for black colleges;
* appointed more blacks to federal posts and high positions than any president, including LBJ;
* adopted the Philadelphia Plan mandating quotas for blacks in unions, and for black scholars in colleges and universities;
* invented "Black Capitalism" (the Office of Minority Business Enterprise)...;
* raised the share of Southern schools that were desegregated from 10 percent to 70 percent.[29]

"The charge that we built our Republican coalition on race is a lie," Buchanan wrote. "Nixon routed the Left because it had shown itself incompetent to win or end a war [Vietnam] into which it had plunged the United States and too befuddled or cowardly to denounce the rioters burning our cities or the brats rampaging on our campuses."[30] Indeed, Nixon showed that civil rights could be advanced in a rational, reasonable way that emphasized cooperation while deemphasizing areas of conflict. His achievements in this area exemplify his nonideological political approach.

Nixon's social liberalism also extended to the other key group then making demands for inclusion, economic opportunity, and political influence—women. Moynihan played a role here, too, in urging Nixon to get out in front of the issue. "Male dominance is so deeply a part of American life that males don't even notice it," Moynihan wrote to the president. "I would suggest you could take advantage of this. In your appointments (as you have begun to do), but perhaps especially in your pronouncements. This is a subject ripe for creative political leadership and initiative."[31]

In today's politics, women's rights have often been seen as synonymous with abortion—an issue on which Nixon vacillated. He believed that the issue should be resolved by the states, though he called New York's Cardinal Cooke in 1971 to express support for repealing the state's liberal abortion law. After the Supreme Court ruled on *Roe v. Wade*, Nixon worried that the decision might encourage promiscuity. (Infamously, he was caught on tape saying that abortions were justified in cases of rape or "when you have a black and a white.")[32] Vocal feminists, like Betty Friedan, certainly did not see Nixon as an ally—yet they overlooked the rest of his record.

Nixon also extended affirmative action to women at educational institutions. Perhaps his foundational achievement here was in signing Title IX, prohibiting sex discrimination in federally funded education programs, in 1972. "It's hard to exaggerate the far-reaching effect of Title IX on American society," wrote longtime sports columnist Allen Barra in 2012. "The number of female athletes at the high school level has increased more than tenfold and at the college level, more than twelvefold.... The year before Title IX was enacted, there were about 310,000 girls and women in America playing high school and college sports; today, there are more than 3,373,000."[33]

Barra concedes that Title IX wasn't Nixon's brainchild; it was pushed primarily by Democratic representative Patsy Mink of Hawaii. "It's almost certain that Nixon signed it into law without considering the potential impact on women's athletics,"[34] Barra wrote, and that's probably true. But it was part of Nixon's broader civil rights efforts on behalf of women—including his support for the Equal Rights Amendment (though Nixon did not push seriously to get the ERA passed).[35]

From 1971 to 1973, Nixon's administration tripled the number of women working in high-level positions.[36] "There is no denying," wrote Joan Hoff, "as with desegregation of southern schools and public institutions, that Nixon's advances in civil and political rights for women and minorities far outweighed those of his predecessors, belying the 'divisive public rhetoric' his administration employed in the process."[37]

Pioneering "Strict Constructionism"

Another reason that Nixon's civil rights achievements aren't better recognized is because, in his efforts to appoint "strict constructionist" Supreme Court justices—meaning that they would interpret the Constitution narrowly—civil rights issues were often the backdrop. That was certainly the case with his first two appointments, Clement Haynsworth and G. Harrold Carswell, neither of whom made it to the court. Both judges were Southerners, and their nominations have been widely seen as a perpetuation of Nixon's Southern strategy. Haynsworth would have been the first Southerner named to the court since the civil rights movement, but civil rights and labor leaders helped sink his nomination. Carswell's nomination imploded on questions of his competence, but also on civil rights grounds: he had given a prosegregation speech in 1948.

The failed nominations were seen as politically damaging, but Nixon was able to rally political support with an angry denunciation of what he saw as bias against Southern judicial candidates. "I have reluctantly concluded," Nixon told reporters, "that it is not possible to get confirmation for a judge on the Supreme Court of any man who believes in the strict construction of the Constitution, as I do, if he happens to come from the South."[38] He said that the only choice left for him was to nominate judicial conservatives from outside the South, since his opponents were biased against that region of the country.

As divisive as these nominations were, Nixon did not look at the court in the hardened ideological terms his public pronouncements sometimes suggested. As with so many other domestic issues, he showed considerable flexibility when dealing with the court—and thus, on the negative side, his flexibility could lead him to subordinate his choices to political considerations, as many assumed he did with these early nominations, as he sought further to strengthen his Southern appeal.

However, Nixon *did* believe in "strict construction"—a phrase and concept that he made familiar to millions of Americans. "It is my belief that it is the duty of a judge to interpret the Constitution and not to place himself above the Constitution," he said. "He should not twist or bend the Constitution in order to perpetuate his personal, political and social views."[39] He meant it, but for Nixon, "strict construction" was not about ideological purity so much as addressing specific issues. In his first term, the two issues that meant the most to him were law and order and antibusing. More broadly, he wanted justices who rejected judicial liberalism in its many manifestations. But he recognized that the most hardline judicial candidates, especially on civil rights issues, would not enjoy the support of the American people.

Eventually, Nixon nominated Harry Blackmun from Minnesota as a justice for the Supreme Court, and he was confirmed unanimously. Blackmun was seen as a law-and-order man, and in the early years of his tenure, he cast mostly conservative votes. But in time, he became a key cog of the court's liberal wing, famously writing the *Roe* opinion legalizing abortion and, two decades later, coming out against the death penalty. The judge would come to exemplify a truism about Supreme Court nominations: no president, no matter how careful his selection, can depend on a justice being "reliable" throughout his tenure.

Perhaps the judicial pick who best exemplified Nixon's own predilections was Lewis Powell, whom the president appointed in 1971. Powell was a centrist, with views often reflective of Nixon's own—he was generally proprosecution in criminal cases and a limited advocate of affirmative action and prochoice, but not at public expense. Warren Burger, whom Nixon appointed in 1969 to replace Chief Justice Earl Warren, also had views that were reflective of Nixon in some ways. He was a dyed-in-the-wool Republican but not an ideological conservative. The justice often frustrated committed conservatives, but he also represented an entirely different sensibility than the departed Warren, who had led a judicial revolution. Burger's chief justiceship, which ran until 1986, brought an end to that era.

But it was William Rehnquist, a committed conservative, who represented Nixon's most vital impact on the court. Rehnquist's nomination ran into serious opposition. He had written a 1952 memorandum supporting the premise of *Plessy v. Ferguson*, the infamous 1896 decision that enshrined "separate but equal" public facilities for whites and blacks. He tended to vote "with the prosecution in criminal cases, with business in antitrust cases, with employers in labor cases, and with the government in speech cases."[40] As John Ehrlichman told Nixon: "If you want to salt away a guy that would be on the Court for 30 years [and] is a rock-solid conservative, he's it."[41]

Once he was joined by more conservative colleagues in the 1980s—when Ronald Reagan appointed Sandra Day O'Connor, Anthony Kennedy, and especially Antonin Scalia—Rehnquist, who became chief justice in 1986, led a more conservative court. Sparked by the "strict constructionist" ideal, which became more commonly described as "originalism," conservatives formed organizations like the Federalist Society to train legal scholars and jurists. But things didn't go entirely as conservatives hoped at the court—they never do. Whether under Chief Justice Burger, Justice Rehnquist, or Justice John Roberts, the court has tended to side with liberals on social issues—abortion, affirmative action, school prayer, and, in 2012, on President Obama's Affordable Care Act. At the end of the 2014–2015 court term, the justices handed down two landmark rulings celebrated by liberals: one effectively upholding a main component of Obamacare (for a second time) and the other declaring a constitutional right to same-sex marriage.

While conservatives currently rue many of these decisions, it is not clear that Nixon himself would have: he had a more traditionally Republican (that is, not ideologically conservative) outlook on most social issues. Yet, while his record of appointments to the court proved uneven, he unquestionably began the push against the Warren-era court's social activism—especially in the area of expanded criminal-defendant rights—and engendered what would become a prevailing critique among conservatives against "activist judges" who interpreted the Constitution and statutory law according to their own predilections.

The critiques Republican candidates make in campaign after campaign—against judges who "legislate from the bench," for instance—have become deeply familiar to millions of Americans, and not in a positive sense. Nixon, then, was the president who put the brakes on the court's liberal momentum; made the court a political field of battle in which certain issues strongly favored conservatives; and discredited the concept of judicial activism in the public mind.

Social Welfare

In 1996, Bill Clinton signed the historic Personal Responsibility and Work Opportunity Act, legislation that reformed the nation's welfare system to encourage work among the poor. The law included a work requirement and a five-year cutoff period for welfare benefits. It was the most sweeping change in the nation's welfare policies since the 1960s. Today, welfare reform is counted among President Clinton's most significant achievements in office. Yet the law had many liberal critics who felt that it stigmatized poor mothers and did not provide adequate job training. And its cutoff period—after receiving two years of consecutive benefits or five years of cumulative benefits—was decried by liberal advocates as too harsh. They saw the Clinton bill as a betrayal of the Democrats' historic commitment to the poor.

What some older Democrats might have recalled was that, a quarter-century earlier, they had had a chance to pass a much more comprehensive, and more generous, welfare plan. But this plan was offered by a Republican president, Richard Nixon, with whom they were often engaged in political war. For various political reasons that I will describe in detail in chapter 4, liberals, who should have been the most reliable supporters of Nixon's welfare reform effort, largely blocked it. Nixon's pioneering effort to transform the nation's welfare system didn't come to fruition, but the effort to do so is an important and fascinating part of his domestic record.

Nixon was not expected to be a voice for the poor, but he began proposing initiatives to assist them when his administration was in its early days. In May 1969, in his "Special Message to the Congress Recommending a Program to End Hunger in America," Nixon called on Americans to support a range of legislation and executive action that would alleviate poverty and especially hunger. "That hunger and malnutrition should persist in a land such as ours is embarrassing and intolerable," Nixon said. "More is at stake here than the health and well-being of 16 million American citizens.... Something very like the honor of American democracy is at issue."[42] On the issue of hunger, Nixon's actions matched his words: he quadrupled spending on food stamps from $610 million in 1970 to $2.5 billion in 1973.

Thus Nixon's most remarkable initiative in social welfare policy came in an area in which, in the end, he failed to win legislative approval: welfare reform. When thinking of Nixon today, few would note that he was a welfare reformer, much less that he was one even before there were welfare reformers. In the late 1960s and early 1970s, welfare was a system largely accepted by liberals; though conservatives detested the welfare system, most didn't envision realistic prospects of changing it. Yet Nixon did. In an August 1969 speech, given over the opposition of his most conservative advisors, he unveiled the Family Assistance Plan (FAP), his attempt to address poverty in America, especially among children. Under Nixon's plan, which would replace Aid to Families with Dependent Children (AFDC), the existing welfare program, all families with children would be eligible for a minimum stipend—$1,600 for a family of four, amended to $2,500 in 1971.

"What I am proposing," Nixon continued in his 1969 congressional message on hunger, "is that the Federal Government build a foundation under the income of every American family with dependent children that cannot care for itself—and wherever in America that family may live."[43]

Yet Nixon's program was more conservative than it looked. All able-bodied heads of families, except for mothers with children younger than six, would be required to accept work or job training—very much in the manner that Clinton later envisioned. And if that parent refused, his or her portion of the welfare benefit would be cut off, even though the child's payment would continue. Moreover, the FAP, unlike the AFDC and later welfare proposals, would have directed a substantial amount of aid to working-poor families, as opposed to solely focusing on non-working-poor families if it had passed. By one calculation, under the FAP, a family of four with an income of $12,652, in 2013 dollars, would have seen its income increase by nearly half—to $18,725, in 2013 dollars.[44]

The FAP was designed to provide the means to guarantee all American children a stable annual income—regardless of the behavior of their parents—and to provide such aid to three times the number of children covered by the AFDC. The FAP, Hoff concluded, "would have revolutionized welfare by switching from providing services to providing income."[45] It was, she wrote, "the most comprehensive welfare reform ever proposed by a United States president."[46]

Initially, editorial pages hailed the FAP as a reform on the order of social security. "A Republican President has condemned the word 'welfare,' emphasized 'work' and 'training' as conditions of public assistance, suggested that the states and the cities be given more Federal money to deal with their social and economic problems, but still comes out in the end with a policy of spending more money for relief of more poor people than the welfare state Democrats ever dared to propose in the past," wrote James Reston in the *New York Times*. "Mr. Nixon has taken a great step forward. He has cloaked a remarkably progressive welfare policy in conservative language.... But mainly he has dealt with the intolerable paradox of American life. He has insisted that poverty in a prosperous country must be eliminated."[47]

The FAP passed the House in April 1970, 243 to 155, but it bogged down in the Senate, where Senator Russell B. Long, who opposed the bill, held long hearings, allowing interest groups from around the political spectrum to organize opposition. Hard-line conservatives saw the FAP as a guaranteed-income handout and opposed it. Liberal opponents also objected to the FAP on various grounds—one being, predictably enough, money. The grants were far too low, they said. They proposed grants of $6,400 for a family of four, an amount that would sink the program's budget and lose support from the American middle class. Radical welfare rights groups also lined up in opposition, and organized labor wasn't crazy about the FAP, either, seeing a guaranteed income as a threat to the minimum wage. Still others objected to the work requirements.

Yet in his 1971 State of the Union address, Nixon pressed on:

> The present welfare system has become a monstrous, consuming outrage—an outrage against the community, against the taxpayer, and particularly against the children it is supposed to help.... So let us place a floor under the income of every family with children

in America—and without those demeaning, soul-stifling affronts to human dignity that so blight the lives of welfare children today. But let us also establish an effective work incentive and an effective work requirement. Let us provide the means by which more can help themselves.[48]

But the partisan hurdles were too much to overcome, and the FAP died in the Senate in October 1972, three years after it was first proposed. "Clearly, partisan politics prevented reform of the country's welfare system," Hoff wrote.[49] By that time, the FAP had taken a pounding in the political debates and was regarded, by conservatives and more and more centrists, as a "guaranteed annual income"—which was anathema to most from the center rightward. In fact, the program *was* a guaranteed annual income, but it came with substantive conditions, and the guaranteed income in question was for children, not adults. Nixon tried to stress these points in defending the FAP, but ultimately the program became enshrined in the public mind as a massive new welfare benefit. Even George McGovern, Nixon's opponent in the 1972 election, who in January of that year had proposed "demogrants" of $1,000—with broader eligibility and fewer conditions—for every poor family in America, retracted his proposal before election day in an effort to disassociate himself with what had become an unpopular (if poorly understood) proposal.

However, the FAP's defeat did not preclude Nixon's achievements in other related programs. The original FAP plan, released in 1969, contained a proposal for supplemental security income (SSI), a new program that would provide regular income for disabled, blind, and aged recipients. On October 17, 1972, just two days after the FAP's final demise in the Senate, SSI passed both houses of Congress. It is likely that SSI had such an easy time because its target population was unambiguously needy—the blind, the old, and the disabled, unlike poor mothers, have few critics. Some didn't even regard SSI as a genuine "welfare" program, seeing it as more of a subset of the most unassailable of all American social welfare programs: Social Security. It seems no accident that SSI's name resembles that of the much larger program. Still, SSI may not have seen the light of day without the momentum—temporary though it was—that the FAP achieved.

Some Nixon critics see the FAP failure as incidental to his presidency. They point out, correctly, that Nixon's true passion was foreign policy. Thus, they claim, his more liberal domestic policies were undertaken solely for political expediency—to blunt liberal initiatives and broaden his political base with moderate policies. Certainly there is some truth to this interpretation—Nixon's domestic moderation *did* broaden his political base—but the critics don't give Nixon enough credit (sometimes any credit) for caring about these issues. On welfare, in particular, the evidence in his presidential papers is that Nixon stayed engaged with the FAP—both in the long and sometimes contentious battle within his administration to formulate the policy and during the political battles that ran for years—to try to get it passed. Welfare reform was definitely something he wished to accomplish, and the time he devoted to it makes that clear. Even more proof of his commitment came in January 1974, when Nixon, already reeling under the Watergate scandal and fighting to save his presidency, still found time, in his State of the Union speech, to urge the Congress once again to take up the cause of welfare reform. This time, for obvious reasons, the effort never got off the ground.

Nixon's mostly unheralded efforts to reform welfare and address poverty and hunger in the United States grew out of his own personal experiences and the suffering he witnessed during his stark childhood. He remembered how his mother and father struggled to put food on the table and clothe their children, and their hardships left a searing mark on him. In an evocative memo to speechwriter Ray Price, Nixon wrote:

> In the depression years I remember when my brother had tuberculosis for five years and we had to keep him in a hospital, my mother didn't buy a new dress for five years. We were really quite desperately poor, but as Eisenhower said it much more eloquently at Abilene in his opening campaign statement in 1952, the glory of it was that we didn't know it.
>
> The problem today is that the children growing up in welfare families receiving food stamps and government largess with social workers poking around are poor and they do know it.[50]

As Nixon saw it, changing welfare from a system of services to a system of income maintenance would alleviate this problem. The state, he believed, should stop reminding the children of modern welfare families that they were poor, and thereby stigmatizing them, when they already had daunting challenges to face in their lives. He sympathized with those in such difficult circumstances—though he also agreed with millions of Americans that the welfare system, as it had evolved by the early 1970s, perpetuated dependency while offering no incentives to poor adults to improve their lives. And he agreed with conservatives that the AFDC was contributing to family breakdown, placing more and more children in undesirable and sometimes precarious circumstances. All in all, his welfare reform proposals were conservative in spirit, if liberal in their means—a description that fits much of his domestic policy.

Nixon, Joan Hoff wrote, sought to use a "peace dividend" that he had gained from the withdrawal of American troops from Vietnam for domestic purposes. Under this moderate Republican president, social welfare spending more than doubled, from $55 billion in 1970 to $132 billion by 1975. It was Nixon, not Lyndon Johnson, Hoff wrote, who more properly deserves the label of "last of the big spenders" on domestic programs. Indeed, from 1970 to 1975, for the first time since World War II, spending on social welfare and other human resources exceeded defense spending.[51] It's never happened again.

Health Care

For years, health care has been a flashpoint of partisan conflict in the United States, and the Obama administration's Affordable Care Act, passed in 2010, has recently elevated the issue to a defining one in American politics. Here again, however, the combatants on both sides are battling over terrain that Nixon had previously trod. And as many commentators pointed out in 2010, the ACA bears more than a passing resemblance to the various health care proposals that Nixon made during his presidency.

These proposals were not incremental reforms but rather transformative new formulations designed to address the growing cost crisis in health care as well as the problem of the uninsured. Nixon's first attempt came in 1971, in his State of the Union address, when he set out an ambitious reform agenda for health care that still sounds remarkably contemporary, over forty years later:

> I will offer a far-reaching set of proposals for improving America's health care and making it available more fairly to more people. I will propose:
>
> —A program to insure that no American family will be prevented from obtaining basic medical care by inability to pay.
>
> —I will propose a major increase in and redirection of aid to medical schools, to greatly increase the number of doctors and other health personnel.
>
> —Incentives to improve the delivery of health services, to get more medical care resources into those areas that have not been adequately served, to make greater use of medical assistants, and to slow the alarming rise in the costs of medical care.
>
> —New programs to encourage better preventive medicine, by attacking the causes of disease and injury, and by providing incentives to doctors to keep people well rather than just to treat them when they are sick.[52]

Nixon called his plan the National Health Insurance Partnership, and included in it the now-familiar set of competing interests: private insurers who write plans for employers, government-provided plans for low-income people, and the then-new concept of health maintenance organizations (HMOs), which Nixon believed held great potential for improving services. In 1973, Nixon signed a bill sponsored by Ted Kennedy pledging federal dollars for the creation of HMOs (unfortunately, forty years later, HMOs haven't quite fulfilled their promise, to put it gently). Nixon's plan was comprehensive and ambitious, the first genuine attempt to provide national insurance since Harry Truman. However, Nixon's 1971 plans never got anywhere in Congress.

Yet again, as with welfare reform, Nixon did not give up. In his 1974 State of the Union address—the last he would give as president, delivered under a swelling cloud of the Watergate scandal—he put health care reform back on the agenda: "I shall propose a sweeping new program that will assure comprehensive health insurance protection to millions of Americans who cannot now obtain it or afford it, with vastly improved protection against catastrophic illnesses. This will be a plan that maintains the high standards of quality in America's health care. And it will not require additional taxes."[53]

Nixon also made clear during the address that he opposed what would come to be known as a "single payer" system—making the government the sole health care insurer in the United States in a vast federal system of nationalized health care:

> Now, I recognize that other plans have been put forward that would cost $80 billion or even $100 billion and that would put our whole health care system under the heavy hand of the Federal Government. This is the wrong approach. This has been tried abroad, and it has failed. It is not the way we do things here in America. This kind of plan would threaten the quality of care provided by our whole health care system. The right way is one that builds on the strengths of the present system and one that does not destroy those strengths, one based on partnership, not paternalism.... Government has a great role to play, but we must always make sure that our doctors will be working for their patients and not for the Federal Government.[54]

One week later, on February 6, 1974, Nixon introduced the Comprehensive Health Insurance Plan (CHIP). Nixon's plan, like subsequent plans that would be proposed by Bill Clinton, Barack Obama, and, in Massachusetts, Governor Mitt Romney, was built around private, employer-provided insurance. CHIP would penalize all but the smallest employers for failing to sponsor insurance for their employees—just as Obama's plan does today—though it would also provide subsidies to small employers and the self-employed to help them cover these costs. Like the ACA, Nixon's plan guaranteed coverage with no exclusions for preexisting preconditions. Nixon's plan had generous coverage as well for mental illness, drug addiction, and alcoholism. But unlike Obama's ACA, the Nixon plan contained no mandate—Americans would enter CHIP voluntarily. When they agreed to participate, they would get a health card that could be used like a credit card to pay for their services. (Bill Clinton copied this detail in 1993, when he pushed for national health insurance reform, and it did not go over well. Twenty years later, millions of Americans had developed more skeptical attitudes toward big government, and they saw the health card as a symbol of an overweening government.)

CHIP had three main parts: an expanded system of employer-provided health insurance, in which employers would pay 75 percent of premiums and employees would pay 25 percent; an improved Medicare program; and, for lower-income Americans or those with special occupations or health status, a new system, Assisted Health Insurance, which, for most services, would replace state-run Medicaid. Nixon felt strongly that the lower-income health insurance coverage benefits needed to be standardized nationally; Medicaid, by contrast, had benefits that varied state by state. To get CHIP started, Nixon envisioned a price tag of about $7 billion. If "promptly enacted by Congress," Nixon said, CHIP would be fully operational by 1976.

The roots of these bold ideas could be found, once again, in Nixon's upbringing. Not only had the struggles of his parents made him sympathetic to those who struggled to make ends meet but he had also seen how medical crises could wipe out a family's savings and leave them in desperate circumstances—to say nothing of the human toll of the tragedy. Nixon lost two of his brothers to tuberculosis, an experience that stayed with him all his life. As an adult, he was heartened by the medical profession's achievement in finding a cure for TB, and he pointed to it and other advances as examples of how government and private industry could work together on health care issues. His interest in the issue dated back to the beginning of his political career: in 1947, as a first-term congressman, he had proposed a system of national health care. "It was something personal for him," said speechwriter Ray Price.[55]

Now, a quarter century later, Nixon stood before the Congress with a better-thought-out, more-comprehensive health care proposal than the one he had floated in 1971. Unfortunately, while his plan was better in 1974, his timing was worse. Watergate already hovered over everything.

"The wagons were not only circling, but they were heavily arming and out for blood," Price remembered. "It was very difficult to get anything through at that point."[56]

But it wasn't just Watergate that brought CHIP down. As had happened with the FAP, Nixon faced opposition from both the Left and the Right on his health care plan—but given the Democrats' edge in numbers in both houses of Congress, it was liberal opposition that really sank the program. In chapter 4, I'll describe in detail why liberals blocked Nixon's health care reform plans, which, as many have noted today, were far ahead of their time and retain relevance for today's political debate.

It's worth noting that Nixon, who is remembered in history as a foreign policy president, did not stop thinking about what might have been possible in health care, even during his postpresidency. In one of his final books, *Seize the Moment*, he wrote with remarkable prescience: "We need to work out a system that includes a greater emphasis on preventive care, sufficient public funding for health insurance for those who cannot afford it in the private sector, competition among healthcare providers and health insurance providers to keep down the costs of both, and decoupling the cost of healthcare from the cost of adding workers to the payroll."[57]

An Inconsistent Economist

"Probably more new regulation was imposed on the economy during the Nixon administration than in any other presidency since the New Deal," said Herbert Stein, chief economic adviser for presidents Nixon and Ford. It should be noted that Nixon was not especially interested in economics. He had no economic background, so he surrounded himself with experts who could help him make decisions without too much personal involvement. Most of his advisers were moderate-to-conservative Republicans, including Paul McCracken, Arthur Burns, Robert Mayo, and David Kennedy. Nixon took office just as America's long economic boom was coming to an end. Throughout the 1960s, the economy had been robust and jobs plentiful. By 1968, though, the federal budget deficit had reached $25 billion, the highest level since the Second World War, and inflation was nearing 5 percent. Nixon believed that standard Republican solutions—tight monetary policy and spending cuts—wouldn't do. As Stein noted, Nixon's aim was "to be a conservative man with liberal policies."[58]

Thus Nixon devised a four-phase "game plan." In Game Plan I (1969), Nixon pursued a traditional conservative laissez-faire, tight-money approach. As a result, unemployment rose, as anticipated, but inflation continued to climb, as well. In 1970 and 1971, Nixon implemented Game Plan II, abruptly announcing, "I am now a Keynesian"[59] and pursuing full employment. He embraced an expansionist monetary policy in the hope of stimulating the economy, possibly with an eye toward improving his electoral prospects for 1972. But Game Plan II proved equally ineffective.

Nixon made another radical departure with Game Plan III, announced in August 1971. Called the New Economic Policy, it aimed both to stimulate the economy and to cut inflation. The plan involved floating the dollar against gold for the first time, imposing a 10 percent import tax, restoring the investment tax credit, providing income tax relief, repealing the excise tax on automobiles, and imposing a ninety-day freeze on wage and price hikes. This last measure, never before done in peacetime, was particularly extreme.

Coming from a moderate Republican who supposedly favored the free market, the wage and price freezes were surprising. Even more oddly, the Democrats helped set the stage for many of these freezes by passing the Economic Stabilization Act of 1970, which granted the president unprecedented power to "stabilize prices, rents, wages, and salaries."[60] The Democrats never believed that Nixon would resort to these measures; they thought they could embarrass him, at no cost to themselves, by giving him tools that he would never use and then blaming him for not using them. But as he so often did, Nixon out-thought the Democrats, and they were forced to go along with his liberal, stimulative policies.

As the 1972 election neared, Nixon increased the fiscal stimulus, hoping to prime the economy and win over voters. By the final quarter of 1972, the economy was growing at a robust 11.6 percent. Nixon won reelection in a landslide. By 1973, however, when the administration finally lifted the price controls, inflation returned and the bill for his artificial overheating of the economy came due. Finally, Nixon implemented Game Plan IV, involving a return to the "old Nixon" of tight fiscal and monetary policies.

On the economy, in particular, the Nixon record has long been a sore spot for conservatives. Nixon's economic policies were all over the map, ranging from traditional Republican approaches, to mainstream Democratic ones, to leftist wage and price controls, and finally back to traditional Republican measures. His economic apostasies alienated conservatives, as did his big-government focus in other areas.

Reviewing Nixon's domestic policy record in full, as I did for a 2013 op-ed I wrote marking the centennial of his birth, I was struck by his willingness to inject government into domestic policy. This was the case whether Nixon was implementing economic measures, as we have just seen, or implementing a vast web of new regulatory and administrative bureaucracies, which have endured in the American economy and had major influence on business and consumer behavior, ranging from the Consumer Product Safety Commission to the Occupational Health and Safety Administration. But it was in the area of environmental protections that the Nixon administration may have left its most enduring regulatory legacy.

The Environmental President

"I hope that you become known as Mr. Clean," Democratic senator Edmund Muskie, a leading environmentalist, told William D. Ruckelshaus at his 1970 confirmation hearing to become the first head of the new Environmental Protection Agency (EPA), which Nixon had announced the creation of earlier that year.[61] "It was not long," Jack Lewis wrote, "before the media were portraying William Ruckelshaus as a knight in shining armor charging out to do battle with the wicked polluters of America."[62]

Today, Democrats and Republicans eagerly tout their environmental credentials, though Democrats, with their more favorable attitudes toward regulation, enjoy, by far, a stronger public identification with proenvironmental "green" policies. Few today realize the irony of this association—most do now know that it was Richard Nixon, not the any of the Democrats, who first forged a strong environmental record for the White House, and it was Nixon who put in place the framework of the modern environmental regulatory apparatus.

As recently as the early sixties, the environment was barely on the American radar screen as a political issue. But in 1962, with the publication of Rachel Carson's powerful bestseller *Silent Spring*, awareness increased and momentum built for environmental legislation. An oil spill in Santa Barbara in 1969 had been the largest in American history up to that point and caused public outrage.[63] In 1970, Wisconsin Democratic senator Gaylord Nelson created Earth Day, putting environmentalism onto the national agenda.[64]

Unlike welfare and health care reform, where past personal experience motivated Nixon, he did not come to the environmental issue with any real passion. He had not regarded the environment as a pressing issue before it came onto the public agenda. As the movement gained momentum, he was slow to become receptive to its message—and, in fact, in private conversations in the Oval Office, was heard calling environmentalists "kooks" and "enemies of the system." It was John Ehrlichman, Nixon's counsel and assistant for domestic affairs, who did the most to get the environment onto the Nixon agenda. Ehrlichman, despite his Watergate infamy, had a progressive side: he had specialized in land-use law, and one forest preservationist even called him "the most effective environmentalist since Gifford Pinchot,"[65] referring to the head of the US Forest Service under Theodore Roosevelt. Ehrlichman's advocacy finally woke up Nixon to the issue's importance, though to Nixon, the importance was political more than anything else. Showing his lack of genuine conviction about the cause, he once told Ehrlichman, "Just keep me out of trouble on environmental issues."[66]

And yet, in 1985 the *EPA Journal* conceded Nixon's achievement in turning his initial reluctance on environmental policy into "a show of visionary statesmanship."[67] The president declared that "our national government today is not structured to make a coordinated attack on the pollutants which debase the air we breathe, the water we drink, and the land that grows our food."[68] Thus in 1970, Nixon created the EPA, installed Ruckelshaus as administrator, and also created the Occupational Safety and Health Administration (OSHA).[69] Eventually, Nixon also supported and signed the Clean Air Act, which required that the EPA establish national air quality standards and set deadlines for reducing automobile emission target levels.[70]

Even though Nixon's critics have pointed out that he vetoed the Clean Water Act, the president generally supported the goals of that law. He vetoed the bill when it came to his desk because he objected to the $18 billion price tag the Democratic Congress had put on it, which he viewed as a budget buster. Congress passed the bill over his veto in 1972, but Nixon's objections later proved to be valid: the $18 billion wasn't even spendable within the time frame for which it was intended, and the cost of the act was in reality closer to Nixon's lower estimates. It is likely that the Democrats set the cost deliberately high to force Nixon into a politically unpopular move. His veto had nothing to do with his views on the issue.

But the Clean Water episode is a good illustration of how Nixon approached environmentalism in true Republican fashion, in the best sense of that term—that is, he endorsed the role and capacity of government to address a public problem, while at the same time insisting that these government efforts should not be so prohibitively expensive or counterproductive to economic growth that they would wind up doing more harm than good. The Nixon administration's rigorous cost-benefit analyses of every environmental proposal infuriated ardent members of the Green movement, who felt that price tags should be irrelevant. The most extreme among them tended to confirm Nixon in his views that environmentalists could be broken out into two groups: antimarket or promarket. The antimarket Greens wanted the most sweeping reforms passed without regard to economic impact, whereas the promarket Greens recognized the need to harmonize environmental protection with economic growth. As Nixon thought of it, when given a choice between "smoke and jobs," he would take jobs. This approach, which movement environmentalists saw as being hopelessly compromised, is responsible for the most important set of environmental regulations ever written in America.

Under Nixon, the federal government joined the environmental movement and gave the force of law and regulatory muscle to controlling industrial pollution and monitoring air and water standards. He passed much of his environmental program with bipartisan cooperation.[71] Nixon's environmental record—"yet to be improved upon by any president," wrote Tom Wicker[72]—is one of his most enduring legacies.

Some environmentalists, however, did appreciate what Nixon had given to the movement. "I doubt seriously whether Richard Nixon ever envisioned the way the environmental movement would develop when he assembled the EPA from a federal hodgepodge of diverse offices," James F. Ryan wrote for the American Chemical Society. "Although Nixon was presumably motivated by politics, he undeniably did a good thing. Meanwhile, you wonder how succeeding presidents will be judged on their environmental records."[73]

Indeed, few presidents have matched Nixon's achievements in this area. For a time, Nixon also inoculated the Republican Party against charges of environmental sensitivity. He provided a template, as he so often did, for how to claim the positions of the center and even some of the Left on an environmental policy issue and use them to strengthen Republicans' stance against unpopular proposals of Democratic opponents. As late as 1988, for instance, George H.W. Bush was able to attack his Democratic opponent for president, Massachusetts governor Michael Dukakis, for the polluted condition of Boston Harbor. Moreover, the Republicans were able to paint Democrats, often, as too liberal and extreme on environmental issues—such as in the late 1980s, when Democrats wanted to stop logging in Washington state in order to save the spotted owl. With so much mainstream environmental ground already covered by the Republicans, moderate American voters found these Democratic positions too extreme.

Since then, however, the Republican Party has lost almost all of its ground on environmental issues. Republicans have become the party of climate change denial, and this position has cost them in public perception. Even Republicans on the Senate Environment Committee have indicated their scorn for climate science. Senator James Inhofe called climate change the "greatest hoax ever perpetrated on the American people," while Senator David Vitter described talk of climate change as "ridiculous pseudo-science garbage that's so common on the left on this issue," adding that, "I think there is beginning to be a serious reconsideration of the science of this."[74]

It's difficult to imagine Richard Nixon taking such positions. More likely, he would have acknowledged the reality of climate change, pushed for serious but reasonable efforts to combat it, and ensured that such measures did not hamper American economic competitiveness. That type of pragmatic approach squared with most Americans' positions on the issue in the early 1970s—and the ones most hold today as well.

The "Warmonger" Who Ended the Draft

Finally, there is the remarkable story of the Republican president whose political adversaries never tired of branding him a warmonger—even though he was actually the one who ended the draft. Nixon, with his fine-tuned political antennae, sensed that abolishing the draft was not only in the public interest but also smart politics. In 1968, he ran, in part, on a promise to bring an end to the draft and transition the US military to an all-volunteer service while also pledging to be the candidate who could conclude the war in Vietnam. "It is not so much the way they are selected that is wrong, it is the fact of selection," he said.[75] In his ever-agile mind, Nixon saw multiple rationales—and multiple benefits—to ending the draft.

One of his reasons was pragmatic. In 1967, during his run for the Republican nomination, Nixon hired as his research director Martin Anderson, a conservative thinker who made an economic case against the draft. Anderson argued that an all-volunteer service would be good for national security, as there were "a high number of trainees and inexperienced men who must constantly be replaced." The research director told Nixon that the reason the draft had been necessary in the first place was "simply that we have not been willing to pay even reasonably fair wages to our men in the military."[76]

Not long after being inaugurated, Nixon set up a commission to explore the idea of a volunteer army. The commission developed a number of compelling proposals, but it is best remembered today for the debate that broke out between two men who came to testify before it, resulting in an all-volunteer army in the United States. The debate was between Milton Friedman, the University of Chicago professor and founder of monetarist economics, and General William Westmoreland, the former commander of American forces in Vietnam. After listening to Friedman argue for the merits of an all-volunteer army—which Friedman believed would both advance personal freedom and national security, Westmoreland replied: "Professor, everything you say makes so much sense, but I'm not sure I'd like to command an army of mercenaries."

"Would you rather command an army of slaves?" Friedman shot back.

When Westmoreland replied that he didn't like hearing patriotic draftees being compared with slaves, Friedman said that he didn't like hearing patriotic volunteers being compared with mercenaries.[77] The exchange showed the strong feelings that existed on both sides of the issue. The commission eventually reported back that, in its view, the United States could maintain its military strength without conscription. The last draft call took place on December 7, 1972. Since then, the US military has been all volunteer.

Nixon's decision to end conscription was hugely popular, and any move to bring back the draft—as some have suggested in the years since—never gets very far. Still, in its forty-plus years, the all-volunteer army has had its critics. Some, like New York congressman Charles Rangel, say that the draft should be reinstituted, because the burden of fighting America's wars has fallen disproportionately on poor and working-class citizens who enlist in the military. Rangel's criticism is not without merit, though it is also ironic: this same criticism—that the poor and working class were doing most of the nation's fighting in Vietnam—contributed to the move to end the inequitable draft system in the early 1970s, on the basis that more privileged Americans could avoid service by obtaining college deferments.

Another criticism of the volunteer army is political. Some say that since only a small proportion of Americans fight the nation's wars, the public can "check out of" foreign policy and pay less attention to our military engagements. Some generals believe that if the draft were still in force, America would never have invaded Iraq in 2003.

These are important considerations, yet there is no denying the success of America's professional military, which remains the best in the world. In the generation since Nixon ended military conscription, the US military has become an unparalleled force, setting a new standard of effectiveness and professionalism. From the Gulf War in 1991—its first great test—to the wars in Iraq and Afghanistan, the all-volunteer American military has proved essentially unbeatable. The wars in which it has engaged, however, have proved intractable, for political and cultural reasons. The military's job is to fight and win, and the American military has never been better at doing that. How the politicians choose to use this power, of course, is another matter.

The American armed forces today are also the best trained and best educated that we have ever had. The mindset of a professionalized army is completely different from that of a fighting force filled with involuntary conscripts serving eighteen- to twenty-four-month tours. The casualty rates for American forces in armed conflicts since the institution of the all-volunteer army began have been dramatically lower than in previous wars.

"The record of the Nixon years," wrote a member of the Gates Commission in a *New York Times* op-ed in 1994, "must include his role in ending compulsion and expanding freedom of choice. Thanks to his actions, the United States armed forces are stronger and more efficient."[78]

★ ★ ★ ★ ★

Of course, it was not just on the draft that Nixon's policies would prove surprising when it came to military and national-defense issues. For it was in the realm of foreign policy itself that he would pave the ground of his greatest achievements. And, just as with domestic policy, his achievements as a statesman often ran counter to the image he had fostered in the public mind.

– CHAPTER 2 –

The Foreign Policy Visionary

Nixon's visit to China is one of the few occasions where a state visit brought about a seminal change in international affairs. The reentry of China into the global diplomatic game, and the increased strategic options for the United States, gave a new vitality and flexibility to the international system.... Consultation between China and the United States reached a level of intensity rare even among former allies.

— HENRY KISSINGER[1]

Nixon and Kissinger's overture forever changed the Cold War by reconfiguring the Communist bloc and bringing Washington and Beijing together to balance Moscow.... The process that Nixon set in motion—the former Red-baiter breaking the taboo on talks with the massive communist power—led to one of those rare times in history when daring leadership actually did redirect the course of events for the better.

— ORVILLE SCHELL[2]

By July of 1959, the American people already had a pretty good idea of Richard Nixon. He had entered Congress in 1947 and risen to fame rapidly as the chief accuser of Alger Hiss, the former high-level FDR aide who had hidden his ties to the Communist Party. Nixon had won a 1950 Senate election by branding his opponent Helen Gahagan Douglas the "pink lady" for her far-left views and sympathies. He had scratched and clawed to keep his place on the presidential ticket in 1952 with his famous televised "Checkers" speech. And now, a year away from the 1960 presidential election, it was common knowledge that Dwight Eisenhower's number two would run for the top job.

By 1959 Vice President Nixon was known, but not necessarily understood. Then he went to Moscow to visit the American National Exhibition. The year before, the Soviets had put up an exhibit in New York; the Americans were reciprocating, as part of an effort by the superpowers to improve relations. On arriving in Moscow, Nixon had met with Soviet Premier Nikita Khrushchev; when Khrushchev visited New York, Nixon took the Soviet leader on a tour of the exhibit.

Khrushchev surprised Nixon with his aggressiveness and belligerence. As the American vice president stood with the Soviet leader at the exhibit showing him the wonders of color television—then a new innovation—Khrushchev scoffed, and then began challenging Nixon on the US sponsorship of Captive Nations Week, in which Americans were asked to pray for "peoples enslaved by the Soviet Union."

Reaching out for a burly Russian worker, Khrushchev asked: "Does this man look like a slave laborer?"

Nixon did not back down, but, trying to be gracious, said: "There must be an exchange of ideas. After all, you don't know everything." And then he smiled, trying to defuse the tension. The two leaders moved across the gallery to a display model of what was billed as a typical American house, complete with a new washing machine. And right there, as he and Khrushchev stood perched by the railing separating the kitchen, Nixon let the Soviet premier have it.

"Would it not be better to compete in the relative merit of washing machines," he asked Khrushchev, "than in the strength of rockets?"

"Yes, but your generals say we must compete in rockets," said the Soviet leader. "We are strong and we can beat you." And in fact, at that moment in history, the Soviets did outpace the United States in rocket thrust. But Nixon was unfazed.

"In this day and age to argue who is stronger completely misses the point," he said. "With modern weapons it just does not make sense. If war comes we both lose." Earlier, Khrushchev had talked over Nixon, but now Nixon turned the tables and cut the Soviet leader off.

"I hope the prime minister understands all the implications of what I just said…," Nixon asserted. "Whether you place either one of the powerful nations in a position so that they have no choice but to accept dictation or fight, then you are playing with the most destructive power in the world…. When we sit down at a conference table it cannot be all one way. One side cannot put an ultimatum to another."

"Our country has never been guided by ultimatums," Khrushchev finally offered. "It sounds like a threat."

"Who is threatening?" Nixon asked.

"You want to threaten us indirectly," the Soviet leader said. "We have powerful weapons, too, and ours are better than yours if you want to compete."

"Immaterial," said Nixon. "I don't think peace is helped by reiterating that you have more strength than us, because that is a threat, too." And then he gently jabbed Khrushchev in the chest.[3]

"We want peace with all nations, especially America," said Khrushchev, now sounding conciliatory.

"We also want peace," said Nixon. But: "In order to have peace, Mr. Prime Minister, there must be a sitting down at the table and a discussion in which each sees the points of the other."[4]

Nixon's showdown with Khrushchev made front pages around the world, and the picture of the two, perched over the kitchen railing, with Nixon looking very much in charge, became the iconic image of what was soon dubbed the "Kitchen Debate." Nixon, *Time* enthused, had "managed in a unique way to personify a national character proud of peaceful accomplishment, sure of its way of life, confident of its power under threat."[5] Khrushchev thought so, too: he didn't forget his encounter with Nixon, whom he now saw as a determined advocate for America and a potentially formidable adversary, should he win the White House. He did whatever he could, he admitted years later, to help defeat Nixon in the 1960 presidential election.

Foreign affairs were always Nixon's deepest interest, and the staunch anti-Communism of his early career had a natural connection with events overseas. In the late 1940s, when Nixon's political career began, it seemed world Communism was on an inexorable march: the Soviets had built their Iron Curtain of Eastern European satellite states, and in 1949, Chinese Communists, led by Mao Zedong, had prevailed in the Chinese Civil War and took power on the Chinese mainland—a shattering blow to freedom for the world. In 1956, Soviet tanks rolled into Hungary to suppress a Democratic movement there. Overhanging all of this was the threat of nuclear annihilation, as the United States and Soviet Union built stockpiles of deadly weapons powerful enough to wipe out any decent concept of human existence.

What Americans saw in the Kitchen Debate was a political leader with the substantive knowledge to go head to head in debate with the leader of Soviet Russia—and to be articulate and resolute in defending the American way of life while doing it. Nixon did not have to worry about whether people saw him as tough on Communism. In fact, when he finally did enter the White House in 1969, many critics had the opposite concern: they felt he would be too much the Cold Warrior, unable and unwilling to manage a more peaceful relationship with the Soviet Union.

Yet the Kitchen Debate provided a clue here as well. "In order to have peace," Nixon had insisted, "there must be a sitting down at the table and a discussion in which each sees the points of the other." And as president, much to the surprise of supporters and critics, Nixon would do precisely that with the leaders of the two great Communist powers—not just with the Soviet Union but also with China. He would do it with an approach that I call visionary realism, whereby he exercised a profound strategic wisdom that somehow balanced big-picture thinking with recognition of the realities of the world. And he would do it at a time when the United States faced not just the daunting Cold War challenges of these relationships but also the ongoing bloodbath in Vietnam, which raged on with no end in sight. Nixon's foreign policy record is large and complex, but for most Americans now, it comes down to three main areas: relations with Russia; relations with China; and the Vietnam War. In each of these areas, Nixon pursued shrewd, strategic, even brilliant policies, though to be sure, this was no guarantee of their enduring success.

Vietnam and Southeast Asia

The Vietnam War paralyzed American foreign policy and traumatized American society. Nixon hadn't initiated the American military presence in Vietnam, let alone escalated it. But he was determined, as president, to get America out of it. And his foreign policy began with that objective.

When Nixon entered office in January 1969, the war in Vietnam was by far the nation's most pressing foreign policy issue. Over sixteen thousand Americans had been killed in combat in 1968, the worst casualty year yet for the United States. Worse, the war wasn't going well; despite years of assurances from the Pentagon and the Johnson administration that a turning point was near, it became clear to the American people in 1968, with the Communist Tet Offensive, that the war would continue to rage on. Even relatively conservative Middle Americans were losing faith in the effort, and they looked to Nixon to find a way out. Most did not favor the Left's calls for unilateral withdrawal, but they did want American troops to start coming home—preferably, after winning the war.

Nixon had promised as a presidential candidate in 1968 that he had a secret plan to end the war, though he didn't really have such a plan—at least, nothing that matched the drama of that description. What he developed, once in the Oval Office, was a plan that addressed Americans' now-prevailing interest: getting Americans home. Thus was born Nixon's policy of "Vietnamization," in which he would bring American troops home by the tens of thousands while preparing the Saigon regime to take on more of the war-fighting burden. However, at the same time, Nixon always privately vowed to himself that he would not be the first American president to lose a war, and thus his Vietnam approach had two prongs, which were somewhat mutually exclusive of each other: (1) to get out while saving face as best as possible, and (2) to win. And these conflicting priorities would overhang everything Nixon and Henry Kissinger did when it came to Vietnam.

In his November 3, 1969, address, Nixon laid out his new approach to the nation's commitment in Southeast Asia:

> In the previous administration, we Americanized the war in Vietnam. In this administration, we are Vietnamizing the search for peace. The policy of the previous administration not only resulted in our assuming the primary responsibility for fighting the war, but even more significantly did not adequately stress the goal of strengthening the South Vietnamese so that they could defend themselves when we left.... We have adopted a plan which we have worked out in cooperation with the South Vietnamese for a complete withdrawal of all U.S. combat ground forces, and their replacement by South Vietnamese forces on an orderly scheduled timetable. This withdrawal will be made from strength and not from weakness. As South Vietnamese forces become stronger, the rate of American withdrawal can become greater.[6]

As American troops started returning home, the pressure on the South Vietnam military to carry the fighting load increased. Nixon hoped that US aerial firepower could help even the odds. He coupled his withdrawal of American troops with massive "carpet-bombing" campaigns against North Vietnamese bases in Laos and Cambodia.

These efforts commenced with Operation Menu in 1969, in which Nixon deployed American B-52 bombers. His efforts were part strategic and part psychological—he wondered whether he could get better results if Hanoi believed that he was a genuine "madman" or "mad bomber." Perhaps, he mused on more on than one occasion to Henry Kissinger, if the North Vietnamese and their Communist allies in the region felt that he might go to any length—including the use of nuclear weapons—they might be more inclined to come to the negotiating table. "Ho Chi Minh himself will be in Paris in two days begging for peace," Nixon told Bob Haldeman.[7] But Nixon's blunter measures—from mining Haiphong Harbor and bombing the Ho Chi Minh Trail in Cambodia to issuing a worldwide nuclear alert—did not make Hanoi back down.

In spring 1970, Nixon upped the ante in Cambodia. Frustrated by the continued presence of large North Vietnamese supply caches in the country and the North's use of portions of the country as staging grounds for attacks, he ordered a joint invasion (he called it an "incursion") of the country by American and South Vietnamese troops. His "secret" bombing of Cambodia in 1970 ignited domestic unrest in the United States, sparking the last great wave of campus protests—the largest in American history—which culminated tragically. National Guardsmen fired at protestors at Kent State University, killing four. Two weeks later, at a protest at Jackson State in Mississippi, police fired again on protestors, killing two.

Nixon expressed sorrow about the incidents, but he also made clear that the increasingly violent antiwar movement bore significant responsibility. "This should remind us all once again that when dissent turns to violence, it invites tragedy. It is my hope that this tragic and unfortunate incident will strengthen the determination of the nation's campuses—administrators, faculty, and students alike—to stand firmly for the right which exists in this country of peaceful dissent and just as strongly against the resort to violence as a means of such expression."[8] Polls showed that the majority of Americans shared his views about the war and the limits of domestic dissent.

The outcry promoted by Nixon's Cambodia policies might have obscured the broader story, at least from an American perspective: the troops were coming home in massive numbers. On his promise to Vietnamize the war and reduce the American troop commitment, Nixon could hardly have been truer to his word. By April 1972, even in the midst of another massive North Vietnamese offensive, Nixon was able to cite the figures to the American people in a nationally televised speech:

> On January 20, 1969, the American troop ceiling in Vietnam was 549,000. Our casualties were running as high as 300 a week. Thirty thousand young Americans were being drafted every month.
>
> Today, 39 months later, through our program of Vietnamization helping the South Vietnamese develop the capability of defending themselves—the number of Americans in Vietnam by Monday, May 1, will have been reduced to 69,000. Our casualties—even during the present, all-out enemy offensive—have been reduced by 95 percent. And draft calls now average fewer than 5,000 men a month, and we expect to bring them to zero next year.[9]

In branding the North Vietnamese offensive "a clear case of naked and unprovoked aggression across an international border," Nixon made clear that the attack was being repelled solely by South Vietnamese forces. "There are no United States ground troops involved," Nixon said. "None will be involved."[10]

These massive troop withdrawals not only lowered American casualties in Vietnam but also slowly drained the life out of the antiwar movement at home—and with that, finally brought a close to the anarchic energies of the late 1960s, which a few years earlier had seemed to threaten the capacity of the United States to govern itself. Yet Nixon received virtually no credit for the twin feats of saving American lives and restoring American domestic tranquility.

The remaining problem, for Nixon, was the outcome of the war itself.

The truth of the matter was that Nixon saw Vietnam, to some extent, as a distraction from big-power, Cold War–related politics—the great matters of state that mattered most to him, and in which he hoped to have the most far-reaching impact. So he wanted to get out of Vietnam for many of the same reasons that the American people did. Unlike them, however, he had to worry about his reelection. Nixon's management of the American withdrawal from Vietnam was at least partially influenced by his concern over electoral politics—namely, that the war not be brought to an end too quickly, lest problems develop in the interim that might reflect badly on the administration's policies.

Documentary evidence suggests that Kissinger convinced the president that total American troop withdrawals should not be completed until after the 1972 elections.[11] And, in fact, twenty years later, during the 1992 presidential primaries, Nixon even told reporters that George H. W. Bush should have kept the Gulf War running through the campaign, as it would have helped his reelection chances.

"We had a lot of success with that in 1972," Nixon said.[12]

Yet Nixon did succeed in bringing the war to an end, even if the process was protracted and difficult. Peace talks in Paris, which had continued off and on for years, finally began to pick up momentum in 1972. In October of that year, just a month before the presidential election—with Nixon holding a commanding lead in the polls over George McGovern—Kissinger held a press conference and announced that peace was at hand. He hadn't apparently cleared that view with South Vietnam's president Thiêu, who objected to terms that would allow Hanoi to retain all of its current territory. But with peace—of a kind—so near to achievement, Nixon knew that he held the advantage, and he pressured Thiêu to accept the agreement by threatening to cut off aid to Saigon. The South Vietnamese president resisted, continuing to push for changes to the tentative agreement; when the North Vietnamese responded by also backing away from the talks, Nixon was left looking for leverage.

He and Kissinger then unleashed the so-called Christmas Bombings in late December to try to bring Hanoi back to the negotiating table. Undertaken a month after Nixon had won the greatest landslide in presidential history, the bombings were some of the most massive in the history of warfare. They did extensive damage to North Vietnamese infrastructure, and Nixon credited the bombardment with bringing Hanoi back to the peace table (others dispute the cause and effect). Perhaps the bombings had the effect Nixon claimed, perhaps not; without question, the momentum for a peace agreement was strong on the American side, and he and Kissinger were determined to bring it to closure. On January 27, 1973, the Paris Peace Accords were signed, bringing an end to American participation in the Vietnam War, the nation's longest military conflict.

The agreement constituted "peace with honor," Nixon said in a televised address to the American people.[13] Others had their doubts. Critics pointed out that the peace terms—under which the North would be permitted to keep 140,000 troops in South Vietnam, even as American troops withdrew their presence down to zero—were essentially the same as the ones on offer in 1969. And since 1969, they said, an additional twenty-five thousand Americans had died in combat. What had been gained?

That question became more haunting as the peace agreement broke down, due largely to blatant violations by the North Vietnamese Communists. By later in 1973, the two sides were fighting again, and President Thiêu declared the agreement null and void. The now fully Vietnamized fighting forces of the South proved, alas, not able to repel the North's march—and Nixon, by now reeling under the Watergate scandal, had lost his political leverage to help Saigon. In August 1974, when Nixon resigned the presidency, the war was going very poorly for the South. By spring 1975, the North Vietnamese were nearing Saigon. Thiêu appealed to President Gerald Ford for assistance, but the new Congress, chock full of new progressive Democratic arrivals, elected on anti-Watergate sentiment, blocked the request—one of the most shameful congressional moments in American history, representing a flat-out desertion of an ally in dire need. Thiêu resigned, accusing the Americans of betraying his country—not only by abandoning him but also by forcing him into the 1973 peace agreement. On April 30, the North Vietnamese overran Saigon. The Vietnam War ended at last with victory for the Communists. The North and South would soon unite to become the Socialist Republic of Vietnam.

In total, fifty-eight thousand Americans lost their lives in Vietnam, and given its tragic outcome, the sense remains that they died in vain. Some blamed Nixon for prolonging a war that, they claimed, he and Henry Kissinger were never fully interested in winning; all they wanted, on this view, was to establish a "decent interval" between final withdrawal from Vietnam and the total collapse of the Saigon regime. Critics claimed that they cared only about securing the release of American POWs and covering themselves from political damage in the 1972 elections. Otherwise, South Vietnam would be left to fend for itself.[14] Of course, even if one accepts this view, it would at most apportion only partial blame to Nixon. The commitments made by Nixon's predecessor, Lyndon B. Johnson, and even Johnson's predecessor, John F. Kennedy, were fateful as well.

I believe, however, that Nixon's own assessment of these events is closer to the mark. He always maintained that the United States had left Paris in 1973 with a solid agreement to win the peace—and he saw a different culprit in the demise of South Vietnam. "By 1973," Nixon would later tell Monica Crowley, his assistant in his final years, "we had achieved our political objective; South Vietnam's independence had been secured. But by 1975, the Congress destroyed our ability to enforce the Paris agreement and left our allies vulnerable to Hanoi's invading forces. If I sound like I'm blaming Congress, I am."[15] Indeed, it is impossible to overlook the magnitude of Congress's decision to wash its hands of the war in 1975.

The American loss in Vietnam was one of the most bitter chapters in American history and continues to haunt our politics today, but Nixon makes a legitimate case in saying that he left the disposition of the war in a manageable state. As the leader of a democracy, he was bound to consult the sentiment of the popular majority, which overwhelmingly desired a drawdown of the American commitment—even if the hope was that such a withdrawal could be done in concert with a victorious outcome. Ultimately, Nixon had to address the American interest first, and in bringing the troops home, reducing American casualties, and securing terms for what, at least in theory, could have been a manageable peace, he achieved as much and probably more than any other president could have done in similar circumstances. It is true that he agreed to a peace in 1973 that he could have had four years earlier—but whether it had been agreed to at the later date or in 1969, Nixon seemed to have gotten the best terms he could have. He extracted the United States from a war that was costing it dearly in human, political, and financial terms. If this doesn't count quite as a resounding triumph, it deserves the more sober term "achievement." It took some doing.

Nixon's conduction of the war had several substantive effects beyond Vietnam. At home, congressional anger about his actions in Cambodia led to the adoption of the War Powers Resolution in 1973, a federal law that reined in a president's ability to wage acts of war without congressional approval. Of course, the Constitution already makes this clear, but the decade of war in Vietnam prompted congressional liberals to make the terms more specific: presidents would have to notify Congress within forty-eight hours of committing forces, and they could not keep them engaged for longer than sixty days without congressional authorization. The law was passed over Nixon's veto. Yet nearly forty years later, it did not prevent Barack Obama from waging an undeclared war in Libya.

More broadly, Vietnam was one of the central drivers of Americans' loss of faith and confidence in government—a confidence that would never again reach the levels of the early postwar period. And, of course, Nixon would be the central player in another driving event: Watergate, which was just beginning to unfold when the Paris Peace Accords were signed. Watergate would not only shatter the confidence of Americans in the honesty and reliability of their government; it would also cripple the remaining American resolve to assist our South Vietnamese ally. Without Watergate, it's unlikely that the Congress would have so brazenly abandoned Saigon in 1975. The two events are unimaginable without each other.

And so Vietnam cannot be scored as one of Nixon's happier chapters—indeed, every American president that touched it has found himself scarred. Yet Nixon did fulfill, however imperfectly, his promise to the American people to end the war. There is much to criticize in how he got it done, but it shouldn't be forgotten that he *did* get it done.

It's safe to say, though, that if Nixon's main foreign policy feat was ending the Vietnam War, his legacy would be checkered at best. But of course, it was not with Vietnam that Nixon left his deepest mark. Nixon will be remembered in history as the American president who ended the global isolation of Communist China, paving the way for normalization of diplomatic relations—with world-historical implications.

China

In 1969, when Nixon took power, many in the American foreign policy establishment still clung to a view of world Communism that held that the Russians, the Chinese, the North Vietnamese, and Communists elsewhere all moved in sync, united in ideology and goals. Yet the Russian-Chinese relationship had imploded earlier in the decade, and it was clear by 1969 that nothing like a Russian-Chinese alliance any longer existed. Quite the contrary: the two Communist powers had become bitter foes. During Nixon's first year in office, the Russians and Chinese came closer than they ever had before to going to war. During the spring and summer of 1969, Chinese troops crossed the disputed Ussuri River to ambush the island of Zhenbao (Damanski). But the Russians retook the territory in a successful counteroffensive two weeks later. The fighting took about a thousand lives on both sides, and according to recently released documents, the Soviets seriously considered a nuclear strike against the Chinese.[16] The United States persuaded the Soviets to stand down.

Nixon saw the Soviet Union's actions as a troubling new phase in the Cold War, reinforcing an idea that had been building in his mind for years: the United States should try to develop constructive relations with the Chinese. It was the Soviets, Nixon told his national-security staff, who posed the greater danger. It would not serve American interests, he stressed, to see the Chinese "smashed" in a war with Russia.[17] The Chinese feared the Soviets, Nixon believed, and these clashes might push China toward developing a better relationship with the United States—and thus help contain Soviet power. The Sino-Soviet Split presented the United States with an opportunity to position itself between the two Communist powers—not only lessening chances that they might become allies again but also reducing the risk to the United States of a three-pronged Cold War. And with the United States and China opening relations, Nixon reasoned, the Russians would be motivated to improve relations with Washington as well.

This was hardly the prevailing outlook in 1969. Not only was it a minority view in the American foreign policy establishment; even Nixon's own top officials didn't share it. At first, Henry Kissinger could not understand the president's desire to reach out to China. "Our leader has taken leave of reality," Kissinger told his staff in 1969. "He thinks this is the moment to establish normal relations with Communist China. He has just ordered me to make this flight of fancy come true...China!"[18]

Years later, Kissinger would write that he and Nixon came to the idea of approaching China independently. But the documentary record offers no support for such claims. By all available evidence, the opening to China was Nixon's idea alone.

Nixon's anti-Communism, while genuine, had always obscured a more pragmatic, realistic side, which he prided himself on as a student of world affairs. As early as 1954, when he was a young vice president, Nixon had suggested a more conciliatory policy toward China. Nixon did, however, oppose President Kennedy's proposal to allow China a seat in the UN, saying that it would "irreparably weaken" the rest of Asia. Well into the 1960s, hardline views on Red China, as it was then known, were firmly in the mainstream. In 1966, a Harris poll showed that 58 percent of Americans opposed giving recognition to mainland China and would vote against a candidate proposing it. Yet, Nixon, during that same year, confided to philanthropist Elmer Bobst that his dream was "to bring China into the world."[19]

Nixon had recognized for some time that China was on the world scene to stay, and that Taiwan leader Chiang Kai-shek's dream of returning to mainland China would never happen. The United States, Nixon had come to believe, had to take the world as it found it—and nowhere did this apply more than to China.

The next year, Nixon authored a seminal article in *Foreign Affairs*, "Asia after Viet Nam," in which he tried to determine the future of Asia—and the US policy toward Asia—beyond the impact of the Vietnam War. Envisioning a future that he would soon help to bring about, Nixon wrote:

> Taking the long view, we simply cannot afford to leave China forever outside the family of nations, there to nurture its fantasies, cherish its hates and threaten its neighbors. There is no place on this small planet for a billion of its potentially most able people to live in angry isolation. But we could go disastrously wrong if, in pursuing this long-range goal, we failed in the short range to read the lessons of history.
>
> The world cannot be safe until China changes. Thus our aim, to the extent that we can influence events, should be to induce change. The way to do this is to persuade China that it must change: that it cannot satisfy its imperial ambitions, and that its own national interest requires a turning away from foreign adventuring and a turning inward toward the solution of its own domestic problems.[20]

From early in his first term, then, Nixon set the machinery to work in a long process to pave the way for improved relations with China. In 1969, Nixon's secretary of state, William Rogers, announced the administration's Two Chinas policy, which conceded the existence of mainland Communist China and a Nationalist China on the island of Taiwan. That year, the United States gradually lifted a twenty-year economic embargo on China, and within a few years, also ended a trade ban. And the two countries restarted ambassadorial talks in Warsaw in 1970—though the talks were short-circuited when the Chinese walked out in protest of the US bombing of Cambodia.[21]

The public knew little about Nixon's overtures. The most high-profile hint of anything like rapprochement between the two countries came in April 1971, when Mao Zedong invited an American ping-pong team, competing in the World Table Tennis Championship in Japan, to visit China. The players were the first Americans to visit China since 1949, when the Communists took over. The press called the goodwill gesture "ping-pong diplomacy."

Yet Mao's gesture was more than window dressing. The aging Communist dictator understood that he could not afford to be at such a sword's point with both the Soviet Union and the United States, and thus he sought out better relations with America. Diplomatic ties slowly and quietly grew between the two countries, and, in December 1970, Mao held high-level talks with US officials and indicated that he was willing to meet with Nixon. To pave the way for the meeting and eventual normalizing of relations, Nixon ended naval patrols of the Taiwan Strait, eased travel restrictions, and began referring to the "People's Republic of China"—a major symbolic milestone.

In June 1971, Kissinger traveled secretly to China to make preparations for a presidential visit. After Kissinger's return, Nixon finally went public with what he had in mind, dropping the bombshell of his presidency: He announced in a national address that he would travel to China the following year and meet with Mao, becoming the first American president to visit the People's Republic. The announcement stunned the world and was greeted largely with celebration.

"This is a turning point in world history—I cannot remember anything in my lifetime more exciting or more encouraging," said Great Britain's Lord Caradon, former ambassador to the United Nations. "This is one of the great moments in the world's history," said Joseph Luns, secretary general of NATO.[22] Many others echoed these sentiments, including the *New York Times*: "By his announcement last night, the President has radically improved the world atmosphere and raised the hopes of all men that the cause of peace in Vietnam and elsewhere will soon be substantially advanced."[23]

Later in 1971, the United States supported the seating of a Communist China representative at the United Nations (though Washington also tried and failed to ensure that a Taiwan delegation be seated as well). Nixon had risen to fame as an anti-Communist, and these announcements shocked many—especially on the conservative right. Millions of others, however, saw the move as a bold and hopeful one to dial down world tensions. Ever since its 1949 Communist Revolution, China had been cut off from the West; now, the president of the world's greatest power was opening the door to diplomatic recognition.

And so Nixon left Washington on February 17, 1972, heading for China after first spending three days in Guam to acclimate himself to the time difference. His plane touched down in Beijing on February 21. (It's worth noting that just as Nixon was leaving Washington to set out on his pilgrimage, US planes were dropping the largest tonnage of bombs on Vietnam since June 1968, thus sending a message to Beijing about American firmness in Southeast Asia.)[24]

The president's statesman's instincts were sharp, and he understood that the symbolism of his arrival—indeed, the symbolism of the entire trip—would likely prove more important than any substantive agreements. He instructed his aides to give priority to television reporters and television cameras over the print press—because he understood that the visual images from the trip would be more important than any written words. As he descended the steps of his plane to meet Chinese premier Chou En-lai, Nixon remembered how, in 1954, Secretary of State John Foster Dulles had insulted Chou by refusing to shake his hand. Now the most powerful man in the world offered his hand first, and Chou took it.

For a week, Nixon met with Chou en Lai and Mao in China, toured the Great Wall, and drank toasts with Chinese leaders. Though most Chinese did not own television sets, they followed the events via radio and the newspapers—causing the *People's Daily* to sell out of copies for the first time in living memory. Back in the United States, and around the world, a global audience of hundreds of millions watched the events—perhaps more people, Nixon said, than had watched any event in the history of the world.

The most important substantive achievement from Nixon's China trip was the trip itself and what it signified. But for all the pageantry, the two sides did formalize some agreements, which were contained in the Shanghai Communiqué. In broad terms, the agreements contained a pledge from both sides to work toward normalization of relations and not to seek "hegemony" in Asia. And, in what many saw as a warning to the Soviet Union, both sides added: "And each is opposed to efforts by any other country or group of countries to establish such hegemony."[25]

On the issue of Taiwan—an irresolvable issue, as the two sides had utterly unbridgeable positions—the American team came up with artful language: "The United States acknowledges that all Chinese on either side of the Taiwan Strait maintain there is but one China and that Taiwan is part of China."[26] Beijing, in turn, acknowledged that "the American people will continue to carry on commercial, cultural, and other unofficial contacts with the people of Taiwan." In effect, Nixon's opening of the US relations with China resulted in an agreement that China indeed existed as one country—while also allowing the United States to maintain that the territories would be overseen by two separate legitimate governments. It allowed the Americans to save face—even though, at the same time, the country was now shifting to a One China policy. Soon after the summit, the United States extended diplomatic recognition and declared that henceforth it would regard the People's Republic, and not Taiwan, as the legitimate national voice of the Chinese. America relinquished its opposition to Chinese entry into the United Nations, and groundwork was laid for the establishment of diplomatic relations (this did not happen until 1979). Many of the agreements struck in the Shanghai Communiqué continue to govern US-Chinese relations today, especially on the Taiwan issue.[27]

The political impact of the trip was immediate and entirely to Nixon's benefit. Nothing he did in office ever approached the acclaim he won for opening relations with China. Nixon had always been respected overseas as a serious political leader, but now he was viewed as a prominent figure in history, as well. At home, too, the trip helped him transform the 1972 presidential race, which once looked like it would be close, into the greatest rout in presidential history. Polls showed 84 percent approval for the China mission—even if conservatives analogized Nixon's outreach to Nuremberg prosecutors making amends with the Nazis. And while the conservative Right expressed disgust, a Gallup poll revealed that 83 percent of Republicans still supported him for reelection. Somehow he had retained most of his conservative support while pulling off a diplomatic feat that even the most liberal president would have been hard pressed to equal.

Nixon's overture to China must rank as one of the most audacious and far-reaching foreign policy moves by any American president. It opened the door for an American-Chinese relationship that exists today (with all the complexity that entails). "Nixon goes to China" has become a political metaphor referring to times when a politician with a staunch reputation in one area does something seemingly out of character with, and even in opposition to, his or her long-held principles—but pulls it off on the basis of credibility. (The classical composer John Adams even wrote a symphony about the events called *Nixon in China*.) Nixon was able to pull it off because as a Cold Warrior, he understood the need to break through a geopolitical state of affairs that had become counterproductive and dangerous. "In Asia, the United States was stuck with a China policy that obliged it to act as though Chiang [Kai-shek] and the other losers of the Chinese civil war were someday going to retake the mainland. The United States was enmeshed in a war in Vietnam that was costing up to 15,000 lives a year," James Mann wrote in his 1998 book *About Face*. "Nixon's initiative was aimed at breaking all of these shackles and creating a world in which American foreign policy would have greater flexibility."[28] This he achieved.

It is no accident that the peace process in Vietnam accelerated after Nixon's outreach to China. The United States had just strengthened its hand by forging relations with Beijing—and thereby putting the Russians, Hanoi's leading benefactor, on the defensive. Beyond the impact on Vietnam was the effect the visit had on the Cold War itself. And here, the effect of Nixon's outreach to China can hardly be overstated. Here was a split in the Eastern bloc; here was a division between the world's two foremost Communist powers, with one of them now openly embracing the United States as if not an ally, at least not a necessary enemy. This was a chess move on the world table that couldn't have come with higher stakes, and it was felt like an earthquake in

Moscow, which saw itself as losing leverage in the standoff with the United States. Moscow would have to think about dialing down tensions and making deals. And shortly thereafter, the general secretary of the Communist Party, Leonid Brezhnev, began reaching out to the Americans to do just that.

Over the long term, too, Nixon's opening of relations with China seems destined for a place in the annals of historic statesmanship. This becomes increasingly clear today, when the role of China in the world has changed so dramatically since Nixon's visit to Beijing forty years ago. A younger generation of Americans doesn't remember a time when China was not an integral, indeed leading, member of the global economic community. Nixon's historic visit can be regarded as the first step in China's amazing journey to becoming a world economic powerhouse—a position unimaginable in 1972.

Of course, for that reason, some rue Nixon's opening communication with Beijing. What, they ask, did the United States get out of it? Haven't we lost innumerable jobs to China, seeing our manufacturing plants shutter and our working people's wages fall? In a geopolitical sense, I believe that Nixon's China gambit bought the United States time and space—with Vietnam, in allowing a way out to be maneuvered; regarding Moscow, in putting more pressure on the Russians to negotiate; and with China itself, in reducing tensions between the two countries. Nixon pursued the national interest relentlessly, without regard to ideological fixations or party preferences.

More broadly, the United States did gain significantly from China's entry into the global economy, in that the massive availability of cheaper consumer goods has been a boon for those of lower or more modest incomes. Critics of free trade often point to the loss of manufacturing jobs as hurting those of modest means, and there is some truth to that, but they fail to account for the countervailing benefit of cheaper goods. And in China, American businesses have found an enormous and lucrative new market. Our exports to China increased over 600 percent between 2000 and 2011, as compared with just 170 percent to places elsewhere during that period. Chinese demand, in fact, may well be one of the principal drivers behind American job growth in the years ahead.[29]

This is not to suggest by any means that all is rosy, or that Nixon's geopolitical achievements have been entirely lasting. Hardly—in my previous book, *The Russia-China Axis*, I argued that the long Sino-Soviet split is over, and that the two former Communist adversaries have drawn closer and closer together into a de facto alliance against the United States and the Western democracies. This is particularly disheartening in light of the success Nixon had in managing the Chinese relationship—and to a substantial extent, the Russian one, too—and it reflects not only several decades of geopolitical trends but also a massive failure of American leadership. To see Moscow and Beijing jointly conspiring to facilitate rogue regimes like North Korea, Syrian, and Iran; to watch as they ramp up their conventional and nuclear armed forces, as we build ours down; and to understand that they are today's two leading practitioners of cyberwarfare is to recognize how far we have fallen from Nixon's successful balancing of these powers. We can only hope that in the presidential election of 2016, the United States gets the foreign policy leadership it deserves and, by now, so desperately needs.

And yet, the failure of Nixon's successors to maintain a constructive relationship with China as it grew into an economic power, and to manage the transition of Russia after the fall of Soviet Communism, does not detract from Nixon's achievement. Nixon himself was never ambivalent about the matter: he always saw his opening of US relations with China as his greatest accomplishment, the one for which he would be remembered to history.

As he put it near the end of the China trip, raising his glass for a toast: "This was the week that changed the world."[30]

Soviet Union

Needless to say, the Soviet Union was knocked off balance by Nixon's bold move. The Russians had long counted on hostility between China and the United States as a truism of international relations. Leonid Brezhnev worried that the Chinese might move closer into the American orbit, leaving Russia the odd player out. Thus he began reaching out to Nixon, just as the president and Kissinger had intended. Nixon's bold opening to Beijing had changed the calculus in Moscow. Pressured by Washington's new relationship with China, Brezhnev wrote Nixon and invited him to the Soviet Union for a week of summits—which would mark the first time a sitting US president visited the USSR.

When Nixon visited Moscow in May 1972, just three months after he had gone to Beijing, American-Russian relations had been stalled for years, especially on the issue of arms reduction. It had been nearly a decade since John F. Kennedy had brokered an agreement with Moscow (with the help of the British) to limit atmospheric nuclear testing. Moscow had always been obsessed with equaling and eventually surpassing American nuclear capacities. When Nixon took office, the Strategic Arms Limitations Talks (SALT) were languishing. But now, with the American-Chinese rapprochement, the Russians showed renewed interest in coming to the table.

Nixon had reasons of his own for pursuing the Moscow visit. On the broadest level, reducing tensions with Moscow was a self-evident benefit. The late sixties had been a difficult time; any lessening of tensions would be a boon for national security and for Nixon's own political standing. But Nixon further hoped to use the prospect of substantive arms control talks as leverage with the Russians in Vietnam. Specifically, he hoped that by making some critical arms control concessions—which he privately believed would not hurt the United States—he could, in turn, win Russian concessions, or at least acquiescence, to American efforts to bring the war to a close.[31]

Nixon knew that leaders in Washington and Moscow were both looking for ways to tamp down the arms race, which had become not just terrifying but also financially ruinous. He approached the Moscow Summit with the same conviction that he had brought to his outreach to China: resolute that he was uniquely suited to the task by virtue of his hardline anti-Communist credentials. He could sell an arms deal with the Russians to the American people, he believed, in a way that a liberal Democratic president couldn't.

Where Nixon's Beijing visit had constituted a landmark event merely for taking place, and for the articulation of a general framework of understanding, the Russian visit was more substantive. Nixon and Brezhnev signed ten agreements, including the Anti-Ballistic Missile Treaty (ABM Treaty), an interim SALT treaty, the US-Soviet Incidents at Sea Agreement, and a billion-dollar trade agreement. This was the dawn of détente, a thaw in the Cold War focused on "peaceful coexistence." The Moscow Summit of 1972 led to two further Nixon-Brezhnev summit meetings, another between Gerald Ford and Brezhnev, and the Strategic

Arms Limitation Talks, resulting in the signing of SALT II in 1979, the details of which had been largely hammered out during the Nixon and Ford administrations. It also served as the model for the very different Reagan-Gorbachev summits a decade later, which laid the groundwork for the end of the Cold War.

Nixon's forging of détente with Moscow coupled with the opening to China are feats difficult to imagine any other American politician of his era achieving. Only Ronald Reagan had comparable anti-Communist credentials, but in the early 1970s Reagan was a California governor still proving his political abilities. At the senior national political level, no Democrat could have pulled off Nixon's overtures to Beijing and then to Moscow. More significantly, the American public widely approved of Nixon's policies, seeing them as courageous efforts to reduce tensions and maintain a fragile peace. On foreign relations, as on domestic policy, Americans saw Nixon as a responsible centrist, a leader poised between irresponsible ideologues to his right and left.

This is not to suggest that the SALT agreements were without flaws. For one thing, the agreements, in "limiting" arms, played a bit with semantics—in that the limits applied to missile production that was already underway. And while the limits applied to the missiles, they did not apply to what were called MIRVs—multiple independently targeted reentry vehicles—the payloads that carried multiple warheads. Thus the Soviets and Americans could still add as many MIRVs as they liked, even if the number of missiles and missile launchers was capped. Both sides could thus produce warheads to an unlimited capacity. As Stephen Ambrose put it, overall SALT was "about as meaningful as freezing the cavalry of the European nations in 1938 but not the tanks."[32]

Yet Ambrose also crystalized why SALT was so important in 1972:

> For all the flaws, for all that he could have driven a harder bargain, for all that he had failed to freeze, much less reduce, nuclear arsenals and delivery systems, Nixon had achieved a symbolic breakthrough, namely that the two sides could set limits on their destructive capability. And he fully intended, in his second term, to move from that position to a treaty that would lead to reductions. Even more important, he had established a wholly new basis for the arms race. The ABM Treaty signified the acceptance by both sides of the concept of

deterrence through 'mutual terror.' In Nixon's words, "By giving up missile defenses, each side was leaving its population and territory hostage to a strategic missile attack. Each side therefore had an ultimate interest in preventing a war that could only be mutually destructive."[33] More than any other individual, Nixon was responsible for that breakthrough.[34] (Note 33 transferred from original text.)

From Nixon's perspective, the benefits of the ABM Treaty, both in national security and in political terms, turned out to be significant. Politically, the trip built on the momentum he already enjoyed from his China visit. Domestically, the concepts of arms control and reducing tensions with the Soviets enjoyed substantial support. However imperfect, the agreement would offer some hope that the superpowers might move away from years of brinksmanship and hostility. The president's speech to the Soviet people, in which he said that "we shall sometimes be competitors, but we need never be enemies,"[35] resonated with Americans back home as well. His approval rating shot into the low sixties.

To be sure, Nixon's moves resulted in a permanent rift between him and the conservative Right, which already saw his toasts with Chinese totalitarians as shameful. And conservatives would always maintain that it was Ronald Reagan's more-confrontational approach that really brought an end to the Cold War, a decade later, rather than Nixon's deal making. After 1972, the president's political capital as an anti-Communist was fully spent; but at least he had it to spend.

Nixon always felt that the conservative Right did not appreciate the context of what he had achieved—that it saw the arms deal monolithically, from the perspective of anti-Communism. He, by contrast, saw a multilayered playing field. His deal with Brezhnev helped get the Russians to back off from deepening the conflict in Vietnam. The Russians didn't stand down by any means, but for the rest of 1972, when American bombing reached some of the heaviest levels in the history of warfare, the Soviets did not push back hard. The arms control agreements had bought if not their acquiescence, then at least their restraint. In Nixon's hands, then, détente was a practical tool—not some dewy-eyed vision of a president who didn't understand the Communists' true intentions. I would argue the contrary: Nixon's détente grew out of a shrewd, tragic understanding of how power in the world worked, and a determination to pursue American national interests. And there is no question that his deals with the Chinese and the Russians, in addition to their other benefits, gave the United States the leverage it needed to end the Vietnam War.

For a brief period after the summit, the détente momentum kept up. Nixon kept a promise to Brezhnev to supply the USSR agricultural credits, and the Soviets reciprocated by purchasing hundreds of millions of dollars' worth of American grain. Détente was useful in the short term, especially as Nixon eased the United States out of Vietnam.

But détente did not prove to have staying power. Whether the results would have been different had Nixon been able to finish his second term, we cannot know. What we do know is that in the hands of his White House successors, and also as a result of a series of adverse events, the new beginning Nixon and Kissinger had forged with the USSR came apart. Détente lost its relevance as the Soviet bear began to roar again.[36]

As American leadership waned in the hands of Gerald Ford and then Jimmy Carter, the Soviets, seeing an end to the Nixon era of strategic balance, began to reassert themselves, especially in Africa and South Asia. Ford did not have the political momentum to pursue Nixon's foreign policy—in fact, Watergate was a serious blow to détente, as it not only discredited Nixon but also emboldened the Republican right wing, which had never supported the policy. Ford even banned use of the word *détente* during his 1976 presidential campaign.[37] The Soviet-American relationship soured further with American pressure on Soviet human rights issues. Though Carter and Brezhnev signed the SALT II agreements—covering strategic nuclear arms—the agreement was not yet ratified by the US Congress when, in December 1979, the Soviets invaded Afghanistan. That brought an end to any hope for SALT II ratification.

Carter, who had prioritized human rights as the basis of his foreign policy for his first three years in office, now shifted to a more "realist" orientation in foreign policy and a more traditional Cold War footing with Moscow. American-Soviet relations moved to a new, more dangerous phase, and the resulting tensions contributed to the election of Ronald Reagan in 1980. And it was Reagan, as conservatives insist to this day, who went on to win the Cold War with his massive arms buildup, unrelenting resistance to Soviet expansionism, and rhetorical anti-Communism.

But imagine how Reagan might have fared if he faced a Soviet Union that didn't have to worry about the growing cooperation between the United States and China. Nixon's opening of China is the silent context for Reagan's victory in the Cold War, the piece of the puzzle that you don't hear much about. It fundamentally altered the Cold War's balance of power, and the shift had a direct impact on the Soviet Union. Washington and Beijing even shared intelligence on the Russians.[38] It's not my intention to minimize Ronald Reagan's accomplishments, or his leadership in helping to bring down the Soviet Union, but only to point out that Richard Nixon authored one of the crucial chapters in that story.

Visionary Realism

Ultimately, what Nixon's foreign policy exemplified is the school of foreign-policy thinking described today as "realism," an approach that emphasizes real-world realities; the balance of power; stability; and a prevailing focus on the national interest—at the expense of ideological frameworks, humanitarian rationales, or hugely ambitious, transformative goals. The foreign-policy realist sees order and predictability as worthwhile goals in themselves, even when that order and predictability are consistent with the presence of dictators or other undemocratic political rulers, because the realist believes that attempts to overthrow or replace such regimes may well lead to more violence and chaos and prove even less manageable than the current order.

As applied to the Cold War, the realists tended to be those who advocated for more constructive relationships with Communist powers, in the interest of minimizing tensions and creating a more manageable framework for coexistence. They clashed often with conservative hawks, who felt that Communism, and the Soviet Union in particular, should be resisted at every turn, and that the ultimate goal of American foreign policy should be an outright triumph in the Cold War. Realists rarely allowed themselves to think that big.

That's a thumbnail version of foreign policy realism, anyway, but what's important in considering Nixon is that he was no more married to a narrow conception of "realism" than he was to other schools of thought. You might say that Nixon was a realist's realist—his prevailing approach was to adopt whatever would work best in any given situation.

"Realism is a sensibility, a set of values, not a specific guide as to what to do in each and every crisis," Robert D. Kaplan wrote. "Realism is a way of thinking, not a set of instructions as to what to think. It doesn't prevent you from making mistakes. This makes realism more an art than a science."[39]

Thus, Nixon was predominantly realist in his understanding that we had to extricate ourselves from Vietnam, but not in a way that would undermine our credibility with our allies. He was realist, though daringly so, in his embrace of détente and arms control with the Russians, and in the opening to China, which he used as a buffer to facilitate deals with the Russians. Kissinger explained how the approach—especially the "triangulation" of America's relationship with the Communist world—represented an elevation of pragmatism over ideology in US foreign policy:

> Our objective was to purge our foreign policy of all sentimentality. There was no reason for us to confine our contacts with major Communist countries to the Soviet Union. We moved toward China not to expiate liberal guilt over our China policy of the late 1940s but to shape a global equilibrium. It was not to collude against the Soviet Union but to give us a balancing position to use for constructive ends—to give each Communist power a stake in better relations with us.[40]

Yet if Nixon's brand of realism sounds like a steady-as-she-goes approach, that is to misread, again, him as having an allegiance to any one prevailing brand of action. Consider the form his realism took in the fall of 1973, when Syria and Egypt attacked Israel in the Sinai Peninsula and Golan Heights, precipitating the Yom Kippur War. Israeli tanks were outnumbered nearly ten to one by those of Syria, and near the Suez Canal, a few hundred Israeli infantry faced off against an eighty thousand-strong Egyptian army.

The Israelis faced a coalition of enemies: Nine Arab nations backed the Syrian and Egyptian aggression. So did Moscow, the chief arms supplier of the Arab world. Nixon did not react like the caricature of a realist president, unconcerned about anything but some narrow construal of the national interest. He recognized instantly that Israel faced a mortal threat—and, moreover, that if Arab victory was achieved, it would be achieved through Soviet arms. He moved decisively to protect Israel, authorizing a massive airlift of arms and munitions, and he made certain that his staff understood that it was the highest priority.

"You get the stuff to Israel," he told Kissinger. "Now."[41]

The massive American resupply effort, which resembled a World War II operation in scale, slowly turned the tide in Tel Aviv's favor. As the Arab armies lost momentum and began to fall back, Leonid Brezhnev appealed to Nixon for a ceasefire. Nixon agreed, and a ceasefire was signed on October 24, but then Egyptian president Anwar Sadat urged the Americans and Soviets to enforce the ceasefire with troops from both countries. When Nixon refused, Brezhnev threatened to send Russian troops unilaterally.

Nixon did not flinch. He ordered that the US military be placed on the highest level of nuclear alert, and he redeployed aircraft carriers to the Mediterranean and put Air Force strike units on standby. A regional desert war had now devolved into a situation where the world seemed poised for a confrontation between the two nuclear superpowers.

But Brezhnev backed down, and the crisis passed. Israel prevailed in the Yom Kippur War, thanks to Nixon. And to this day, Nixon, though notorious around the world to many people for his misdeeds during Watergate, remains popular in Israel. Israeli prime minister Golda Meir called him "My President."[42]

As Stephen Ambrose summarized:

> Those were momentous events in world history. Had Nixon not acted so decisively...[t]he Arabs probably would have recovered at least some of the territory they had lost in 1967, perhaps all of it. They might have even destroyed Israel. But whatever the might-have-beens, there is no doubt that Nixon...made it possible for Israel to win, at some risk to his own reputation and at great risk to the American economy.[43]

Indeed, Arab members of OPEC slapped an embargo on the United States in retaliation for its support of Israel, hurting the US economy and making Americans aware of their dangerous dependence on foreign oil for the first time. Yet Nixon stood firm, even as the Watergate crisis was draining his political support at home.

What Nixon's bold actions on behalf of Israel showed was that he was a statesman who could adapt to different situations. It was not a matter of being a pure Cold Warrior, which he wasn't, or a dyed-in-the-wool realist, which he wasn't entirely, either. It was about bringing the entire complex of strategic and political analysis to bear on geopolitical questions, with the American national interest as the guiding principle.

Since Nixon, the United States has had few successful foreign policy presidents, and the country has paid the price for it. Jimmy Carter was run aground by naïveté, George W. Bush by ideology, and Barack Obama, in a sense, by both: the naïveté was his own, and the ideology, in his case, was a determined rejection of American preeminence as a lead actor in world affairs. George H. W. Bush and Bill Clinton did enjoy some successes in foreign policy; neither possessed Nixon's overarching strategic vision but both were able to forge successful policies in trouble spots around the world. As for Ronald Reagan, he is the one post-1974 president whose accomplishments bear any comparison with Nixon's. But, as I noted previously, his achievements should not be divorced from their Nixonian context, nor should it be forgotten that Reagan became a statesman only when he began doing what Nixon had done in 1972—putting ideology aside and reaching out to the enemy, not in a self-destructive way but as a means of determining whether a genuine path toward peace could be found.

And yet, if Nixon often approached foreign policy from a position beyond ideology, he was never unaware of the ideological *impact* of his policies, especially as they translated to American domestic politics. Having summarized Nixon's domestic and foreign policy record, I'll now take an extended look, in the next section of this book, at how Nixon's domestic and foreign policies reshaped the two major political parties—starting with the Republicans.

SECTION II

THE

NIXON

INFLUENCE

CHAPTER 3

Nixonizing the Republicans
Part One: The Southern Strategy and the Silent Majority

Out there the juke boxes don't play "New World Coming"; they play "Welfare Cadillac." In the heartland, it's all Agnew put to music.

—KEVIN PHILLIPS[1]

It is time for America's silent majority to stand up for its rights.

—VICE PRESIDENT SPIRO AGNEW[2]

With one rhetorical stroke, Nixon identified a new populist category that redefined how political groups strive for influence.

—MATTHEW D. LASSITER, "WHO SPEAKS FOR THE SILENT MAJORITY?"[3]

The Nixon revolution in the Republican Party started out with an insight about weakening Democratic appeal within a key demographic: white men. As he prepared for another presidential run in 1968, Nixon began formulating a strategy that could peel off a large portion of whites—especially working-class whites and Southerners—from the Democrats. Before 1968, the idea that blue-collar workers might come out for the GOP was considered fanciful. But what Nixon and his team would then identify was a fault line, and a strategy to exploit it, that would redefine American politics. The evidence of their success, over forty years later, is clear in the continued difficulty today's Democratic Party faces in attracting white male voters, especially those in the working class.

"Democrats are for a bunch of freeloaders in this world as far as I'm concerned," said a sixty-three-year-old Avis bus driver, interviewed for a March 2014 *New York Times* feature. "Republicans make you work for your money, and try to let you keep it." Another white working man who was interviewed criticized the Democrats' obsession with social issues: "I don't see why that's at the top of our priority list," he said.

"But you say that out in the open, and people are all over your back." And a Republican Party spokesman put it: "When you're spending 60 percent of your time talking about birth control and Obamacare, not a lot of men are paying attention to you."[4]

Where the Democrats have managed to win elections with poor results among white working-class men—President Obama won reelection with a stunningly low 38 percent of the overall white vote—Democrats like Frank Houston, a Democratic Party chairman in Michigan's affluent Oakland county, worry that the losses among white men must be contained to some degree, lest the party rely too heavily on its "ascendant coalition" of women, gays, and minorities.

"There's a whole cadre of us—of young, white men political leaders in Oakland County—who are saying, 'We can't just write off 30-year-old to 40-year-old guys, let alone anyone who's older,'" Houston said.[5] The writer of the *Times* feature, Jackie Calmes, reminded readers that Democrats often win the votes of fewer than four out of ten white men in elections, and that they haven't won a majority of white men since it was done by Lyndon Johnson in 1964.

And yet, this very cohort was once the bedrock of Franklin Roosevelt's Democratic coalition that won five consecutive presidential elections between 1932 and 1952, and seven out of nine elections between 1932 and 1964. During that era, it would have sounded exotic to suggest that the Republican Party—a motley coalition of upper-crust business and financial types and Northeastern elites, along with a small-but-intense coalition of ideological conservatives—could break through with this demographic, let alone come to own it. Yet that is precisely what happened over the last half century.

And that brings us back to Richard Nixon. It was Nixon's 1968 campaign that first shifted this well-worn pattern and his 1972 landslide victory that made the reversal permanent. Many factors, policies, and decisions played a role in this transformation. But two key approaches paved the way:

- **The Southern Strategy:** An approach that took shape among Nixon advisor Harry S. Dent Sr.—a veteran of Barry Goldwater's 1964 campaign—and the shrewd young political operative Kevin Phillips.

- **The Silent Majority:** A phrase Nixon first used to refer to a broad spectrum of American voters in a 1969 speech about the Vietnam War.

These approaches—one electoral, the other rhetorical—helped make possible not only Nixon's electoral victories but also the wholesale transformation of the Republican Party, and, indeed, of the American political landscape. They made up a landscape that, with some alterations, remains in place today.

The Republican Party has deeply internalized the concept of the silent majority, and the party's ideological commitments and communication style have been directly shaped by it. Inevitably, the identification of this majority involved a separating of the electorate into us-versus-them camps. But what made Nixonian polarization so remarkable was that the "us" comprised a huge majority. Perhaps that's why Nixon's vice president, Spiro Agnew, called this sorting of desirable and undesirable voters "positive polarization."[6] While the men spoke in polarizing terms, their words did not serve to narrow but to expand their political base—at least until Watergate intervened.

But the coining of the term "silent majority," and its derivatives, was only the rhetorical portion of the Nixon polarization strategy. On the electoral side, he and his team also found a way to draw sharp lines while expanding their political support. They did so by looking to the beleaguered South. Nixon's Southern strategy forged the most dramatic political realignment since the New Deal and changed the Republican Party forever. The presidencies of Ronald Reagan and George W. Bush are unimaginable without it, and later presidential candidates, like John McCain and Mitt Romney, would also rely on the South as their electoral bedrock.

The Southern Strategy

The Southern strategy's genesis was as simple as arithmetic and as methodical as typical political calculation. Ever since Reconstruction, the South had been a "solid" bet for the Democratic Party, as white Southerners voted steadfastly against the party of Lincoln and the liberal Republican architects of Reconstruction, black suffrage, and civil rights. No region of the country was such a lock: in every presidential election from 1876 to 1964—a span of eighty-eight years—the South went Democratic. There is no parallel for this kind of long-running regional dominance by a major party. Even in elections where the Republican Party won the White House smashingly—in 1924, with Calvin Coolidge; in 1928, with Herbert Hoover; and in 1952 and 1956, with Dwight Eisenhower—it did so without the South.[7]

But by 1968, the Democrats had reached a crossroads with their disparate coalitions. They maintained the support of Southern "Dixiecrats," but this support was threatened by their growing electoral reliance on the North, particularly on blacks, who had come north by the millions in the Great Migration starting around 1910—and then, from the 1940s on, in the Second Great Migration. In the early sixties, the civil rights movement changed the calculus. The 1964 Civil Rights Act and 1965 Voting Rights Act, along with desegregation and growing national support for the civil rights movement, threatened the South with a political and social revolution rivaling anything since secession. Many Southern whites saw their way of life under attack, and more than a dozen Southern governors and senators boycotted the 1964 Democratic Convention. Most of the Alabama delegation refused to pledge support for the Lyndon Johnson/Hubert Humphrey ticket. Some were already talking about becoming Republicans.[8]

"We have lost the South for a generation," President Johnson is said to have told an aide after signing the landmark 1964 civil rights legislation. If anything, LBJ was being overly optimistic: the South began drifting away from the Democratic party immediately. The Southern strategy's dry run came later that year, with Barry Goldwater's presidential campaign. Goldwater was far to the right of most American voters in 1964, and, though an honest and thoroughly decent human being, he was a crude politician. In one of the greatest presidential routs in history, Goldwater was trounced around the country, but not in the five core states of the Deep South: Louisiana, Mississippi, Alabama, Georgia, and South Carolina. Goldwater won them all, in addition to his home state of Arizona. Johnson took everything else.[9]

By 1968, the Democratic Party's turmoil was driving white Southerners en masse to the GOP. If the Voting Rights and Civil Rights acts weren't enough, there was the 1968 Democratic Convention in Chicago. The convention chaos, marked by infighting between the liberal mainstream of the party and its more militant left wing, convinced many working-class Americans—especially in the South—that the Democrats could no longer be trusted with national leadership.[10] As longtime Democratic advisor Ted van Dyk put it in a 2008 *Wall Street Journal* article, "Democratic presidential candidates have not since 1968 been able to restore the party that was broken that year."[11] That remains true even today, recent Democratic wins notwithstanding.

Richard Nixon and his advisors thought they saw the outline of a new political alignment. Their goal was to capitalize politically on the alienation of Southern whites resulting from the civil rights movement and Washington liberalism generally—which seemed bent on forcing radical change on the South. Aware that many Southern whites would cast protest votes against Democratic candidates, Nixon and his advisors hoped to convert this demographic into a solid base of loyal Republican supporters. Their timing was good: demographic changes since World War II made the South highly amenable to such a strategy. By 1970, the South was less than 20 percent black.[12] At the same time, white transplants relocated to the South—many of them Republicans already, lacking any generational loyalty to Democrats.[13] Nixon and his team did not just pursue the Southern strategy among voters but also among political leaders, wooing prominent southern Democratic politicians into the Republican Party. These included former South Carolina senator Thomas A. Wofford,[14] Texas attorney general Will Wilson,[15] future Mississippi senator Trent Lott[16]—and most important, South Carolina senator and former Dixiecrat Strom Thurmond.[17] Thurmond's support would be crucial in the 1968 election. In addition, some formerly Democratic representatives became the first Republican congressmen from their states since Reconstruction.[18] And other prominent Southern Democrats eventually became Republicans, such as Texas governor John Connally.

Unlike Goldwater, who came out explicitly against the Voting Rights and Civil Rights acts, Nixon did not question these legislative achievements. Instead, he appealed to Southern whites' concerns about the effects of broad-ranging liberal reforms as well as the federal government's impositions on local authority. Nixon threaded the needle between accepting existing federal legislation—especially legislation narrowly tailored to protect basic rights—and opposing the newer efforts with more expansive goals, like forced busing and desegregation mandates. He spoke out against Washington's attempts to direct state Republican parties that were more conservative on civil rights. "Washington cannot dictate," Nixon said to state parties. He sometimes couched his positions as a defense of the two-party system: "I will go to any state in the country to campaign for a strong two-party system, whether or not I agree with local Republicans on every issue."[19]

He carved out nuanced positions on civil rights court decisions. He spoke of *Brown* v. *Board of Education* as settled law, but he also said that the federal government, under a strict reading of the Constitution, had only limited ability to enforce it.

The Southern strategy is widely regarded today as racist, even by many Republicans. (Few Democrats seem as eager to condemn their own party's exploiting of the Solid South for a century, at a time when the region was immeasurably more racist and more violent than it was by the time Republicans began winning there.) For many liberal critics, Nixon's commercials from 1968 on crime, in particular, only strengthened the impression that the candidate was using race to stoke white fears—and win white votes.

"It is time for a proper look at the problem of order in the United States," Nixon said in a voice-over for his most provocative ad. As quick-cut photos of urban crime scenes, bloody faces of protestors, police, and conflagrations splashed across the screen, Nixon intoned: "Dissent is a necessary ingredient of change. But in a system of government that provides for peaceful change, there is no cause that justifies resort to violence. Let us recognize that the first civil right of every American is to be free from domestic violence." As the frightening imagery continued, Nixon concluded: "So I pledge to you: we shall have order in the United States."[20] The use of the word "order," not to mention the use of the phrase "civil right" in a different context than black rights, leaves room for interpretation about the ad's intentions.

However, in my view, the Southern strategy was far more nuanced—politically and ethically—than its liberal critics have long maintained. Certainly Nixon and his men were, at minimum, politically unsentimental; at such a delicate moment in the nation's social history, to forge ahead with the Southern strategy so unapologetically was, at the least, opportunistic. Nixon's own reputation for private racism—his statements about blacks on Oval Office tapes, for example—and the hard-boiled attitudes of his men, like Patrick Buchanan and Kevin Phillips, didn't alleviate that impression. Phillips was prone to saying things like: "The more Negroes who register as Democrats in the South, the sooner the Negrophobe whites will quit the Democrats and become Republicans. Without that prodding from the blacks, the whites will backslide into their old comfortable arrangement with local Democrats."[21] But from a purely arithmetical standpoint, Phillips was right.

On the left, the Southern strategy's notorious reputation was enshrined by Lee Atwater, who said in an infamous 1981 interview:

> You start out in 1954 by saying, "N–ger, n–ger, n–ger." By 1968 you can't say "n–ger"—that hurts you, backfires. So you say stuff like, uh, forced busing, states' rights, and all that stuff, and you're getting so abstract. Now, you're talking about cutting taxes, and all these things you're talking about are totally economic things and a byproduct of them is, blacks get hurt worse than whites..."We want to cut this," is much more abstract than even the busing thing, uh, and a hell of a lot more abstract than "N–ger, n–ger."[22]

These are offensive and shameful formulations—but they shouldn't obscure the fact that Nixon had no desire to run a campaign based on racism. Whatever his private views of blacks may have been, he could not afford to alienate more liberal Republicans in the rest of the country. Nixon's own civil rights record in Congress had been strong. Martin Luther King Jr. had even called to thank him for his support of the 1957 Civil Rights Act. Moreover, as noted in chapter 1, Nixon would go on to achieve substantial—even remarkable—progress on civil rights, from massive school desegregation to the promotion of black entrepreneurship.

Perhaps the most vivid testimony to Nixon's true intentions comes from White House Communications Director Pat Buchanan, who worked closely with Nixon on his 1968 presidential campaign and was at the center of the historic strategy developed that year:

Among the malevolent myths about Nixon is that he set out to build the Republican Party in Dixie on a foundation of racism. That is not the man I knew and it is the antithesis of what I saw. While Nixon approved of my writings on law and order, he expressed an emotional empathy with black Americans. It was in his DNA. His Quaker mother's family had been active in the Underground Railroad in Indiana. On coming to Congress he agreed to Adam Clayton Powell's request to be part of a five-man team that would take the floor to answer the racist rants of Mississippi's John Rankin. His record as vice president, working behind the scenes for the Civil Rights Act of 1957, for which Dr. King sent him a personal letter of gratitude, marked him as a progressive. I recall him storming out of his office in a rage one morning over a story he had read about an Alabama town that had refused to bury a black soldier killed in Vietnam in its whites-only cemetery.... Nixon's visceral recoil at what he thought was a moral outrage was genuine and unforgettable.[23]

Indeed, far from a crudely racist appeal, Nixon's Southern strategy should be seen as an instrument of political realism—one, that, like all pragmatic efforts, has more- and less-salutary elements. Nixon and his men were going where the votes were, as politicians have always done, and saying what they say to secure those votes. Indeed, as Joan Hoff and others have argued—I think persuasively—Nixon deserves less credit for formulating a Southern strategy than for *recognizing* one—that is, he saw that a political realignment was already in force, and he capitalized on it.

Buchanan continued:

What the Left never understood, or would never accept, is that Nixon brought the South into the Republican column not because he shared their views on segregation or civil rights. He did not. What we shared was the South's contempt for a liberal press and hypocritical Democratic Party that had coexisted happily with Dixiecrats for a century but got religion when conservative Republicans began to steal the South away from them. The Goldwater-Nixon party in which I enlisted was not a segregationist party but a conservative party. Virtually every segregationist in the eleven states of the old Confederacy and every Klansman from 1865 to 1965, belonged to the party of Woodrow Wilson, Franklin Roosevelt, and Harry Truman.[24]

Hoff pointed out how, before October 1960—when Jack Kennedy, in her view and Nixon's own view, "grandstanded" by telephoning the jailed Martin Luther King Jr.—both King and Jackie Robinson "had openly praised Nixon above all other presidential candidates in 1960 for caring about the race issue."[25] Indeed, the Southern strategy is another instance of Nixon running to the right but also governing from the center. Nixon's conservative critics would excoriate him for doing exactly that throughout his presidency.

The journalist David Frost, who got to know Nixon well, viewed it that way:

> Nixon was among the most sophisticated presidents ever to seek higher office in the USA and clearly he discerned the elements of what Kevin Phillips called "the Emerging Republican Majority." Nixon did what he could to capture the process and speed it along. Clearly he succeeded. But his contribution to what I believe was an inevitable process consisted of little more than saying some nice things about the South, holding hands with Southern districts ordered to desegregate, and seeking to appoint Southern judges to the US Supreme Court. Yes, Nixon also went after the Northern white ethnic voter and yes, in 1972 and 1984 they voted Republican in mammoth numbers. But again, I think the Voting Rights Act of 1965 was the catalytic ingredient in realigning constituencies from four into two essential voting blocs.... Nixon for the most part simply rode the crest of events.[26]

Put another way: Few presidents have run more provocative, polarizing campaigns, yet few presidents have achieved more centrist, mainstream policy goals. It is a paradox worthy of Nixon himself.

However one understands it, there is no denying the impact of the Southern strategy on Nixon's electoral fortunes. Despite the candidacy of the Southern populist and segregationist governor of Alabama George Wallace—whose appeal to whites was overt and enormously polarizing—the Southern strategy was astonishingly successful for Nixon in both 1968 and 1972. While Wallace took the Deep South (and many working-class votes in the North[27]), Nixon captured Virginia, North and South Carolina, Kentucky, Tennessee, Missouri, Oklahoma, and Florida.[28] In 1972, Nixon won the entire South, along with the rest of the country except Massachusetts and the District of Columbia.[29] The Democrats had lost their Solid South—and with it, their lock on the White House, which they had comfortably held for twenty-eight of thirty-six years before 1968.

Moreover, the Southern strategy would survive Nixon and become, with modifications, the guiding electoral model for the Republican Party up to the present day.

The Southern Strategy since 1968

It would be difficult to think of a political strategy that has had a longer "tail" in American politics than the Southern strategy. The strategy first identified, and then shaped, the most enduring political realignment since Franklin Roosevelt's New Deal Coalition. Consider how it has played out in elections since 1968.

Democrats have won the Deep South in a presidential election only once since Nixon—in 1976, when Watergate and Gerald Ford's pardon of Nixon helped propel Jimmy Carter into the White House. Democrats— notably Bill Clinton—have managed to pick off some Deep Southern states, but they have never won the region outright. In all the election cycles since 2000, they have been shut out entirely in the Deep South.

The move to the South that Goldwater started and Nixon completed was locked in by Ronald Reagan—a fitting inheritor of the strategy since he had been a Goldwater supporter in 1964 and given a powerful televised speech that helped launch his own political career. When Reagan came within a whisker of taking the 1976 GOP nomination from President Gerald Ford, he built his base of support with primary victories in Southern states, starting in North Carolina. And he famously, or infamously, launched his 1980 campaign at the Neshoba County Fair in Philadelphia, Mississippi—the same town where three civil rights workers had been killed in 1964. Reagan spoke that day mostly about the economy, but he also expressed his support for "states' rights." Liberals ever since have branded the episode as an explicit appeal to Southern racism. But Reagan and his campaign team were trying to win Mississippi, which the GOP had lost in 1976, while also hoping to build stronger black support. Reagan's appearance there, like Nixon's Southern strategy itself, is more complex than usually portrayed.

If anything, the contours of the Southern strategy have only hard-ened in the years since Reagan, and they have affected far more than elec-toral math. They shape the communications and dialogue of presidential campaigns. For Democrats, Republican appeals to white Southerners are often dismissed as "dog whistles"—that is, as coded language or imagery that speaks to the concerns of Southern whites, concerns which include, however subtly, racist connotations. Republicans, on the other hand, see these appeals as both legitimate—they point out that Southern whites are a voting bloc like any other and deserve consideration—and more broad minded than Democrats allege.

A case in point for the negative interpretations is the 1988 George H. W. Bush campaign ad concerning the convicted murdered and rapist Willie Horton. At that time Bush was engaged in a difficult presidential campaign against the Democratic nominee, Massachusetts governor Michael Dukakis. At one point in the summer, Bush trailed Dukakis in polls by seventeen points, but by early fall he had pulled even and then begun pulling ahead. The race still looked competitive in early October, when an independent Republican group ran the most provocative cam-paign ad since Nixon's "We will have order in America" spot in 1968. The ad showed the mug shot of a frightening-looking man who happened to be black—Willie Horton, a convicted murderer serving a life sentence, who had nonetheless been granted a weekend furlough from prison in Dukakis's Massachusetts. He didn't return from furlough; instead, he raped a woman and stabbed her fiancée, whom he bound throughout the ordeal, before finally being recaptured.

"Weekend furloughs for convicted murderers," the ad warned. "Dukakis on crime."

Liberals howled that the ads were racist, using the mug shot to tap into white fears of black crime. Republicans countered that Dukakis's furlough policy—which he had inherited from a predecessor and kept in place—was highly relevant, a part of his record and an insight into his priorities. Implicit in the ad was a conservative critique of the weak-willed liberalism that Dukakis seemed to embody.[30]

The Horton ad proved especially potent in the South, reminding Southern voters of the racial violence of the 1960s and 1970s. Bush's campaign manager, the always-acerbic Lee Atwater, called the Horton ad campaign "a wonderful mix of liberalism and a big black rapist."[31] Bush beat Dukakis in a near landslide, winning forty states.

Dukakis's flameout, on the heels of Minnesotan Walter Mondale's forty-nine-state defeat to Ronald Reagan in 1984, convinced the Democrats that if they were to have a chance at the White House, they ought to give Southern candidates a serious look. Thus came the Bill Clinton-Al Gore tickets of 1992 and 1996, offering voters not one but two Southerners. Clinton won some Southern states in his two presidential races, but he did not fundamentally alter the outline of what was now the GOP's Solid South. What success Clinton did achieve in the South he managed through a two-pronged approach: rallying nearly universal support from Southern blacks, while convincing just enough white Southerners that he was no bleeding-heart liberal, making it clear to voters that he supported the death penalty and strong policing, among other centrist gestures. Rather than dismantling the Southern strategy, then, Clinton mostly confirmed it.

George W. Bush, Clinton's successor, ran two of the most Southern-inflected campaigns of modern times. A proud Texan, Bush already had a natural Southern base, though some conservative Southerners were leery of another Bush in the White House; his father had proven less than a stalwart conservative. But George W., with his strong ties to Southern Republicans, his unabashed evangelical Christianity, and his stout patriotism, which reminded many in the GOP of Reagan, was a much better fit. Easygoing and tolerant, Bush made serious efforts to appeal to blacks—but he still felt the need to secure his religious voters with a visit to Bob Jones University in Greenville, South Carolina, during the 2000 campaign. Bob Jones had become infamous among liberals for its efforts to bar interracial dating among students. Yet Bush, who had survived a furious primary battle in South Carolina with John McCain, knew that the visit would reassure Evangelicals and white Southerners. He would try to make broader appeals elsewhere.

It was under George W. Bush that the nation became acquainted with the color-coded electoral map—the Red-Blue division of conservative- and liberal-voting states—that since his election in 2000, hasn't changed terribly much. A few states shifted here and there, but under Bush, the Republican Solid South remained the ultimate firewall.

Given the nation's dramatic demographic shifts of recent decades, the Republicans' stranglehold on the South has finally become a mixed blessing. The GOP was able to reelect Bush in 2004 by maxing out in the South—but the Republicans needed every one of those votes. Despite campaign pitches featuring black Americans, Bush drew fewer than one in ten black voters in 2000, the party's worst showing since 1964.[32] He did marginally better in 2004, getting 11 percent of the black vote. By pursuing an unprecedented voter outreach and registration effort targeting rural white Evangelicals, the Bush campaign assembled an untapped goldmine of votes to push their man over the top in toss-up states like Ohio, which decided the election against John Kerry. Such an effort was not likely to be duplicable, as Bush mastermind Karl Rove himself admitted. Besides, national demographics were moving against the GOP.

Barack Obama's two presidential victories offered eloquent testament to the changing face of the American electorate—especially in the 2012 election, when Obama won a paltry 38 percent of the white vote and still defeated Mitt Romney by a comfortable margin. Only 12 percent of Romney's support came from nonwhite voters—well within the 10–20 percent minority-vote range that Kevin Phillips had once projected as necessary for Republicans to hold the White House. But Phillips was writing in 1969, when whites were a substantially larger portion of the electorate. Today, 12 percent isn't good enough. In the wake of their second loss to Obama, Republicans have acknowledged the need to reach out to minority voters. Nonwhite talent within the GOP now includes figures like Marco Rubio, Bobby Jindal, and Nikki Haley, but the true test for Republicans will come through policies, not personalities. It is not yet clear that the party has much chance of attracting minority support—or, conversely, if any serious moderation of its core positions could survive the resulting backlash from its base. The Southern strategy continues to cast a long shadow. Republican efforts to win minority voters in larger numbers won't be easy.

The Southern strategy no longer appears to be a sufficient strategy, at least in itself, for Republicans to win the White House. Yet the strategy has almost certainly not seen its sunset. The Republican hold on the white Southern base remains a lodestar for the party's presidential campaigns. Nixon designed it and put it into place.

The Silent Majority

The Southern strategy sometimes overlapped with a related Nixon conceptual formulation—one less about electoral math than it was about rhetoric and imagery. For Nixon wanted to court a new constituency even broader than Southern whites or the South generally: he wanted to reach those Americans united not by class or income or even race but by culture. If the Southern strategy was initially based substantially in grievance, the silent majority was grounded more positively in identification. For there was not just a social revolution going on, symbolized by the civil rights movement; there was also a cultural war, one that has continued up to the present day. Nixon was determined to align himself with the Americans in whom he saw himself reflected—and he was convinced that these Americans constituted an overwhelming majority.

This new constituency had political roots tracing back decades, to some of the formative liberal-conservative battles of the early postwar years. Nixon was at the forefront of many of them, especially the Alger Hiss case, in which he played a leading role on the House Un-American Activities Committee interrogating the former FDR state department official about his ties to the Communist Party. Hiss had been a prominent figure in the FDR administration and played an important role in the founding of the United Nations; HUAC was attacked by President Harry Truman and many in the media for defaming Hiss. But Nixon, listening to Hiss's testimony and watching him interact with the committee, wasn't satisfied with his denials of Communist activity. Further, he found Hiss "insolent," "condescending," and "insulting in the extreme."[33] Nixon's suspicions lay at the heart of what became the famous showdown between Hiss and the writer and editor Whittaker Chambers, who had accused him of being a Communist. History would prove Chambers (and Nixon) correct, but at the time—and even today, for some diehards—the Hiss-Chambers case was a flashpoint of the culture wars. Hiss was the champion of liberalism and tribune of the well-educated, well-placed elites; Chambers and Nixon were the unglamorous, often-despised representatives of Middle America who lacked the social pedigrees but had enough common sense to understand when they were being lied to. The showdown between opposing values that Hiss versus Chambers represented would eventually take larger form in the electorate itself.

In 1950, Nixon won a Senate seat against Helen Gahagan Douglas in a bitter campaign in which he accused her of Communist sympathies and derided her as the "pink lady." The Nixon/Douglas contest was another testing battle between liberals and Middle Americans—or, to use the terms that Nixon remembered from his time at Whittier College, between the Franklins (the liberals) and the Orthogonians (the "straight shooters"), whom Nixon represented. At the national level, Nixon first fashioned himself in this way in 1952, when, as Dwight Eisenhower's vice presidential nominee, he delivered his famous nationally televised "Checkers" speech at a time when he was fighting to stay on the ticket. At issue was Nixon's acceptance of an expense fund from political backers and whether his use of it had been improper.

What made the "Checkers" address extraordinary was Nixon's personal appeal to the American people—a tactic never before tried so dramatically and extensively, and magnified by the new technology of television. After addressing the specifics of the fund and defending its propriety, he went on to describe, in revealing detail, his personal finances and the lifestyle of his family. He had come from a family of modest means, he said. He went through his assets and liabilities, his mortgage, his bank account. No American political candidate had ever revealed himself this nakedly. But then Nixon went for the kill, adding the touches that have been remembered for sixty years.

First, he said that his wife, Pat, didn't have "a mink coat"—a clear dig at elite, wealthy liberals, many of whom were calling for his head. He added, "She does have a respectable Republican cloth coat. And I always tell her that she'd look good in anything."[34] To millions listening, Nixon came across as a humble public servant who loved his wife. But the best was yet to come:

> One other thing I probably should tell you because if we don't they'll probably be saying this about me too, we did get something—a gift— after the election. A man down in Texas heard Pat on the radio mention the fact that our two youngsters would like to have a dog. And,

believe it or not, the day before we left on this campaign trip we got a message from Union Station in Baltimore saying they had a package for us. We went down to get it. You know what it was?

It was a little cocker spaniel dog in a crate that he'd sent all the way from Texas. Black and white spotted. And our little girl—Tricia, the 6-year-old—named it Checkers. And you know, the kids, like all kids, love the dog and I just want to say this right now, that regardless of what they say about it, we're gonna keep it.[35]

The speech, which Nixon originally worried was a failure, was instead a smashing political success. Telegrams coming in afterward ran *seventy-five to one* in his favor. He stayed on the ticket and served two terms as Eisenhower's vice president.

As effective as "Checkers" was, most ordinary Americans didn't see themselves as beleaguered in 1952. They responded to Nixon because *he* seemed beleaguered—and he seemed like he was one of them. By 1968, however, the inhabitants of what had come to be called Middle America were feeling ignored, embattled—and angry. They wondered what had happened to the country they had known. Everywhere they looked there was disorder and anger—in the decaying cities, in the burning American flags and furious anti-Vietnam War rallies, in the spiraling crime rate, in the drug subculture that threatened to take a generation of young Americans down with it. These Americans, located around the country, now had serious doubts about the Democratic Party—the party they and their parents had been voting for, more or less, for a generation. Millions of Americans, Democrat and Republican, had become alienated from politics.

In naming Middle Americans as "Man of the Year" for 1970, *Time* magazine described them as tending "toward the middle-aged and the middlebrow. They are defined as much by what they are not as what they are. As a rule, they are not the poor or the rich."[36] The Middle Americans were the small business owners; hardworking college students; sons and daughters of blue-collar workers who were helping pay some of their school tuitions through part-time jobs; and parents everywhere worried about the seeming collapse of American standards, order, and optimism. They were neither John Birchers nor Young Americans for Freedom; neither members of Students for a Democratic Society nor antiwar protestors. They were, as Nixon described them once, "the nonshout-ers"[37]—the silent majority.

"If they had a message," *Time* wrote, "it was this: 'This,' they will say with an air of embarrassment that such a truth need be stated at all, 'is the greatest country in the world. Why are people trying to tear it down?'"[38]

Nixon first identified this vast constituency in May 1968, calling them the "silent center," and describing them as "the millions of people in the middle of the American political spectrum who do not demon-strate, do not picket or protest loudly."[39] The idea of protesting had never occurred to them, since they had always been grateful to America and assumed that their fellow citizens regarded it with the same mix of love and gentle criticism. But during the 1960s, they came to endure, as Rick Perlstein put it, "the humiliation of having to defend your values that seemed to you self-evident, then finding you had no words to defend them, precisely because they seemed so self-evident."[40]

It was Nixon's chief of staff, H. R. Haldeman, who formulated the plan to mobilize these Americans in 1970. Aware that many blacks were being "shouted down by a handful of militants," the administration also created the National Black Silent Majority Committee.[41] White House operative Charles Colson incorporated silent majority political offices around the country and created organizations like Americans for Winning the Peace and the Honor America Committee.[42] As these names suggested, the original focus of the silent majority strategy was on the Vietnam War, the nation's top source of division as Nixon took office. At the same time, the antiwar movement was stepping up its activities, holding huge rallies and moratoriums in Washington—even as polls showed that Nixon's approach of standing firm with our Saigon allies while pursuing peace negotiations had the support of most Americans.

After a major antiwar rally in October 1969, Nixon delivered a tele-vised address on November 3 in which he made his silent majority appeal explicit. Speaking from the Oval Office, he told his audience:

> If a vocal minority, however fervent its cause, prevails over reason and the will of the majority, this Nation has no future in a free society.... And so tonight, to you, *the great silent majority* of my fellow Americans, I ask for your support. I pledged in my campaign for the Presidency

to end the war in a way that we could win the peace. I have initiated
a plan of action, which will enable me to keep that pledge. The more
support I can have from the American people, the sooner that pledge
can be redeemed; for the more divided we are at home, the less likely
the enemy is to negotiate at Paris.[43] (Emphasis added.)

The speech was Nixon's most successful as president. Polls showed
strong support for his policy in Vietnam, and his appeal to the silent
majority resonated with Middle Americans, who sent supportive telegrams and letters to the White House.[44] Emboldened, Nixon felt he could
afford to be blasé about the massive protest that took place twelve days
later, on November 15, 1969, when five hundred thousand war protesters gathered at the Washington monument. The president, his spokes-
men told the press, was busy that day watching the Purdue-Ohio State
football game.[45]

Nixon's overt dismissal of the protest movement was intentional:
Within his silent majority, no group of Americans was more unpopular
than the student Left, which by 1969 had become thoroughly radical-
ized against the war. Between their radical politics, their disrespect for
institutions, and their indulgence in sex and drugs, the student Left had
become the most despised subgroup in the country. Nixon sent Agnew,
in particular, to lambaste them and their adult liberal enablers.

"A society which comes to fear its children is effete," Agnew said
at Ohio State University. "A sniveling, hand-wringing power structure
deserves the violent rebellion it encourages." On the campaign trail for
the 1970 midterms, Agnew painted liberals with a broad and devastating brush, lambasting them with a series of alliterative put-downs that
were as humorous as they were memorable. War protesters, he said,
were "an effete corps of impudent snobs." Liberals, more generally,
were called "pusillanimous pussyfooters," "vicars of vacillation," and
"nattering nabobs of negativism." Finally, he confined "ultraliberalism"
to his own private ash heap of history, saying that it translated into "a
whimpering isolationism in foreign policy, a mulish obstructionism in
domestic policy, and a pusillanimous pussyfooting on the critical issues
of law and order."[46]

Richard Nixon was the first presidential candidate to voice a broad,
adversarial critique of the power of the media, calling out print and

broadcast journalists for being politically biased. He voiced much of this criticism through Agnew, who may have delivered the most famous formulation of it. In a speech in November 1969, the vice president laid down a blueprint for conservative media criticism that sounds familiar even today:

> Are we demanding enough of our television news presentations? And are the men of this medium demanding enough of themselves?... They can elevate men from obscurity to national prominence within a week. They can reward some politicians with national exposure and ignore others.... Nor is their power confined to the substantive. A raised eyebrow, an inflection of the voice, a caustic remark dropped in the middle of the broadcast can raise doubts in a million minds about the veracity of a public official or the wisdom of a government policy.
>
> Is it not fair and relevant to question its concentration in the hands of a tiny enclosed fraternity of privileged men elected by no one and enjoying a monopoly sanctioned and licensed by government? The views of the majority of this fraternity do not—and I repeat, not—represent the views of America.... As with other American institutions, perhaps it is time that the networks were made more responsive to the views of the nation and more responsible to the people they serve.[47]

Agnew's branding of television commentators—the liberal media, though he didn't use that term—as representatives of "a tiny, enclosed fraternity of privileged men elected by no one and enjoying a monopoly sanctioned and licensed by government" was a serious critique from a man whose adversaries refused to regard him seriously.

Yet for all the fire they trained on protesters and the young, Nixon and Agnew were also aware that not all students were radicals by any means—and that some of those inclined to support Nixon were young themselves. "Forget Harvard and Columbia and the long-haired kids driving Jaguars their permissive dads gave them," Kevin Phillips advised. "Concentrate on the kid working his way through Eastern Kentucky University—he's for Nixon and social conservatism."[48] Thus, even within the student demographic, the silent majority made up a significant caucus.

The silent majority represented a much broader rhetorical strategy than is commonly realized. Its eventual targets would cover an entire range of liberal pursuits—social activism, permissiveness, drugs, racial militancy. A favorite target was the Supreme Court, whose chief justice, Earl Warren, was already a conservative bogeyman for his rulings on race, criminal rights, and sexual mores. Nixon consistently pledged to name justices to the court who would not "legislate from the bench." He became the first president to make the court a key component in political campaigns.

And there was another division that Nixon identified, one that has endured right up to today, most evocatively in the contrast between a Republican figure like, say, Sarah Palin and a Democrat like Barack Obama: that between "ordinary Americans" and "elites." Nixon wasn't alone in seeing these oppositions. His wife, Pat, sensed them, too, as Gloria Steinem discovered when she interviewed Mrs. Nixon in 1968 for the *Atlantic.*

Steinem spent time with Mrs. Nixon on the campaign trail. She was interested in learning more about what made Pat Nixon tick, but she found the candidate's wife to be guarded. Looking for a way to connect with her, she asked Mrs. Nixon to name the woman in history she most admired and wished to emulate. Mamie Eisenhower, the interviewee replied. Stunned, Steinem asked why. "Because she meant so much to young people," she explained. Steinem replied that she was in college during the Eisenhower years and couldn't recall a single young woman who looked up to Mrs. Eisenhower. Mrs. Nixon insisted that young women admired the former first lady for her courage while her husband was away at war. Steinem fell silent for a moment, wondering how to respond, and then Mrs. Nixon cut loose:

I never had time to think about things like that—who I wanted to be, or who I admired, or to have ideas. I never had time to dream about being anyone else. I had to work. My parents died when I was a teenager, and I had to work my way through college. I drove people all the way cross-country so I could get to New York and take training as an X-ray technician so I could work my way through college. I worked in a bank while Dick was in the service. Oh, I could have sat for those months doing nothing like everybody else, but I worked in the bank and talked with people and learned about all their funny little customs. Now, I have friends in all the countries of the world. I haven't just sat back and thought of myself or my ideas or what I wanted to do.... I don't have time to worry about who I admire or who I identify with. I've never had it easy. I'm not like all you... all those people who had it easy.[49]

Steinem, to her credit, wrote that this moment helped her understand the Nixons: "For the first time," she described,

I could see Mrs. Nixon's connection with her husband: two people with great drive, and a deep suspicion that 'other people had it easy,' in her phrase, 'glamour boys' or 'buddy-buddy boys' in his, would somehow pull gracefully ahead of them in spite of all their work.... It must have been a very special hell for them, running against the Kennedys; as if all their deepest suspicions had been proved true.[50]

Middle Americans shared many of the same suspicions, identifications, and resentments. They were on Nixon's side in fundamental ways, and the administration worked hard to reach them—especially those among them who, economically liberal but socially conservative, still identified as Democrats. The silent majority strategy proved most effective in the West and Midwest, as well as in parts of Appalachia. Nixon convinced constituencies that had benefited from Democrats' economic policies that having someone in the White House who shared their *values*—hard work, thrift, respect for institutions, patriotism, religiosity, moral restraint—was the most important thing. Rural and suburban voters, especially outside the North, flocked to Nixon and the Republican Party during the president's first term, especially as the Democrats moved further left.

In 1972, Nixon expanded his silent majority call, pushing hard to win over Democrats troubled by their party's leftward turn. He appealed to "those millions who have been driven out of their home in the Democratic Party... to join us as members of a new American majority."[51] Nixon's appeal on issues like crime and public order, patriotism, moral decency, and skepticism about federal government power helped him win over many George Wallace–leaning voters—working-class Democrats, for the most part, many of whom had traditionally not been accessible to the Republican Party on economic grounds.

They were people who benefited from government even if they were not aware of it, but who were also angry and anxious about social and cultural changes.

While appealing to Wallace-leaning voters, Nixon was also able to co-opt the conservative movement, at least for a time. Although the conservatives, of the Goldwater/Bill Buckley variety, questioned Nixon's convictions and motives, his masterful drawing of lines between groups in the electorate made clear to most of them where their political fortunes lay. Most stayed with him in 1968 and 1972.

It is remarkable that the Nixon team was able to make this pitch to the Wallace faction and the movement conservatives, while at the same time holding onto the traditional constituency of the Republican party—the Northeastern monied elites, the business roundtable and Wall Streeters, and the old-money WASPs.

With these three planks in place, Nixon built a coalition that, in 1972, produced a national share of the vote almost as large as what LBJ got in the aftermath of the Kennedy assassination. Nixon's smashing forty-nine-state victory in the 1972 election—in which he won 60.7 percent of the popular vote and an eighteen-million-vote margin, both setting records—indicates how effective the silent majority was as a rhetorical and political device. If it was divisive, as its critics charged, it did not divide evenly. The majority may have been silent but it was also immense.

Not even Watergate could negate the silent majority's power. As the political commentator Kevin Phillips had presciently warned: "For a long time the liberal-conservative split was on economic issues. That favored the Democrats until the focus shifted from programs which taxed the few for the many, to things like 'welfare' that taxed the many for the few. In the future, the liberal-conservative division will come on social issues; Middle America and the working class are socially conservative." Phillips saw an opening for the GOP to embrace populism for the first time in its history—but this would be a populism made up "of the middle class, which feels exploited by the Establishment."[52]

Nixon's downfall did not change this emerging dynamic. Neither party could afford to ignore the political fault lines that Nixon had identified. In 1976, Jimmy Carter became the only Democrat who got elected president between 1964 and 1992 by appealing substantially to Nixon's silent majority, culturally and economically. Carter ran a relatively centrist campaign in 1976, well to the right of George McGovern's ultra-left 1972 effort. Enough of the silent majority came home to the Democrats to give Carter a narrow win over Gerald Ford.

But Carter imploded in office, his presidency a rolling disaster of legislative ineptitude, skyrocketing inflation and interest rates, and finally, the American hostage humiliation in Iran. It would be left to the Republican Party to reclaim the silent majority. Patrick Buchanan, perhaps Nixon's greatest barometer of American anxieties, understood the stakes. "The last best hope of the Republican Party," Buchanan wrote in 1975, was to "place itself at the head of the middle-class revolution boiling in the countryside."[53] For forty years now, that is precisely what the GOP has sought to do.

The Silent Majority's Long Afterlife

Few rhetorical framing devices have had a longer afterlife than the silent majority, even if the term itself did not survive the Nixon years. The silent majority's legacy can be found across the political spectrum, though it has had far-more resonance for Republicans than for Democrats—not least in the area of religion.

For a long time, traditional East Coast Republicans kept Evangelical Christians at arms' length, if that; they wanted little to do with overt expressions of religiosity in the public sphere and tended to be most comfortable with the East Coast Protestant churches, which declaimed little on public morality and generally confined themselves to charitable giving and socially liberal causes. Nixon was the first Republican to change that, opening the White House to conservative Christians. Nixon called on Billy Graham to build bridges to conservative Protestants, found common ground with the Southern Baptist Convention, and used White House church services to send a message of religious tolerance to Evangelicals, who felt increasingly estranged by secular culture.

In the late 1970s, concerned by the moral direction the United States was taking, Baptist Minister Jerry Falwell began hosting a series of "I Love America" rallies across the country. The strong response he got convinced him to found the Moral Majority in 1979—an explicitly religious, Christian, Evangelical organization dedicated to halting progressive momentum in areas like abortion, sexuality, and secularism. The Moral Majority's arrival changed the history of Fundamentalist Christianity in the United States; such Christians had usually stayed out of politics. Falwell's organization built on the Nixonian formulation. Here was another way of uniting what, as Falwell saw it, included the vast majority of Americans—by focusing on moral attitudes toward social issues.

It turned out, of course, that Falwell's estimate of a "majority" was much less accurate than Nixon's. Even so, the Moral Majority helped create the Christian Right, which, starting in the 1980s, became a fundamental constituency of the Republican Party. This move of Christian conservatives to the GOP was also strongly Southern—so both the silent majority and the Southern strategy came together, a decade after Nixon left the White House. In 1988, Christian televangelist Pat Robertson made a surprisingly strong showing in the Republican presidential primaries; the following year, he founded the Christian Coalition, which played an important role in GOP politics for two decades.

Of course, the greatest inheritor of Nixon's silent majority imagery was Ronald Reagan. But whereas Nixon had been the stern, gloomy messenger, Reagan's sunny disposition and Happy Warrior politics brought a much more optimistic tone to similar messages. Reagan had a seemingly endless supply of one-liners at liberals' expense:

- "It isn't so much that liberals are ignorant. It's just that they know so many things that aren't so."
- "I have wondered at times what the Ten Commandments would have looked like if Moses had run them through the US Congress."
- "Republicans believe every day is the Fourth of July, but the Democrats believe every day is April 15th."[54]

On a more serious note, Reagan exploited the divides that Nixon had identified between the vast American mainstream and the much smaller progressive cohort, increasingly isolated on the coasts and within other major metropolises. His identification with ordinary Americans; his heartfelt expressions of patriotism—in contrast, it was widely perceived, to the attitude of his Democratic opponents; and his pledge to "make America great again" resonated with those Americans who had responded to Nixon's plea a decade earlier that the United States not be cowed by war protesters and defeatists.

Where Nixon's skillful appeals helped create a short-lived Democratic group—Democrats for Nixon—Reagan's political appeal created an entire new voting bloc, the Reagan Democrats, which was made up of those who could not bring themselves to pull the lever for Jimmy Carter in 1980. They were famously profiled by Democratic pollster Stanley Greenberg, who in 1980 analyzed voters in Macomb County, Michigan (north of Detroit). Most of Greenberg's Macomb voters were white, ethnic, unionized auto workers. Nearly two-thirds of them had voted for Jack Kennedy in 1960; by 1980, two-thirds went the other way and pulled the lever for Reagan. In Macomb, Greenberg felt he had found the story underlying the two parties' shifting White House fortunes: The Reagan Democrats no longer saw their party as the party of the working man. Instead, they saw it as the captive of narrow special interests—blacks, Latinos, welfare recipients, feminists, environmentalists. In a country reeling under sky-high inflation and interest rates, the Democrats seemed out of touch with ordinary people trying to make a living.

In his 1981 inaugural address, Reagan crystallized his appeal and his philosophy when he said: "Government is not the solution to our problem; government is the problem."[55] Millions who had once voted for the party of FDR now agreed.

The only two Democratic presidents since Jimmy Carter both won by running to the center—where the silent majority resides—and by championing the middle class and Middle American values in their campaign rhetoric. Bill Clinton promised to listen to the "quiet, troubled voice of the forgotten middle class."[56] His Family and Medical Leave Act put him on the side of working people who wanted to be able to hold onto their jobs after medical emergencies. His proposal of the V-chip allowing viewers to selectively block television programs was mocked by sophisticates but supported in the nation's heartland by parents concerned about the escalating quantity of offensive, sexed-up content on network television.

Barack Obama said of the middle class that they have "a right to be frustrated because they've been ignored"[57]—implying that Republicans had turned their backs on Middle America. His health care law, as hotly contentious as it remains, was sold as a deserved benefit for hardworking, ordinary Americans—the same people Nixon championed and made the fundamental voting bloc of American politics.

This identification with ordinary Americans, and their sense that policy elites in Washington don't have their interests at heart, remains crucial to electoral politics, especially for Republicans.

During the 2008 campaign, John McCain and Sarah Palin both tried to appeal to nonpolitical citizens. Seeking to regain popularity among the stricken working class, McCain made a hero out of Joe the Plumber, an Ohio worker who asked candidate Obama about his small-business tax policy and wasn't happy with the response: "When you spread the wealth around, it's good for everybody," Obama said.[58] Joe the Plumber became an iconic figure, representing the "forgotten" American whose tax dollars would be squandered on liberal social programs. This became a constant theme for McCain.[59]

Meanwhile, McCain's running mate, Sarah Palin, updating Spiro Agnew's role, often made support for the GOP ticket a matter of patriotism and implied a cultural critique of the other side. She made references to subgroups within this silent majority—"soccer moms," "hockey moms," "Wal-Mart moms," and "Nascar dads."[60] It was another attempt to identify Republicans with those Americans opposed to the "elites."[61] It was best represented in a speech Palin made in North Carolina in October 2008, in which she extolled the virtues of what she called "real Americans":

> We believe that the best of America is not all in Washington, D.C. We believe that the best of America is in these small towns that we get to visit, and in these wonderful little pockets of what I call the real America, being here with all of you hard working very patriotic, um, very, um, pro-America areas of this great nation. This is where we find the kindness and the goodness and the courage of everyday Americans. Those who are running our factories and teaching our kids and growing our food and are fighting our wars for us.[62]

It is a Nixonian spirit, too, that animates the Tea Party today: millions of middle-class Americans who, like his silent majority of the early

1970s, feel disgusted by failed political leadership—and most of all, by a prevailing belief that Washington doesn't care about them and is only interested in protecting its favored interest groups. One rallying slogan for the Tea Party, in fact, has been: "*Silent majority* no more!"

Tea Partiers are also motivated by an overarching concern of Nixon's silent majority: the fear that the America they know and love is becoming unrecognizable. As a candidate, Nixon described their fears on the campaign trail in 1968, in words that could apply just as well to 2016:

> The new voice that is being heard across America today... is not the voice of a single person, it's the voice of a majority of Americans who have not been the protesters, who have not been the shouters. The great majority finally have become angry, not angry with hate, but angry, my friends, because they love America and they don't like what has been happening to America for the last four years.[63]

At the same time as it has championed humility and ordinary virtues, the silent majority has rejected what it sees as the growing number of Americans who live off government largesse. This, too, was an equation Nixon made: his people were neither elites nor welfare recipients.

And that brings us to one of the most notorious moments of the 2012 presidential campaign: the *47 percent* video of Mitt Romney speaking at a fundraiser. In September 2012, in the midst of a hard-fought campaign, Romney and his team were blindsided by the release of the unauthorized video, taken by cell phone, of the candidate speaking at a fundraiser that past spring. In the video, Romney, addressing a room of wealthy donors, is trying to explain the challenge he faced in winning an electoral majority:

> There are 47 percent of the people who will vote for the president no matter what ... who are dependent upon government, who believe that they are victims, who believe the government has a responsibility to care for them, who believe that they are entitled to health care, to food, to housing, to you name it. That's an entitlement. And the government should give it to them.... These are people who pay no income tax. My job is not to worry about those people. I'll never convince them they should take personal responsibility and care for their lives.[64]

The *47 percent* video quickly went viral, becoming the talk of the campaign and putting Romney on the defensive, as he tried to explain that he was *not* writing off 47 percent of the electorate. Democrats condemned the video, arguing that it showed the candidate had contempt for the middle and lower middle class. He was, in their telling, a classic Republican presidential candidate: he spoke for the rich. While few Republicans defended Romney's comments outright, they tried to make clear the real target of his words—the country's massive and ever-expanding entitlement state. This was a point worth making, they said, even if Romney made it crudely and divisively. It's arguable how much Romney's "47 percent" comments may have cost him in the 2012 election, which he lost by a clear but not overwhelming margin to President Obama.

The 47 percent episode was just the latest in a long string of gaffes that made Romney appear unsympathetic to ordinary Americans. But what the 47 percent controversy showed most strikingly was how degraded the Republican understanding of Nixon's silent majority approach had become (at least in Romney's hands). Republicans were still trying to play the Nixonian game of "positive polarization," but their application of the strategy had become completely self-defeating. Romney was dividing the electorate in a way that suggested that he could not win and should not win. If you write off 47 percent of the electorate, it's very hard to win over everyone else.

What Nixon did by appealing to the silent majority, by contrast, was to broaden the base of his political coalition. He did this by tapping into the extraordinary support George Wallace had received in the 1964 and 1968 primaries—generating enough support, in the 1968 campaign, to marginalize Wallace's independent candidacy, which had polled as high as 25 percent. Whereas Nixon's approach was strategic, shrewd, and massively inclusive, Romney's was ham handed, ill considered, and totally divisive. He may as well have put a "Don't vote for me!" sign on his back.

The problem Romney was trying to solve in 2012 was one that Nixon intuitively understood and solved in a way that no Republican other than Reagan has been able to since: how to unite a vast bloc of American voters concerned, variously, with economic hardship and cultural decline. It is a bloc whose members might not ordinarily fit together in most other contexts but who can be rallied to support the same presidential candidate—for their own sometimes-mutually exclusive reasons.

A GOP Transformed

The old Republican Party began its death throes in the Nixon years. It has never been the same since, and judging by its presidential run from 1968 to 2004, it has Nixon to thank. Put simply, the party, which had spent most of two political generations in the electoral wilderness, identified a winning coalition and sustained it for the better part of thirty-six years. Nixon created that coalition, which, as Buchanan described it, was comprised of "the solid centrist GOP base that had stood by Nixon in 1960, the rising conservative movement, to which I belonged, the 'northern Catholic ethnics' of German, Irish, Italian, Polish, and other East European descent, and the Southern Protestants, who saw themselves as abandoned by a Democratic Party moving leftward."[65]

It was a new center-right coalition, in opposition to the center-left coalition first forged by FDR, and it captured the social momentum of the American people. Though the GOP was much smaller than the Democratic Party in terms of party registrants, beginning with Nixon it assembled the pieces of an unbeatable majority. GOP stalwarts like Buchanan also saw other advantages:

> Not only would this constitute a new governing majority, displacing FDR's, but liberal Republicans, finding themselves in a party no longer defined by Rockefellers, Scrantons, Romneys, Javitses, and Lindsays, might drift away. And if they did, they would leave behind a party more antiestablishment and populist. Remaking the GOP into the party of anti-elitists, of forgotten Americans and Middle Americans, was what some of us had long had in mind.[66]

Buchanan's vision came true, of course—the GOP became a more conservative party. Yet Nixon's political and rhetorical strategies also helped achieve a curious and ironic outcome—they helped create a Republican party in which Republicans like Nixon were no longer welcome. The moderate Republican has mostly vanished from the national GOP today, just as Buchanan and others had wished, largely due to tactics pioneered *by* a moderate Republican. In fact, moderates have become scarce in both parties, replaced, for the most part, by more ideological figures.[67] The resulting polarization in Washington has been the backdrop for the failures and paralysis of recent years—from the government shutdown to the debt-ceiling standoff.

I've written about this polarization in previous books, particularly in *Hopelessly Divided*. There, I argued that the polarization we often hear about among the American electorate—between the Red states and the Blue states, whose inhabitants watch different news sources and have nothing in common—has been driven by, and exacerbated by, the divisiveness in Washington. I described how the growing polarization in Washington rendered government impotent and often incompetent; how this bred frustration among members of the electorate, who then looked for other solutions; how these solutions often tended to be extreme ideologically; and how the politicians in Washington, seeing the energy coming from these populist movements, doubled down on ideology, eager not to be washed away in the tide. The result is what we see today: a government that doesn't work and a populace that has lost faith in the nation's institutions to solve its problems.

Perhaps the key recent figure in the polarization of Washington today is a man enormously influenced by Nixon: Newt Gingrich. Research has shown that Gingrich's 1994 House freshmen had a political impact not confined to the House. New Republican senators winning office in the epochal 1994 midterm elections were found to be 62 percent more conservative than Republicans entering the Senate in prior years. The Gingrich Senators, as some called them, were, like their House colleagues, committed to strong ideological positions and intense partisan warfare.

Today's intense polarization between the parties developed in substantial degree during this period. And who was one of Gingrich's guiding lights? Richard Nixon.

Few remember that Gingrich worked on Nixon's 1960s campaign as a teenager. He often told of how he learned about politics by observing Nixon. In the 1980s, as Gingrich laid plans for a congressional takeover, he consulted Nixon on strategy and tactics. Nixon's advice? The GOP needed to become "more idea oriented." No one ever accused Gingrich of being short of ideas.[68]

Jon Meacham, as well as others, have pointed out the cultural and temperamental similarities between the two men:

> Like Nixon, Gingrich is smart, with a wide-ranging and entrepreneur-
> ial mind. Like Nixon, Gingrich is a striver who seems insecure around
> traditional establishment figures even though he has achieved much
> more than nearly all the politicians, editors and reporters he seems to
> at once loathe and fear. Like Nixon, Gingrich is fluent in the vernacular
> of cultural populism, brilliantly casting contemporary American life
> in terms of an overarching conflict between "real" people and distant
> "elites" bent on the destruction of all that is good and noble about
> the U.S.[69]

Even the Republican national figures who tried to soften the edges of this critique—Bob Dole, George W. Bush, John McCain, Mitt Romney— inevitably found themselves having to sound some of its themes, lest they lose credibility with what had become the dominant power center in the Republican Party. In a sense, then, Nixon nationalized his oldest political formulation: the Orthogonians versus the Franklins—the us- versus-them division that he first articulated at Whittier College. This division remains central to conservative political identity—and thus to Republican political identity.

I'll explore the second part of the rightward move in the GOP that Nixon helped shape—this time, mostly inadvertently—in chapter 5. But next, I'll turn to his transformative impact on the other side. For if Nixon helped make the Republicans more right wing, he had an equal, if opposite, effect on the Democrats. By the time he ran for reelection in 1972, he faced a Democratic opposition well to the left of where the party had been in 1968 or 1964—in no small part because of his policies.

– CHAPTER 4 –

Nixonizing the Democrats

Part One: Stealing the Domestic Center from Liberals

Tory men and liberal policies are what have changed the world.

—RICHARD NIXON[1]

Nixon comprehensively outmaneuvered his political opponents through the daring appropriation of their purposes, constituents, and chosen policy instruments. Domestic presidential politics provides few more dramatic demonstrations of . . . a skilled president's use of lawful authority.

—MELVIN SMALL, *A COMPANION TO RICHARD NIXON*[2]

This country is going to go so far right you won't even recognize it.

—JOHN MITCHELL[3]

Watch what we do, not what we say.

—JOHN MITCHELL[4]

[Nixon's] proposals on national health insurance and welfare reform were so far in advance of his time that congressional liberals preferred to oppose them than to allow Nixon to take credit for upstaging them.

—JOAN HOFF[5]

"Are you the most liberal president in US history?" Bill O'Reilly asked Barack Obama in February of 2014.

"Probably not," said Obama.

"Probably not? Who would be?"

"You know," the president replied, "the truth of the matter is when you look at some of my policies, in a lot of ways Richard Nixon was more liberal than I was. He started the E.P.A., you know, started a whole lot of the regulatory state that has helped make our air and water clean."

"That's interesting, Nixon," said O'Reilly. "I thought you were going to say F.D.R."[6] Of course, Obama could have said FDR or LBJ, and no one would have blinked. But his mention of Nixon was telling, as was

O'Reilly's surprise—because even forty years after Nixon left office, the nature of his policies, especially in the domestic realm, is not well understood. As I described in the previous chapter, Nixon's domestic record would be regarded, in the political landscape of 2015, as that of a liberal. That fact has much to do with the shifting ideological ground since then, a process that Nixon did much to shape. But in his time, Nixon viewed his domestic policies as centrist and *practical*.

That last word might be the most important—because Nixon's "liberal" domestic policies had other benefits beyond their own merits. Most particularly, they acted as a positioning tool to put Nixon squarely in the domestic center, identifying him as essentially a moderate. It was a paradigm-shifting political approach. Democrats were caught off balance by Nixon's approach to domestic policy and forced either to support a president who defended—and in some cases expanded—the Great Society or to forge new positions further left. Most chose the latter course. The vast majority of voters preferred Nixon's moderate centrism, even moderate liberalism. Former Bill Clinton advisor Sidney Blumenthal, writing decades later, described Nixon's ability to "run right and left at the same time, by occupying a movable center... to play both ends against the middle."[7] Indeed, Nixon didn't just take the center away from liberals; he took a good portion of the Left as well, leaving little but the more leftist, ideological margins. He forced the party to choose between political accommodation and political ideology. In the process, he drove moderates away from the Democrats and built an historic national coalition, laying the foundation for what would become a generation in the presidential wilderness for the party of FDR. In this way, Nixon became as important to the direction of the American Left as Lyndon Johnson.

And he was aided in his approach and philosophy by a man who might have been seen as the representation of all Nixon detested: Daniel Patrick Moynihan, a liberal intellectual, sociologist, former Kennedy administration official, and Harvard professor. Moynihan became an index of liberalism's disillusionment, and he had the candor to share his thoughts with the incoming Republican president. The partnership they developed, while short-lived, was highly consequential and illustrative of the conflict within liberalism—a conflict that Nixon exploited masterfully.

Nixon, Moynihan, and Liberalism's Demise

One reason why Nixon was able to marginalize the Left so effectively was because liberals themselves, in the late 1960s and early 1970s, were coming face to face with the limits of their ideology. Race riots, intractable inner-city poverty, an unpopular war, and the radicalism of the student movement made liberalism's failings difficult to ignore. These events also proved to be increasingly divisive within the Democratic coalition, which by the late sixties was beginning to split. On one side were the mainstream, Cold War internationalists and traditional liberals; on the other, the New Leftists and the counterculture. Moynihan counted himself firmly in the traditionalist camp.

What would eventually draw Nixon to Moynihan was not only his intellect but also his willingness to reexamine his ideas and admit his mistakes—which were often the areas where liberal ideology failed. Moynihan caused a sensation with his 1965 report, "The Negro Family: The Case for National Action," which examined the roots of black poverty and warned—presciently, as it turned out—that rapidly increasing rates of out-of-wedlock childbirth were deepening the crisis of poverty in the black community. Moynihan found that fatherlessness in black homes was spiraling upward, that inner-city pathologies like drug use and violent crime were spiking, and that welfare, rather than lifting blacks out of poverty, was keeping them mired in it. The report became particularly controversial for its identification of the cultural role in poverty—Moynihan was later charged with "subtle racism" and being an "apologist for the white power structure."[8] He was regarded warily by African Americans and civil rights activists from then on.

For all its controversy, the Moynihan report was not so contentious as its critics suggested. Moynihan's real transgression was to cite facts that most liberals didn't want to admit and to ask questions that they would rather not answer. He would continue to hold a mirror up to his fellow liberals in the coming years.

In 1967, Moynihan delivered a speech called "The Politics of Stability" to Americans for Democratic Action, a liberal activist group, focusing on the rising racial disorder in cities. In it, he surprised many by declaring that liberal pieties about civil rights and equality wouldn't resolve the problems of the black underclass, and he pushed liberals to recognize that their "essential interest" should be in social stability, not just social reform.[9] It was a call to avoid the excesses of radicalism, the appeal of which had been growing throughout the decade, especially in regard to the situation of blacks. Moynihan warned that liberals "must somehow overcome the curious condescension which takes the form of sticking up for and explaining away anything, howsoever outrageous, which Negroes, individually or collectively, might do."[10]

Moynihan also urged liberals to find common ground with conservatives. "Liberals [must] see more clearly that their interest is in the stability of the social order, and that given the threats to that stability, it is necessary to make more effective alliances with political conservatives who share that concern, and who recognize that unyielding rigidity is just as much a threat to the continuity of things as is an anarchic desire for change," he said.[11] The speech was foundational to what became the neoconservative movement—made up of former liberals who felt political realities pushing them rightward. In 1969, Nixon hired Moynihan as his counselor for urban affairs.

Moynihan influenced Nixon's thinking in many areas, including the importance of restoring faith in American institutions.[12] "In one form or another," he began one letter to the president over the course of a fascinating correspondence,

> all of the major domestic problems facing you derive from the erosion of the authority of the institutions of American society. This is a mysterious process of which the most that can be said is that once it starts it tends not to stop.... All we know is that the sense of institutions being legitimate—especially the institutions of government—is the glue that holds societies together. When it weakens, things come unstuck.[13]

Moynihan gave Nixon a copy of *Disraeli*, Robert Blake's biography of Benjamin Disraeli.[14] Always an avid reader, Nixon found much of value in the book, and he concluded that "Tory men and liberal policies are what have changed the world"[15]—clearly seeing himself as part of both traditions. He spoke to reporters of his desire to be a "Disraeli conservative," by which he meant his desire to foster "a strong foreign policy, strong adherence to basic values that the nation believes in, combined with reform, reform that will work, not reform that destroys."[16]

The influence of Moynihan—whether on actual policy or simply in approach—showed in multiple domestic areas. In chapter 1, I outlined Nixon's domestic policy achievements in civil rights, social welfare, health care, the environment, and the draft. Let's look now at how Nixon's policies affected the Democratic Party, beginning with the issue that, with the exception of the Vietnam War, remained the nation's most pressing when Nixon took office: civil rights.

Civil Rights

"I wanted to eliminate the last vestiges of segregation by law, and I wanted to do it in a way that treated all parts of the nation equally," Nixon wrote in his memoirs. "I was determined that the South would not continue to be a scapegoat for Northern liberals."[17] As we have seen previously, Nixon's record on school desegregation should give him the undisputed title as the man who desegregated America's schools. The numbers don't lie. His achievement is even more impressive considering that it came in the face of strong advocacy for busing, especially among liberals. Nixon's refusal to expand busing, and his eventual request for a moratorium on new busing mandates, drew ire from the Left; on the Right, meanwhile, he was criticized for not pushing back harder. If it was a difficult situation for Nixon, it was a torturous one for Democrats, who could not resolve the competing tensions within their coalition.

The Democrats' response to civil rights issues, but in particular to the federal government's policies on busing and school desegregation, broadly reflected the emerging split within the party: Whereas Southern and some Northern and Western Democrats from rust-belt states were wary of these policies, as they were susceptible to angry suburban electorates, the liberals further to the left and African American Democrats were more likely to support them. Once busing mandates became applicable to schools outside the South, cracks in the Democrats' and moderate Republicans' civil rights coalition began to show. For example, several non-Southern Congressional Democrats supported a 1972 House measure that would prevent Washington from cutting funds to schools that failed to meet integration targets via busing.

"The Civil Rights Coalition in the Senate—that group of Northern Democrats and moderate Republicans that, for a decade, has formed the majority on nearly every major piece of civil rights legislation—is in danger of collapse over this year over the issue of school busing," a January 1972 *New York Times* article opened.[18] Published two months before Nixon's proposed moratorium, the article reported on three House measures that would limit the ability of what was then the Department of Health, Education, and Welfare (HEW), later to become the Department of Health and Human Services, to withhold funds in nonintegrating districts. According to the *Times*, the senators "leading the anti-busing assault" were all Southern Democrats (including John Stennis of Mississippi, Samuel Ervin of North Carolina, and David H. Grambell of Georgia), whereas the more liberal senators (Walter Mondale of Minnesota and Jacob Javits of New York) had hoped to "dilute the House package enough so that it will sound like a strong policy against busing but in reality be innocuous."[19]

Once Nixon announced his moratorium, the Democratic split became evident again. The president wanted "to turn back the clock on civil rights," said Congressman William F. Ryan of New York, even accusing Nixon of attempted nullification of the 1954 *Brown v. Board of Education* ruling against segregated schools.[20] Referring to Nixon's statement that busing would be a test of the American character, James C. Corman of California said that the president had "flunked his own test."[21] Ted Kennedy charged Nixon with perpetuating segregated schools—against all evidence—and said that, in announcing his proposal of $2.5 billion to upgrade inferior schools, the president had "in a real sense duped the American public." Kennedy acknowledged that he himself had opposed "indiscriminate busing" but also recognized that "in many situations, busing has been, and still is, the only possible device to end outright segregation and discrimination in the public schools of local communities."[22]

Civil rights leaders chimed in. Congresswoman Shirley Chisholm called Nixon's moratorium "final evidence of [Nixon's] desire to shut the door to racial equality in this nation."[23] Jesse Jackson, then a prominent civil rights leader, called the president's speech "the most dangerous speech that I have heard in this century, or that I have read." He went on to say, "Beware of any issue that George Wallace and Richard Nixon agree on."[24]

Thus spoke the Democratic Party's liberals. On the other side, Democratic senator James Eastland of Mississippi, chairman of the Senate Judiciary Committee, also criticized Nixon's moratorium— because it didn't go far enough. The moratorium would offer no relief for the South, Eastland said, because it did not affect current busing mandates. The only "real cure," he said, would be a constitutional amendment banning busing.[25] Democratic politician Sam Ervin of North Carolina made similar statements.

Mentioned almost as an aside in the *Times* piece was the observation, apparently off the record, by House leaders, that Nixon's busing moratorium, combined with his $2.5 billion proposal for upgrading inferior schools, was "*politically unbeatable*" (emphasis added). Indeed, it was masterful triangulation on a hugely divisive issue. But, as often was the case with Nixon's domestic policies, his "triangulation" was also in the service of genuine moderate centrism. Most Americans *did* oppose busing; most Americans *did* want inferior schools improved and all kids to have an equal chance. What they did not want was transformative, destabilizing, divisive social engineering in the service of these goals.

Busing became a prominent political issue just as Democrats were fighting out the 1972 presidential primary—where the divisiveness of the issue was apparent in the careful and sometimes-tortured positions articulated by the three main contenders: Edmund Muskie, Hubert Humphrey, and George McGovern, the eventual nominee. Humphrey, the most socially conservative of the three, at first expressed general agreement with Nixon's approach, but within days, he was temporizing. He believed that it was "fit, right and proper that you bus a child from an inferior school to a good school," but not the other way around. Lest that worry more centrist listeners, Humphrey called busing a phony issue. The real issue, he said, was the need for "more and better schools not more buses." As *Time* magazine observed, "Humphrey, in short, was on both sides."[26]

Muskie, too, tried to dodge the issue, suggesting that busing was a distraction; the real problem, he said, was "to bring quality education within the reach of every child." But the millions of Americans opposed to busing, and affected by the existing mandates, didn't think that the issue was "phony." When pushed, Muskie allowed that "busing is a legitimate tool that has been endorsed by the courts, supported by the courts and so long as it has been, I think we have to be willing to use it in a common-sense way."[27]

McGovern also sought to steer clear, blaming Nixon for engaging in a "frantic effort to capitalize on this emotional issue."[28] But he later revealed his liberal position: "I believe that school busing and redistricting as ordered by the federal courts are among the prices we are paying for a century of segregation in our housing patterns."[29]

The Democrats would struggle with the busing issue for years. They battled internally about whether to include a probusing plank in their 1972 national platform, which was almost universally liberal. Reflecting the momentum of the liberal flank that year, the busing statement did make it into the platform. It stayed there in 1976, too, though by then busing was described as a "last resort," and the party's nominee, Jimmy Carter, avoided discussing it whenever possible.

Nixon's championing of black capitalism, as embodied in the Philadelphia Plan—geared toward guaranteed fair hiring practices in construction jobs—put the Democrats even more off balance. What made the plan objectionable to conservatives, of course, was its designation of definitive "goals and timetables" for minority inclusion. Despite Nixon's denials, many on the right felt that his administration was imposing quotas. The Philadelphia Plan was the first federal-level attempt to implement affirmative action policies.

If the Philadelphia Plan was anathema to many Republicans, especially to conservatives, it put Democrats in a quandary that exposed a split between party constituencies—and Nixon, ever aware of political opportunity, in part pursued the plan for that reason. The split in this case involved the civil rights coalition, on the one hand, and organized labor, on the other. For civil rights advocates, the Philadelphia Plan represented what many leaders, including Martin Luther King Jr., before his death in 1968, had spent years calling for: preferential hiring. For labor, affirmative action violated the seniority system and threatened the structure of advancement within the union framework. Nixon knew this and pushed the plan even harder because of the divisions he knew that it would cause. In part, he was motivated by anger at the unions for their opposition to his Supreme Court nominee Clement F. Haynesworth. Labor and civil rights coalitions helped sink Haynsworth's nomination in the Democrat-controlled Senate. The Philadelphia Plan, in part, was Nixon's way of putting these two crucial Democratic constituencies at loggerheads. Nixon succeeded, John Ehrlichman wrote later in his memoirs, in "constructing a political dilemma for the labor union leaders and civil rights groups by 'tying their tails together.'"[30]

AFL-CIO chief George Meany called the Philadelphia Plan a "concoction and contrivance of a bureaucrat's imagination,"[31] and suggested that Nixon had formulated it to cover up his poor civil rights record. But the plan forced Meany into alliance, at least temporarily, with probusiness Republicans and conservative Southern Democrats—not his usual allies. Together they tried to pass a rider to a Senate bill that would block implementation of the Philadelphia Plan, but the rider died in the House. The Philadelphia Plan survived and was soon extended to other cities. The Democrats got nothing for their opposition except more intraparty warfare.

Social Welfare

When Nixon first unveiled the Family Assistance Plan, it was met with considerable acclaim across the political spectrum. Moynihan summed it up best: "A Republican President, elected in significant measure out of distaste for the dependent poor, thus proposed the adoption of a guaranteed income," he wrote after leaving the Nixon White House, "F.A.P. was a kind of domestic trip to China, a triumph of pragmatism over ideology."[32] Early on, the FAP had Congressional momentum, too: it passed through committee rapidly and was then approved by the House.

But the FAP ran into trouble in the Senate, first from conservatives (though the bill was more conservative than many of them seemed to appreciate). The conservatives helped to drive out HEW secretary Robert Finch, who had become identified with the bill and prompted the administration to trim its sails, reining in its scope and cost. But the modified FAP lost the liberals, who already thought that the original bill should have been more expansive. They argued that the FAP did not offer enough funds and was too restrictive (it was limited to families, excluding singles and childless couples). So the revised FAP pleased neither faction, and it failed to get out of the Senate Finance Committee, sunk by the combined opposition of conservatives and liberals, who opposed it for entirely different reasons.[33] The liberals' objections were well captured in the words of New York congressman William F. Ryan.

"Accepting the concept of income maintenance and establishing the mechanics for implementing that concept are two far different things," Ryan said. He had been the first legislator to introduce legislation for a guaranteed annual income, and he believed passionately in the idea. But he saw Nixon's plan as "seriously flawed." Instead, Ryan pointed to proposals by the radical National Welfare Rights Organization (NWRO), which was pushing for a much higher annual-income guarantee of $5,500 per year—the equivalent of a guaranteed income of $32,910 in 2013. To Ryan and others, such a stipend should not be regarded as a "privilege" but as a "right." Anything less, he suggested, was to sentence the poor "not to be able to have a life with dignity."[34]

On the Senate Finance Committee, liberals like Walter Mondale railed against the Nixon plan's supposed stinginess. Mondale also thought the FAP should offer a higher guaranteed income, and he detested the workfare requirement, though this would only affect a small number of welfare recipients. The bottom line, for Mondale as well as others, was that the FAP simply wasn't big and generous enough. The bill would leave "millions of people in destitute circumstances," he warned, and expanded: "The real question returns to how much substance we are willing to give to these programs. We authorize dreams around here and we continue to appropriate peanuts."[35]

Remarkably, this staunch liberal push back did not even encompass all of the opposition on the left to the FAP. Organized labor came out in full force against the FAP, but for different reasons. George Meany's AFL-CIO feared that the FAP would subsidize sweatshop labor.[36] And a guaranteed annual income, Meany and other union leaders worried, might come to be regarded as an alternative to the minimum wage. Even more vital was the opposition of the welfare coalition, as led by the National Welfare Rights Organization, or NWRO. It saw the FAP, with its radical plan to remake the welfare system, as a direct threat to the jobs of its caseworker members—so the NWRO organized against the plan, too, concealing its self-interest with trumped-up criticisms of the bill's supposedly punitive treatment of the poor.

Crucial to the NWRO's power and clout within liberal circles was George Wiley, head of the organization and a former college professor turned radical organizer. The NWRO was a mostly black organization, and in the style of the times, Wiley wore a dashiki and mastered what the *New York Times* called "Mau Mau tactics," which included unleashing groups of welfare mothers to "shout down or cry down or stare down any opposition." Wiley's shock troops broke up meetings of other liberal groups around Washington that were considering taking positions opposed to the that of the NWRO. He was divisive, intimidating, and totally uncompromising, and his positions foreclosed any possibility of centrist accommodation. Most liberals were loath to take him on. As the *Times* put it, "Privately, liberals denounce Wiley and the N.W.R.O.... In public, they tiptoe around him."[37]

In the end, Moynihan blamed the FAP's demise on the liberals, whom he felt had sunk the bill because they were too devoted to the status quo and too beholden to interest groups—like social workers and welfare rights activists—to come along on the task of reform that Nixon set out. The failure of the Nixon administration's brave attempt at welfare reform was a bitter domestic defeat, but if it had a silver lining—and Nixon couldn't have been unaware of it—it was that such policy proposals were wreaking havoc on the once-unified liberal coalition. That was even more in evidence when it came to what was perhaps Nixon's boldest domestic policy initiative: health care reform.

Health Care

Few senators in American history have served longer or put their name to more legislation than Ted Kennedy. When the "lion of the Senate," as John McCain called him,[38] died in 2009, he had served in the upper chamber for forty-seven years and built a legislative record that dwarfed those compiled by his more famous brothers, John and Bobby. But Kennedy had also seen plenty of low points, both personally and professionally. When asked, over the years, what his greatest regret was as a legislator, he usually gave the same answer: his decision to spurn a deal with Richard Nixon that would have reformed the nation's health care system in the 1970s.

It's no wonder that Kennedy would list health care as his key regret: few issues were more important to him during his long career, and when he died, in August 2009, Washington was embroiled in an intense political debate about the Obama administration's proposed Affordable Care Act. At the same time, "town halls" across America exposed congressional legislators to the anger and fears of their constituents about the Obama health care plan. Kennedy regretted the lost chance to reform health care with Nixon even more because he had two cracks at it: in 1971 and in 1974. Both times, due in substantial part to liberal intransigence, the dream of health care reform failed to materialize.

As I detailed in chapter 1, Nixon first proposed a system of national health insurance in 1971, which he called the National Health Insurance Partnership. His initial plan called for a private employer mandate to purchase health care plans for their employees—and cover 75 percent of premiums—along with an expansion of Medicaid. Low-income workers would get federal subsidies to purchase health plans. The Nixon proposal, Robert Reich argued, was "in essence, today's Affordable Care Act," in which "all but the smallest employers would provide insurance to their workers or pay a penalty, an expanded Medicaid-type program would insure the poor, and subsidies would be provided to low-income individuals and small employers. Sound familiar?"[39]

Nixon's health care politics were not free of self-interest: They had much to do with Nixon's concern that he might be running against Ted Kennedy in the 1972 presidential race. Kennedy had already proposed national health care. There was no love lost between Nixon and Teddy, but the president tried to win his support for the proposal, which he thought would bring along other Senate liberals.

The problem in 1971 was that the left wing of the Democratic Party wanted more from the Nixon plan, and Kennedy was the party's spokesman. He stood firm against the health care plan, dismissing it as a sop to the health insurance industry. The plan, Teddy said, "is really a partnership between the administration and the insurance companies. It's not a partnership between the patients and the doctors in this nation."[40] Countering Nixon, he proposed a plan of straight-up national health insurance funded through payroll taxes. Unlike the Nixon plan, which had various cost-control mechanisms and cut-off points for coverage, Kennedy's plan spurned cost sharing and made coverage unlimited. Rather than a system of private health insurers, it operated through the centralized authority of a health security board, appointed by the president.[41]

The bottom line, in 1971, was that liberals, and Kennedy himself, saw no point in compromising with Nixon on a health reform plan that they saw as hopelessly inadequate. They held firm congressional majorities; if they couldn't win universal health insurance in 1972, they could do so in 1974 or 1976.[42] And so, in 1971, Nixon's National Health Partnership died on the vine, never even making it into formal legislation.

In 1974, things were different. Nixon revived his health care reform package in his State of the Union address in January of that year; this time calling it the Comprehensive Health Insurance Plan. But as I noted in chapter 1, that address was given under the cloud of Watergate. Nixon was a hobbled president by now, and yet here he was, offering liberals another chance at one of their holy grails. This time, Ted Kennedy was willing to meet Nixon halfway. He didn't get behind Nixon's bill on his own, but he did cosponsor, with Wilbur Mills, the chairman of the House Ways and Means Committee, an alternative plan that did not differ from Nixon's plan nearly as radically as their competing 1971 versions had. The Kennedy-Mills plan was more generous than Nixon's and cost more, but not by dramatic amounts, and Kennedy had dropped his insistence on national health insurance and his resistance to private insurers.

Kennedy had learned an important lesson from the 1971 standoff: When given a chance at major social legislation, get the best deal you can, but don't sink an agreement over details that might be worked out or amended later. The key goal is always to address a fundamental problem; big pieces of social legislation, like Social Security and Medicare, are always being revised and updated. If you didn't make some kind of deal, you have nothing.

The problem on the left in 1974 was that organized labor was dead set against any compromise plan—which included both Nixon's and the one sponsored by Kennedy and Mills. For the unions, it would be their own Health Security Act—consisting of universal, national health insurance—or bust. And they made clear that they would rather see no progress made on health care reform than a bill they disliked made into law. Once again, they held out for the future: if the act didn't make it through in 1974, it might in the next congress, which figured to be more liberal.

Labor's uncompromising position was on display in a hearing before members of the House Ways and Means Committee, when Andy Biemiller, the AFL-CIO's director of legislation was called to testify. The conversation proceeded as follows:

> CONGRESSMAN BURLESON (D-TEX). Mr. Biemiller, your attitude is unless you get the full adoption of that measure [Health Security Act], you would prefer that there be no bill at all in this session.... Is that your attitude?
>
> MR. BIEMILLER. We do not think that any of the bills that are being offered as a compromise bill, including Mills-Kennedy, meet the basic principles that we think ought to go into a sound health insurance bill.

Citing recent experience—especially the Medicare legislation of a decade before—Biemiller made explicit the union's position: if it couldn't get precisely what it wanted this time, it would sink the whole process.

> MR. BIEMILLER. We have not forgotten, for example... that in 1964 the Congress did not want to pass any kind of a Medicare bill. A big flap went on over the fact and, as a result, a bill that would have increased social security benefits got held up and did not pass in 1964.
>
> By the time 1965 came around, many of those who had fought Medicare very hard had become advocates of Medicare, and we have a feeling that the same kind of thing can prevail with national insurance.
>
> CONGRESSMAN CLANCY (R-OH). Mr. Biemiller, [you're saying that] organized labor is not going to approve of any national health program this year short of [the Health Security Act], because labor feels that the climate next year will be much better to get what it wants. Now, is that a fact?
>
> MR. BIEMILLER. As I stated earlier... the years 1964–65 demon-strated to us pretty effectively that we do gain sometimes by having to delay for a year or so the enactment of legislation.[43]

The unions were so intransigent that even the *Washington Post* came out against them. "Labor's leaders should stop painting its utopias with a broad brush," the paper editorialized, "and get into the practical realistic debate that is taking place on Capitol Hill right now. With union support, a comprehensive bill preserving the best features of the Kennedy-Mills approach would stand a good chance of passage."[44]

Alas, such union support was not to be. In early fall 1974, after Nixon had resigned, Congressman Mills merged versions of the Kennedy-Mills and Nixon plans and made one last push to get it passed. With a thirteen-to-twelve vote, the bill barely cleared Ways and Means, and Mills felt that such a narrow margin was in effect a defeat, and that the bill wouldn't stand a chance of passage. He publicly excoriated organized labor for sinking the bill, and the *New York Times* and other sympathetic liberal voices agreed. The unions had scuttled an historical chance for health care reform by gambling that national health insurance could be achieved by a more liberal Congress. (On the right, pressure from small business owners and the American Medical Association played a role, too, but given the Democrats' powerful majorities, union opposition was the key driver.)

After the post-Watergate midterm elections of 1974 swept a wave of new Democrats into office, labor's arrogance looked like it might pay off. But it would be nearly twenty years before the nation would see another serious attempt at health care reform—and by then, the electorate had grown more conservative about new big-government programs. Despite strong initial momentum, Bill Clinton couldn't get his health care reform plan—ironically also called the Health Security Act, the same name the unions had given their universal-coverage plan—through Congress in 1994. Health care reform seemed to be dead again for Democrats. It would take a financial crisis rivaling the Great Depression to make it a viable prospect again, in the hands of Barack Obama, the most liberal Democratic president since Franklin Roosevelt.

Obama's Affordable Care Act passed in March 2010, six months after the death of Ted Kennedy. Writing a few days after Kennedy's death in the *Washington Post*, Steven Pearlstein marveled at how the political terrain had shifted since Kennedy and Nixon had wrestled with health care reform: "It should tell you how far the country has moved to the right that the various proposals put forward by a Democratic president and Congress bear an eerie resemblance to the deal cooked up between Kennedy and Nixon, while Nixon's political heirs vilify it as nothing less than a socialist plot."[45]

Pearlstein had a point, but what shouldn't be overlooked in the story of the 1970s attempts at health care reform is that liberals had majorities in Congress that they would not hold for much longer. You can give credit to Kennedy for learning from his mistakes, but his intransigence in 1971 exemplified the way that Nixon's domestic policies had put liberal Democrats into a box. To liberals, moving left of this Republican president seemed like a natural impulse, but their self-indulgence proved costly. No episode illustrates it better than the historic failure of Democrats to achieve health care reform a generation before Obama.

The Environment

"The great question of the seventies is, shall we surrender to our surroundings, or shall we make our peace with nature and begin to make reparations for the damage we have done to our air, to our land, and to our water?"[46]

Nixon put that question to Congress in his 1970 State of the Union address, setting the stage for a remarkable offensive on environmental issues that remains unparalleled today among his presidential successors. Pledging to implement "the most comprehensive and costly program in this field in America's history,"[47] Nixon outlined a sweeping, technology-centered plan to address water and air pollution as well as concerns about garbage disposal, sewage, despoliation of land, and protection of park land. Nixon's advocacy turned out to be a shrewdly moderate and appealing pitch to the middle-class constituency, whose support he relied upon. In becoming the first president since Theodore Roosevelt to put the full power of the White House behind environmental protection, Nixon incorporated a liberal concern—the environment—into policy choices that pleased not only many mainstream Democrats but also the centrist Independents who made up a good portion of his silent majority.

As I detailed in chapter 1, Nixon's record on environmental legislation put all of his successors to shame, though it's certainly true that a good deal of his work in this area was politically motivated. He urged John Ehrlichman, his counsel and assistant for domestic affairs, to keep him out of trouble on the issue, and privately called the Green movement "crap for clowns."[48] But by getting out in front of the environmental issue, he could undercut opponents who may successfully have run presidential campaigns against him on the issue—especially Maine senator Edmund Muskie, a longtime environmental champion and the odds-on favorite to be Nixon's Democratic challenger in 1972.

Nixon came into office at a time when the environmental movement was finally reaching mass public awareness. As a political pro, he recognized a winning issue when he saw one, and his White House polls showed burgeoning support among the American public for environmental action. And Nixon took action. It is true that many of the measures that would shape Nixon's environmental legacy—the EPA, the Clean Air Act, and the Clean Water Act—originated in the Democratic Congress, and, in the case of the Clean Water Act, it was actually vetoed by Nixon because of its cost. For dedicated liberal environmentalists, Nixon's environmental record was incomplete and inadequate, a series of half measures driven mostly by self-interest.

But Nixon was, again, positioning himself in the center; he was in tune with a broad spectrum of public opinion, and slightly ahead of it in some areas. At the same time, his caution and skepticism resonated with conservative-minded Americans. The version of the Clean Air Act that he did sign was not as draconian in its standards as the version that the Democrats preferred. (And, never losing sight of the politics, Nixon, for good measure, refused to invite Muskie to the bill's signing ceremony.) Nixon's battle with Congress over the Clean Water Act, described in chapter 1, also showed that he was pursuing a centrist course: he pushed back on the Democrats' funding demands, which proved to be unrealistic. The president positioned himself, again, as a sensible moderate, occupying the middle ground between those who rejected all environmental appeals as statist interference with business and those who wanted much-more-radical ecological measures. He took serious action on an important issue while also using restraint in formulating federal policy. The Democrats too often sounded alarmist by comparison.[49]

From a political standpoint, Nixon's environmental push was undeniably shrewd. By addressing the issue so comprehensively, he took it off the table for most Americans and deprived Democrats from using it against him. The editors of *Mother Earth News* understood this in 1972, writing that Nixon had "made the question of preserving the environment boring for the voters and suicidal for the Democrats."[50] Moving to the left of such a president would make Democrats look extreme to the American public.

His wide-ranging environmental policies put Nixon in a good position to defend himself against the Democrats' leading environmentalist, Edmund Muskie. Indeed, while Muskie was in the race, he avoided taking Nixon on about the environment. The best he might have been able to claim was that Nixon was a Johnny-come-lately to the cause—but American voters never have tended to care much about such distinctions if the substance is there. As it turned out, Nixon didn't have to worry about Muskie. The Maine senator, regarded as the Democratic front-runner, imploded on his way to the nomination—with help from some Nixon-team "dirty tricks." Neither Hubert Humphrey nor George McGovern had much in the way of environmental records. Nixon had effectively tabled the environmental issue for the 1972 race.

Ending the Draft

"By upholding the cause of freedom without conscription," Nixon wrote in his 1970 "Special Message to the Congress on Draft Reform," "we will have demonstrated in one more area the superiority of a society based upon belief in the dignity of man over a society based on the supremacy of the State."[51]

Democrats had been divided on compulsory military service even before Nixon entered office. The issue of the draft shaped the split that developed between Democrats in 1968, when chaos erupted in Chicago over a proposed "peace plank" to the party platform. The dividing lines on the draft were the same ones as on other issues—it was a split between the old-line national-security Democrats in the FDR, Truman, and Kennedy/Johnson molds and the newer faction more devoted to the worldviews of men like Eugene McCarthy and George McGovern. The Democrats were undergoing a civil war (which I'll look at more closely in chapter 6) over what some have called "liberal internationalism" and what I call "national-security liberalism": the view that America should play a leading role in the world to shape an international order along the lines of democratic values and institutions. The Vietnam War shattered the faith in this view for many in the party. Those Democrats who wanted an immediate end to the American presence in Vietnam also pushed for a fundamental transformation of the Selective Service System—specifically, an end to involuntary military conscription.

They could not have expected that Nixon himself would champion the cause.

But in promising an end to conscription, Nixon saw that he could position himself against the New Left and the antiwar movements by removing what was, for many, the main source of their angst—their fear that they, too, would be called up soon to fight in Vietnam. Nixon also believed, and history has largely proved him correct, that antiwar movements in America would be much harder to start and sustain when the army fighting those wars was all-volunteer. And finally, the president saw that ending the draft would enable him to reach out to millions in the middle class who worried that their sons would be called up next.

Nixon also offered a vision of the long term in ending the draft. While he maintained that he would end the Vietnam War on honorable terms, he also suggested that wars like Vietnam would soon be a thing of the past. Future conflicts would either be mostly high-tech nuclear conflicts or guerrilla struggles. Neither would require mass conscription. This didn't turn out to be the case—Americans would fight a brief war against Iraq, for example, in 1990 and then a much longer one beginning in 2003—but the vision was part of a broader appeal to young people. Nixon was demonstrating that he was able to think innovatively about the nation's defenses and that he did not view involuntary conscription as some kind of national birthright. He was once again playing against type, and he had once again stolen a substantial portion of the Left on a crucial issue—bringing American troops home from Vietnam, ending the war itself, and changing the arrangements by which American troops fought wars in the first place.

In all of these areas—civil rights, welfare, health care, the environment, and the draft—Nixon proved himself, at least shrewd and nimble, and at best innovative and even visionary. These policies were also extraordinarily effective politically, in positioning him in the great center of American politics—in stark contrast to a fracturing Democratic

Party that, as the 1972 campaign approached, was poised to nominate the most radical presidential candidate from a major party in the twentieth century.

The Fracturing Democrats and the McGovern Train Wreck

In January 1972, Gallup showed Nixon running in a dead heat with Edmund Muskie, the favored Democratic nominee. But ten months later, in the greatest landslide in presidential history, Nixon won the election over South Dakota Senator George McGovern, the eventual Democratic nominee. How did it happen?

To a substantial degree, Nixon's change of political fortunes had to do with his foreign policy achievements later in 1972: the historic outreach to China, followed by his conciliation with Moscow and pursuit of détente between the superpowers. These were hugely visionary and important moves, and they forever changed the way Nixon was regarded, as I described in chapter 2.

But Nixon's foreign policy was not the only factor contributing to the landslide. Domestically, as we have seen, Nixon outflanked the Democrats on issue after issue, leaving them precious little ground on which to stand (or run). By the time 1972 rolled around, the president had taken much of the mainstream political terrain away from liberals. The most activist portions of the Democratic Party hungered for political change—for a true idealist candidate, a true cause to rally around. They found both in George McGovern. Part of the ground for his candidacy had been paved four years earlier, in the ashes of the Democrats' bitter defeat to Nixon.

The 1968 campaign was a nightmare for the Democrats. Not only did they lose the White House but their dysfunction was also paraded on national television at the infamous Democratic National Convention in Chicago. Moreover, party leaders spurned a candidate who had competed in the primaries, Eugene McCarthy, and nominated another, Hubert Humphrey, who ignored the primaries completely. The party rank and file demanded reform. Democratic National Committee chairman Fred Harris appointed a commission to study the nominating process and named George McGovern to chair it. The McGovern Commission, as it came to be known, declared that the party's nominating procedures were undemocratic.[52] It opened up the delegate-selection process to all party members and mandated that nominations be mostly determined by individual state elections—thus elevating the primary system to its current stature in presidential politics. Most controversially, McGovern's commission required that the representation of minority groups and women in state delegations be proportionate to their population within each state.

By revolutionizing the way the party chose delegates, the McGovern Commission stripped power from the labor unions as well as the old-line party bosses and big-city machines—Chicago Mayor Richard Daley exemplified both—and put it in the hands of grassroots activists, progressive organizers, and civil-rights and single-issue groups. These included not just feminists and environmentalists but also the huge peace faction, advocates for drug legalization, and the nascent gay rights movement.[53]

"The faces of the party had been Chicago Mayor Richard J. Daley and AFL-CIO president George Meany—old slabs of well-done beef," Rich Yeselson wrote. "After the commission reforms, it was Bella Abzug and Jesse Jackson."[54] The transformation became apparent for all to see at the 1972 Democratic National Convention in Miami.

During Ronald Reagan's presidency and for years afterward, the Republicans would often deride what they called "San Francisco Democrats," meaning Democrats who were extremely liberal. The term derived from the party's 1984 convention in San Francisco, in which it nominated Walter Mondale and ran on a staunchly liberal national platform. It's a wonder, though, that the phrase "Miami Democrats" didn't catch on first since the 1972 Democratic convention in that city made the Mondale gathering look practically corporate—and conservative—by comparison.

The 1972 platform itself outstripped anything the Democrats ran on in 1984. It was "a liberation movement wish list," Joyce Milton wrote.[55] It began ominously, with: "We are not sure if the values we have lived by for generations have any meaning left."[56] Amid this general despair and loss of faith in anything resembling the American vision, there was left only a mass undifferentiated assertion of rights. The party platform claimed rights including "the right to be different, to maintain a cultural or ethnic heritage or lifestyle, without being forced into a compelled homogeneity... [and] [t]he rights of people who lack rights: Children, the mentally retarded, mentally ill and prisoners, to name some... [and]

the development of new rights of two kinds: Rights to the service itself and rights to participate in the delivery process."[57]

It was the most liberal campaign platform in American history.[58] McGovern advocated immediate withdrawal from the Vietnam War in exchange for the return of American prisoners of war, amnesty for draft evaders, across-the-board reductions in defense spending, guaranteed jobs, and a guaranteed minimum income. The underpinning of the Miami convention was New Politics, a result of the liberal reforms that Democrats had instituted to their nominating practices. The goal was to ensure greater inclusion in party decision making. The most symbolic moment came when a delegation led by Jesse Jackson unseated Daley's men from the Illinois contingent—a development unimaginable before 1972. The young activists and firebrands were convinced that the party had lost to Nixon in 1968 not because of its liberalism but because of its *insufficient* liberalism. In Miami, it had the convention it had always wanted. State delegations, shorn of old-style Democratic machines, were now a motley collection of interest groups, marginal characters, and kooks. As Steven Hayward described them:

> There were no farmers in the Iowa delegation, only a handful of Poles or Italians in the Illinois delegation, no elected official among the Virginia delegation, while nine members of the New York delegation were associated with a gay rights group. Two welfare mothers were on the Washington DC delegation, and two Native Americans (the media still called them "Indians") anointed the delegation from McGovern's home state of South Dakota. Tip O'Neill quipped that the Massachusetts delegation "looked like the cast of 'Hair.'" (O'Neill skipped the convention.) California's delegation included actress Shirley MacLaine, who remarked that her delegation "looked like a couple of high schools, a grape boycott, a Black Panther rally, and four or five politicians who walked in the wrong door." She meant it as a compliment. One old time Democrat remarked that the key decisions were still made in smoke-filled rooms, "only the smoke smelled different."[59]

A spirit of self-indulgence and outright zaniness prevailed. Every conceivable interest group had to have its say—and to get equal time saying it. Delegates placed names like Jerry Rubin, Dr. Benjamin Spock, and Archie Bunker into nomination for the vice presidency. Feminists demanded that a woman's name be placed in nomination, even if there was no chance of her being nominated. "Every nutball constituency and street theater artist got into the act," Hayward wrote.[60]

"We lost the election at Miami," Democratic congressman James O'Hara later said. "The American people made an association between McGovern and gay liberation, and welfare rights and pot-smoking and black militants, and women's lib, and wise college kids."[61] The prevailing sense was of a free-for-all.

Because every hyper-Democratic process had to be observed, consequences be damned, the party's nominee didn't get to address the convention until three in the morning. That's what time it was when George McGovern, his nomination finally confirmed, addressed the delegates with his acceptance speech, featuring the memorable refrain, "Come home, America!" Only four million Americans saw it. One of them was Richard Nixon, who felt that it "had the air of a college skit that had gotten carried away with itself and didn't know how to stop."[62] Nixon must have been amazed—or even frightened—by how successfully he had marginalized the Democrats.

Nixon played a significant role in motivating this far-left movement. He did this, first, by taking the responsible, mainstream, centrist liberal positions away from the national Democratic Party: on economic policy, where he had proved Keynesian; on school segregation, where he had proved visionary and judicious; on environmentalism, where he had set up vast new federal agencies and mandates to ensure clean air and water and protection of federal lands; on women's rights, where he had done more for the cause than any president before him; on social welfare, where he had made bold attempts to address poverty while also strengthening the social safety net; and on ending the draft, a moral cause that shaped so much of the national trauma over Vietnam. Thus, as I have argued, Nixon forced the Democrats to look to further to the left for differentiation—and in George McGovern, they found it.

Second, and more subtly, Nixon's centrist-liberal positions also confirmed, in the minds of the McGovernites and other devotees of the New Politics, that mainstream liberalism—and indeed, the American political process—was bankrupt. For many of the forces involved in the

New Politics, the truest enemy was not conservatism but liberalism. As they saw it, conservatives were simply reactionaries, easy to oppose. But liberals—incrementalists, deal makers, takers of the half loaf—were the true moral sellouts. They were the ones who made dramatic social change in America truly impossible. For the Students for a Democratic Society (SDS) alumni in the McGovern ranks, slow-and-steady progressive change would never be enough. That is what they hated about Humphrey and even Johnson. They saw even Great Society programs as deceitful compromises with the status quo, window-dressing social reforms that didn't bring about the dramatic changes that American society needed.

If they needed any further proof of their critique, Richard Nixon himself—the ultimate political pragmatist—had adopted many of these same policies. How worthwhile could such policies be if even Nixon espoused them? True social change would require much more. And so George McGovern became the Democrats' standard bearer.

The grand dreams of the McGovernites, and the bizarre trappings of the 1972 Democratic National Convention, struck most Americans as profoundly unserious, as well as dangerous. McGovern's well-meaning but radical call for change simply "frightened too many Americans," as Theodore White put it.[63] It frightened core Democrats, too. The AFL-CIO was so troubled by McGovern that it sat out the election—the only time in history that the labor group watched from the sidelines.

"The Democratic Party has been taken over by people named Jack, who look like Jills and smell like Johns," said George Meany.[64] Even Democratic Party stalwarts like Tip O'Neill refused to attend the convention. Rank-and-file Democrats' distaste for the party's presidential nominee was made most explicit by Democrats for Nixon, a group led by former Texas governor John Connally, who was then serving as Nixon's Treasury secretary. Connally said that he had polling data showing that as many as twenty million Democrats would cross over with him and vote for Nixon because of their fears of a McGovern presidency—particularly on issues of national security and social welfare spending. The Democratic Party, Connally said, was "becoming an ideological machine closed to millions who have been the party's most loyal and steadfast members."[65]

Soon, McGovern became known to many in Middle America as the candidate of "acid, amnesty, and abortion."[66] A World War II hero and a man of dignity and integrity, he was far from such a caricature, but he presided over a party that had had something like a nervous breakdown.

On November 7, 1972, American voters returned Nixon to the White House by an historic margin. Nixon won 60.7 percent of the popular vote, beating McGovern by a staggering eighteen million votes. His winning percentage just missed LBJ's record of 61.1 percent in 1964 and FDR's record of 60.8 percent in 1936. Nixon won forty-nine states and 520 electoral votes, outstripping LBJ and falling just short of FDR's 523 electoral votes (which Reagan topped in 1984, with 525). But for Massachusetts and the District of Columbia, McGovern's "Come home, America!" message was answered by voters with: "Go home, McGovern!"

Nixon's smashing victory came ten years to the day after his political career had been thought finished: when he lost the 1962 California governor's race to Pat Brown and, in a postelection press conference, famously told the press that it wouldn't "have Nixon to kick around anymore."[67] Six years after his declaration, he had clawed his way to his first presidency, running an ingenious political campaign but taking the White House in wartime as a minority president, winning just 43 percent of the popular vote. Now, he had completed one of the most remarkable reversals of political fortune in American history.

On the other side, an equally transformative political reversal had been consummated. Just eight years earlier, the Democrats had returned President Lyndon Johnson to the White House in a massive landslide. Pundits wrote the political obituary of the Republican Party. Now it was the Democratic Party whose future seemed in doubt, in part due to its own failures of leadership and ideas during a time of extraordinary change and social upheaval—but also in part due to the genius of Richard Nixon.

The Post-1972 Democrats

Though he lost by a crushing margin, McGovern brought together a new base of the Democratic Party—one composed of young people, African Americans, women, and gay activists—that would put Barack Obama in the White House in 2008. The party now defined itself along the lines of the McGovern coalition.[68] Indeed, ever since the McGovern campaign,

Democrats have struggled to overcome the stigma of being the party of elites—rather than the party of workers, as they had been known before the 1960s. This burden has proved fatal at the polls: between 1968 and 2004, Republican candidates have won seven out of ten presidential elections and the GOP has gained power in Congress.

In subsequent chapters, I'll sketch out the history of the post–Nixon era Democratic Party, which, in reaction to its electoral routs of 1972, and later, of 1980, 1984, and 1988, finally moved to the center again under the direction of the Democratic Leadership Council and Bill Clinton. Clinton, running as a New Democrat, was able to rebrand the party as moderate to centrist, promarket, strong on defense, and a staunch defender of middle-class values. He won two terms and left office with enviable approval ratings in the high fifties. Not many two-term presidents can say that. (I examine Clinton's presidency in chapter 7). Clinton was successful because he recognized the political opportunity that polarization created; hence his approach of "triangulation," in which the president positioned himself as the moderate alternative between unreconstructed liberals (like Ted Kennedy) in the Democratic Party and the New Right conservatives (led by Newt Gingrich). Yet in adopting this strategy, he was only relearning the lessons of Nixon, who had first modeled the centrist paradigm in a time of deep partisan division. Thus Nixon's dual legacy, of confrontation and co-optation, remains the most powerful and influential one in American politics.

For some, the Clinton presidency seemed to bring to a close a painful chapter of Democratic history, post-McGovern. The Democrats had taken a while to learn the lessons of 1972, but they had finally reclaimed the political center. At least, that's the way it looked when Bill Clinton left the White House. Yet while Clinton skillfully pivoted between perceived extremists on the right and the left to become the consummate centrist, most of his Democratic colleagues didn't take this path. The national party has moved further left since Clinton: not only is the party more liberal today, thanks in part to redistricting and party polarization, it has also doubled down on its McGovern-era identification with liberals and cultural elites. There is one crucial difference between now and 1972, however: the national demographics are now in the Democrats' favor, as became clear with President Obama's election in 2008 and his reelection in 2012.

Obama's victories in 2008 and especially in 2012 represented the maturation of the McGovern coalition. The difference thirty-six years later was that America's demographics had changed so much that a McGovernesque coalition could prevail. "If you look at the map of states where McGovern ran ahead of his national average, you see something very much like the map of the states carried by Obama in 2008," wrote political analyst Michael Barone in 2012, as the November vote approached. "A claim can be made that the McGovern candidacy and the peace movement sowed the seeds for later Democratic triumphs and contributed importantly to the Democratic majorities that have emerged from time to time—and which could not have been produced by the pre-1968 Democratic Party."[69]

When Obama did go on to win reelection, Peter Grier wrote in the *Christian Science Monitor* that

> the lesson of his victory for both parties, but particularly Republicans, may be this: The primacy of white male voters has passed. In the modern era, it takes a diverse coalition to win the White House. Look at the basic breakdown of Mr. Obama's victory, according to exit polls (which may yet be revised). He won 93 percent of African Americans, 71 percent of Hispanics, and 73 percent of Asians. He took 55 percent of the overall female vote, down only one percentage point from his comparable 2008 showing. Mitt Romney, meanwhile, won about 59 percent of the white vote. That's the best a GOP nominee has done among whites since 1988, and not too long ago such a performance might have guaranteed a winning margin of 270 electoral votes.[70]

The Democrats have aggressively courted their new coalition in ways that suggest, as Ross Douthat put it, "a form of 'positive polarization,'" not unlike what happened when the Republicans galvanized the silent majority. Retreating from the political center, the Democrats have, ironically, taken a page from the Nixon playbook. The result has been a more ideological party that has done its share to contribute to national polarization:

Where the Clinton-era Democrats still tried to win working class whites outright, the Obama-era Democrats mostly just used scorched-earth campaigning to try to minimize the G.O.P.'s margin and/or keep these voters on the sidelines. Where the pre-Obama party still made room for immigration skeptics and coal-country populists, the Obama-era Democrats have pushed in policy directions calculated to alienate many of the swing voters who cast ballots for Byron Dorgan in the past, or Joe Manchin or Mark Pryor in the present. Where the pre-Obama party spoke the language of "safe, legal and rare" on abortion and basically set gun control aside as a losing issue, the Obama Democrats have mostly dropped the "rare" part and, post-Newtown, taken up the gun-control cause anew.[71]

This pursuit has given the Democrats "a presidential-level majority that they did not enjoy before," Douthat conceded, even if it comes with a precarious balance: Obama lost non-college-educated white voters by *forty points* in 2012.[72] A generation ago, those voters didn't like George McGovern, either, and though they're a smaller portion of the electorate today, the Democrats probably can't afford to let that gap grow much larger. But for now, Democrats have embraced positive polarization, confident that demographic trends in the electorate give them a powerful advantage, at least in presidential elections.

That's a comfort George McGovern didn't have, but his surviving supporters must see today's Democratic Party as his vindication. A little more than forty years after the 1972 catastrophe, demographically at least, it has become McGovern's party—which is another way of saying that, all these years later, the Democrats remain Nixonized.

CHAPTER 5

Nixonizing the Republicans
Part Two: The Conservative Revolt

Nixon has followed the policies of the Democrats and has carried us from disaster
to disaster.

—**JOHN ASHBROOK**[1]

Flexibility is the first principle of politics.

—**RICHARD NIXON TO A NEW STAFFER, RICHARD WHALEN**[2]

O n September 20, 1971, some of the leading lights of the American
conservative party—*National Review* publisher William Rusher;
Tom Winter from *Human Events*; Young Americans for Freedom's
Randal Teague; and Daniel Mahoney, founder of the New York State
Conservative Party—gathered for dinner at the Manhattan apartment
of the brightest conservative light of all: William F. Buckley Jr., editor of
National Review. They had gathered to explore the possibilities, as one
attendee described it, "for political action against Mr. Nixon"[3]—including supporting a conservative candidate to run against the president in
the Republican primaries.

These were not men normally given to rebel candidacies or politically quixotic pursuits—especially Buckley, the best-known member
of the group, who loathed the idea of opposing a sitting Republican
president. The group gathered in his apartment had supported Nixon
in 1968, misgivings and all, because they believed that he was the best
choice available. But they had been losing confidence and faith in the
president as his first term unfolded, especially during 1971. Only a few
months earlier, in July, some of these same men had met at Manhattan's
University Club to draw up a statement declaring their "suspension of
support" for the president. In an editorial in *National Review*, they presented their defection as "an act of loyalty to the Nixon we supported
in 1968."[4]

It was no accident that they referenced the Nixon of 1968. To win
the White House in that fractious year, Nixon knew he needed to win
over conservatives—especially those who had passionately supported
Barry Goldwater in 1964, and who remained, despite the 1964 results,
proud of their involvement. Indeed, the Goldwater campaign was in
many respects a reaction to Nixon's narrow defeat in 1960. Conservatives
saw their opportunity to take control of the Republican Party, and they
succeeded, at least temporarily; however, Goldwater was trounced in
November by Lyndon Johnson. In 1968, Nixon came knocking at the
conservatives' door. Through his Southern strategy, his appeals to law
and order, his attacks on Earl Warren's Supreme Court, and his defense
of conservative cultural values, Nixon succeeded in gathering enough
conservatives in his corner—while holding onto Republican moderates.
And he won.

But three years later, the conservatives felt used. In their view, Nixon
owed them: they had defended him during tumultuous times, but he had
rewarded them, for the most part, by speaking one way and governing
another. During the campaign, for example, Nixon had decried "the
welfare mess," and implied that the massive welfare levels of the Great
Society were untenable. But then, as president, he had proposed the
Family Assistance Plan—a guaranteed annual income for all Americans.
Conservatives saw it as universalized welfare. He had spoken out against
busing, and even taken measured action against it as president, but then
instituted affirmative action policies that pursued the same goals. He
had presented himself as a disciplined spender and budget cutter, but
then vastly expanded social welfare spending, including for Medicare
and Social Security, as well as for food stamps and Medicaid. And as a
candidate he had announced a "secret plan" to end the Vietnam War, and
to bring "peace with honor"—but as president, he declared that America
did not seek victory in Vietnam, and proceeded to bring troops home.

In 1971, two presidential actions, one foreign and one domestic,
finally pushed conservatives over the edge. Nixon announced in July that
he would visit Peking to begin normalizing relations with Communist
China, and in August, he moved the United States off the gold standard and announced temporary wage and price controls in an effort
to control inflation. These policies were so far afield from conservative
principles that, for Buckley's group—which called itself, half-jokingly,

the "Manhattan Twelve"—and other conservatives, it became impossible to support Nixon for reelection.

In Buckley's apartment, the Manhattan Twelve began a search for a candidate willing to challenge the president. This was no easy task. Like most incumbent presidents of recent times, Nixon had built a juggernaut reelection campaign with financial and political support that few, if any, figures from the president's own party would wish to challenge. And conservatives, by their nature, were less given to such pursuits than others. All the big conservative names were already on board for Nixon's reelection: Barry Goldwater, Ronald Reagan, and Texas senator John Tower.

But the Manhattan Twelve settled on a candidate: John Ashbrook, a forty-three-year-old Ohio Congressman and conservative movement stalwart. A veteran of the Goldwater campaign, Ashbrook had served as chairman of the American Conservative Union, and he was a popular speaker at Young Americans for Freedom (YAF) events. By early December, the Manhattan Twelve and Ashbrook were talking seriously about a candidacy. Upping the ante further, William Loeb, editor and publisher of the conservative newspaper *Manchester Union Leader*, ran a front-page editorial calling on Ashbrook to challenge Nixon.[5] On December 29, 1971, Ashbrook announced his candidacy for president. He explained his run by alleging that Nixon the 1968 candidate and Nixon the president were two different people.[6]

Ashbrook, of course, would not go on to deny Nixon the Republican nomination. But he and the Manhattan Twelve symbolized something far-reaching: a renewed, expanded, and ultimately victorious conservative movement. The groundwork for what would become the Reagan Revolution in 1980 was crucially laid during the 1970s, when conservatives often felt disdained, first by Nixon and then by Gerald Ford. It was Nixon's insufficient conservatism that galvanized the Republican Right, helped it define itself more clearly, and ultimately propelled it to power.

Thus Nixon, who had congealed so much conservative support in 1968, now congealed conservative momentum again, even more strongly, in opposition to his pragmatism and moderation. By the late seventies, the stage was set for the Reagan Revolution and the conservative takeover of the Republican Party. It's a story most often told with two key protagonists: Barry Goldwater and Ronald Reagan. Yet the crucial intermediary figure—at the center of everything that happened between 1964 and 1980—was Richard Nixon. Neither a committed moderate nor a true-believing conservative, only Nixon could navigate along the crossroads that separated the party factions.

How Nixon Courted the Right

From the beginning of his political career, Nixon knew that courting the right wing of the Republican Party was essential. In the late 1940s, when Nixon was starting out, a resurgent but small conservative movement saw promise in him—and he showed willingness to attack his early political opponents, like Jerry Voorhees and Helen Gahagan Douglas, as Communist sympathizers.

At the same time, he had a keen understanding of party dynamics and an unsentimental assessment of how to exploit political realities. "Richard Nixon always knew where the political power was," said conservative historian Lee Edwards.[7] In 1960, as he geared up to pursue the presidency against John F. Kennedy, Nixon knew that he needed conservative support but also that he needed to assuage party moderates, whose champion was New York governor Nelson Rockefeller. Since Nixon's hardline rhetoric put many moderates off, he made a deal with Rockefeller in 1960 that came to be known as the "Pact of Fifth Avenue," ensuring the moderate faction's support. In the deal, Nixon agreed to some platform changes requested by Rockefeller, and he pushed the GOP platform committee to incorporate them. Rockefeller publicized the deal, causing a conservative backlash against Nixon, but he had demonstrated his willingness to navigate between factions in the GOP. He would go on to anger various factions at different times, but he would unify the party behind his candidacy. Like no Republican before or after him, Nixon had the ability to move in all directions at the same time.

By 1968, though, with the Vietnam War spinning out of control and American cities burning, the GOP's moderate wing was on the defensive. Nixon made a renewed conservative push. "A Republican can't win without the conservatives—1962 taught me that," he told an aide, referring to his defeat that year in the California gubernatorial race. But in the next breath, alluding to Goldwater's landslide presidential defeat, he said, "a Republican also can't win with the conservatives alone—1964 showed that."[8] He set out to win over conservatives early on before tacking gradually to the center for the general election. But, as Lee Edwards put it, "Nixon's center moved to the right."[9]

He had seen it coming. During Nixon's first presidential run, in 1960, William F. Buckley's *National Review* had refused to endorse him, calling him "an unreliable auxiliary of the right."[10] The GOP's conservative wing, smarting from the narrow 1960 defeat, vowed to nominate a true conservative in 1964. No more Nixons, they said.

In 1964, they got their wish with Barry Goldwater, who ran the most conservative presidential campaign in the twentieth century. The Goldwater campaign would become a landmark moment in the history of modern conservatism, the proving ground for a generation of young conservatives like Pat Buchanan, Phyllis Schlafly, Edward Feulner (who would go on to found the Heritage Foundation), and Ed Crane (who would found the libertarian Cato Institute). And even as the clouds of defeat hung heavy in the air in the campaign's final week, the conservatives discovered another hero: fifty-three-year-old Ronald Reagan, whose televised speech for Goldwater, "A Time for Choosing," was one of the most electrifying political addresses in American history. Reagan made the case for conservatism better than Goldwater himself had, and he did it in a conversational style—in fact, he delivered the address from notes, not from a script—that resonated with millions. Reagan, who had honed his timing and delivery over a decade of giving political speeches for General Motors, sounded to many Americans like one of them, especially when he said: "This is the issue of this election: whether we believe in our capacity for self-government or whether we abandon the American revolution and confess that a little intellectual elite in a far-distant capitol can plan our lives for us better than we can plan them ourselves."[11] The Reagan speech brought the campaign to a close on a high note.

And yet, the following week, the Goldwater campaign was buried under what was, at the time, the worst presidential landslide in history. Reagan's eloquence and passion had not swayed nearly enough people that Goldwater was the man to lead the country. As Republicans and conservatives looked toward 1968, some at *National Review* were determined to avoid a replay of the Goldwater debacle—notably Frank Meyer, originator of the concept of fusionism, essentially a "big tent" theory of conservative unity. For Meyer, it was less important to get a candidate who was a true-blue conservative than it was to get a candidate who would "owe his victory to the conservatives." In reasoning that Nixon would have appreciated, Meyer made clear that, in 1968, Ronald Reagan was his ideal candidate—but that Nixon was an acceptable backup choice. The main thing, he wrote, was the pressure that a Reagan candidacy would exert on Nixon: "The solider the support for Reagan at the Republican convention, the greater the possibility that he may be nominated—but also the certainty that any liberal candidate can be vetoed; the assurance that, if Nixon is nominated, he will owe it to conservative support; and the guarantee that conservative control of the Republican party will be consolidated."[12]

But Nixon wasn't waiting for other conservatives to come around to Meyer's way of thinking. So, as he prepared to run for the White House again, Nixon reached out to Buckley and Rusher of *National Review* to win their support. Rusher, if anything, was even more skeptical than Buckley. He wasn't buying, and he used his influence to block a formal endorsement of Nixon in the journal. Buckley, on the other hand, as practical as he was staunchly conservative, seemed to see a winner in Nixon. He invited him on the show *Firing Line* and ran a sympathetic profile of the candidate in the magazine. "As a result," Edwards wrote, "conservative opinion makers linked Nixon and *National Review*."[13]

The outreach to *National Review*—then as now, the leading journal of conservative opinion in the United States—was part of a broader outreach strategy. Nixon tirelessly met with and built bridges to conservative politicians, journalists, and thinkers. A year before the critical *National Review* meeting, Nixon was conducting informal policy sessions with conservative journalists and youth leaders around the country—a regular feature of these talks was a sixty-minute, off-the-record presentation by the candidate about international affairs and foreign policy. Always delivered without looking at any handwritten notes, Nixon's presentation was generally regarded by all who saw it as a "tour de force."[14]

In short, the courtship proved successful. Nixon convinced most Republicans that he was the party's best hope in 1968—especially in swing states. Even Reagan, running against Nixon in the primaries (and winning more popular votes overall, due to his margin in California), saw some of his hardline conservative support go to Nixon in the South, a consequence of Nixon's shrewd liaison with Southern power broker

Senator Strom Thurmond. A Southern partisan who had defended segregation, Thurmond was also a calculating judge of politics and electoral
math. He knew that Democrat George Wallace would likely win the
Deep South against any Republican candidate, even Reagan, and that
a more moderate Republican, like Nixon, would stand a better chance
against him in the North and Midwest, especially in toss-up states.
Thus Thurmond supported Nixon over Reagan, though he was closer
to Reagan ideologically. Most conservatives, while they couldn't have
Reagan, who was their favorite, on the ticket, took heart that Nixon was
well to the right of the party's liberal Northeastern establishment. He
may not have been Reagan, but he wasn't Nelson Rockefeller, either.

Human Events, a longtime conservative newsletter, endorsed the
Nixon-Agnew ticket in 1968, calling it "the best vehicle for implementing the conservative philosophy and saving this country from the ills
that beset it."[15] Nixon prevailed narrowly on election day, though George
Wallace did capture the five Deep South states, along the way garnering
nine million popular votes—a sure sign that the electorate, at least in
parts of the country, was moving rightward. "It's ridiculous," opined a
National Review editorial, "to talk about these nine million as if they are
all Ku Kluxers, illiterates and foaming racists."[16] It was now Nixon's job
to find a way to keep conservatives happy while also serving as president
of two hundred million people.

Once in office, Nixon tried to signal that he understood his debt
to conservatives, in part through his hires. Perhaps the most dramatic
of these hires was Patrick J. Buchanan, then a young speechwriter and
editorialist for the *St. Louis Globe-Democrat*. A gifted political polemi-
cist—as he remains today, nearly fifty years later—Buchanan had cut his
political teeth in the 1964 Goldwater campaign.[17] Nixon used his team to
work closely with a constellation of conservative organizations—from
National Review and *Human Events* to the American Conservative Union
and the Buckley-created Young Americans for Freedom—to draw up
lists of prospective conservative appointees and administrators.

Despite the early good signs, though, true-blue conservatives like
William Rusher from *National Review* always doubted Nixon's conservative credentials. In fact, prior to Nixon's inauguration, the ACU published a report claiming that the combined Nixon-Wallace vote—nearly
57 percent of the popular vote—represented "the outright repudiation of

the Johnson-Humphrey policies." The ACU called on Nixon to "remake the Republican Party as the majority party."[18] He was well on his way to doing that, in fact—but not in the way that the ACU and other conservative groups had hoped.

The Break

After the 1968 election, Rusher told a friend that he doubted conservatives had made a "wise" choice in settling for Nixon. L. Brent Bozell was even harsher. Writing in the conservative Catholic magazine *Triumph*, he lambasted conservatives for supporting Nixon and declared that by doing so, they had "ceased to be an important political force in America."[19]

For his part, Nixon was hardly enthused about conservatives, either. The suspicion, and sometimes contempt, that he felt for hard-core right wingers ran deep. Sitting with his aide John C. Whitaker on a plane in 1965, the day after William F. Buckley lost his mayoral race in New York City, Nixon gave him an earful.

"The trouble with far-right conservatives like Buckley," Nixon said, "is that they really don't give a damn about people and the voters sense that. Yet any Republican presidential candidate can't stray too far from the right-wingers because they can dominate a primary and are even more important in close general elections."

"Remember, John," Nixon lectured, "the far-right kooks are just like the nuts on the left, they're door-bell ringers and balloon blowers, but they turn out to vote. There is only one thing as bad as a far-left liberal and that's a damn right-wing conservative."[20]

Whitaker felt that Nixon's contempt for conservatives' thinking, particularly on domestic policy, was balanced by his pragmatic, hardheaded respect for the power they held in elections. Nixon would straddle the fence throughout his presidency, pushing against conservatives often, but then coming back to them—sometimes symbolically, sometimes substantively—to prevent a full-scale desertion.

White House Chief of Staff H. R. Haldeman was already sensing Nixon's disdain early on, as shown in his diary. In February 1969, Haldeman wrote that Nixon was "obviously concerned about reports (especially Buchanan's) that conservatives and the South are unhappy.

Also he's annoyed by constant right-wing bitching, with never a positive alternative. [He] ordered me to assemble a political group and really hit them to start defending us."[21] A year later, the chief of staff wrote that the White House needed to "build our own new coalition based on Silent Majority, blue collar, Catholic, Poles, Italians, Irish. No promise with Jews and Negroes. Appeal not hard right-wing, Bircher, or anti-Communist. Need to study the real base.... [Nixon] feels he's getting coverage on his trip because he attacked the press and forced them to pay attention."[22]

But at the policy level, conservative Nixon watchers likewise had grounds for complaint early on. The president's policies, especially in the areas of the economy, social welfare, and foreign policy, would soon drive a wedge between him and his conservative backers and prompt a conservative revolt within the GOP—one that would set the stage, in the years to come, for the conservative takeover of the Republican Party.

Fiscal Policy

"You see to it," Nixon told Arthur Burns, whom he had tapped to take over the Fed in 1970, "no recession."[23] That statement sums up Nixon's level of interest in, and expertise about, economic matters. He knew how important the domestic economy was to his chances for reelection, but he had little passion for economic matters. In this he was like most other presidents, and also like them he would prove willing to subordinate sound and consistent economic policy to what he saw as his bigger political interests.

Conservatives knew, even before he entered the White House, that Nixon was not likely to please them on economic policy. But they didn't expect him to announce, as he did in January 1971, that "I am a Keynesian"[24] and embrace a full-employment approach toward the economy, with massive deficit spending.

Nixon had his reasons for this pragmatic and calculating approach. For one thing, he thought the reason he had lost the 1960 election to Kennedy was because of the recession that year, and he blamed the financial managers at the Federal Reserve for prioritizing cutting inflation over cutting unemployment. "He attributed the recession, or at least its depth and duration, to economic officials, 'financial types,' who put

curbing inflation ahead of cutting unemployment," wrote economist
and Nixon advisor Herbert Stein.[25] He was determined not to make the
same mistake in 1972. But as he prepared his reelection campaign, he
was facing a situation many economists thought impossible: high inflation of 5 percent, along with unemployment of 5 percent—substantially
higher than its 3.5 percent average in the 1960s.

To control both the level of inflation and the unemployment rate,
Nixon embraced federal wage and price controls. He was aided in this by
the Democratic Congress, which in 1970 gave him the power to impose
wage and price freezes, assuming his commitment to the free market
ideals of his party would prevent him from enacting them. They were
wrong.

In this, Nixon was led by Burns, who had always previously opposed
such interventions but had concluded, by the early 1970s, that the
economy had structurally changed. Labor unions and private-sector
corporations were driving up wages and prices, Burns told the president,
and traditional fiscal and monetary prices would no longer suffice. He
proposed a wage-price review board composed of prominent citizens
that would "pass judgment" on wage and price increases, though they
would not have policy-making power—their input would be advisory,
though influential. Only such a measure, Burns believed, could tame the
rampant inflation as well as the mounting joblessness stemming from
employers' unwillingness to pay high wages.

As inflation continued to rise in 1971, Nixon began to seriously
consider a step he had previously promised conservatives was out of
the question in his administration: wage and price controls. No matter
how "politically expedient that may seem," he promised the Right, he
wouldn't resort to such a step. But with the annual inflation rate reaching 6 percent and beyond and many constituencies demanding that some
action be taken, he felt the pressure to impose the controls, along with
"closing the gold window." Overseas governments had been accumulat-
ing dollars far in excess of the US gold reserve, and Nixon's team was
seriously worried about the possibility of a gold run.

Finally, in what he would call the New Economic Policy, Nixon
announced a ninety-day wage and price freeze and the delinking of the
dollar to gold—ending the postwar Bretton-Woods financial system
in a single stroke. It was not a step that met with unanimous support

even within the administration—its leading opponent was Burns, who warned the president that going off the gold standard would be celebrated in Moscow as a sign that free market economies could not sustain themselves. "Pravda would write that this was a sign of the collapse of capitalism," he fumed. But the other Nixon men overruled him. "Going off the gold standard and giving up fixed exchange rates," Daniel Yergin and Joseph Stanislaw would later write, "constituted a momentous step in the history of international economics."[26]

Ever practical, Nixon explained to his aides: "Philosophically... I was still against wage-price controls, even though I was convinced that the objective reality of the economic situation forced me to impose them."[27] That exemplified the attitude that conservatives had come to loathe in his leadership.

The policy itself, however, or at least the announcement of it, gained huge popular support—despite the speech's preempting *Bonanza*, then among the most watched programs on television. Americans felt that the administration was taking action to protect their pocketbooks against high prices. The Dow Jones Industrial Average registered a one-day record gain of 32.9 points, and the mainstream media, led by the *New York Times*, cheered Nixon's leadership. "We unhesitatingly applaud the boldness with which the President has moved," the *Times* editorial declared.[28]

The daring policy move proved to be just what Nixon needed for his reelection campaign in 1972, though it came at a heavy long-term cost. Nixon's direction to the Fed to loosen the money supply led to runaway inflation; when he resigned office in August 1974, it stood at 11 percent—the first indication of the crippling inflation rates of the 1970s which, at their worst under Jimmy Carter, would reach an incredible 18 percent. Nixon's utilitarian fiscal moves in August 1971—the ending of Bretton Woods and the imposition of controls—would come to be known as the "Nixon shock." Assessing its impact forty years later, Roger Lowenstein wrote in *Bloomberg Businessweek* that the Nixon shock "spelled the end of the fixed relationships that had governed the financial universe."[29]

And thus another irony of Richard Nixon's presidency: This Republican and nominally "conservative" president may have turned out to be our most "statist" president of the postwar period. No president has so transformed the nation's fiscal and monetary policy, and the effects of these sweeping measures still shape the landscape today.

Social Welfare

In chapter 1, I described Nixon's failed attempt to pass comprehensive welfare reform legislation with the Family Assistance Plan (FAP). The plan would have provided a guaranteed minimum income for all American families with dependent children—including those with fathers still in the household, in stark contrast to the established welfare program Aid to Families with Dependent Children (AFDC). Nixon saw the FAP as a "small-c conservative" reform, a practical and humane attempt to address poverty while also reinstating incentives to family cohesion that AFDC had undermined.

But the Right hated the plan. Libertarians and market-oriented conservatives saw the program as socialistic, a perpetuation of Great Society policies, rather than, as Nixon saw it, a reform of those policies. The FAP didn't make it out of Congress; it never reached the president's desk. Ironically, both the Right and the Left claimed something of a victory in defeating the FAP—conservatives because they saw the program as too redistributive of wealth, and liberals because it wasn't redistributive enough.

But Nixon wasn't through rankling conservative sensitivities on social welfare.

Concurrent with FAP's long-running on-again, off-again status in Congress, another bill cherished by liberals came to the fore: the Comprehensive Child Development Act, sponsored by Democratic senator Walter Mondale of Minnesota and Republican representative John Brademas of Indiana. The CDA would establish a national network of child care centers to provide early childhood education—what we call pre-K today—as well as nutrition and medical services. Mondale saw the CDA as the first step in a move toward universal child care. Congress passed it on a bipartisan vote and allocated expansive funding for it.[30] It looked like a sure bet for Nixon's signature—especially since the administration had helped write the bill.

But the right wing rebelled, and the first stirrings of what would become the John Ashbrook candidacy began here. Congressman

Ashbrook derided the CDA as the "child control" or the "parent replace-ment" act.[31] Conservative columnist James J. Kilpatrick wrote that the CDA was the boldest and most far-reaching scheme ever advanced for the "Sovietization of American youth."[32] As opposition bubbled up on the right, Pat Buchanan intervened, urging Nixon to veto the CDA as a show of solidarity with the right wing. Some in the administration agreed that the bill should be vetoed, but along purely practical lines; they opposed it solely based on its cost. For the Right, that wasn't suf-ficient; Buchanan urged the president to reject the bill in the strongest ideological terms.

In his veto message of December 1971, Nixon warned that the CDA "would commit vast moral authority of the National Government to the side of communal approaches to child rearing over against the family-centered approach."[33] The president said that federal policy should "cement the family in its rightful position as the keystone of our civilization." He called the CDA "a long leap into the dark" and "the most radical piece of legislation to emerge from the Ninety-Second Congress."[34]

Back in Minnesota for the holiday recess, Mondale was not shocked that Nixon had vetoed the bill, but he was surprised by the ideologi-cal language. He and Brademas didn't give up; they rejiggered the bill, downsized its scope and cost, and tried to move it through Congress again. But the American Right was fully awakened now. In a Senate debate with conservative New York senator James Buckley, brother of the *National Review* editor, Mondale struggled to fend off the conserva-tive accusations. Buckley accused Mondale of backing a bill that would "encourage women to put their families into institutions of communal living."[35] The revised CDA did not pass the House.

Along with the defeat of the FAP, the demise of the CDA proved heartening to movement conservatives. By now, few felt that the presi-dent was one of them; most had come to the conclusion that he was not. What mattered, then, was whether they could influence him, and the CDA victory showed that they could. The drive against the CDA had drawn power and force from a grassroots push in the nation's heartland, and it had featured the prominent participation of conser-vative women—who were, up to now, a nearly invisible portion of the electorate. Typical of their efforts was Women Who Want to be Women, a fundamentalist Christian women's group whose Oklahoma chapter entered national politics for the first time by fighting against the CDA.

The late Paul Weyrich, cofounder of the Heritage Foundation and originator of the term *Religious Right*, pointed to the CDA episode as the birth of family-based social conservatism in the political arena.[36] Others remembered it less fondly.

"That was really the beginning of the Tea Party," a frustrated Mondale said many years later. "The right wing started to turn on this thing viciously. They said it was a socialist scheme. They were really pounding the members of Congress and a lot of people got cold feet."[37] The Right was pounding, yes—but in the minds of many of its leading lights, it was also *taking a pounding* from the Nixon White House. The president had given conservatives satisfying language to go along with his veto message, but he'd clearly been coerced into the decision by conservative political opposition. And for some committed conservatives, a bombshell foreign policy announcement from Nixon marked a point of no return.

Foreign Policy

On July 15, 1971, Nixon asked NBC for a few minutes of television time. Standing stiffly before a lectern, he said that he wanted

> to announce a major development in our efforts to build a lasting peace in the world. As I have pointed out on a number of occasions over the past three years, there can be no stable and enduring peace without the participation of the PRC [People's Republic of China] and its 750 million people. That is why I have undertaken initiatives in several areas to open the door for more normal relations between our two countries.[38]

And then he read from an announcement being simultaneously unveiled in Peking: stating that he, Richard Nixon, had accepted Chou en Lai's invitation to visit Peking sometime before May 1972. He would take the trip, he said, in the "profound conviction that all nations will gain from a reduction of tensions and a better relationship between the United States and the People's Republic of China."[39]

Nothing Nixon did as president met with anything like the resounding approval, even celebration, across the political divide that was generated by his trip to China. Liberal Senate Majority Leader Mike Mansfield said he was "flabbergasted... but very pleased and happy that the President has accepted Peking's invitation." House Republican Minority Leader Gerald Ford called the trip "singularly significant in the pursuit of world peace."[40] Even the *New York Times,* Nixon's bête noire, gave Nixon full credit for his vision and daring.

But one group did not join in the celebration—in fact, they deplored it. For the American Right, Nixon's move was the last straw.

"I am just phoning to say... goodbye," *National Review*'s Rusher told Buchanan after the announcement.[41] Rusher and others could see where the Nixon trip was likely to lead: a diplomatic recognition of the PRC as the legitimate national entity of the Chinese people; an eventual move to a One China policy at the expense of Taiwan, long an ally of the United States; and legitimization for Mao and Red China in the world community, along with integration in the world economy.

All of this would indeed come to pass.

"This newspaper considers President Nixon's proposal to visit Communist China and the change in policy toward Red China to be immoral, indecent, insane and fraught with danger for the survival of the United States," William Loeb wrote in the conservative *Manchester Union Leader.*[42]

Coupled with Nixon's conciliatory move toward détente with Moscow, the opening to China was the body blow to the Right from which there was to be no recovery. Visiting China represented an abandonment of the cause that Nixon had begun his career fighting for and that, for the American Right, was as close to a raison d'etre as anything else: anti-Communism. Of course, the Nixon announcement, bombshell that it was, didn't come out of nowhere. It had been preceded by two years of determined diplomacy on the part of Nixon and Secretary of State Henry Kissinger. The two men sent secret envoys to Peking, often using Pakistan or Romania as conduits.[43] As information on those extensive and hard-won efforts spilled out into the news, conservatives could only wonder at the priority Nixon had placed on normalizing relations with a regime they regarded as totalitarian and genocidal.

"The United States spends billions to go to the moon. Mao just waits—and the moon comes to him," wrote a deeply disappointed Dr. Water H. Judd, chairman of the Committee of One Million against the Admission of Communist China to the United Nations.[44]

Outside of the geostrategic considerations, Nixon also knew that the China overture would be political gold for him in the looming 1972 campaign. His longtime political reputation as an anti-Communist red-baiter had already started to fade among centrist voters, but for liberals it remained a reliable trope. Now, with the China announcement, the caricature of "red-baiting Dick Nixon" just wasn't going to have the old power. Nixon's image transformation couldn't have been better timed: In mid-1971, polls showed him trailing his presumptive Democratic opponent, Maine senator Edmund Muskie, by 47–39 percent. "A presidential visit to China," wrote conservative historian Lee Edwards, "with all its attendant publicity and television coverage, might lose Nixon some votes on the right but would gain him far more votes from the center."[45]

All that meant little to conservatives. They had had enough, and they aimed to make Nixon pay. The August 10, 1971, *National Review* editorial "We Suspend Our Support" cited the administration's many domestic apostasies—wage and price controls, rampant inflation, high taxes, and what it called "inordinate welfarism"—but made clear that the "overtures to Red China" and the overall decline of American military power were the chief offenses. Nixon had cut Pentagon spending by 30 percent.[46]

A few weeks later, YAF held a mock presidential convention at which it nominated Vice President Agnew and his "running mate," Senator James Buckley. Over fifteen hundred YAF members pledged to raise $750,000 to mount a primary challenge to the president. "Dump Nixon!" members chanted as others made speeches criticizing administration policy. "Dump Nixon!"[47]

In a *New York Times Magazine* feature story in August 1971, "Say It Isn't So, Mr. President," Buckley wrote: "Does the bond of anti-Communism simply not mean anything anymore?"[48] He concluded that the challenge facing Nixon was to put to rest the growing "superstition" among conservatives that he had adopted the liberal view—that the Communists wanted peace in the same way liberals did. How long,

Buckley wondered, could Nixon allow such a suspicion to fester "before the American right comes to the conclusion that he is not one of us?"[49]

William Buckley's brother James, the conservative senator from New York, was more circumspect about the fallout. As a sitting senator, he made clear that he understood the complexities of governing and the compromises that any president had to make. Even so, he warned that the suspension of support by conservatives could have "serious implications" for Nixon's reelection chances. Nixon should consider it a "warning signal," James Buckley wrote. If the conservative revolt becomes full blown, he said, "it will be virtually impossible for the President to regain their credible support." The men stepping away from Nixon were not far-right crackpots, Buckley stressed; on the contrary, they were "thoughtful men, responsible men," and their desertion of a Republican president "was made with the greatest reluctance and only after the most careful deliberation, because the individuals in question have from the beginning wished the President well."[50]

And so the conservative revolt against Richard Nixon began.

The Conservative Revolt

The Manhattan Twelve made one more attempt to sway the Nixonites. They sent *Human Events* editor Allan Ryskind to meet with White House advisor Charles Colson. Ryskind presented a list of demands from the angry conservatives, chief of which was the retention of Spiro Agnew on the 1972 presidential ticket—rumor had it that Nixon wanted to give Agnew the boot in favor of Treasury Secretary John Connally. They also demanded a clear signal that the administration would stand with Taiwan, and, most cryptically, they wanted a clear "demonstration by action" that the administration had not bought into the "illusion of détente."[51] What that demonstration should be they did not say. But the best Nixon could do was promise them that yes, Agnew would remain on the ticket, in addition to pledging a small increase in Pentagon spending.

It wasn't enough.

"Some of the Nixon men have implied they don't care about us, that we have no place to go," said Walt Hintzen, a businessman and chairman of United Republicans of California. "There are quite a few conservatives that are going to show Nixon that they have several places they can go."[52] Hintzen called Nixon's opening to China "obscene" and said, "I wouldn't walk one inch for that man [Nixon] if he was running against Brezhnev. No one trusts him anymore."[53]

Like many of the conservatives backing him, John Ashbrook felt that he had stuck his neck out for Nixon and gotten little in return.[54] Ashbrook considered himself "an American first, a conservative second, and a Republican third."[55] He knew that he faced an uphill battle, but he wasn't really running to win—he was running to pull Nixon back toward the right, to show that the conservative movement was too powerful for a Republican president to ignore.

Even so, the Ashbrook campaign was "one of the most effective political operations conservatives have ever undertaken," a Nixon aide later recalled—at least up to that time.[56] The campaign pioneered direct-mail fundraising, which would become, in the 1970s, one of the principal tools of conservative grassroots political organizing. The effort was led by the direct-mail visionary Richard A. Viguerie, whose efforts lost money overall but vastly expanded the network of conservative donors. Viguerie helped the Ashbrook campaign stay afloat on just $5,000 per week. His commitment came from his own dissatisfaction with Nixon. "I felt isolated and frustrated," he said years later. "I kept looking for people who could lead, who could make things happen. Finally, reluctantly, I began to call my own meetings."[57]

Meanwhile, criticizing Nixon for adopting "liberal policies in the verbal trappings of conservatism,"[58] Ashbrook took just under 10 percent of the vote in the New Hampshire, Florida, and California primaries—although it was no threat to Nixon, it was an indication of a groundswell of dissatisfaction, exactly what conservatives like Rusher had hoped for.

At the same time, however, the Ashbrook insurgency may have helped Nixon with the broader electorate. The president was also facing a challenge from the Republican Left—in the person of Congressman Peter McCloskey of California. As Geoffrey Kabaservice noted, "Both campaigns ultimately seemed to confirm Nixon's claim to speak for the broad center of both the Republican Party and the American populace."[59]

And Nixon was able to stave off the scenario that he dreaded most: a challenge from California governor Ronald Reagan, the darling of the right wing. Nixon was careful to keep Reagan placated, on the one hand, and at arms' length, on the other. He stayed in touch with the popular

Californian and sent him on foreign trips, increasing Reagan's profile. At all times, Nixon was careful to convey to the governor that he valued his views, but in private he derided his "typical right-wing simplicity."[60]

Though electorally unsuccessful, the Ashbrook campaign proved an important training ground for young conservatives. Thanks to Young Americans for Freedom, the campaign attracted strong enthusiasm among students. Many young conservatives had formative experiences in the campaign, including Charles Black, later chairman of the Republican National Committee. Just twenty in 1972, Black ran Ashbrook's Florida campaign and went on to play important roles in the Reagan campaigns to come.[61]

How Anti-Nixonism Became Modern Conservatism

With Nixon's smashing victory in 1972, conservatives could take heart in the vanquishing of McGovern, a far-left candidate, and in the strong evidence from polls that the American people were, at minimum, center-right in their views. Conservatives were under no illusion, though, that Nixon, in a second term and no longer facing reelection, would feel more inclined to devote himself to them than he had been in his first term.

And of course, soon enough, Nixon had far-bigger problems to worry about: the Watergate scandal and the looming evidence that the White House inner circle, and perhaps Nixon himself, was involved from the beginning. For the Right, there had to be painful symbolism in the fact that one of the leaders of the Republican congressional delegation to the White House that advised Nixon to resign was none other than Barry Goldwater—the man whom conservatives had always wanted to be president in the first place.

The Right could take little solace in the end of the "long national nightmare" of Watergate. Gerald Ford was a committed Republican moderate. He needed a vice president, now that he had acceded to the top job himself, and conservatives hoped he might pick one of their own for that position. Instead, Ford tapped the man synonymous with the party's moderate Northeastern wing: Nelson Rockefeller. In 1964, at the Republican National Convention that nominated Goldwater, Rockefeller had warned the delegates of "the extremist threat" and its "danger to the party."[62] They booed him lustily.

So things looked bleak for conservatives at the end of 1974. But the Rockefeller nomination was more proof that they needed to organize and build their movement outside of the mainstream Republican Party establishment. And though they were loyal Republicans, and had on their hands an "accidental" president whose chances for election in his own right in 1976 would be uphill at best, they refused to stand on the sidelines when they saw the administration tacking leftward.

In fact, it was the Ford years that saw the rise of what Paul Weyrich later dubbed "the New Right." Weyrich, along with Viguerie, Phyllis Schlafly, Howard Phillips, and others, saw themselves as radicals working to change the status quo. Some had experience in conservative politics going back to the 1950s; some did not become political until the late 1960s or the 1970s. Nixon's career was inextricably linked with the history they had lived through. Their passion, commitment, and know-how transformed the conservative movement in the United States from a serious but often toothless minority into a political powerhouse determined to remake the Republican Party.

"We are radicals who want to change the existing power structure," Weyrich said. "We are not conservatives in the sense that conservative means accepting the status quo."[63] They found out that they had company: the conservative reaction to Nixon in the seventies marked the entry into Republican politics of many wealthy conservatives who remain central today—the Koch brothers, John Olin, Joseph Coors, Richard Scaife—and the founding of the first conservative think tanks, like the Heritage Foundation.[64] By the late 1970s, the National Conservative Political Action Committee (NCPAC) had become the largest and best-funded political action committee in the United States. The committee grew its power and influence by grabbing hold of issues that traditional, mainline Republicans—like Gerald Ford—would never have dreamed of contesting.

One of the key flashpoints for the Right against the Ford administration—and an unexpected impetus for the conservative revival—was the Equal Rights Amendment. The ERA had long been a goal of feminists dating back to the 1940s. With its unequivocal pledge—"Equality of rights under the law shall not be denied or abridged by the United States or by any state on account of sex"[65]—the amendment passed the House 352–15 in 1970. It passed the Senate 84–8 in 1972. Polls showed strong support, especially among American women. Nixon supported it, too, though his support was mostly verbal.

Gerald Ford had voted for the ERA in the House, and his wife, Betty, a former model, was a fervent advocate. By the time Ford took office in 1974, the ERA had already been ratified in twenty-eight of the thirty-eight states needed for passage. Its advocates considered its adoption a foregone conclusion, as did Ford.

Conservative women activists saw it differently. They argued that the polls were inflated and that when more mainstream American women understood what was in the amendment and its implications for women and families, they would oppose it. Phyllis Schlafly's Stop ERA campaign got started in 1972, when the amendment had already been passed by twenty-four states. She argued that the ERA presented grave threats to the traditional family and that it was unnecessary anyway. Women's rights and equal opportunity were already guaranteed, she said, by the Equal Pay Act, Title VII of the Civil Rights Act, the Equal Employment Opportunity Act, and Title IX of the Education Amendments.

People magazine called Schlafly the "velvet fist" behind the anti-ERA movement. "What I am defending," she had said, "is the real rights of women. A woman should have the right to be in the home as a wife and mother."[66] By 1973, Schlafly had set up Stop ERA organizations in twenty-six states. Evangelical Christians, becoming active in politics for the first time, joined the anti-ERA efforts in many of these states.

The anti-ERA push took supporters by surprise. Mail coming into the White House ran three to one against ERA adoption. Betty Ford was undeterred. She began campaigning for the amendment, visiting states where it was under consideration to speak at fundraising rallies and lobby legislators. Her hard-core advocacy backfired, however. Speaking to *Good Housekeeping* about her support for the ERA, she said that she understood "the low status of the homemaker in today's society and would like to find ways to raise it."[67] Most American "homemakers" didn't see themselves in this way, and they resented Ford's condescending assumption that she was doing this for their own good.

Mrs. Ford had offended conservatives in the same way that liberals and moderate Republicans would do countless times over the coming decades: She had suggested, even if unintentionally, that she was better than her constituency. In short, she was an "elitist."

"ERA advocates could not understand opposition to the amendment, especially when it came from women," Donald Critchlow wrote. "As a result, they were caught off guard by the anti-ERA movement, which spread like wildfire among traditional women.... The anti-ERA campaign tapped into a growing resentment among traditional religious women that their values were being threatened."[68]

As conservative opposition mounted, the ERA's momentum slowed. Thirty-five states had signed on by 1977, but five had rescinded their ratifications in the meantime, bringing the total back down to thirty. "The battle had succeeded in making feminism a suspect term for mainstream America," Critchlow wrote.[69] More important, Schlafly and her conservatives had stopped the ERA's forward progress. No more states adopted it after 1977, and the amendment died when its ratification deadline expired in 1982.

Though Ford himself, unlike his wife, kept himself at a distance from the ERA advocacy, the groundswell of conservative opposition threw his administration off balance. Underlying the administration's misjudgment was a fundamental underestimation of the growing power of the right wing—as well as its increasing anger and dissatisfaction with moderate Republicans of the Nixon/Ford variety.

The Ford foreign policy was a continuation of Nixon's—a commitment to détente and conciliation with Moscow, especially. "We are a nation in retreat," conservative commentator John Chamberlain wrote in *Human Events*. "Because we have been soft in the head and weak in will, our retreat is in danger of becoming a rout."[70]

The cries for Ronald Reagan to enter the 1976 campaign went up. "The Republican Party is in serious danger of extinction because it has ceased to represent anything more than a broad based pragmatism," Mickey Edwards, board member of the American Conservative Union, wrote in a letter to Reagan in which he urged him to get into the race. "If Gerald Ford becomes the Republican nominee, I see a disastrous defeat that will end the Republican Party. Because the Republican Party is, at its roots, a party of conservative principle, I believe that would be tragic."[71]

The Reagan challenge forced Ford to the right—at least rhetorically. "We are going to forget the use of the word détente," Ford said, an astounding statement from the custodian of the Nixon-Kissinger foreign policy.[72] Reagan, who called Communism a "disease," had long ridiculed détente. "Isn't that what a turkey has with his farmer until Thanksgiving Day?" he asked.[73]

Ford's moderate and practical small-*r* republicanism was no match rhetorically for Reagan's committed conservatism. "Reagan's candidacy," Kabaservice wrote, "illustrated both the gathering strength of the conservative movement within the Republican Party and its ability to stir the blood of voters with emotional appeals that moderates conspicuously lacked."[74] Ford barely prevailed over Reagan at the party's nominating convention in Kansas City, but Reagan's appeal forced the president to invite him down to the podium. Reagan responded by making one of his great speeches, telling the delegates that it was their responsibility as Republicans to ensure that the American heritage of free expression and individual liberty survived. His stirring words left many in the convention hall wondering why they hadn't nominated him.

When Ford lost the election to Jimmy Carter in November 1976 by a razor-thin margin, conservatives felt emboldened. They argued that Reagan would have won if he had been the candidate, even if polls didn't support that claim. But more important than claiming that Reagan could have won was the irrefutable fact that Ford had lost—the moderate, reasonable Republican hadn't been able to get the job done.[75] From the moment Ford conceded the race, the Reagan forces were busy at work planning for 1980.

Tax Revolts and Prairie Fires

The conservative tide that would propel Reagan to the nomination that year showed itself long before then, nationally and locally, for those who knew where to look. Its most seminal outbreak came in California, where crippling property taxes sparked a citizens' protest movement— what Reagan liked to describe as a "prairie fire" of aroused citizens. In California, personal income taxes had risen 150 percent between 1973 and 1977, and sales taxes had gone up 188 percent in that same period.[76] Californians had had enough, and they got behind a new initiative, Proposition 13, under which property would be taxed at a flat 1 percent of its actual value, and state and local government would need a two-thirds majority vote to institute new taxes. The measure promised property-tax relief of more than $6 billion.

It was led by Howard Jarvis, a seventy-five-year-old, longtime conservative activist and a self-described "rugged bastard who's had his head kicked in a thousand times by the government."[77] A Goldwater campaign veteran, Jarvis had never drawn much popular support for his causes. In part, that was because he was an antitax zealot: He had campaigned over the years against public financing of libraries, parks, garbage collection, and even schools, and he had staunchly opposed Medicare in the 1960s. But now, instead of attacking taxes on a philosophical basis, as a threat to freedom, he simply argued that Californians were being extorted by the high rates. His 1978 book, *I'm Mad as Hell*—borrowing the famous line from the 1976 film *Network*—gave him his platform. But Jarvis was also a gifted campaigner and talker.

"Now we know how it felt when they dumped English tea in Boston harbor!" he told his ecstatic supporters at one campaign event in Los Angeles. "We have a new revolution. We are telling the government, 'Screw you!'"[78]

"We have seen the trauma of high taxes on older people," Jarvis said in a calmer moment. "The deteriorating state of mind. The disease. The ulcers. When elderly people get those tax bills on their meager homes that demand another $1,500 a year, they get a cloud over their heads. Many of them give up the spirit and quietly die. One woman had a heart attack in front of me back in 1962 right in the assessor's office." Then, getting worked up again, he said: "Even the Russians don't do that, run people out of their homes for no reason. It is a goddamned crime! It is grand-felony theft."[79]

In June 1978, California voters cut off the tax hikers' heads, figuratively at least, approving Proposition 13 by a nearly two-to-one margin. In November, fifteen other states put antitax resolutions on their ballots. Eighty percent of the measures passed.

More significant for the party, in the midterm elections, a conservative tide powered a fifteen-seat gain for Republicans in the House and a pickup of three seats in the Senate. Equally telling was the character of the gains. Conservative Republicans moved into the Senate in greater numbers, while moderate Republicans, like Edward Brooke of Massachusetts, were turned out. In addition, conservatives like Jesse

Helms made it known that they would pursue leadership positions, and moderates like minority leader Howard Baker were required to win the support of the expanded conservative bloc to keep his job. "It's a new ball game," said one moderate. "It doesn't take much to change things around."[80]

Charles Percy, a moderate Republican from Illinois, inadvertently symbolized what was driving the voter when, facing a tough reelection fight, he made a campaign commercial that somewhat desperately appealed for conservative support. As *Time* described it:

> There, in a 30-second television commercial, was the usually dapper and composed Senator Charles Percy of Illinois looking haggard and close to tears. Staring straight into the camera, the onetime presidential aspirant implored millions of unseen viewers: "I got your message and you're right. Washington has gone overboard, and I'm sure that I've made my share of mistakes, but your priorities are mine too. Stop the waste. Cut the spending. Cut the tax."[81]

Somehow, Percy survived. But moderate Republicans were on the run. As *Time* summarized the election's message: "The American people had soured on costly government and demanded relief—now. That was, as much as any, the message of last week's off-year elections." Ronald Reagan's moment had arrived.

The Reagan Revolution

By 1980, the American people had had enough: enough of double-digit inflation under Jimmy Carter, enough of high unemployment, and especially enough of the sense that they had gotten from Carter's White House that the nation was not in the hands of a capable and determined leader. Nothing fed that perception more powerfully than the 444-day-long ordeal of the American hostages in Tehran, whom Carter could not get released. A daring special-operations rescue mission (the first for the new Delta Force) in April 1980 ended in disaster, with helicopter malfunctions causing the effort to be aborted. Even worse, the whole endeavor ended in tragedy when one of the helicopters crashed into a transport aircraft in a desert sandstorm, killing eight American servicemen. Never in the postwar era had an American president seemed so impotent.

"I will not stand by and watch this great country destroy itself under mediocre leadership that drifts from one crisis to the next, eroding our national will and purpose,"[82] Ronald Reagan said—words that resonated, as earlier words of resolution from Richard Nixon had, with America's silent majority.

Reagan's crushing victory over Carter in November 1980—he won forty-four states and 489 electoral votes—was not just a rejection of Democratic leadership or a vindication of the Republican Party, post-Watergate. It also represented an historic transformation of the Republican Party, as Reagan, long the right wing's conservative standard bearer, became the most conservative figure elected president in the twentieth century. The conservative tide reached far beyond Reagan, too: the GOP took control of the Senate for the first time in a quarter century and gained thirty-four seats in the House of Representatives—beginning the process that would result, fourteen years later, in the Republican capture of the chamber. The landslide put out of office some famous Democratic names, including Birch Bayh in Indiana, Frank Church in Idaho—and George McGovern, who won just 39 percent of the vote in South Dakota in his bid for another Senate term.

"The disaster," wrote *Time*, "left the Democratic Party, which has held the presidency for 32 of the 48 years since 1932, badly in need of a new vision and a new agenda."[83] Indeed, Democrats not only struggled to define effective policies for a new era, they also faced the most formidable political leader the nation had seen since Franklin Roosevelt. This time, the man the nation loved was a Republican.

A defining aspect of Reagan's appeal was his profoundly effective communication skills. Americans had first seen his skills in 1964, when he gave the televised address on behalf of Barry Goldwater. They saw them again in 1976, at the Republican Convention in Kansas City, when Reagan just missed taking the party's nomination away from the sitting president, Gerald Ford. They saw them in the 1980 debate with President Carter, when Reagan framed the entire election with one question: "Are you better off than you were four years ago?" And they heard them over and over again in his campaign speeches, as he articulated a clear, consistent, and principled political vision: about excessive government, about the evils of Communism, about the gifts of individual freedom liberty, and about the blessings of America itself—"the shining city on a hill," as he liked to call it. The "great communicator," as Reagan came to be called, spoke to Americans with an intimacy and sense of personal connection that no president since has ever quite matched.

Reagan's gifts were different than Nixon's. And what made them even more potent was that Reagan, by and large, delivered on his political promises. He cut taxes as he had proposed—in what, in fact, were the largest tax cuts in American history—which helped spark an unprecedented economic boom. In 1981, he slashed the top rate from 70 percent to 50 percent; in 1986, he cut rates further, getting the top rate down to a remarkable 28 percent. The top marginal rate has gone up since then, but it has never come anywhere near 70 percent (or even 50 percent, for that matter). Reagan's 1986 reforms also broadened the tax base, generating more tax revenue without raising rates.

Reagan's much-derided "supply-side" economic policies—cuts to marginal tax rates, along with deregulation and spending cuts in discretionary programs (except for the Pentagon budget)—revitalized America's private-sector economy. For a quarter century, from 1983 to 2008, the US economy enjoyed unprecedented growth, interrupted only by a few brief recessions. Sixteen million new jobs were created during Reagan's two terms in the White House. The foundation was laid in the private investment markets for the technology boom that would take shape the 1990s. And Reagan vanquished the inflation that bedeviled the nation in the 1970s, eroding Americans' savings and threatening their faith in the future. In his first term in office, inflation plunged from an average of 13 percent in 1980 to 4 percent. It stayed low throughout his second term as well.

Reagan also rebuilt American military strength—to be sure, spending a staggering sum to do it. Many worried about his confrontational Cold War rhetoric, but the president's commitment to military strength and tough stance on Communist expansionism put the Soviet Union on notice. In Reagan's second term, he enjoyed better relations with Moscow, and he and Mikhail Gorbachev signed the historic INF control accords. Always underestimated, and thought of as a mere ideologue, he showed that he could be a savvy statesman—and that he could channel Nixonian pragmatism when he needed to.

Finally, Reagan reinvigorated a sense of pride and optimism among Americans that had been missing, I would say, since 1972—when Nixon united the country by winning forty-nine states. Nixon's victory in 1972 is not commonly regarded as a moment of optimism in America, but it was, and I remember it well. But the eight years between 1972 and 1980 were some of the most demoralizing of the postwar years—seeing everything from Watergate, to oil shocks, to the disastrous Carter presidency. When Reagan won in 1980, and especially when he won his even more smashing reelection in 1984, the nation was reaffirming broad goals and values and its belief in a leader who was committed to them. Reagan's victories ushered in an era of American renewal. He represented then, and he still does today, ideas that Americans revere: individuality, creativity, optimism, and the freedom to forge one's destiny.

No wonder, then, that Reagan duplicated Nixon's electoral feat, when, running for reelection in 1984, he won forty-nine states, just as Nixon had, and even outdid Nixon on electoral votes, winning 525 of them (however, Nixon's popular-vote percentage of 61 percent still topped Reagan's 59 percent). It is unlikely that such an historic rout will ever be equaled. Reagan won so overwhelmingly because, four years later, so many Americans could answer the question he posed in the 1980 debate with a simple affirmation: Yes, we are better off.

It's worth noting, too, that when Reagan left office in January 1989, Americans *still* felt that way. When he left Washington, he flew to his new home in Bel Air, California, with an approval rating of 64 percent. In the quarter century since he left office, his influence continues to loom large—not just for Republicans but for Democrats, too. In my work in the White House for President Bill Clinton, I saw the Reagan influence: when Clinton famously announced that the "era of big government is over," he was consciously echoing Reagan and even tacitly endorsing the changes he had wrought. Politicians from both parties try to claim the Reagan mantle whenever they can. As a candidate in 2008, Barack Obama linked himself with the "transformational" presidency of Reagan rather than with the incremental approach of his fellow Democrat, Bill Clinton.

Today, Reagan remains a conservative icon. And yet, many conservatives forget or overlook that Reagan, while certainly more conservative than Richard Nixon, was not the absolutist of his popular image. No less than Nixon, he approached issues from a pragmatic perspective. He did, after all, raise taxes twelve times while in office; he worked with Tip O'Neill and moderate Republicans to save Social Security; and while his foreign policy is remembered as tough and uncompromising, it was much more subtle than his language often suggested. Reagan fulfilled the Nixon vision of arms control that began a decade and a half earlier with the first SALT agreements. And it's worth remembering that when Reagan began making agreements with Gorbachev, his conservative backers threatened to revolt—just as they had in the early 1970s when Nixon made overtures to the Communist world. Reagan had built up a deep well of trust with conservatives, and he was able to weather their disapproval. Still, it's a reminder that Reagan and Nixon had more in common than it may first appear. (Indeed, in chapter 10, I'll examine Nixon's impact on Reagan's approach in his second term.)

The most dramatic link between Nixon and Reagan can be found in their mirror-image reelection victories of 1972 and 1984. Both victories were not only resounding endorsements of their leadership but also reflections of the rise of a new governing coalition in American politics. Nixon organized this coalition; Reagan revived it.

"Nixon Conservatives"

Reagan's 1980 election marked a watershed for the American conservative movement—the first time it had gotten one of its own into the White House. Only sixteen years before, after the Goldwater debacle, few would have dared predict that conservatives would wield this kind of political power. After 1964, many analysts had written off the Republican Party, especially its conservative faction.

Republicans recovered, in crucial degree thanks to Richard Nixon. His congressional campaigning in 1966 forged alliances with dozens of Republican candidates and helped the party roll to impressive midterm wins over a suddenly limping Democratic Party. Then, as I discussed in chapter 3, he threaded the needle in 1968—capturing the presidency by uniting middle-class and working-class northern whites with Southern whites and by bringing together moderate and conservative Republicans around powerful themes like law and order, national security, and

Middle American values. He wouldn't have been able to do it without conservative support, and his campaign drew heavily on conservative themes. This coalition would come to full strength in 1972 and prove to be nearly as enduring as FDR's—and certainly more conservative. Thus, many on the right felt justified in seeing Nixon's victory as, in part, their victory. While they didn't see him as a true believer, they felt that he owed them something.

As president, Nixon *did* in fact do much for the Right—but not in the way that conservatives would have expected. Moving leftward domestically, economically, and internationally, he first frustrated, then alienated, and finally galvanized American conservatives to action. Much of the political organizing and grassroots activism that forged today's Right got started during the Nixon years and the Ford and Carter years that followed. It was in the 1970s that the American Right found its footing as a political movement determined to take control of the Republican Party and win the White House.

Nixon himself probably wouldn't want to take credit for this. But the evidence suggests that right wing energy in the 1970s drew heavily on opposition to Nixon and the sense that he had betrayed his conservative supporters. He had Nixonized the Republican Party for a second time, albeit this time inadvertently.

There was nothing inadvertent, though, about Nixon's impact on the opposition party. As we saw in chapter 4, Nixon consciously set out to take most of the domestic center, and even some of the Left, away from the Democratic Party. In foreign policy and national security, he acted less from such political calculation than from his own well-developed statesman's instincts. He acted, in other words, based on how he saw the world. But the impact of his policies, as I'll show in the next chapter, was similar: he left Democrats marginalized on national-security matters, with little to hold onto but a resolute antiwar pacifism that few Americans supported.

Nixonizing the Democrats

Part Two: Vietnam, McGovern, and the End of National-Security Liberalism

We believe that war is a waste of human life.... We will end that war by a simple plan that need not be kept secret: The immediate total withdrawal of all Americans from Southeast Asia.

—DEMOCRATIC PARTY PLATFORM OF 1972[1]

Let us be united for peace. Let us also be united against defeat. Because let us understand: North Vietnam cannot defeat or humiliate the United States. Only Americans can do that.

—RICHARD NIXON[2]

Inasmuch as a neoconservative is a liberal who votes for the defense budget, it is possible to clarify the whole matter for your readers by describing such persons as patriots.

—DANIEL PATRICK MOYNIHAN[3]

Liberal idealism need not be identical with masochism, and need not be incompatible with the defense of freedom and the national interest.

—JEANE KIRKPATRICK[4]

It is true, of course, that the Democratic Party's shift leftward on foreign policy—a shift from which the party has never really recovered—has its roots in the Vietnam War, and not, in a directly causal sense, to Richard Nixon. Yet Nixon lies at the heart of the Democrats' generational collapse on national-security matters, in which they slowly abandoned a proud tradition of robust foreign policy and lost the faith of millions of Americans that they could keep the country safe. No single cause for this development was as dramatic and as damaging as the war. Yet perhaps no other cause was as instrumental and as enduring as Nixon's magisterial foreign policy, which heightened and exacerbated the Democrats' foreign policy divisions.

Such were Democratic divisions on the Vietnam War by 1968, when Nixon won the presidency, that when he took office, he became the symbol of the war for the growing antiwar caucus within the party. In time, Nixon came to stand as antiwar Democrats' bête noire, the summation of everything they opposed in foreign policy. Yet, since Nixon's own foreign policy was, similar to his domestic policy, a mostly nonideological mixture of pragmatism and strategic vision, this meant that the Democrats were reacting not against a right wing national-security policy so much as a centrist one—and to move left of it was to move far left indeed. Unpopular as the Vietnam War became, most Americans were similarly repelled by a Nixon-hating, increasingly anti-American Democratic Party that moved further and further left on national security—and made itself unviable at the national level.

To be sure, this did not describe all Democrats, and the party's lurch leftward, especially on national security, precipitated a battle for the soul of the party between the liberal antiwar Democrats and a more hawkish faction that found itself increasingly outnumbered, and eventually isolated, within the party. Many would cross over to support Nixon in 1972 against George McGovern. Most stuck with the party through the 1970s, hoping that the McGovern debacle would not prove enduring, and looking to Jimmy Carter to restore Democratic foreign policy principles. But when Carter foundered too, Democratic hawks deserted him for Ronald Reagan in 1980, desperate to support a candidate who believed in American leadership in international affairs.

The Democratic hawks were trying to recapture a foreign policy vision under which the party had once owned national security. Democrats led American efforts in World War II and the early years of the Cold War. There were setbacks in these years, too, as with the "Who lost China?" debate, in which Republicans blamed Democratic administrations for the victory of the Red Chinese under Mao. And the early 1950s, of course, was the era of McCarthyism, when the Wisconsin senator accused many liberals of harboring Communist sympathies. When Republicans nominated Dwight Eisenhower for president in 1952, the greatest soldier of the age gave the GOP an edge on national security that it had never before possessed. Yet even during the Eisenhower years, when Democrats were out of the White House for the first time in two decades, most leading politicians in the party stood behind a Cold War consensus that emphasized national security.

Democrats—especially those with national ambitions—generally espoused what has been variously called "liberal internationalism" and "national-security liberalism." This philosophy sought to expand American influence in the world, which it saw as morally and politically desirable, believing in American exceptionalism, and embracing the role the United States had inherited after World War II as the defender of the free world. National-security liberalism underpinned the foreign policy of Harry Truman, John F. Kennedy, and Lyndon Johnson—and later, of Bill Clinton. "We are the indispensable nation," Clinton's secretary of state, Madeline Albright, said in 1998. "We stand tall and we see further than other countries into the future."[5]

But between LBJ and Clinton lay a wilderness of Democratic foreign policy history, in which leading Democrats deserted their allegiance to national-security liberalism and became almost-unrestrained doves— costing them dearly in national elections. Whereas national-security liberals had seen America as the key player in maintaining international stability, and American democracy as the hope for millions enslaved by Communism or other authoritarian systems, the new liberals saw America as one of the world's chief villains, culpable for a chronicle of atrocities against the Third World and equally responsible—perhaps even more responsible—for the tense nuclear standoff with the Soviet Union.

It wasn't just the fact that the Democrats disastrously lost an election in 1972 because they suicidally embraced an extreme dovishness that was rejected by voters. That was just the start. The Vietnam War was the fulcrum that sent cadres of Democratic hawks streaming out of the Party of Roosevelt. And Nixon's foreign policy philosophy, positioning, and substantive successes hollowed out the Democratic Party rhetorically, ideologically, and institutionally—setting the stage for a generational rout, especially after conservatives took over the GOP. Once Ronald Reagan added an expanding economy and fresh optimism, the Republican Party became hard to beat.

Moving Left: The Democrats' National-Security Journey

The Vietnam War was not much on Americans' radar screens until 1965, when Lyndon Johnson drastically escalated the American troop presence in Vietnam in the wake of the Tonkin Gulf incident of the previous year. By the end of 1965, there were more than 180,000 troops in Vietnam, and that number would double by the end of 1966.[6] Yet opposition to the war was initially muted and mostly confined to the student-activist Left, not then a major presence in national politics. But as the war dragged on and the American troop commitment grew, a sense of futility about the war's purpose and outrage over its conduct and costs—human and otherwise—slowly began to mount.

In January 1968, the Tet Offensive, a failed North Vietnamese and Vietcong attack on the South Vietnamese, catalyzed American war fatigue. Even so, public sentiment against the war, while growing, was still a distinct minority: in the early years of the conflict, doves made up just 28 percent of the public, but by April 1968, their numbers had swelled to 42 percent, edging out the hawks, who stood at 41 percent. Johnson's approval rating on the war had plunged to 28 percent.[7]

Antiwar Democrats in Congress began speaking out. Democratic senator William Fulbright convened the first of what would be years of hearings on Vietnam in 1966. Fulbright was perhaps the emblematic figure for the journey the party was about to take. Not only had he voted for the 1964 Tonkin Resolution that gave LBJ the authority to expand the war in Vietnam, he had *sponsored* it—and now here he was, just two years later, spearheading inquiries that would open up the war to scrutiny across the country. And Johnson soon faced a progressive insurgency, as Wisconsin senator Eugene McCarthy announced that he would seek the party's nomination in 1968.

Though few gave him a chance, McCarthy stunned the nation—and Johnson—by getting 42 percent of the vote in the New Hampshire primary, to Johnson's 49 percent. A few days later, Bobby Kennedy, who had hesitated to enter the race, announced that he, too, would run as an antiwar candidate.

By the time McCarthy's challenge to Johnson emerged in early 1968, it was already clear that the Democrats were facing deepening divisions. The party's base was fracturing and becoming two separate, increasingly irreconcilable bases. On one side were the increasingly troubled remnants of the FDR coalition: labor unions, working- and middle-class families, and minorities. On the other was the smaller but growing coalition of the young, political radicals, intellectuals, and minorities, whose outlook became known as the "New Politics." The split would separate the traditional Democratic liberal Left from what would become the new post-1960s liberals.

Where the old Democratic Left had championed the working man, the New Politics types tended to disdain this figure. The New Left was a movement heavily made up of youth, and its cadres tended to be drawn from the college campuses; it championed minorities and women and stressed personal liberation from bourgeois morality. If anything, it seemed embarrassed by the socially conservative white working class—whose sons (along with the sons of working-class blacks) were doing most of the fighting in Vietnam. One of McCarthy's aides said that the labor movement wasn't worth "the powder it would take to blow it to hell."[8]

The new liberals' views on foreign policy reflected this absolutist attitude. At a board meeting for Americans for Democratic Action, a stalwart progressive group that had helped shape the party's agenda for a generation, arguments broke out about whether to withhold support for Johnson, who was "the greatest presidential champion of liberalism since Franklin Delano Roosevelt," in Rick Perlstein's words. The war overwhelmed all other considerations in the debate. "People who agreed on about 98 percent of everything else were throwing schoolyard taunts at one another," Perlstein wrote.[9]

The younger members of the ADA advocated an immediate "negotiated settlement" to the war, rejecting the mainstream liberal position seeking a coalition government in Vietnam. The ADA's older membership retained its identification with the muscular foreign policy of Harry Truman. Yet 40 of the ADA's 143 board members voted for a resolution pledging to support a candidate from *either* party who "offered hope for restraint in the conduct of the war in Vietnam."[10] Some union and civil rights leaders urged the ADA to overturn the resolution, but the younger cadres ignored them.[11]

Finally, on March 31, 1968, Johnson made the shocking announcement that he would not seek reelection. His vice president, Hubert Humphrey, now stepped into the breach as the candidate of the Democratic mainstream—and of national-security liberalism—but with both McCarthy and Kennedy in the race, the contest became wide open. Kennedy might have gone on to unite the Democrats, or at least to hold together, however delicately, the party's hawk and dove factions. He was that kind of candidate, possibly a man of political destiny, if his destiny hadn't turned out to be martyrdom. On June 5, 1968, he was assassinated in Los Angeles, after winning the California primary. Now the progressives had only McCarthy to fall back on, but the enigmatic Wisconsin senator seemed to lose interest in seeking the presidency after Kennedy's death. The antiwar Left also refused to support Humphrey, who called for maintaining the Johnson war policy.

"Dump the Hump!" they chanted, as the Democratic National Convention in Chicago approached. Humphrey's power base lay with the traditional constituencies—the labor unions and the white working class and the established Democratic Party institutions. He got the nomination, of course—but not before presiding over the most traumatic political convention in American history, where protesters fought outside with Chicago police, who unleashed tear gas strong enough to seep into the convention floor. Viewers at home watched in astonishment as the city of Chicago seemed to be up for grabs—both in the streets and in the convention hall, where the Democrats' internal divisions over Vietnam were ripping the party apart.

So determined were the New Politics types that they genuinely believed that it would be better for Humphrey to lose. But wouldn't Humphrey's defeat deliver the presidency to Richard Nixon, a man reviled by everyone from mainstream liberals to the movement activists of the antiwar Left? Yes, but this was all to the good, at least as those on the far left saw it—all the better to bring about the remaking of the Democratic Party and the transformation of American politics. Were Nixon to become the president, the American people, they reasoned, would blame Nixon for the collapse of what they called the "system."

These extravagant ideas sound ridiculous today, but in 1968, many on the left put stock in them. Ronald Radosh suggested that the New Left types felt that by withdrawing support for Humphrey and ensuring the election of Nixon, "they had taught the Democrats a lesson... and they were heartened that their efforts alone had caused defeat for their own party. Surely in the annals of American party history there has never been such a naïve view of defeat.... [I]t was another step on the slide to the left that would continue to burden the Democratic Party for two decades."[12]

Some major players in the Democratic Party today remember the millenarian energies of those days. As Lanny Davis recalled:

> President Johnson's outstanding liberal record creating the anti-poverty program, the Great Society social programs, and the Civil Rights Acts of 1964 and 1965 were completely ignored.... The only thing that mattered was the Vietnam War. Even in the general election, when the great Democratic liberal, then Vice President Hubert H. Humphrey, was the nominee against the hated Richard Nixon, the purist anti-war left spoke openly that it would be better to elect Nixon and "purge" the Democratic Party of the impure pro-Vietnam War moderates and lose in 1968 rather than compromise and support Humphrey, who was overly apologetic about Johnson's tragic Vietnam War policies.[13]

Nixon, McGovern, and the Democratic Crack-Up

Richard Nixon had seen the Democratic split coming for some time. In 1966, campaigning for the midterms, he had suggested that the party was breaking down across prowar and antiwar lines and that it would be vulnerable in 1968. On his way to a narrow victory in 1968, he fully exploited that vulnerability.

In his campaign advertising, Nixon tied Humphrey closely to the Johnson war policies. His most famous spot, called *Convention*, by documentarian Eugene Jones, cut back and forth between stills of Humphrey and chaotic, disturbing images of the war, as well as riot and disorder in the United States, including the incidents at the party convention in Chicago. The ads evoked feelings of uncertainty and associated Humphrey with the war. In a voice-over, Nixon excoriated the Johnson administration for pouring resources into Vietnam, with nothing to show for it.

"Never has so much military, diplomatic, and economic power been used so ineffectively as in Vietnam," Nixon said. "If, after all of this time and all of this sacrifice and all of this support there is still no end in sight, then I say the time has come for the American people to turn to new leadership, not tied to the policies and mistakes of the past." Taking an apocalyptic tone, the Nixon ads ended each spot with the quote: "This time, vote like your whole world depended on it."[14] The ads drove home themes that have reverberated in our national politics ever since: suggesting that the Democrats could not be trusted with leadership, especially when it came to national security, and that Republicans were the party of order, strength, and responsibility.

Once in office, as I described in chapter 2, Nixon remained determined to lead the United States to victory in Vietnam. But he also pioneered the Vietnamization of the conflict—the shifting of the manpower burden from the Americans to the Vietnamese. He made clear how his approach differed from that of his predecessor, Lyndon Johnson—and by extension, from that of the Democratic Party. In his speech on December 3, 1969, one of the best of his presidency, Nixon said: "Many believe that President Johnson's decision to send American combat forces to South Vietnam was wrong. And many others—I among them—have been strongly critical of the way the war has been conducted.... The defense of freedom is everybody's business—not just America's business. And it is particularly the responsibility of the people whose freedom is threatened."[15]

It was a centrist speech, one that emphasized the nation's responsibilities in the war while also acknowledging the divisions that the war had caused and the need for a change of policy. As such, it positioned Nixon as the Vietnam moderate within a roiling debate that pitted those who felt that America should take an even-firmer military hand in Vietnam against those who wanted an immediate withdrawal from the war—many of them now prominent Democrats, who along with some liberal Northeastern Republicans, began pushing legislation to end the war.

Indeed, a succession of legislation seeking to end the war came about following the speech. Liberal Republican congressman Charles Goodell of New York proposed a bill establishing a December 1970 deadline for withdrawing American troops from Vietnam. Congress repealed the Gulf of Tonkin Resolution, which had established Johnson's authority for expanding the war in 1971, and the Cooper-Church Amendment cut off funding for American air or troop support for Cambodia. And the proposed McGovern-Hatfield Amendment, colloquially known as the "amendment to end the war," would have ended funding of US military operations in Vietnam by the end of 1971 and mandated a complete withdrawal of American troops by middle of the year.[16]

"Every Senator in this chamber is partly responsible for sending 50,000 young Americans to an early grave," said George McGovern, the bill's cosponsor. His tone was far harsher than most speeches delivered in the Senate, which highly valued decorum.

"This chamber reeks of blood," McGovern continued, and then elaborated:

> Every senator here is partly responsible for that human wreckage at Walter Reed and Bethesda naval and all across our land—young men without legs, or arms, or genitals, or faces or hopes. There are not very many of these blasted and broken boys who think this war is a glorious adventure. Do not talk to them about bugging out, or national honor our courage. It does not take any courage at all for a congressman, or a senator, or a president to wrap himself in the flag and say we are staying in Vietnam, because it is not our blood that is being shed. But we are responsible for those young men and their lives and their hopes. And if we do not end this damnable war those young men will someday curse us for our pitiful willingness to let the Executive carry the burden that the Constitution places on us.[17]

McGovern's speech left his Senate colleagues stunned. He stepped down from the lectern and went back to his seat in a silent chamber. "You could have heard a pin drop," said John Holum, a staff advisor for the candidate. One senator, angered by the speech, approached McGovern and told him that he was personally offended. "That's what I meant to do," McGovern replied.[18] Nonetheless, his amendment failed.

George McGovern was an admirable man, but his excoriation of his Senate colleagues and the defeat of his amendment symbolized his broader failures: First, he was self-righteous to a degree that made practical politics enormously difficult; second, inspiring as he might be to the like-minded, he never had much success convincing others of his beliefs. Yet both of those qualities would not prove to be sources of resistance to the New Politics caucus that powered him to the nomination of the Democratic Party in 1972. For them, at long last, here was a candidate who was morally pure—and his moral purity began with his anti-Nixonism. McGovern exemplified it when he compared

Nixon's Vietnam bombing campaign to "Hitler's campaign to exterminate Jews."[19]

The chaos that had overrun the 1968 convention led to reforms—spearheaded by the commission McGovern cochaired—that enshrined party primaries as the nominating mechanism and imposed quotas for blacks, women, and the young in each state's convention delegations. These reforms not only steered McGovern to the nomination; they also "disenfranchised" traditional working-class Democrats, in Ron Radosh's words, who "relied on representation at conventions by union leaders and professional politicians."[20] The old party system served their needs and goals; the new one did not. Traditional Democrats began a Stop McGovern movement.

At the same time, Nixon divided the Democrats further with his surprisingly moderate foreign policy in other areas than the war—especially on détente with the Soviet Union and China. In the first half of 1972, while the Democrats were fracturing between their New Politics and Stop McGovern factions, Nixon enjoyed the most successful months of his presidency. During the Democratic primaries, Nixon made his historic trip to Peking while also planning a summit with Leonid Brezhnev in Moscow, at which he would sign the SALT I agreement. Answering a North Vietnamese offensive, Nixon bombed Hanoi and mined Haiphong Harbor—with the broad support of the American public. His war policies had the support of 52 percent of American voters, with only 39 percent disapproving.[21] His popular standing rose further in October 1972—by which time he enjoyed a wide lead in the polls over McGovern—when Secretary of State Henry Kissinger announced, "We believe that peace is at hand" in Vietnam.[22]

Nixon's peaceful overtures to America's Communist adversaries put the New Politics Democrats in a bind: in principle they agreed with such moves, yet to support Nixon was to undercut their own case for change. More hawkish Democrats, led by Senator Henry "Scoop" Jackson of Washington, were troubled by Nixon's moves, especially the SALT agreements, as were Republican conservatives. Jackson, in fact, pushed for amendments to SALT. He objected to the treaty's unequal terms, which, under a five-year "interim" agreement, allowed the Soviets to accumulate substantially more nuclear missiles than the United States. Jackson's amendment said that Congress "urges and requests the president to seek a future treaty that... would not limit the United States to levels of intercontinental strategic forces inferior to the limits provided for the Soviet Union."[23] The amendment passed.

Herein lay the split that would transform the Democratic Party, driving many of its foreign policy hawks into the Republican camp and making others increasingly lonely voices for a robust national-security posture within the party. They found themselves more in agreement with the Republican Right on foreign policy than with the liberals of their own party. And by now, Nixon had the liberals spinning in confusion. Nothing set them more off balance than his trip to China in 1972.

In addition to the strategic and national-security implications of Nixon's trip to China discussed in chapter 2, the visit also had domestic political implications, especially on the Democrats, who had long painted Nixon as an unreconstructed Cold Warrior. In fact, as McGovern told famed China journalist Edgar Snow, he had sought to visit China himself in 1972. When he was there, McGovern told Snow, he planned to announce that, if he became president, he "would be prepared to recognize Peking as the sole legitimate government of China, leaving the future status of Taiwan to a peaceful resolution by the Chinese people."[24] McGovern believed this would dramatically illustrate the differences between him and Nixon. But the Chinese were already negotiating, secretly, with Nixon and Kissinger, and they had little interest in visiting with a far-left Democratic senator.[25]

McGovern and his liberal supporters had assumed that Mao Zedong would never welcome someone like Richard Nixon. Yet Mao told Edgar Snow: "'I don't like the Democratic Party, I prefer the Republican Party. I like Nixon in power. Why? Because though he is deceitful, he is a little bit less so. He resorts more to tough tactics, though also some soft ones."[26]

McGovern now faced a president who had revised his image as a dangerous hawk—a man who had met with the Communists in Moscow and Peking and had drawn down American troops in Vietnam, but had also promised Americans that he would end the war honorably. That combination would have presented a stiff challenge for a centrist Democrat—but for McGovern, it was insurmountable, especially after Nixon's approval ratings shot up into the low sixties.

I described the McGovern march to the nomination in chapter 3. What's important to note here is how the McGovern campaign reflected the kind of insular self-righteousness that today's liberals have too often embodied on national-security policy—a quality that has contributed to the Democrats' reputation as unreliable on national defense. Traced back, this tendency is difficult to disentangle from the party's broader reaction to Nixon himself—a figure Democrats had already hated for a generation, who now sat in the White House conducting a war they saw as evil.

In fact, the entire McGovern campaign—with its isolationist slogan "Come Home, America!"—was an explicit rejection of the Nixon approach to Vietnam, both substantively and stylistically. Polls showed consistently that Americans felt that the president's approach— Vietnamizing the war and slowly reducing the American footprint while helping our ally continue the fight—represented the best course. But McGovern wanted an immediate, unconditional, and complete withdrawal of American troops. The majority of Americans understood that peace could not be attained in Vietnam without a strong American presence, but McGovern openly declared that he would "crawl on his hands and knees" to Hanoi and beg for peace.[27]

Looking at these factors in hindsight, it's easy to conclude that the Democrats never had much of a chance in 1972, but this judgment overlooks the influence of Nixon's strategic vision on the defeat of the Democrats. Thematically clear, psychologically powerful, and politically shrewd, the president's dominant message was that McGovern, the antiwar Left, and by extension, the Democratic Party were reckless and irresponsible in their pursuit of "peace at any price." Meanwhile, he and the Republicans spoke in a robust language about national security, patriotism, and American values. Those themes were evident in the 1972 Republican platform, which differed from its Democratic counterpart the way oil does from water. The Republicans defended the Vietnam War as an honorable cause and touted the leadership they had brought to American foreign policy.

"When our accomplishments are weighed—when our opponents' philosophy, programs and candidates are assessed—we believe the American people will rally eagerly to the leadership which since January 1969 has brought them a better life in a better land in a safer world," the

Republican Party Platform stated in 1972.[28] Republicans also reminded Americans about the domestic disorder that had preceded Nixon's presidency and the successes that the administration had had in restoring domestic tranquility. Nixon employed themes and symbols, which Republicans have used ever since, to portray Democrats as recklessly dovish: suggesting that the antiwar movement had devolved into a dangerous, anti-American effort that threatened the nation's security; that while Democrats had gotten us into the mess overseas—Vietnam was Kennedy and Johnson's war, after all—Republicans were cleaning it up; and that the silent majority of Americans would not be fooled by the loud and self-dramatizing behavior of the radical Left.

"Let us be united for peace," Nixon himself had said in his 1969 "Silent Majority" speech, but he continued to say, "Let us also be united against defeat. Because let us understand: North Vietnam cannot defeat or humiliate the United States. Only Americans can do that."[29]

Nixon harnessed his attack dog, Vice President Agnew, once again to deliver some of his toughest campaign lines. Agnew lambasted McGovern's self-identification as the "peace" candidate. McGovern's pacifist positions would endanger peace, according to Agnew, embolden the North Vietnamese, and spell defeat for American efforts. He reminded his audiences that Nixon was the man responsible for bringing home half-a-million American troops since 1969, for reducing casualties, and for bringing an end to the US combat role—all while forging peace with the Red Chinese and the Russians. How would George McGovern improve on that record?

Agnew's lines were crisp and devastating. "No reasonable, informed person can believe that our nation's defense expenditures can be slashed 30 per cent without inviting aggression and chaos in the world, dissolving our partnerships with other nations, and imperiling our security," he told one audience. McGovern's proposals, Agnew said, were so naïve as to be "nothing short of frightening." The way to confront the Soviet Union, he said, was through strength, not "drastic, unilateral disarmament." He added: "The Soviet Union is not moved by mere smiles or frowns from any president of the United States." He painted McGovern as almost a child. Reminding voters that the candidate had willingly said that he would "beg" the North Vietnamese for peace, Agnew snarled: "A strong nation need never beg at the bargaining table."[30]

These images of Nixon, the Republican candidate, as the strong, tragic realist in a harsh world and of McGovern, the Democrat, as the naïve and peace-focused candidate had lasting effects on the public opinion of the parties' attitudes toward national security.

Nixon's words in 1969, in his appeal to the silent majority, should be recalled: "If a vocal minority, however fervent its cause, prevails over reason and the will of the majority, this Nation has no future as a free society."[31] Many members of the "vocal minority" were students or youth organizers who had engaged in violent protests such as the 1969 "Days of Rage" in Chicago. By courting the silent majority, Nixon effectively segmented this population and portrayed the Democratic Party in the public mind as the party of antiwar demonstrators, flag burners, and student radicals.[32]

Capping it all off was the Nixon advertising campaign, the shrewdest and most effective in presidential history up to that point. An ad entitled *McGovern Defense* showed toy soldiers and ships representing the respective branches of the US military: the Marines, the Navy, the Air Force, and the Army. A voice-over described McGovern's plans to cut each branch by at least one-fourth, sometimes more. A hand then appeared and swept away the quantity of troops or aircraft or ships that McGovern would do away with. The voice-over proceeded to cite a major critic of the cutbacks, Hubert Humphrey, saying: "It isn't just cutting into the fat. It isn't just cutting into manpower. It is cutting into the very security of this country." Next the ad showed Nixon standing on a real battleship, and the voice-over intoned that he didn't think we "should play games with our national security."[33]

The ads were doubly powerful since they were produced by Democrats for Nixon, a committee set up by former Texas governor John Connally. The governor had long been a Nixon supporter and represented the substantial segment of the Democratic Party who found it impossible to support McGovern in 1972. Connally told the *New York Times* that because of his plans to drastically cut the Pentagon budget and reduce the number of US troops stationed abroad, Democrats were "afraid of George McGovern."[34] "He's made some statements that frankly are quite frightening," Connally said. These included the McGovern pledge that if elected, he would have all Vietnam POWs home in ninety days. The governor thought that such statements undermined "efforts of this Administration and of the peace negotiators in Paris to try to bring the war to an end on a negotiated basis." He also railed at McGovern's plan to give amnesty to evaders of the draft. "This is a glorification of men who refuse to serve their nation," Connally said.[35]

Summing it up, Connally said bluntly: "It is in the best interests of this country that the President be reelected this year."[36]

What made Democrats for Nixon significant was its broad-based support, not just from some prominent Democrats—including Johnson administration cabinet members and two of Franklin Roosevelt's sons—but also, crucially, from elements of the Democratic rank and file. "Day by day," the New York Times reported, "[Democrats'] phone calls, telegrams, letters and checks pour into the committee's headquarters a few blocks from the White House. Their correspondence shows that many are disaffected, disgruntled, disillusioned Democrats who find only doom and despair in Senator George McGovern, their party's nominee, and have turned instead to the President and his re-election campaign."[37]

The prevailing reason for supporting Nixon for these Democrats came down to national security. The president's frequent pledges to protect American military supremacy resonated with them. Even as his lead swelled and the prospect of a landslide became loomed, Nixon told his team to "step up attacks" on McGovern.[38]

McGovern's historic defeat by Nixon—he won just one state, liberal Massachusetts, and he was beaten by nearly twenty points and eighteen million popular votes—was the inevitable fate for a candidate and a party that had gotten far to the left of the American electorate. In his survey of the campaign, The Making of the President 1972, Theodore White wrote that McGovern had lost because he had simply "frightened too many Americans" with his radicalism. As for Nixon, White wrote, the president had "convinced the Americans, by more than 3 to 2, that he could use power better than George McGovern."[39] White concluded that "the beautiful Liberal Idea of the previous half-century had grown old and hardened into a Liberal Theology which terrified millions of its old clients."[40]

Many of those old clients now began streaming out of the party of Roosevelt to the Republicans. Those who didn't make the switch labored on within the Democratic Party, increasingly outnumbered but trying to revive the traditions and concerns of national-security liberalism. Theirs would be a lonely battle.

Democratic Dissenters

Democrats for Nixon was a short-term organization, built around a specific purpose: the 1972 campaign. The Coalition for a Democratic Majority, however, took the long view. Created by Scoop Jackson and LBJ speechwriter Ben Wattenberg in the ashes of McGovern's defeat, the CDM was an attempt to revive a centrist, even conservative, Democratic Party. Pushing back against the increasingly left-wing tilt of groups like the ADA, it sought to reconnect with the party's traditional base voters, especially in the working class. And on foreign policy, the CDM, which took a dim view of détente, wanted a return to the muscular defense policies of Truman, Kennedy, and Johnson. Hubert Humphrey was also in that tradition, and he was the most high-profile member of the group, which also included civil rights activists like Bayard Rustin and A. Philip Randolph and noted liberal intellectuals Seymour Martin Lipset and Daniel Bell. The CDM's motto was a repudiation of the McGovern campaign: "Come Home, Democrats!"

Henry "Scoop" Jackson, senator from Washington, was probably the emblematic member of the disgruntled Democrats. Unlike some other members, especially in the South, he would never leave the party, but he found himself ever more at odds with its pacifistic and neoisolationist foreign policy. And his disagreements weren't just with Democrats; he also objected to the Nixon administration's détente drift, which he felt was unwarranted, based on the Soviet behavior, and would prove disastrous.

Jackson would prove to be a consistent critic of the Nixon administration's foreign policy. He supported Nixon on Vietnam but otherwise opposed what he saw as a dangerous abandonment of America's Cold War posture, especially concerning Moscow, and, after 1972, in regard to Beijing as well. He found the Nixon policy amoral in that it made America complicit in Soviet human rights violations, and he rallied traditional liberals to their identification with an American mission in the world.

Jackson also pushed to make the treatment of Soviet Jews, who were not allowed to emigrate, central to any trade agreements between

Washington and Moscow.[41] The result was the 1974 landmark Jackson-Vanik Amendment, which linked the Soviet most-favored-nation trade status with concessions on Jewish emigration. After Nixon's departure, Gerald Ford tried to stop the amendment, but it became law, and Scoop Jackson became a hero to Jews in the Soviet Union, the United States, and around the world.

That wasn't the last time Jackson would embarrass the Ford administration. In 1975, one of his strongest political allies, AFL-CIO leader George Meany, invited Soviet dissident Alexander Solzhenitsyn to tour the United States. Meany organized a banquet in Solzhenitsyn's honor and invited President Ford—but the president and Kissinger worried that the leader's appearance would anger Moscow and jeopardize what was left of détente. After an agonized internal debate, the White House cancelled Ford's appearance, claiming his schedule was too busy. The cop-out led to a firestorm of criticism from conservatives, and from Democratic hawks like Jackson.[42]

The senator carried the liberal-internationalist banner into two presidential campaigns, in 1972 and 1976. Trying to halt McGovern's drive to the nomination, Jackson, his campaign manager said, wanted to be "seen as the man crying out against the left/berserk flank of the party."[43] In 1976, he seemed to have a better chance at the nomination, but he was outflanked by Jimmy Carter, who skillfully occupied Jackson's centrist positions and adopted his human rights appeals. Carter was a better campaigner and a more charismatic figure than Jackson, and his identity as an outsider helped him appeal to the New Politics faction, which detested the senator and saw him as a conservative.[44]

In time, a good number of "Scoop Jackson Democrats," feeling unwelcome in the Democratic Party, switched over to the Republican side. Perhaps Jackson would have done so himself had he not died of a heart condition suddenly in 1983. But his shadow loomed heavily over his party on foreign policy and national defense issues, representing the road not taken—or more aptly, the road abandoned. Despite the stalwart advocacy of Jackson heirs like Senator Joseph Lieberman of Connecticut, the defense establishment would become more Republican oriented and less trusting of Democrats.

Another significant figure in the fissuring of the Democrats, post-Nixon, was none other than Daniel Patrick Moynihan, who had, of course, worked for Nixon in the White House. As Moynihan saw it, the party was doubling down on the tendencies that troubled him most, including anti-Americanism and self-indulgence. Like Jackson, and others who would follow, he sought to preserve the Democratic Party for those who saw the United States as a positive force in the world.

In a 1975 essay in *Commentary* magazine, "The United States in Opposition," Moynihan addressed the sense that America was put off balance in the Third World by a strong bias toward socialist-oriented redistribution, and that this bias, strongly present at the United Nations, tended to make American diplomats defensive. Moynihan felt that they should instead take the offensive. "*The United States goes into opposition,*" he started,

> This is our circumstance. We are a minority. We are outvoted. This is neither an unprecedented nor an intolerable situation. The question is what do we make of it. So far we have made little—nothing—of what is in fact an opportunity. We go about dazed that the world has changed.... We rebound with the thought that if only we are more reasonable perhaps "they" will be.... But "they" do not grow reasonable. Instead, we grow unreasonable.[45]

Moynihan felt that the United States should speak up for liberty and democracy. "It is past time we ceased to apologize for an imperfect democracy. Find its equal.[46]

In 1975, President Ford named Moynihan the American ambassador to the United Nations. Moynihan's tenure was brief, stormy, and historic. As the American representative to the body, Moynihan was determined that he would be feared "for the truths he might tell," and he denounced Idi Amin as a "racist murderer" and the PLO as "an amorphous terrorist organization."[47] But his most memorable moment was when he stood to oppose the UN's infamous Resolution 3379, which declared that "Zionism is a form of racism and racial discrimination."[48] The UN motion gained the votes of Arab and Islamic-majority countries, as well as the Soviet bloc. It stayed in force until 1991.

But Moynihan rose in opposition to it. "The Abomination of anti-Semitism has been given the appearance of international sanction," he said, and then he made clear that the United States found the resolution appalling and unforgivable: "The United States of America declares that it does not acknowledge, it will not abide by, it will never acquiesce in this infamous act."[49] *National Review* named him its "Man of the Year,"[50] and *Time* put him on the cover with the headline, "GIVING THEM HELL AT THE U.N."[51]

Moynihan would win the New York Senate seat the following year and serve four terms, during which time he retained his penchant for independent thought. He stayed in the Democratic Party, and at times, especially in the 1990s, he seemed to be veering leftward again. But he never lost his fundamental orientation toward liberal internationalism and an unapologetic American role in the world—convictions that often put him at odds with other liberal Democrats and that got him labeled as a neoconservative, though he never liked the identification. His disclaimer, which he wrote to the *New York Times*, speaks volumes about how old-fashioned, Kennedy-era liberals like himself now seemed out of place in the Democratic Party: "Inasmuch as a neoconservative is a liberal who votes for the defense budget," Moynihan wrote, "it is possible to clarify the whole matter for your readers by describing such persons as patriots."[52] The tensions between that viewpoint and the newer form of post-Nixon liberalism became even more pronounced during the Carter years.

Jimmy Carter and the Long McGovern Hangover

Despite McGovern's crushing defeat in 1972, the momentum of like-minded McGovern voters and supporters within the party remained strong. And within two years, they got what they saw as glorious vindication: Nixon's resignation, under threat of impeachment for his actions to cover up the Watergate affair. Democrats, especially progressives and young radicals, celebrated the president's demise. Nixon's own self-crippling had helped save, it seemed, the crippled Democrats.

In the 1974 midterm elections, Democrats rolled to huge gains in the House and Senate, bringing into Congress a new class of young progressives, called the Watergate Babies. Of the ninety-two new members of Congress elected that year, an incredible seventy-five were Democrats and just seventeen Republicans.[53] The Democrats included stalwart liberals like Patrick Leahy, elected to the Senate, and Tom Harkin and

Chris Dodd, elected to the House and later to become senators, as well as Congressman Henry Waxman.

Americans soon found out what it meant to have a resurgent Democratic Party empowered to make decisions on national defense. By April 1975, North Vietnamese forces were closing in on Saigon. Faced with the resurgent Democratic majorities, Gerald Ford's ability to maneuver was limited. He tried to issue emergency funds to Saigon before it was too late, but Congress rebuffed him. On April 30, Saigon fell, and the Communist North won the Vietnam War.

The South fell because, less than a year earlier, in the wake of Nixon's resignation, the Democratic Congress had voted to drastically cut its funding for the South Vietnamese army. Our Saigon ally was essentially left helpless against the Communist onslaught. Disgusted by the liberals' betrayal of a staunch and beleaguered ally, Richard Armitage compared the South Vietnamese to "a pregnant lady, abandoned by her lover to face her fate."[54] This critique, widely shared, expressed a moral dimension not normally associated with foreign policy realism—it was an argument about national character as well as policy. Yet the American abandonment, spearheaded by Democrats, was inspired by the same principle that had been governing focus of George McGovern's presidential campaign: peace at any price, with results just as Richard Nixon had warned in 1972. Nixon and Henry Kissinger had brought the war to the brink of victory for the South while also removing almost all American combat troops. It would have been a feat for the ages, but in Vietnam, the Democratic Left got its revenge, of sorts, on behalf of McGovern.

And, after that, the anti-Watergate momentum was still strong enough to carry the Democrats back to the White House in 1976, when Jimmy Carter beat Ford in a razor-thin election. It is important to remember that Carter was no McGovernite. His brief but successful political career, forged in Georgia's conservative political environment, had mostly been an exercise in Democratic centrism. He was an appealing candidate to the national-security Democrats, like those in the Coalition for a Democratic Majority, some of whom had voted for Nixon in 1972. CDM members Ben Wattenberg and Jeane Kirkpatrick helped shape the 1976 Democratic platform with "tough-minded ideas." The CDM saw Carter as a leader who would return the party to a muscular foreign policy.[55]

Carter won in 1976 running not as a liberal or even so much as a Democrat, but more as an "outsider," a man with no links to the domestic or foreign policy debacles of the past decade. "Going from total anonymity, to being President of the United States in less than twelve months, is unprecedented in American history," said one of Carter's pollsters, Patrick Caddell. "If it weren't for the country looking for something in '76, Carter could never have gotten elected."[56]

Carter also won by appealing to idealism—and by running implicitly against Nixon in at least two ways: First, he made an impossible pledge to the American people—"I will never tell a lie," one of his campaign commercials promised, "I will never make a misleading statement. I will never betray the confidence any of you has in me."[57] Second, borrowing from Scoop Jackson, Carter made human rights the central platform for his foreign policy. But unlike Jackson, who saw human rights especially in the context of Communist abuses of religious and political liberty, Carter was more interested in cleansing American of its impurities, especially its affiliations with unsavory foreign leaders. The president's focus was a rebuke to the foreign policy realism represented by Nixon and Kissinger—and a weak attempt to get the Democrats back into the foreign policy game by emphasizing soft issues palatable to the antiwar base. As time would reveal, the Carter vision did not represent a viable foreign policy.

Carter's outsider appeal obscured these troubling signs in 1976, but once in office, he almost immediately began disappointing muscular Democrats—and pleasing doves like George McGovern, who cheered the appointments Carter made to fill policy-making positions at the State Department, calling them "excellent... quite close to those I would have made myself."[58] It was a sign that the New Left, though defeated at the presidential level, was making deeper inroads within the Democratic establishment.

Ben Wattenberg and others at the centrist CDM were dismayed almost immediately by Carter. Wattenberg had even considered disbanding the coalition after Carter's victory; it looked like its purpose had been accomplished, especially when the president named one of its members, Zbigniew Brzezinski, as his national-security adviser. But he also named Cyrus Vance, a dove, his secretary of state. Carter seemed to swing between hawkish and dovish orientations, but over time, the predominantly liberal tilt of his policies convinced Wattenberg that the CDM needed to stay in business.[59]

Centrist Democrats were also distressed when Carter considered naming Paul Warnke to a top Pentagon post. Warnke had advised McGovern on national security in the 1972 campaign and was a staunch advocate of cutting defense spending and "unilateral disarmament" to end the arms race. He had also compared the Soviet Union and the United States to "apes on a treadmill," equating them as mutually deluded in a moral sense. The CDM and other groups—including the Committee on the Present Danger—mobilized against Warnke and halted his Pentagon nomination. But Carter ended up naming him to head up the Arms Control and Disarmament Agency, a position in which he became the chief SALT II negotiator in the United States.[60]

Carter sent more disturbing signals in high-profile speeches. Just months after he took office, he delivered the commencement address at Notre Dame, where he spoke to the graduates about American power in the world, describing the Cold War in terms reminiscent of McGovern. "Being confident of our own future," he said, "we are now free of that inordinate fear of Communism which once led us to embrace any dictator who joined us in that fear. I'm glad that that's being changed."[61]

The fissures that Nixon promoted in the Democratic Party reasserted themselves as Carter revealed himself as a weak and vacillating leader. His apparent unwillingness to look at the Soviet Union realistically came back to haunt him in 1979, when the Soviets invaded Afghanistan. "This action of the Soviets," Carter told ABC News, "has made a more dramatic change in my own opinion of what the Soviets' ultimate goals are than anything they've done in the previous time I've been in office."[62] Though he never used the word "shocked," Carter acted as if he was shocked by the Soviets' aggression. His dismay in turn dismayed Republicans and millions of Americans, who couldn't believe he could be so naïve. Clearly, the West's fear of Moscow had not been "inordinate," after all.

By that point, the Carter foreign policy had already run aground, and centrist and conservative Democrats had been grousing about its fecklessness for some time. The Soviet invasion occurred only a month after Iranian militants seized the American embassy in Tehran, precipitating the infamous Iranian Hostage Crisis. Carter first won praise for his calm under pressure and refusal to do anything hasty or reckless, but as the months dragged on without the hostages' release, and with the nightly videos on network news of Iranians burning Carter's image in effigy and American flags, the public became angry.

So did the Democratic hawks, especially those in the CDM. One of Carter's most vocal CDM critics was Jeane Kirkpatrick, a political science professor at Georgetown, lifelong Democrat, and advocate of the bold liberal internationalism of men like Hubert Humphrey and Scoop Jackson. Like so many other Democrats of this orientation, she had grown more and more dismayed by the direction of the party, and she blamed the New Left and the McGovernites, who, she said, proposed "utopian schemes for the reform of almost everything."[63] She turned against Carter, whom she had initially supported, for his inconstancy against Communism and his passion for arms control. The Carter foreign policy, she said, amounted to "McGovernism without McGovern."[64]

Kirkpatrick also took issue with Carter's elevation of human rights as the guiding principle in American foreign policy. That sounded good, Kirkpatrick wrote in her seminal essay "Dictatorships and Double Standards," but in practice, privileging human rights over other strategic considerations (of the kind Richard Nixon considered paramount) often led to the desertion of loyal friends in dangerous parts of the world and their replacement by adversarial and more extreme rulers. The situation in Iran, where the pro-American Shah had been overthrown by the Islamic Revolution of Ayatollah Khomeini, vividly illustrated this dynamic.

Kirkpatrick's essay appeared in *Commentary*'s November 1979 issue—the same month as the embassy seizure—opening starkly:

> The failure of the Carter administration's foreign policy is now clear to everyone except its architects, and even they must entertain private doubts, from time to time, about a policy whose crowning achievement has been to lay the groundwork for a transfer of the Panama Canal from the United States to a swaggering Latin dictator of Castroite bent. In the thirty-odd months since the inauguration of Jimmy Carter as President there has occurred a dramatic Soviet military buildup, matched by the stagnation of American armed forces, and a dramatic extension of Soviet influence in the Horn of Africa, Afghanistan, Southern Africa, and the Caribbean, matched by a declining American position in all these areas.

The closing sentence provided the most eloquent summary of the position of the liberal hawks: "Liberal idealism need not be identical with masochism, and need not be incompatible with the defense of freedom and the national interest."[65]

Not long after publishing the essay, Kirkpatrick received a fan letter from Ronald Reagan, who was then gearing up to make one more attempt at the presidency. Reagan suggested they meet, and Kirkpatrick agreed. After long consideration, she decided, in 1980, to support Reagan for president.[66] When Democrats in the Carter administration called her to ask if she would participate in the party's national convention in New York, she acidly replied: "I already have a date."[67] Not all of the CDM members took Kirkpatrick's course; Wattenberg stuck with Carter, though it was dawning on him that Democrats like him "don't seem to be a majority any longer."[68]

The rolling disaster of Carter's foreign policy hit its nadir in April 1980, when Carter authorized an attempt to rescue the hostages in Iran—an audacious plan. Desert One, had it succeeded, may well have gotten him a second term. Unfortunately, Desert One became an American military tragedy, as first the mission was aborted due to sandstorms and then several malfunctioning helicopters crashed, costing the lives of eight special-forces operatives. It was a devastating psychological blow to a nation already reeling under high unemployment and inflation rates. Few blamed Carter personally for the mission's failure, yet it seemed that everything he touched turned to ashes.

By this point, Carter didn't just have the centrist and hawkish Democrats to worry about; he also faced a challenge from his left in the person of Ted Kennedy. Though Kennedy was not a McGovernite per se, his appeal owed much to the New Left takeover of the Democratic Party. Kennedy's campaign against Carter bruised the already-wounded president, especially since Kennedy insisted on taking his challenge all the way to the convention in New York, though he had no real chance. The Democrats were acting as if they would have liked anyone but Carter to be their nominee.

Millions of Americans eventually came to feel the same way about having Carter as their president. In the final week of Carter's presidential campaign against Reagan, the race was still close, according to the polls. But the sole debate between the candidates, on October 28, 1980—one week before the election—likely turned the tide in Reagan's favor. The debate is remembered today for Reagan's quip, "There you go again," as well as for his closing statement, in which he asked the famous question: "Are you better off than you were four years ago?"[69] But what may have swayed the audience even more was something Carter said about national security—something so off-base and odd that it might have come from George McGovern.

The candidates were discussing the nuclear arms race when suddenly Carter interjected: "I think to close out this discussion, it would be better to put into perspective what we're talking about. I had a discussion with my daughter, Amy, the other day, before I came here, to ask her what the most important issue was. She said she thought nuclear weaponry—and the control of nuclear arms."[70] The weird aside "gave the impression to some voters that Carter was consulting with his daughter about nuclear strategy," wrote Donald Crichtlow.[71] A week later, Reagan won one of the greatest landslides in American history—forty-four out of fifty states, 489 electoral votes to Carter's 49.

The Scoop Jackson Democrats, many of whom had crossed over to vote Republican in 1980, heard in Reagan a leader who shared their view of Soviet Communism—and their conviction that American democracy needed and deserved to prevail. Reagan articulated an impassioned, eloquent defense of Western values and individual liberty and pledged the American people's willingness to defend them. Contrast, for example, Carter's 1977 Notre Dame speech, in which he had espoused being free of the fear of Communism, with Reagan's 1982 Westminster address:

> The objective I propose is quite simple to state: to foster the infrastructure of democracy, the system of a free press, unions, political parties, universities, which allows a people to choose their own way to develop their own culture, to reconcile their own differences through peaceful means.... Who would voluntarily choose not to have the right to vote, decide to purchase government propaganda handouts instead of independent newspapers, prefer government to worker-controlled unions, opt for land to be owned by the state instead of those who till it, want government repression of religious liberty, a single political party instead of a free choice, a rigid cultural orthodoxy instead of democratic tolerance and diversity?[72]

In the same speech, Reagan inspired his audience and listeners around the world with an audacious vision of a world without Communism: "What I am describing now is a plan and a hope for the long term—the march of freedom and democracy which will leave Marxism-Leninism on the ash-heap of history as it has left other tyrannies which stifle the freedom and muzzle the self-expression of the people."[73]

Reagan's philosophy of national security could be boiled down to the mantra he repeated often: "Peace through strength," a concept that had the benefit of being both wise and easy to understand—while putting Democrats on the defensive. Why, millions of Americans wondered, couldn't Democrats explain themselves on national defense? Democrats continued to rationalize away the foreign policy deficit they now faced with the voters. Reagan had only won, many of them argued, because of the hostage crisis... and the energy crisis, and the bad economy—a unique set of woes that would have brought any sitting president down, not just Jimmy Carter. They dismissed Reagan's appeal and felt confident that they could beat him in 1984. They didn't reckon with his leadership abilities—or with the mounting evidence that, post-Nixon, Americans did not trust Democrats on national security.

Thus the Democrats saw fit to nominate as their challenger to Reagan, in 1984, Carter's vice president, Walter Mondale—a man with a more consistent and more distinguished liberal career than his boss had ever compiled. Before he served under Carter, Mondale had been an influential Democratic senator, earning a 96 percent approval rating on foreign policy from the left-liberal ADA.[74] Nominating Mondale in 1984 seemed utterly out of step with the national mood, and Jeane Kirkpatrick felt that the Democrats ought to hear about it from one of their own. Kirkpatrick had already made her choice: not only had she voted for Reagan in 1980, she had also gone on to serve as his UN ambassador, enduring a term as stormy as Moynihan's was under Gerald Ford. Now, in the summer of 1984, a month after the Democrats had nominated Mondale in San Francisco, Kirkpatrick stood at the lectern of her first Republican National Convention and let her old party have it. In a speech called "Blame America," she railed against the "San Francisco Democrats":

When our Marines, sent to Lebanon on a multinational peacekeeping mission with the consent of the United States Congress, were murdered in their sleep, the "blame America first crowd" didn't blame the terrorists who murdered the Marines, they blamed the United States.

But then, they always blame America first.

When the Soviet Union walked out of arms control negotiations, and refused even to discuss the issues, the San Francisco Democrats didn't blame Soviet intransigence. They blamed the United States.

But then, they always blame America first.

When Marxist dictators shoot their way to power in Central America, the San Francisco Democrats don't blame the guerrillas and their Soviet allies, they blame United States policies of 100 years ago.

But then, they always blame America first. The American people know better.

They know that Ronald Reagan and the United States didn't cause Marxist dictatorship in Nicaragua, or the repression in Poland, or the brutal new offensives in Afghanistan, or the destruction of the Korean airliner, or the new attacks on religious and ethnic groups in the Soviet Union, or the jamming of western broadcasts, or the denial of Jewish emigration, or the brutal imprisonment of Anatoly Sharansky and Ida Nudel, or the obscene treatment of Andrei Sakharov and Yelena Bonner, or the re-Stalinization of the Soviet Union.

The American people know that it's dangerous to blame ourselves for terrible problems that we did not cause.[75]

Kirkpatrick was right, not only in her critique of her former party but also of her analysis of Americans' understanding of these issues. In November 1984, voters returned Reagan to the White House in a forty-nine-state wipeout reminiscent of Nixon's demolition of George McGovern.

Nixonized until the Nineties

So popular was Reagan—and so trusted, by now, were Republicans on national defense—that he even got his vice president, George H. W. Bush, into office in 1988 for what some called a "third Reagan term." The election of 1988 once again demonstrated the chasm that separated the parties on defense and security—the chasm that had been opened wide by George McGovern's candidacy and Richard Nixon's presidential leadership.

A story in the *Chicago Tribune* illustrated how widespread the public perception of Democratic weakness on defense had become. The Democratic nominee, the hapless governor of Massachusetts, Michael Dukakis, was not the man to redefine the party on national security. When Dukakis was campaigning with John Glenn at a General Electric defense plant outside of Cincinnati, he tried to convince his listeners that he would preserve the nation's defenses—but they weren't buying. They booed him, and when Dukakis insisted that he supported a strong national defense, the crowd responded with: "Bush, Bush" and "Give us a break!"[76]

The ultimate Dukakis moment, however—and the capstone to two decades of Democratic ineptitude on national security and in presidential elections—was the Massachusetts governor's infamous tank ride, in which he dressed in General Dynamics coveralls and donned a helmet for a photo op that would, he hoped, demonstrate his commitment to defense. But Dukakis looked unnatural, to put it generously, sitting in the tank—one commentator compared him to Rocky the Flying Squirrel—and the contrived pose made perfect fodder for a Bush campaign ad.

Sid Rogich, working for the Bush ad team—headed by Roger Ailes, who had gotten his start with Nixon in 1968—saw the Dukakis footage and thought, "I can't believe they put him in that position." Rich Bond, Bush's deputy campaign manager and later head of the Republican National Committee, remembered a staff meeting in which someone said, in reference to Dukakis in the tank, "My God, he looks like Alfred E. Newman."[77] Everyone dissolved in laughter.

It didn't take long for Rogich and Ailes to get an ad together called "Tank Ride" showing the footage of Dukakis in the tank with a voiceover highlighting the incongruity. The effect was heightened by scrolling the text:

> Michael Dukakis has opposed virtually every defense system we developed.

He opposed new aircraft carriers.

He opposed antisatellite weapons.

He opposed four missile systems, including the Pershing Two missile deployment.

Dukakis opposed the Stealth bomber and a ground emergency warning system against nuclear attack.

He even criticized our rescue mission to Grenada and our strike on Libya.

Now he wants to be our commander in chief?

America can't afford that risk.[78]

Dukakis was beaten in forty states, winning just 111 electoral votes to Bush's 426.

The defeat capped off a decade of presidential drubbings for the party of FDR, Truman, and Kennedy: the Democrats lost forty-four states in 1980, when Carter ran for reelection; forty-nine states in 1984; and forty in 1988. And, in the period from 1968 to 1988, the Nixon-scarred Democrats lost every presidential election but one. The American center had drifted away from Democrats in presidential elections, and a new voting bloc was recognized, the Reagan Democrats, who identified with the party of FDR but voted for "the Gipper." Among their other reasons for voting Republican—including economics, culture, and taxes—was the prevailing view that the Republican Party was better trusted with the nation's defense. The GOP had practiced the principle of peace through strength, and, through three presidencies, had gotten results. The Democrats could not say the same.

The only question, after 1988, was whether Democrats could ever get out from under the shadow of George McGovern—and by extension, from that of Richard Nixon. As it happened, a centrist movement had been growing within the party throughout the eighties, and Dukakis's smashing defeat left the opening its advocates needed to move to the forefront. These centrists, working in a group called the Democratic Leadership Council, would finally succeed in taking the party back to the center—at least for a time. In doing so, they would adapt Nixon's lessons to their own party, and see the rise of the most popular American politician since Ronald Reagan.

– CHAPTER 7 –

Triangulation Redux

How Bill Clinton Became a Nixon Heir

[Clinton] came from dirt and I came from dirt. He lost a gubernatorial race and came back to win the Presidency, and I lost a gubernatorial race and came back to win the Presidency. He overcame a scandal in his first campaign for national office and I overcame a scandal in my first national campaign. We both just gutted it out. He was an outsider from the South and I was an outsider from the West.

—**RICHARD NIXON**[1]

I think [Nixon] really cared about America as a whole, and he was a flat-out communist compared to the crowd running his party today.

—**BILL CLINTON**[2]

The two presidents sat in the White House family quarters, talking about the challenges of war and peace, and especially about America's challenge—and opportunity—in forging a new relationship with Russia. It was March 1993, and Bill Clinton had been president barely fifty days. But he had already learned that in the presidency, one had to learn fast and take lessons from whoever had the best insights—even if they came from a man still regarded as a pariah by the Democratic Party. By 1993, Richard Nixon's name was less toxic than it had been in the late 1970s, but he still wasn't the kind of figure who made White House guest lists. Only once, in 1979, had he been officially welcomed back to the White House, and then only because the visiting Chinese vice premier had requested his presence. He visited Ronald Reagan at the White House in 1987, but that meeting had been kept top secret. By contrast, Clinton made it no secret that he was about to host the only man to resign the presidency. Nixon's name appeared on the White House guest list, and his visit was publicly confirmed.

The White House released a photo of the meeting afterward, one that became iconic: it showed the two men sitting in wingback chairs in a shadowy room lit by a large table lamp. Clinton would later call their

meeting "the best conversation I've had in the White House."[3] And, for
the next year, Clinton and Nixon would stay in touch, the young president seeking the foreign-policy counsel of a man whose wisdom and
clarity of thought he came to hold in the highest regard.

Few Americans knew about the Clinton-Nixon relationship at the
time, though, so many were surprised to hear Clinton's generous words,
in April 1994, as he eulogized the thirty-seventh president at Nixon's
funeral in Yorba Linda, California.

"May the day of judging President Nixon on anything less than his
entire life and career come to a close," Clinton said,[4] speaking to an audience that included, in the front row, all four living former presidents:
Gerald Ford, Jimmy Carter, Ronald Reagan, and George H. W. Bush.
Henry Kissinger and Bob Dole also spoke about Nixon that day, but it
was Clinton's eulogy that got the most attention. In part, of course, this
was because Clinton was president and would have the last word. But
more importantly, it was Clinton's magnanimous treatment of Nixon's
life and career that struck listeners.

"Oh, yes, he knew great controversy amid defeat as well as victory,"
Clinton said of Nixon, and continued:

> He made mistakes, and they, like his accomplishments, are a part of
> his life and record. But the enduring lesson of Richard Nixon is that
> he never gave up being part of the action and passion of his times....
> May we heed his call to maintain the will and the wisdom to build
> on America's greatest gift, its freedom, and to lead a world full of dif-
> ficulty to the just and lasting peace he dreamed of.[5]

Liberals and die-hard Nixon haters were stunned, and even some of
Clinton's own aides were surprised by his treatment of the man who had
symbolized political corruption, if not evil itself, for a generation.[6] His
eulogy offered the most public evidence of something that keen observers had already begun noting: that Bill Clinton—who had protested
against the Vietnam War, gotten his political start working for George
McGovern's 1972 presidential campaign, and married a feminist icon
who served on the Watergate committee—was, in many ways, Richard
Nixon's political heir.

Just as Nixon had led the GOP out of the electoral wilderness after the 1964 drubbing of Barry Goldwater, laying the ground for a new majority, Clinton had brought a halt to his party's long-running presidential slump, achieving three blowouts in a row, in 1980, 1984, and 1988, and five losses in six elections. And he did it with Nixonian political savvy—moderating his own party's worst tendencies while co-opting the best ideas of the other side.

Each president was also the target of more vitriol and hatred from the opposition party than any other politician of his time. The Left hated Nixon and the Right despised Clinton for reasons that went deeper than mere politics. Part of it was the suspicion of their Machiavellian characters, but another part had to do with culture: Nixon and Clinton aroused contempt in their opposition because they seemed to represent, personally and politically, everything that their opponents despised. That hatred, along with character flaws, would force both men to battle for their political survival.

For all of that dislike, Nixon and Clinton possessed unrivaled instincts for locating the American political center. These instincts were often derided as the product of calculation and insincerity—Nixon was "Tricky Dick," and Clinton was "Slick Willie." But whatever their awkwardness or imperfections, they affirmed and defended unifying American values during periods of great uncertainty. The electorate rewarded them for it.

"I was convinced that if we could escape the 'alien' box the Republicans had put us in since 1968, except for President Carter's success in 1976, we could win the White House again," Clinton wrote.[7] It was Richard Nixon who had first put Democrats in that box, and no one knew it better than Bill Clinton. His entire presidency was an effort, largely successful, to reconnect with the middle-class Americans—the silent majority—that Nixon had originally lost for the Democratic Party.

Two Men with Common Themes

"What did you think of him?" Roger Stone asked Nixon in 1993, after the former president had met Bill Clinton for the first time. Nixon didn't answer directly, but his response spoke volumes about the connection he felt with the new president.

"You know," Nixon told Stone,

> he came from dirt and I came from dirt. He lost a gubernatorial race and came back to win the Presidency, and I lost a gubernatorial race and came back to win the Presidency. He overcame a scandal in his first campaign for national office and I overcame a scandal in my first national campaign. We both just gutted it out. He was an outsider from the South and I was an outsider from the West.[8]

The identifications didn't end there. It's rare that two presidents so different in personality have so much in common in their career trajectories and political circumstances. Their respective presidential crises—impeachment for Clinton and Watergate for Nixon, which led to his resignation before he could be impeached—were both tied to issues of integrity. Ultimately, it was their character that was questioned: Clinton was easy to like but difficult to trust, while Nixon was both difficult to like and to trust.

Despite their perceived shortcomings, both men won two terms and enjoyed, at different times in their presidencies, high popularity ratings, because their policies were considered the right ones, especially in comparison with those of their opposition. "Nixon's moral character was more questionable than Humphrey's in 1968, but the people elected Nixon on the basis of the issues," Diane Hollern Harvey wrote. "In 1992 and 1996, Bill Clinton's opposition was regarded as far more moral and ethical, but more people selected Clinton, with his flawed character but popular programs."[9]

Their popular policies didn't dissuade their political enemies from waging all-out war against them. That warfare cultivated, in both men, intense suspicion, even paranoia—a sense that enemies always lurked near. For Clinton, it was "the vast right-wing conspiracy," in the words of his First Lady. For Nixon, it was the counterculture, the media, and the Eastern elites—the people who looked down on him, his origins, and his values. Clinton's adversaries derided his origins and values, too; they just happened to be different ones. Both men spent their presidencies under siege—and both men, with their siege mentalities, exacerbated and worsened their problems.

"Since the day he entered politics, Nixon hadn't liked people much," David Gergen wrote, "and they in turn didn't like him. By the time he was elected president, he had a legion of work enemies. No one drew as much venom until Bill Clinton was elected in 1992." Nixon, Gergen wrote, "made a manageable problem infinitely worse by assuming he had more enemies than he did."[10] Clinton would do the same.

In waging political war, neither man could always count on the support of his party—because they were often at odds with one faction or another. Conservatives never trusted Nixon, as we have seen, and when he veered leftward, confirming their worst suspicions, they turned on him. Likewise, liberals soon learned to distrust Clinton and his centrist inclinations. But ideological disputes were only part of it. Both men also inspired antipathy that was "purely personal," as William Schneider observed. "With Nixon," he wrote, "the joke was, 'Would you buy a used car from this man?' With Clinton, it's endless variations on, 'I didn't inhale.' What's odd is that the two represent such different character types. Nixon was cold, distant, calculating, formal and synthetic. Clinton is warm, open, approachable, laid-back and touchy-feely."[11]

Thus both presidents waged lonely battles at times, finding allies not in ideological soulmates but in a small inner circle of trusted aides. It was, in part, this sense of being cut adrift, of taking up arms against a sea of troubles, that led to both men's self-identifications as "survivors." Both famously took to the airwaves when their political survival hung in the balance: Nixon in 1952, with the "Checkers" speech, and, less successfully, with various Watergate-related appeals; Clinton in 1992, in his *60 Minutes* interview with Hillary by his side, and with more mixed results, in 1998, when he admitted to having an affair with Monica Lewinsky. Both portrayed their opposition as vindictive and destructive—and themselves as defenders of the national interest. Many saw the parallels between Clinton's *60 Minutes* appearance and Nixon's "Checkers" speech forty years earlier. "Both men made shrewd use of their wives for political advantage," William Schneider wrote. "Nixon did Clinton one better, however. He threw in his dog."[12] (Eventually Clinton, too, would employ a dog, Buddy, to good effect.)

But the Nixon-Clinton linkage goes deeper, to more substantive political traits. Bill Clinton was known in his time as the "great triangulator." Richard Nixon could just as easily have earned that nickname twenty years earlier for navigating the ideological splits within his own party and the political hemorrhaging on the other side with even-greater deftness than Clinton. Both men were shrewd, sophisticated political operators who positioned themselves as the reasonable, statesmanlike alternative to the ideological leadership of both parties. And they made their marks in history by doing so.

The Triangulators

This concept of triangulation is what links Nixon and Clinton most closely at the political level: their positioning of themselves between ideological and political poles, both within their own parties and in regard to the opposition party. They did this rhetorically and substantively, by positioning themselves not just in the middle politically but also as the champion of the ultimate middle in American life: the middle class. Nixon's appeal to the silent majority resonated with the tenor and conflicts of the times, the early 1970s, with the national discord over the Vietnam War. Clinton, two decades later, appealed to the "quiet, troubled voice of the forgotten middle class," which, as he described it in 1992, had been trampled by the harder edges of Reaganomics and forgotten by Washington politicians.[13] He called his pursuit of the White House a "campaign for the future, for the forgotten hard-working middle-class families of America."[14]

Before Clinton, Democratic presidential candidates Walter Mondale and Michael Dukakis had given lip service to middle-class concerns, but voters read between the lines and sensed that what really motivated them were the interests of the Democrats' special constituencies—minorities and women. By appealing to those who "work hard and play by the rules,"[15] Clinton made the middle class flesh and blood again, and he won back millions of Reagan Democrats who had deserted the party for three presidential elections. By appealing to the vast American middle, a unifying strategy—since most Americans are middle class or at least consider themselves to be—Nixon and Clinton managed to position themselves as protectors of middle-class voters, against those hostile to middle-class interests. In Nixon's time, the enemy was the progressive Left—the war protestors and student demonstrators, and the radical black-power and feminist activists, for whom, many Americans felt, the Democratic Party had abandoned them. In Clinton's time, the enemy was both Republican "trickle-down economics" advocates and far-left Democratic liberals who had deserted the middle class.

This brings us back to Nixon's 1969 speech to the American people. "For almost 200 years," he said,

> the policy of this Nation has been made under our Constitution by those leaders in the Congress and the White House elected by all of the people. If a vocal minority, however fervent its cause, prevails over reason and the will of the majority, this Nation has no future as a free society.... And so tonight—to you, the great silent majority of my fellow Americans—I ask for your support.[16]

And as for those who stood outside the silent majority—the radicals and demonstrators—Nixon left no doubt as to where he stood.

"It isn't just the radicals that set the bomb in the lighted, occupied building who were guilty," Nixon said in 1970, speaking of one of the leftist bombings of the time. "The blood is on the hands of anyone who encouraged them, anyone who talked recklessly of revolution, anyone who has chided with mild disparagement the violence of extremism, while hinting that the cause was right all the time."[17]

Clinton took some time to develop the same knack. Listen to Clinton in 1994, talking about the opposition to his health care plan: "The interests—the violent, extremist interests in this country that are trying to keep health care out of reach of ordinary American working people are a disgrace to the American Dream."[18] Those were strident words on an issue that divided the country. But if you listen to the president a year later, after the Oklahoma City bombing had taken place, you can hear how he has channeled the Nixonian technique of aligning himself with the vast middle. Lamenting those voices—such as Rush Limbaugh's—who "keep everybody torn up and upset all the time, purveying hate and implying at least with words that violence is all right,"[19] Clinton went after what he saw as right-wing extremist movements and their Republican enablers.

"It's very interesting to me," he said at a town meeting in Billings, Montana, "to see that there are some public officials in our country who are only too happy to criticize the culture of violence being promoted by the media in our country or the rap lyrics that are coming out in some of our recordings... but are stone-cold silent when these other folks are talking and making violence seem like it's OK."[20]

In pursuing the center, both Nixon and Clinton were willing to remain aloof from, and even alienate, their own parties. Nixon, of course, as we have seen, kept conservatives in the Republican Party alternately appeased and outraged. Clinton, two decades later, kept his party's liberal wing at arm's length—and in so doing shifted the party's center of gravity rightward, at least for a time.

Both men were also adept at marginalizing the opposition party, by co-opting so much political space in the center that their opponents were left with little ground on which to stand. Nixon did it as early as the 1968 campaign, giving policy speeches in which he quoted whom he called "new liberals," or thinkers who embraced private-sector solutions. "Tory men and liberal policies," he said, "are what have changed the world."[21] Once he was in the White House, Nixon's guaranteed annual income proposal put liberals off balance. Though it never became law, the proposal helped Nixon establish moderate credentials and blunted Democratic attacks against GOP economic policies.[22] Similarly, as John Pitney pointed out, "Clinton snatched a major issue from Bob Dole when he reached an agreement with the GOP on comprehensive welfare reform. But by promising to seek future changes to make the law more generous, the president also appeased liberals."[23]

And Nixon and Clinton employed similar against-the-grain policies regarding the size of government—Nixon growing it, in contravention of Republican orthodoxy, and Clinton shrinking it, much to Democratic disgruntlement. "Clinton outflanked the Republicans with proposals to streamline government," Pitney wrote, "just as Nixon had stayed ahead of the Democrats by establishing bureaucracies such as the Environmental Protection Agency."[24] As John Ehrlichman urged in a 1970 memo, "We will try to co-opt the opposition's issues... if the political cost is not too great."[25]

In short, Clinton and Nixon fashioned themselves, variously, as liberal-moderates and moderate-conservatives, often exasperating their own parties while confounding their opponents—in contrast with George W. Bush and Barack Obama, Clinton's successors, who never mastered unifying rhetoric. Bush and Obama almost never surprised their opposition, either. They represented a certain portion of the American electorate, a large one, to be sure; but Clinton and Nixon transcended narrow partisan identities. At their best, they knew that their true constituency was the American people, writ large—not the Republican or Democratic party establishments. That's why they are the two great centrist American presidents of modern times.

Policy Centrism

Nixon and Clinton both sought the center but came to it from different directions.

Nixon found the policy center by supporting and expanding the welfare state constructed by FDR and LBJ. He did it using somewhat-conservative principles, but nonetheless, the end result was a strengthening of the administrative state that the Right loathed. Clinton found the center by putting real substance into policies to lighten the weight of government on the American economy and the American taxpayer, as well as by finding more commonsense solutions to the problems, like poverty, that the liberal administrative state had failed to heal. Clinton pursued these goals on somewhat-liberal principles—he wanted government to work better, he said—but nonetheless, the end result was real progress toward conservative reforms that the Left feared.

Clinton made his orientation explicit in his 1996 State of the Union speech. "We know big government does not have all the answers," he told both houses of Congress. "We know there's not a program for every problem. We know, and we have worked to give the American people a smaller, less bureaucratic government in Washington. And we have to give the American people one that lives within its means. The era of big government is over." It was a landmark statement from a Democratic president.

Not many remembered what Clinton said next.

"But we cannot go back to the time when our citizens were left to fend for themselves. Instead, we must go forward as one America, one nation working together to meet the challenges we face together.

Self-reliance and teamwork are not opposing virtues; we must have both."[26] Clinton's moderation and pragmatism were exemplified in a frequent refrain through his presidency—"Opportunity, responsibility, community"—a vision both liberal and conservative. It was the role of government, Clinton believed, to fashion the conditions that fostered opportunity—but it was the role of citizens to reciprocate by taking responsibility and, ultimately, by giving something back. This reciprocal vision, which most Americans supported, also had political advantages, in that it allowed Clinton to position himself as the reasonable alternative between two unappealing and unrealistic warring camps. Nixon had been there before him.

Welfare Reform

There may be no better example of how Nixon and Clinton broke free of the ideological constrictions of their respective parties than each of their efforts to reform welfare. As I described earlier, Nixon's Family Assistance Plan, which failed to become law, would have represented the most transformative change to welfare policy in history. Nixon broke with conservatives in the Republican Party—and even some moderates—who saw the proposal as a massive government giveaway that would foster dependency. They failed to acknowledge the potential it held to change the dynamics and incentives of welfare.

A quarter-century later, in August 1996, Clinton broke from a generation of liberal gospel when he signed into law the Personal Responsibility and Work Opportunity Reconciliation Act, reforming the nation's welfare system. The new law set a five-year time limit for those receiving benefits, imposed tough new work requirements, and gave states incentives to create jobs for people on welfare while transitioning much of the responsibility for public assistance to the state level.

Welfare had been one of the first hooks on which Bill Clinton hung his new centrist candidacy in 1992. He often referred to poor people as being "trapped" on welfare. His oft-repeated promise to "end welfare as we know it" sounded like something a Republican would say. As governor of one of the nation's poorest states, Clinton, by all accounts, felt passionately about the issue. He had even worked with the Reagan administration in the 1980s on earlier welfare reform efforts—which he eagerly noted on the campaign trail, hoping to attract long-straying Reagan Democrats. It worked. Clinton's welfare proposals presented voters with a Democrat who talked about poverty policy in the way a normal American would—the way members of the silent majority would. Clinton's victory in battleground states like Ohio owed to his positioning as a New Democrat; his ideas on welfare reform were central to that identity.[27]

As leader of the Democratic Leadership Council in the 1980s, Clinton had forced Democrats to recognize that they needed to change. Bruce Reed, who worked on Clinton's 1992 campaign, saw "a growing consensus among Democrats that we have an obligation to end dependency and reform welfare, to move beyond the rhetoric of the right and the mistakes of the left."[28] Indeed, just as Nixon had found broad support on issues like the environment, health care, and workplace safety, Clinton's welfare position appealed to Americans who saw the system as fundamentally flawed but who also blanched at right-wingers who seemed to want to cut millions of dollars off the rolls at a moment's notice. By advocating welfare reform, Clinton could erase a stigma dating back to McGovern: that Democrats coddled the poor and minorities, that they expected nothing in return, and that they wanted the middle class to pay indefinitely for an entire population of able-bodied, nonworking adults.

Clinton also tried to make clear to liberals that he was not abandoning their traditional concern for the vulnerable. As he put it: "I believe we must also provide childcare so that mothers who are required to go to work can do so without worrying about what is happening to their children. I challenge this Congress to send me a bipartisan welfare reform bill that will really move people from welfare to work and do the right thing by our children. I will sign it immediately."[29]

Clinton would sign the act on August 22, 1996, after vetoing two previous bills because they lacked sufficient funding, as he saw it, for child care. "This is not the end of welfare reform, this is the beginning," the president said at a signing ceremony in the White House Rose Garden. "And we have to all assume responsibility."[30]

Clinton's historic signing won a chorus of praise from the political middle but impassioned dissent on both sides of the aisle. Some conservatives thought the bill's financial incentives to states were too generous and that the law's enforcement mechanisms had no teeth. For liberals, the law's work requirements were too harsh and the child-care and protection provisions too weak. On the Senate floor, Senator Ted Kennedy called it "legislative child abuse."[31] Liberals also saw the five-year time limit as a punishment for the vulnerable. They objected, it often seemed, to the very spirit behind the bill: the belief that everyone ought to contribute something to his or her own well-being, and that work was a good in itself—that it ennobled, disciplined, and matured people.

Three members of the Clinton administration resigned in protest over the president's decision. Women's groups and poverty groups protested along Pennsylvania Avenue, carrying signs and vowing to disrupt the Democratic National Convention, which would take place in Chicago the following week. Other constituencies that Clinton needed as he sought reelection in November—civil rights groups, unions, liberal churches, and immigrant advocates—also lamented the move. They felt betrayed by their vote, they said, though they conveniently seemed to forget that Clinton had been promising welfare reform long before coming to Washington.[32]

Ten years later, in 2006, Clinton looked back on welfare reform, by then regarded as major success, in a *New York Times* op-ed. He saw it as a triumph of bipartisanship and took pains to point out that neither side got entirely what it wanted. "Most Democrats and Republicans," he said,

> wanted to pass welfare legislation shifting the emphasis from dependence to empowerment. Because I had already given 45 states waivers to institute their own reform plans, we had a good idea of what would work. Still, there were philosophical gaps to bridge. The Republicans wanted to require able-bodied people to work, but were opposed to continuing the federal guarantees of food and medical care to their children and to spending enough on education, training, transportation and child care to enable people to go to work in lower-wage jobs without hurting their children.

Clinton saw "a great lesson to be learned, particularly in today's hyper-partisan environment.... Simply put, welfare reform worked because we all worked together. The 1996 Welfare Act shows us how much we can achieve when both parties bring their best ideas to the negotiating table and focus on doing what is best for the country."[33]

The Crime Bill

No one who remembers the 1968 presidential election can likely forget one of Richard Nixon's famous ads calling for a return to law and order in an increasingly lawless nation. Nixon pioneered "law and order" as a Republican issue, and for a generation afterward Republicans owned it. Democrats were the party, seemingly, of laxity when it came to crime fighting, more interested in the rights of the accused than in the rights of victims, more devoted to *Miranda* processes than to stopping violent perpetrators. Clinton ended this association in voters' minds, at least temporarily.

Like many Democrats, Clinton supported gun control, but unlike most of them, he positioned his views on the issue as part of a broader anticrime focus. The 1970s, 1980s, and early 1990s were an era of high crime, especially in cities, and many Americans saw Democrats as a party of excuse makers for miscreants and murderers. In addition, the now-familiar scourge of shootings using semiautomatic weapons began around this time. In pushing for stronger measures against crime and gun violence, Clinton was savvy enough to campaign with a key constituency of the old silent majority: police officers. They were outgunned by criminals, he protested, who enjoyed easy access to semiautomatic weapons. Clinton pushed for an assault weapons ban.

Predictably, the NRA pushed back. But Clinton won public support by framing the issue as one pitting cops and law-abiding citizens against criminals. He expressed support for gun owners and hunters—noting that he was one himself—but stressed safety and cutting crime. "I know the difference between a firearm used for hunting and target shooting," the president said, "and a weapon designed to kill people."[34]

The centerpiece of Clinton's accomplishments was the Violent Crime Control and Law Enforcement Act of 1994, popularly known as the "crime bill," the largest of its kind in American history, providing for "100,000 new police officers, $9.7 billion in funding for prisons and $6.1 billion in funding for prevention programs, which were designed with significant input from experienced police officers," according to the Justice Department.[35] Americans liked the crime bill, especially for its increased federal penalties for many crimes. The law added crimes to the category of federal offenses—especially "drive-by" shootings and carjacking, so prevalent in the 1990s—and added new offenses that could be punished by death. It boosted funding for federal law enforcement, including for the Border Patrol and Immigration and Naturalization Service (INS), and provided fresh funding for the construction of additional state prisons.[36]

Passing the law was an impressive feat, especially because Clinton had to do it not only over the opposition of conservative groups like the NRA but also over the opposition of liberal interest groups, which objected to the law's stiff penalties for offenders. He had to make some concessions, too, surrendering on the assault weapons ban in the interest of winning the broadest-possible congressional support for the crime bill.

It may seem that Clinton's getting the crime bill through was no great feat; Americans are reflexively anticrime, after all, so it follows that the bill would be inherently popular. But that view overlooks the political significance of what he accomplished: by championing police, on the one hand, while decrying violent crime, on the other—including crime committed with assault weapons—Clinton positioned himself nearly unassailably at the political center of a volatile issue in American life.

NAFTA

If welfare reform highlighted Clinton's break with the Left on poverty, and social spending and the crime bill moved him away from liberals' unwillingness to confront Americans' fears about urban violence, his championing of the North American Free Trade Agreement put the Democratic Party squarely back into the economic mainstream—where it hadn't been since at least Jimmy Carter. Clinton once again appealed to the center, leaning neither left nor right, with the passing of the agreement—and, as with the crime and welfare bills, faced down critics from both sides, but especially within his own party.

NAFTA is the most significant economic trade deal of our generation and perhaps the most important since World War II. In brief, the agreement, signed by the United States, Canada, and Mexico, phased out most tariffs and other import barriers to commerce between the three nations, and would take effect over a fifteen-year period, beginning on January 1, 1994. By removing most tariffs placed on Mexican goods coming into the United States, NAFTA would force US companies and workers to compete with Mexican firms, which usually paid their workers a fraction of what American workers earned. At the same time, though, most Mexican tariffs assessed on US products would be phased out—and US companies saw lucrative opportunities in this emerging market. Joined by most Republicans and conservatives, the Clinton administration argued that Mexico would become more prosperous as the result of the disappearing tariffs on its products and would thus become a stronger consumer market for US products. Clinton's embrace of NAFTA, and his willingness to put political skin in the game to fight for it, aligned him with the advocates of free trade and globalization. A Democratic president was championing an essentially conservative vision of an economic future based in competition.

"We cannot stop global change. We cannot repeal the international economic competition that is everywhere," Clinton said. "We can only harness the energy to our benefit. We must recognize that the only way for a wealthy nation to grow richer is to export, to simply find new customers for the products and services it makes."[37]

Critics of the agreement suggested that NAFTA would create a "race to the bottom" that would devastate the US manufacturing base and depress blue-collar wages. Some of this criticism came from around the political spectrum, most notably from Ross Perot, who put his political credibility on the line—running as an independent, he had earned 19 percent of the popular vote in the 1992 presidential election—to campaign against NAFTA. Perot famously went on *Larry King Live* to square off against Vice President Al Gore in November 1993, on the eve of the congressional vote on the bill. But most of the bill's opponents were Democrats, who saw it as an assault on working Americans. Typical dissenters were two leading Democrats, House Majority Leader Richard A. Gephardt of Missouri and House Majority Whip David Bonior of Michigan.

"It will cost jobs. It will drive down our standard of living. It will lock in place a Mexican system that exploits its own people and denies them the most basic political and economic rights," Bonior said.[38] "Drawn down by the lower wages in Mexico," Gephardt warned, "our standard of living will continue to stagnate or decline."[39] Even Clinton's persuasive skills could not sway them; they both voted against the agreement.

Much as Nixon had pursued initiatives that went against GOP orthodoxy in the early 1970s, Clinton persisted in his break from liberal orthodoxy. His support came mostly from Republicans. "This is a vote for history, larger than politics, larger than reelection, larger than personal ego," said Newt Gingrich, no ally of Clinton's.[40]

Clinton also reached out to his 1992 foe, former president Bush— who had supported an initial version of the agreement—as well as to former presidents Carter and Ford. All supported NAFTA. Repeatedly, Clinton sounded the theme that the agreement was good for the country. He stressed a bipartisan theme in September 1993, when he signed preliminary accords to the agreement, before the congressional vote. With the three former presidents looking on at the White House, Clinton said: "These men, differing in party and outlook, join us today because we all recognize the important stakes for our nation in this issue."[41]

Meanwhile, in the Larry King debate, Gore was widely judged to have pummeled Perot. Perot seemed angry and ill-mannered, and Gore suggested that his opposition to NAFTA was based on self-interest. The debate helped Clinton pick up more support, both in Congress and in the public.

In the end, the House approved the agreement 234–200—a wider margin than expected (218 votes were needed for passage). Republicans voted for NAFTA by a three-to-one margin; Democrats opposed it by five to three. By signing it, Clinton sent a message to the country that he was willing to go against his party in pursuit of the national interest.

NAFTA was part of a broader Clinton vision, one that harkened back to Nixon: an understanding of the increasingly symbiotic relationship between economic and trade policy, on the one hand, and foreign policy, on the other. Nixon had made that clear in moving off the Bretton Woods financial system, and most profoundly in his opening to Beijing—seeing Chinese relations as not just a crucial step in managing the Cold War but also as an opening to rich new markets for American trade. Likewise, Clinton saw the globalization of the world economy as something not to resist but to embrace. He understood that the foreign and domestic economies were becoming inextricable from each other, and he wanted America to take the primary role in shaping the new global economic order. Clinton's support for free trade went hand in hand with his vigorous support for democracy overseas—including the

use of force to enforce international norms on human rights, free elections, and democratic governance. He would demonstrate his commitment to these principles with his intervention in the Balkans.[42]

In pursuing these policies, Clinton said years later, he "sought guid-
ance in the example of President Nixon, who came to the presidency at
a time in our history when Americans were tempted to say, 'We've had
enough of the world.' But President Nixon knew we had to continue
to reach out to old friends and to old enemies alike. He knew America
could not quit the world."[43]

A dedicated liberal would not have pursued these policies. But
Clinton didn't govern as a liberal Democrat; he couldn't afford to. Nor
was he a conservative by any definition. He was, like Nixon, a pragmatic
visionary who saw the complexities of global and domestic politics
and the necessity for acting with firm principles but free of ideological
commitments. That freedom from ideology is also what distinguished
him from his Republican opposition—and especially from his chief foil,
Newt Gingrich.

Triangulating and Marginalizing

On November 8, 1994, the House of Representatives fell to the
Republicans in an electoral earthquake: the GOP picked up an amazing
fifty-four seats, gaining its first majority since the 1950s. The new House
speaker would be Newt Gingrich, whose Contract with America was
the campaign platform for many incoming House freshmen. Gingrich
set out a legislative agenda in which he sought to pass into law as many
items from the contract as possible. Many commentators compared it
with FDR's first one hundred days in office. *Time* and *Newsweek* put
Gingrich on the cover; he was a star player on the front page of the *New
York Times* seemingly daily. To some, it even seemed that Gingrich was
president, not Clinton.

This was a time of crisis in Clinton's presidency. In the winter of
1994 and 1995, I was called in as a strategic advisor for the president's
reelection campaign, which at that time looked problematic: Clinton's
approval ratings had dipped below 40 percent. He knew that he had
moved too far left since his centrist campaign for president. "I'm way
out of position," he told me in our first meeting. I made a broad range

of recommendations, all built around repairing his image and reminding voters that he was not an ideological liberal but could govern practically and effectively—and in ways that had direct bearing on their lives. I urged the president to present himself as a fiscal conservative and push for a balanced budget. We did a skillful ad buy for the crime bill that helped turn the public in Clinton's favor on the issue. But it took some time to slow down Gingrich's momentum.

In April 1995, Clinton held a prime-time presidential news conference that only one of the three major networks thought worth carrying. One reporter asked Clinton whether he felt he was still "relevant." It was a stark question to ask a president in just his third year, but he fielded it in dead earnest.

"I am relevant," he insisted. "The Constitution gives me relevance. A president, especially an activist president, has relevance."[44] He didn't sound very convincing.

The next day, an explosion ripped apart the Alfred P. Murrah Federal Building in Oklahoma City, killing 168 civilians, including children in a day care center. It was the worst terrorist attack on American soil in the nation's history. Within a few days, the perpetrator had been caught: Timothy McVeigh, a Gulf War veteran who for years had harbored a growing fury against Washington and its policies, its treatment of veterans, and its betrayal, as he saw it, of America's founding principles. McVeigh thus became the most infamous face of the militia movement of the 1990s, whose members often trained in paramilitary style, stockpiled ammunition, referred to Washington as a tyrannical government, warned about violent confrontation—and sometimes sought it.

Though Gingrich and his House caucus had never openly defended militia groups or other extremists, their over-the-top antigovernment rhetoric, especially as magnified on talk radio, seemed, at least thematically, to be of a piece with it. In the ashes of Oklahoma City, as Clinton moved to comfort survivors and grieving families with his formidable interpersonal gifts, he began to find his political footing. As speechwriter Michael Waldman recalled: "It was the nation's first exposure to Clinton as mourner in chief.... In fact, it was the first time Clinton had been a reassuring figure rather than an unsettling one."[45]

It was also, as Clinton saw it, the first opportunity he had had in months to strike back at his opposition. And, in a Nixonian gambit, he took it. He warned the public about the dangers of extremist political rhetoric—whether from talk radio hosts like Rush Limbaugh or from right-wing GOP congressmen. While Clinton made clear that he was not blaming Republicans for Oklahoma City, he skillfully suggested a linkage between extremist rhetoric and extremist *behavior*. And some Republicans *did* say things that sounded like defenses of the militias; Clinton made them pay for it.

"There is nothing patriotic about hating your country," Clinton said at a Michigan State commencement, "or pretending that you can love your country but despise your government."[46] Many years later, in his memoir, *My Life*, Clinton wrote that "the haters and extremists didn't go away, but they were on the defensive, and, for the rest of my term, would never quite regain the position they had enjoyed after Timothy McVeigh took the demonization of government beyond the limits of humanity."[47]

Oklahoma City was the turning point of Clinton's presidency. His compassionate dealings with the victims; his outrage at what had occurred; and his eloquent rhetoric against extremism and antigovernment fanaticism resonated with millions of Americans—many of whom were already becoming worried about how far the Republicans really wanted to take their Gingrich revolution. It turned out that McVeigh, Peter Keating wrote years later, hadn't just destroyed the Murrah Building; he had also "detonated his own fringe," discrediting extreme right-wing politicians in the eyes of millions of moderate voters and positioning Clinton as the viable presidential candidate in 1996. Before Oklahoma City, Clinton's chances in 1996 looked uncertain. After the bombing, it slowly became evident that no Republican had much chance to beat him.

Clinton kept twisting the knife in, too—another Nixonian lesson. He made sure that the Republicans, and the voters, would never forget Oklahoma City. The following year, during his State of the Union address, he spotlighted an individual American hero—Richard Dean, a Vietnam veteran who had rushed in and out of the Murrah Building several times that day to pull survivors to safety. The House chamber stood as one to acknowledge the hero. But Clinton wasn't through.

"Richard Dean's story doesn't end there," Clinton said. "This last November, he was forced out of his office when the government shut down. And the second time the government shut down, he continued helping Social Security recipients, but he was working without pay." The chamber grew quiet, and the president said: "I challenge all of you in this chamber: Never, ever shut the federal government down again."[48]

The shutdown had taken place a month earlier, in December 1995. It stemmed from the inability of the Republicans and the Clinton administration to come to an agreement on a budget deal. From the start, the shutdown was unpopular with Americans—many of them federal employees who couldn't go to work. So when Clinton highlighted an individual victim of the shutdown, he chose a potent symbol. When that victim also happened to be a hero with ties to the rescue effort in Oklahoma City, the symbolism was devastating. One could almost sense Republicans wanting to crawl under their seats.

The shutdown was the beginning of the end for Gingrich. He had begun 1995 seeming to hold all the cards in his battle with Clinton, but he ended it reeling from a shift in political momentum that could scarcely be imagined. Gingrich and the GOP had pushed hard for a balanced-budget amendment, and Gingrich came up with a budget proposal that would cut *$1 trillion* and eliminate 280 federal programs. The conservative caucus in the House was strong enough to pass the bill, but it got no further. Clinton went on the attack, armed with polling that I had done with him, showing that the American people were with him on the issue. He warned that the Republican proposals were callous to the poor and elderly. The president skillfully tapped into seniors' fears about Medicare cuts, and Republican poll numbers dropped as the battle intensified into the fall. Finally, with Clinton refusing to come to terms with Republican proposals that he considered extreme and unacceptable, Gingrich went nuclear—he threatened a government shutdown.

"President Clinton can run the parts of the government that are left, or he can run no government," Gingrich boasted. "Which of the two of us do you think worries more about the government not showing up?"[49]

But Gingrich misread the situation. He was slow to realize that even before the shutdown, Americans placed more of the blame on him and his party for the impasse than they did on the White House. The first shutdown lasted for five days and the second shutdown for twenty-one; in all, eight hundred thousand federal workers were idle.

Gingrich's ego and vision, which had propelled him to power, were also his downfall, because their flip side was egomania and petulance. The moment that crystalized Gingrich's volatility—and Clinton's comparative steadiness—was an imbroglio on Air Force One, on the flight home from Israel for the funeral of Yitzhak Rabin. Accounts vary, but Gingrich let it be known that he was "insulted" and "appalled" that the president didn't invite him and Senate Majority Leader Bob Dole to the front of the plane to discuss the budget impasse. He also objected to having to leave the plane by the back exit, though Clinton said that that the back exit was closer to the cars waiting to take the passengers home. At any rate, Gingrich made a stink about it, and he was pilloried in the media for doing so, especially by the *New York Daily News*, which ran an infamous cover cartoon showing Gingrich wearing diapers, with the headline "CRYBABY: NEWT'S TANTRUM: HE CLOSED DOWN THE GOVERNMENT BECAUSE CLINTON MADE HIM SIT AT THE BACK OF PLANE."[50]

Republicans never recovered from the shutdown, which infuriated millions of Americans. Heading into his reelection campaign, Clinton would skillfully use the Nixon lessons of triangulation, tailoring Republican policies to make them more responsive to voters' concerns, while also distinguishing himself from traditional liberals. His signing of the welfare bill in August 1996, just weeks before the traditional Labor Day kickoff for the general election campaign, sealed the deal. Enough Americans now believed that Clinton was a true centrist—and a more balanced, moderate, and compassionate leader than Bob Dole, his 1996 Republican opponent. They reelected him by a wide margin in the election.

I've always been proud of my role in helping President Clinton get reelected, and as a lifelong Democrat, I've always rejected the argument, made by some on the left, that Clinton ran as a Republican. Hardly. Bill Clinton was and still is a Democrat all the way. He always believed that government had a role to play in people's lives. And this was, in a sense, the purpose of his presidency: to redeem government as a limited-but-active, practical, and positive force in American life.

Winning a second term was sweet vindication for Clinton, as sweet as Nixon's reelection had been in 1972, even if Clinton's margin came nowhere near what Nixon had achieved. Yet, like Nixon, Clinton would face a constitutional crisis in his second term. Where Nixon's had been caused by his paranoia, Clinton's was the product of hubris. The Monica Lewinsky affair would force Clinton, just as Watergate had forced Nixon, to fight for his political life using every instinct at his command.

The Survivor

The parallels between Nixon and Clinton became truly dramatic in 1998, when Clinton faced a crisis that culminated in impeachment, an outcome Nixon had avoided only by resigning. And, as it had with Nixon, the scandal that led to the crisis damaged the considerable success Clinton had achieved in bipartisan leadership; after the Monica Lewinsky scandal, he had more difficulty transcending partisanship, since he had become such a lightning rod himself. Watergate and the Lewinsky matter effectively prevented both men from capitalizing on their hard-earned resurrections after others had written them off. Now, they had to rise from the ashes again.

I won't rehash the extensive details of the Monica Lewinsky episode. Presumably, most readers know the broad outlines: that the matter stemmed from an earlier sexual harassment suit filed against Clinton by Paula Jones; that the Jones suit would likely have petered out had not the Supreme Court, on May 27, 1997, unanimously denied Clinton's request to delay the lawsuit until he left office; that Lewinsky, who was having an affair with the president, had sworn an affidavit in the Jones case; that when Lewinsky's friend and fellow Pentagon employee, Linda Tripp, discovered this, she delivered secretly recorded telephone conversations between Clinton and Lewinsky to Kenneth Starr, the independent counsel investigating Clinton on Whitewater and other matters; and that Starr then pursued testimony from the president himself regarding his relationship with Lewinsky, testimony in which, so Starr and his team alleged, the president had committed perjury.

News on Lewinsky first hit in January 1998, and Clinton, like Nixon before him, vigorously denied all charges. At this point, long before his legal difficulties in the case, Clinton firmly denied that he had any relationship with Lewinsky. He angrily denied the allegations put forth in brief questions from reporters:

> Now, I have to go back to work on my State of the Union speech. And
> I worked on it until pretty late last night. But I want to say one thing to

the American people. I want you to listen to me. I'm going to say this again. I did not have sexual relations with that woman, Miss Lewinsky. I never told anybody to lie, not a single time—never. These allegations are false. And I need to go back to work for the American people.[51]

It was hard to miss the parallels to Nixon's televised denials of culpability for Watergate, including his most famous disavowal: "People have got to know whether or not their President is a crook. Well, I'm not a crook. I've earned everything I've got."[52]

Armed with the Tripp tapes, Starr eventually deposed the president in the matter, and in August 1998 Clinton was forced to deliver grand jury testimony to Starr and his investigative team. Barely concealing his contempt, Clinton gave Starr responses worded with excruciating care, including the infamous "It depends on what the meaning of the word 'is' is," as a reply to Starr's request that the president characterize the truthfulness of the statement "There is not a sexual relationship, an improper sexual relationship or any other kind of improper relationship."[53] That put the president in line for perjury allegations, which would eventually be used, along with obstruction of justice and two other charges, as grounds for impeaching him. Polls showed that Americans had lost respect for Clinton on character and integrity but opposed any attempt to drive him from office.

Republicans, confident that they had the president reeling, made impeaching Clinton a campaign issue in the midterm elections, traditionally a good time for the party out of the White House. When the returns came in, though, they had lost four seats, barely holding their House majority. It was one of the only times in the twentieth century that the president's party picked up seats in an off-year election. The midterm defeat spelled doom for Gingrich, who would complete one of the most precipitous falls in American political history by resigning as speaker and then from Congress. It was later revealed that he was having his own extramarital affair during this time.

Still, the Republicans were undaunted and pushed on for impeachment. It is impossible to dismiss the lingering power of Watergate in motivating them to destroy Clinton. For twenty years, they had lived under the shadow of Nixon's fall, which many felt—with some justification—had been driven by Democrats' desire to destroy him. Now they found the temptation to go after a Democratic president irresistible. In December 1998, the House approved two articles of impeachment, charging Clinton with perjury and obstruction of justice. The twenty-one-day impeachment trial began in the Senate in January 1999, but Clinton was acquitted of all charges brought in the impeachment. Remarkably, his standing in polls only improved, reaching the high point of his presidency—73 percent—while Republicans saw their numbers plummet. Clinton would finish his second term with a 68 percent approval rating, the highest of any departing president measured since Harry Truman.[54]

Here the Watergate-Lewinsky parallel breaks down: Watergate ended Nixon's political career; impeachment damaged Clinton, to be sure, but its impact proved more destructive, at least in the near term, to the Republicans. Where Nixon had to wait for an extended postpresidency to achieve some measure of redemption—the subject of chapter 10— Clinton revived his fortunes while president, surviving the impeachment ordeal and rallying in his final two years in office. Not that there weren't costs: Clinton saw them firsthand in 2000, when he was unable to get his vice president across the finish line in a presidential election that should have been the Democrats' for the taking. The ultimate victim of impeachment was not Clinton or the GOP, but Al Gore.

It would have been fascinating to see Nixon's reaction to the Clinton impeachment and to Clinton's battle for survival. Though Nixon would have been repulsed by Clinton's behavior, he also would have admired the president's bare-knuckled determination to fight back and his effectiveness at turning the tables on his enemies. We'll never know for certain what his reaction would have been, since Nixon died in 1994, four years before the impeachment saga began. But we do know that in Clinton's brief presidency up to that time, the two men had forged an unlikely—or not so unlikely—relationship.

The Clinton-Nixon Relationship

"The test of great leadership is to overcome adversity," read a handwritten letter that president-elect Bill Clinton received on November 4, 1992. "The strongest steel must pass through the hottest fire. In enduring that ordeal you have demonstrated that you have the character to lead not just America but the forces of peace and freedom in the world." It was signed Richard M. Nixon.[55] Nixon was determined to reach out to the new president and have an influence. In his note, he invoked the relationships of past presidents and current White House occupants. While Nixon was laying it on a bit thick, he genuinely admired Clinton's political skills—especially since, in January 1992, with Governor Clinton reeling under scandals involving alleged extramarital affairs, Nixon had considered his presidential candidacy to be finished.

"Clinton is a pretty boy who doesn't quite have it together," Nixon had said to Monica Crowley. "He's a waffle and an opportunist, and I don't think he has much of a chance. This race is Bush's to lose."[56] Nixon also considered Clinton to be a "moral disaster." As he told Crowley,

> A candidate for the presidency, a man seeking to be commander in chief of the armed forces, should have a higher sense of honor than that displayed by Bill Clinton in his young adulthood. His opposition to the war was not the issue. Those who joined the service made the choice and made the sacrifice. Draft resisters who went to jail or into exile made their choice and made sacrifices for their principles. But those children of privilege who defrauded the draft board and, like Clinton, demonstrated against the war on foreign soil evaded the choice, the sacrifice, and the honor.[57]

But when Clinton became "the comeback kid," rallying to become the front-runner in the Democratic primaries and eventually securing the nomination, Nixon could sense a political kinship between them. Even if he hadn't, he would have pursued a relationship with the new president, anyway. He had done that with each of his successors, though none of them had wanted him to visit the White House. At first, it seemed that Clinton would be no different.

Nixon's initial overture went unanswered. Disappointed, he blamed the nonresponse on Hillary, whom he considered "a real lefty, like Eleanor Roosevelt."[58] She had, after all, served on the staff advising the House Judiciary Committee during Watergate. But Nixon persisted. He enlisted some old Washington hands—Bob Dole, Roger Stone, and others—to prevail upon Clinton to reach out to the former president. That didn't work, either, so finally Nixon put the word out that he was writing an op-ed for the *New York Times* on foreign policy, summarizing his insights from a recent trip to Russia. He could be harsh or gentle toward Clinton when he wrote the article, he said; that would depend on how the administration treated him. The prospect of Nixon undermining Clinton's foreign policy in the *New York Times* did the trick: The White House got in touch with Nixon immediately, setting up a phone call. Nixon would describe it as "the best conversation with a president I've had since I was president."[59] As he later told Monica Crowley:

> [Clinton] was very respectful but with no sickening bullshit. To give you a quick overview, he only spent one third of the time on foreign policy, mostly Russia, but he asked about China also. He said that he was worried that his defense cuts may be too steep; of course he may just have said that because I'd be against cutting defense too much. But he likes to talk, and he was candid on aid to Russia. I gave him the highlights of what we found. He asked what I thought of Yeltsin, and he said he admired his guts for seeing him when Clinton was a candidate.[60]

Nixon was clearly flattered and pleased that Clinton would consult him. "I *never* had such a conversation with Reagan," he told Crowley, and he described his discussions with President Bush as stilted. "This was a different cup of tea," he said. "He really let his hair down." And then he paid Clinton what might be, in the Nixon universe, the ultimate compliment: "This guy does a lot of thinking."[61]

He was impressed by Clinton's intellectual curiosity. Perhaps more than anything else, a Clinton gesture at the end of the phone call made the most lasting impression. "He invited me to the White House," Nixon told Crowley. "In twelve years, neither Reagan nor Bush *ever* put me on the White House schedule or put a picture out."[62]

A few days later, on March 8, 1993, Nixon met with Clinton in the White House family quarters. They spoke mostly about Russia, but the two presidents also covered China, health care, and even Clinton's weight during the past year's primary campaign.[63] Nixon came and went by a back entrance, but the White House made no effort to cover up the visit, disclosing both the in-person meeting and the earlier phone conversation.[64]

"More than anything else," the journalist R. W. Apple Jr. wrote, "it was Russia—long a preoccupation of Mr. Nixon, now one of the biggest problems facing Mr. Clinton—that sealed their relationship."[65] Clinton considered it "the best conversation I've had in the White House." In his *Times* op-ed, Nixon praised Clinton's "gutsy support" of Boris Yeltsin and attacking the "advocates of inaction" in Russian affairs.[66] As Nixon saw it, American support for Yeltsin, a democratically elected, Western-friendly leader, could not be strong enough.

After the meeting, Nixon sent Clinton a follow-up letter. Clinton told his aides, "I was incredibly impressed with the energy and rigor he brought to analyzing [Russia]."[67] Indeed, Clinton often expressed admiration for what he called Nixon's "lucidity." When Nixon had a stroke in April 1994, Clinton told David Gergen, "I hope it hasn't affected his mind."[68]

Though he would have his frustrations with Clinton, Nixon was generally impressed. A few weeks after their White House visit, Nixon received a signed photo from Clinton, asking Nixon to reciprocate. "In the end," Roger Stone wrote, "Mr. Nixon came to like Mr. Clinton and had enormous respect for his political talents. 'You know that bit he does where he bites his lip and looks like he is pondering the question?' he asked me. 'I think it's practiced, but let me tell you, it's great television.'"[69]

Clinton gave Nixon new legitimacy by inviting him back to the White House and consulting him as a sage on foreign policy. "Clinton had done more to restore Nixon to the center of power than anyone else had apart from Nixon himself," Crowley wrote.[70] "What's interesting," commented David Brinkley, "was how Nixon was able to start rehabilitating himself and had been shunned largely by Reagan and Bush and was welcoming an overture with the new Democratic president. And Clinton took it."[71]

Thus one could hear the note of regret in Clinton's voice on the evening of April 26, 1994, when he stepped outside the White House Rose Garden to meet briefly with the press and announce Nixon's death. "It's impossible to be in this job without feeling a special bond with the people who have gone before," he said, noting how he had called on Nixon many times and always relished hearing his thoughts on matters of the day.[72] Years later, at a video tribute at the Nixon Presidential Library, Clinton said: "After he died, I found myself wishing I could pick up the phone and ask President Nixon what he thought about this issue or that problem, particularly if it involved Russia. I appreciated his insight and advice and I'm glad he chose, at the end of his life, to share it with me."[73]

Clinton even offered to give Nixon a state funeral, which the Nixon family graciously declined. They did accept the president's declaration of a national day of mourning for Nixon.[74] Clinton was eager, as David Gergen remembered, "to do this in a first-rate way."[75] His eulogy for the former president, given at the funeral held for Nixon in Yorba Linda met that standard. It was hard to miss the symbolism of the first baby boomer president eulogizing a man who had come to represent everything that generation had taught itself to hate. Yet Nixon had died honorably, defiant to the end, and at least one representative of the generation that had helped bring him down, Bill Clinton, had found it necessary to beat a path back to his door.

The parallel lines of the Clinton and Nixon presidencies—and with them, two generations in American postwar history—finally intersected in the eighteen months of their fascinating relationship. More than anything else, the Clinton-Nixon relationship underscored the prevailing influence of Richard Nixon on American political life.

The Road Not Taken

"Richard Nixon and Bill Clinton were the two most gifted presidents of the past thirty years," David Gergen wrote. "Each was inordinately bright, well read, and politically savvy. Each reveled in power. Nixon was the best strategist in the office since Eisenhower and possibly since Woodrow Wilson; Clinton was the best tactician since Lyndon Johnson and possibly Franklin Roosevelt. Yet each was the author of his downfall. Nixon let his demons gain ascendance, and Clinton could not manage the fault lines in his character."[76]

Despite his failings, Bill Clinton left office in January 2001 with the highest approval ratings of any departing president since the statistic began being measured. Though his tenure was marked by partisan warfare, political scandal, and finally impeachment, his policies exemplified centrism, compromise, and ideological moderation. Clinton had learned the Nixon lessons well: redeem your own party's public appeal by isolating its most untenable factions; co-opt the good parts of the opposition party while marginalizing the rest; and above all, speak to central American concerns and values. Clinton's outgoing approval numbers testified to his success on all these counts.

And yet, the Clinton model, like the Nixon model before it, would not be emulated by his successors—and here we come to the final parallel between the two presidents. In the same way as Nixon left the White House with partisan warfare boiling, and resurgent liberals winning seats in Congress and the ground shifting toward conservatives in the GOP, Clinton left office with a conservative movement hungry to regain the White House and a liberal wing of the Democratic Party that was resentful of its marginalization, eager to reclaim power. In both cases, these determined ideological forces—along with world-changing events—would shape the American political landscape in the decade to come.

CHAPTER 8

They Didn't Listen to Nixon

Foreign Policy and Polarization under Bush and Obama

So it is the policy of the United States to seek and support the growth of demo-cratic movements and institutions in every nation and culture, with the ultimate goal of ending tyranny in our world.

—PRESIDENT GEORGE W. BUSH, 2005[1]

My kind of realism would look at what are the most likely consequences of push-ing out a government. What will replace it?

—BRENT SCOWCROFT[2]

The pendulum always swings too far. Obama the restrainer has been the great corrective to Bush the decider. Far from the magician imagined back in 2008, Obama has been the professional moderator. But the president has gone too far; and in so doing has undersold the nation, encouraged foes, disappointed allies, and created doubts over American power that have proved easy to exploit.

—ROGER COHEN[3]

The presidencies of George W. Bush and Barack Obama mean dif-ferent things to different people, but in ways rarely remarked upon, they both represent a failure to learn from Nixon's lessons, especially in foreign policy, but also in domestic political coalition building. By fail-ing in this latter area, Bush and Obama helped to polarize the American electorate to levels not imagined in Nixon's day. As I have written before, while Nixon certainly polarized the parties, he used the polarization to build majorities —at the peak of his power, this amounted to a vast and unrivalled majority in American electoral history. Bush and Obama did nothing of the kind. Instead, they polarized to maximize their base turnout, ensuring their reelections but little else. They did not expand their party's coalitions.

It is in foreign policy, however—with which I will be predomi-nantly concerned here—that we see most starkly how Nixon's achieve-ments were so difficult to maintain and perpetuate. Bush's presidency, framed by the 9/11 attacks, became defined by the Iraq War, a preemptive war of choice that highlighted a Republican Party split between the neoconservatives, who supported the 2003 invasion, and Nixonian realists, most of whom opposed it. The neoconservatives had been riding nearly two decades of momentum by 2003, heartened by the bold and successful foreign policy of Ronald Reagan. Once the planes hit the Twin Towers in September 2001, the case for an aggressive, even crusading American foreign policy held a strong hand. But the Iraq War became a national catastrophe, undermined by the administration's overly ambitious goals and extreme negligence in postinvasion planning and consideration of contingencies, especially the insurgency that would rip Iraq apart. Though Bush made a courageous, and to a considerable extent successful, effort to salvage Iraq with the surge of 2007, by the end of his presidency only his devoted loyalists would call his foreign policy a success. The war had simply been too costly, in blood, treasure, and political capital.

Obama, meanwhile, would campaign for the presidency in 2008, running explicitly against the Bush neoconservative vision and often sounding like he wanted to restore the realism of Nixon and of Bush's father, George H. W. Bush. Once in office, however, Obama proved to be neither a consistent neoconservative nor a realist. His foreign policy would show a predominant lack of vision and consistency, fatally undermined by his lack of conviction about the role of American power in the world—a subject about which, it should be said, realists and neoconservatives had strong views, if different ones. Obama's failure to appreciate the role of deterrent capability in foreign policy led to a series of damaging decisions, such as his drawing of a "red line" in Syria and then backing away from it; his premature withdrawal of troops in Iraq—which set the stage for the rise of Isis, or the Islamic State; his unwillingness to confront Vladimir Putin; and his needless antagonism toward proven allies, especially Israel. The result is a less secure United States, for entirely different reasons than under George W. Bush.

Nixon wouldn't have made such negligent moves, because he understood the uses of power much better than Obama has. Conversely, he wouldn't have launched the Iraq War, because he understood the limits of power much better than Bush did. He also had better advisers than both Obama and Bush have had. Nixon, after all, was the president who opened relations with the Communist Chinese, a world-shaping event that also gave him leverage with the principal adversary of the United States, the Soviet Union. Nixon's forging of what he would later call "hard détente" brought him his share of criticism from hawkish critics—but then, in 1973, during the Middle East's Yom Kippur War, he showed his own hawkishness, demonstrating his understanding of how power had to be exercised in different ways in different situations. His foreign policy, as I previously mentioned, magisterially blended practicality with vision and strategic clarity.

In their own ways, then, Bush and Obama spurned the lessons of Nixon—which were complex and subtle, involving the most vital issue facing any president: the uses and limits of American power. The presidents each represented, in their own ways, their own parties' reactions to Nixonian realism: a neoconservative rejection of realism, in Bush's case, and, in Obama's case, a rudderless—and faithless—exercise of American power. And, beyond foreign policy, both Bush and Obama presided over the most polarizing eras in recent American history, heading up parties that seemed relentlessly driven by their ideological poles—continuing a process that Nixon had set in motion.

George W. Bush and the Rejection of Nixonian Realism

George W. Bush entered the White House with a partisan target on his back. He had won the presidency only after the Supreme Court halted an historic recount in the state of Florida. The knowledge that Bush only prevailed in Florida after the court stepped in—leaving the final result of a recount forever unknown—and, perhaps worse, the fact that he had lost the popular vote to Al Gore, made many liberals view him as an illegitimate president. He wouldn't have enjoyed much bipartisan feeling even if these things weren't the case—the campaign had been hard fought and close, and the bitter feelings between the parties after the Clinton impeachment saga remained strong. Still, the extraordinary circumstances of his victory put Bush in an unenviable position.

Bush's first eight months on the job were relatively uneventful, though they involved plenty of partisan battles. Democratic bitterness over the election remained, and Bush's policy proposals—like implementing sweeping tax cuts and oil drilling in Alaska—ignited furious opposition. In the first days of September of 2001, the president's approval rating was at 51 percent, a decent number, though low for such a new president, and one reflecting an already-sharp partisan divide. Then the planes hit the towers in New York.

What many Americans don't remember today about Bush is that he ran for office in 2000 touting a realist foreign policy. In the presidential debates, he talked of his belief in a "humble" foreign policy and disdained the practice of "nation building." It would have been challenging for any president, even the most committed realist, to maintain a sense of restraint after the attacks, which transformed Bush, for a time, from a polarizing president to a unifying national leader. Most Democrats and Republicans agreed that the administration had to go after the Taliban in Afghanistan, as Bush would order starting in October 2001. He moved with nearly unprecedented national support: The week after the attacks, his approval rating had gone up an unprecedented thirty-five points, to 86 percent. For the next twelve months, his rating would not dip below 65 percent, and even on the eve of the midterm elections of 2002, it stood at 63 percent.[4] By then, Bush had shepherded the American war in Afghanistan that overthrew the Taliban, decimated al-Qaeda training camps there, and nearly captured Osama bin Laden. (Only in later years would our gains in Afghanistan come to look ephemeral and the failure to capture bin Laden become a damning indictment of the administration.) Now, Bush was eyeing the next step in what he had dubbed the "War on Terror"—a potential invasion of Iraq.

Here was where the realist-neoconservative fissure became unavoidable.

The neoconservatives differed from the realists in definitive, fundamental ways. Principally, the difference involved how they saw the role of American power in the world. Neoconservatives embraced a forceful exercise of American power, both because our military might was unequalled and because our democratic values represented the best hope for the world. Democratization, the neoconservatives believed, would bring peace and eventually prosperity to trouble spots in the world, especially in the Middle East.

After 9/11, the argument became more urgent: Not only did the United States need to combat terrorism where it existed, the country also needed to take the long view. The only way to stamp out the problem of Islamic extremism and terrorism, according to the neoconservatives, was to bring democracy to the autocratic regimes of the region—especially the ones hostile to the United States—over time. The regime that headed this list, for the neoconservatives, was that of Saddam Hussein, ruling Iraq. And even as American forces routed the Taliban from Kabul, plans were afoot in the Bush administration to pursue "regime change" in Iraq, where Hussein would be overthrown and the way would be paved for what, neoconservatives believed, would be a pro-American democratic state in the heart of the Middle East. Iraq would then serve as the tipping point for a regional transformation.

It would be hard to come up with a vision more at odds with the Nixon-Kissinger realist foreign policy vision—a vision advocated, with subtle variations, by such advisers of post-Nixon presidents as Brent Scowcroft, Zbigniew Brzezinski, Strobe Talbott, and James Baker. Yet the seeds of the second Iraq war were sowed during the first—the Gulf War of 1991, when the United States under President George H. W. Bush drove Saddam Hussein from Kuwait but stopped short of Baghdad, leaving the dictator in place. The advocates of the new war in Iraq were in effect offering a critique of the limited, bloodless approach of the realists backing George H. W. Bush. One of those realists had been Dick Cheney, who had been the elder Bush's defense secretary and was now Bush the younger's vice president. In 1991, Cheney had defended the decision not to go to Baghdad; now he was the principal advocate for invading Iraq and deposing Saddam Hussein.

The Iraq War can be seen as the culmination of two decades of conservative disquiet that came about with the approach of the Nixonian realists, motivated initially by the Iranian Revolution and Soviet invasion of Afghanistan. Even before 9/11, the neoconservative critique grew in power and force, greatly emboldened by the principled and idealistic foreign policy of Ronald Reagan. The Nixonian realists had been skeptical about Reagan—as had Nixon himself—seeing him as simplistic and, worse, as dangerously confrontational. Yet the Cold War had ended in a spectacular victory for the United States and the West, and it had brought about the dissolution of the Soviet Union itself—an almost-unimaginable result even a decade earlier, yet one that Reagan had predicted would happen someday. Thus came the newfound confidence of the neoconservatives in shaping an international environment more in line with American values.

"To many," wrote William Kristol and Robert Kagan, two leading neoconservative critics and thinkers, "the idea of America using its power to promote changes of regime in nations ruled by dictators rings of utopianism. But in fact, it is eminently realistic. There is something perverse in declaring the impossibility of promoting democratic change abroad in light of the record of the past three decades."[5]

In retrospect, it seems clear that the momentum toward a second Iraq war was almost inevitable after 9/11. It was a war that had its genesis in the ideas of a spectrum of figures with loose or direct ties to the Nixon administration: former Nixon staffers Dick Cheney and Donald Rumsfeld, described by Francis Fukuyama as "Jacksonian nationalists,"[6] though more commonly identified today as neoconservatives, and also by traditional neoconservatives, embodied by people like Elliott Abrams, Paul Wolfowitz, Richard Perle, and Paul Bremer. Some of the latter group, like Abrams, started out as aides to Scoop Jackson before switching over to Nixon. The neoconservative caucus also included leftover JFK Democrats, most prominently Senator Joseph Lieberman, author of the 1998 Iraq Liberation Act, which made the rollback of Saddam's regime the policy of the United States—in name at least—even before 9/11. Both groups grew in stature because of Reagan's achievements and the conservative critique of the realists.

The odd group out, of course, in the run-up to the Iraq War was the realists, though they were not completely unrepresented. After all, Bush's secretary of state was Colin Powell, a skeptic about invading Iraq and a former aide to Bush's father, whom he had served as head of the Joint Chiefs during the Gulf War.

"I tried to avoid this war," Powell wrote years later—perhaps self-servingly, since he previously climbed on board to support the war and made a famous, or infamous, presentation at the UN to justify the American invasion. The former secretary of state, having left office, now cast himself as a reluctant participant in the run-up to the Iraq invasion:

> I went to the president in August of 2002, after coming back from a trip and seeing all the planning that was under way, and we had a long meeting upstairs in the residence.... For the better part of two and a

half [hours], I took him through not only the military planning that was being done in the Pentagon but... through the consequences of going into an Arab country and becoming the occupiers.[7]

As for George H. W. Bush, the dialogue that took place between the two presidents, father and son, leading up to the war has never been revealed. But clearly George W.'s decision to invade Iraq represented a break with the cautious and generally realist foreign policy of his father. Outside the administration, Brent Scowcroft, former national-security adviser under Bush's father, was vocal in his opposition to invading Iraq. Scowcroft's reasoning was classic realism: no nation, not even America, could remake the world.

In the aftermath of the war, many would criticize the Bush administration for its shifting arguments in favor of the invasion. One argument stressed removing Saddam's weapons of mass destruction (WMD), which were said to pose an imminent threat to the United States, especially since, the administration claimed, Saddam might give such weapons to al-Qaeda; another argument promoted the war as an objective to bring democracy to the Middle East. At other points, too, the administration stressed that Saddam had been in violation of UN resolutions on arms for years and should be punished. None of these goals, in the end, would be served, save the deposing of Saddam—punishment enough, one could suppose, for his flouting of UN resolutions. Every other goal of the administration's in Iraq went up in smoke as the insurgency became increasingly grisly, and as domestic support for the venture slowly began to ebb as the horrors increased. Clearly, the fears underlying the realist vision of a world order based in stability, in which rash actions—however ambitious and idealistic—might well do more harm than good, seemed to have been borne out in Iraq. In a 2004 interview with the *Financial Times*, Scowcroft called the war a "failing venture" that had damaged relations between the United States and its allies, especially in Europe.[8]

Scowcroft also told Jeffrey Goldberg of the *New Yorker*:

> I believe that you cannot with one sweep of the hand or the mind
> cast off thousands of years of history.... This notion that inside every
> human being is the burning desire for freedom and liberty, much less

democracy, is probably not the case. I don't think anyone knows what burns inside others. Food, shelter, security, stability. Have you read Erich Fromm, 'Escape from Freedom'? I don't agree with him, but some people don't really want to be free.

Summing up, he said: "My kind of realism would look at what are the most likely consequences of pushing out a government. What will replace it?"[9]

By 2006, the majority of people in the United States had come around to Scowcroft's point of view, and as the years passed, more and more in this country would regard the Iraq War as a mistake, something that America would have been better off not doing. But Bush had won a second term in 2004—at a time when the war had already taken a serious turn for the worse but was not yet viewed as unsalvageable. Despite his administration's mistakes and mismanagement, Bush was able to run as a war leader and gain reelection—especially since the Democrats could not persuade the electorate that in the aftermath of 9/11 they would be the party better suited to handle national-security challenges.

If his foreign policy represented a rejection of Nixonian realism, Bush did channel Nixon politically when it came to the politics of national security. For the better part of six years, he was able to keep the Democratic Party on the defensive about Iraq and the War on Terror, utilizing many of the same themes and motifs that Nixon had deployed in the early 1970s against Democrats in urging withdrawal from Vietnam.

Bush's Nixonian Politics

Americans had never been overwhelmingly in favor of the venture in Iraq, but a solid majority, in 2002, gave the president strong marks on national security, and it seemed clear that, should Bush insist that taking on Saddam Hussein was necessary, Americans would back him.

Democrats seemed to realize it, too, and they found themselves, in the fall of 2002, backed against a wall. Most prominent Democrats were skeptical about the administration's claims that Saddam's WMD—which it was widely assumed he possessed—presented an "imminent" threat to the United States, and they were even more skeptical that a full-scale American invasion was necessary to protect the "homeland" from a terror attack. They questioned why Bush wanted to open a new front in the war, when the battle against al-Qaeda was still raging and Afghanistan needed to be secured further. We hadn't captured bin Laden yet, either—and weren't bin Laden and Saddam enemies, anyway? Yet the Bush administration argued adamantly that there was a terror "nexus" between Iraq and al-Qaeda. That supposed nexus, along with Saddam's purported WMD stockpiles, made for a potent threat, in the minds of many.

And Democrats knew it. They had spent nearly two decades in the "alien box," as Bill Clinton put it, that Richard Nixon had entrapped them in. During the Clinton years, they had begun to come out of it. The American people still gave the GOP an instinctive vote of confidence on national-security issues, but the gap was no longer large enough to do meaningful damage. Democrats wanted to maintain their identity with the American voter as reasonable, patriotic, and tough on national defense.

As Iraq moved to center stage in the political debate, the Democratic Party's most prominent figures would have to make a choice: oppose the administration's policy on Iraq or stand with a Republican president whom they instinctively distrusted and whose aggressive posture was already making them uncomfortable. But Bush's approval rating was still high, and voters still listed terrorism as the top national issue. How could Democrats afford to oppose him?[10]

Republicans, especially Bush strategic guru Karl Rove, could see the opportunity to do what Richard Nixon had done a generation earlier: in effect, to unify the country by dividing it—that is, by marshaling the broad majority of Americans who supported the president post-9/11 and isolate those on the other side who seemed to be on the wrong side. Nixon had done this with Vietnam in his "Silent Majority" speech, proposing policies that the vast majority of the electorate supported, and a smaller, if vocal, minority opposed. Rove now sought to do it in the run-up to the midterm elections, elections in which the party in the White House traditionally fares poorly. Though many expressed doubts about going to war with Iraq, Rove wanted to frame the Iraq issue within the broader context of national security.

"We can go to the country on this issue," Rove told Republicans in strategy meetings, because the voters "trust the Republican Party to do a better job of strengthening America's military might and thereby protecting America."[11]

Perhaps the most infamous formulation of this idea came in the fall of the year, in the Georgia Senate race between Saxby Chambliss and incumbent Democrat Max Cleland, a triple-amputee Vietnam veteran. Painting Cleland, who had been critical of President Bush, as soft on defense and insufficiently focused on winning the War on Terror, the Chambliss ads showed pictures of Cleland just after images of bin Laden appeared on the screen—an old psychological ploy to create a linkage in viewers' minds. In one of the ads, the voice-over warned: "As Americans face terrorists and extremist dictators, Max Cleland runs television ads saying he has the courage to lead." Then it listed Cleland's statements and votes against President Bush, before asserting: "The record proves Max Cleland is just misleading."[12] Cleland and the Democrats were outraged, but the ads were effective, and Chambliss went on to victory, taking a Senate seat away from the Democrats.

Cleland's fate was the nightmare scenario for Democrats. They were determined not to be caught on the wrong side of the new national-security fervor. But they also didn't want to rubber-stamp Bush's "march to war." They resolved to back the president with their votes while laying down warnings with their words.

And so, in the fall of 2002, with the Iraq showdown coming to a head, most leading Democrats took the plunge and voted to give the administration the power to use military force in Iraq. The House endorsed the measure on a 296–133 vote. Only six Republicans voted against it. The Democrats were more split, with 81 siding with Bush and 126 voting against him.[13]

In the Senate, every serious Democratic presidential prospect—along with Democratic Senate leader Tom Daschle—lined up with the White House. The chamber voted for the resolution, 77–23, with twenty-nine of fifty Democrats supporting it.

Not that they didn't try to couch their votes with every nuance they could muster. In her floor speech endorsing the measure, Hillary Clinton laid down some eloquent markers that, she must have hoped, would serve her in good stead should events turn the other way. "Even though the resolution before the Senate is not as strong as I would like in requiring the diplomatic route first and placing highest priority on a simple, clear requirement for unlimited inspections," she said, "I will take the President at his word that he will try hard to pass a UN resolution and will seek to avoid war, if at all possible." She called it "probably the hardest decision I have ever had to make," but cautioned that her vote was not "a vote for any new doctrine of pre-emption, or for unilateralism, or for the arrogance of American power or purpose."[14]

In sum, as Senate staffer Peter Zimmerman put it, "The Democrats were afraid of being seen as soft on Saddam or on terrorism. The whole notion was, 'Let's get the war out of the way as fast as possible and turn back to the domestic agenda.'"[15] But there would be no turning back, both because "getting the war out of the way" would prove impossible and because American voters saw through the Democrats' insincerity.

Now that the war was on, the Democrats did their best to stand behind the effort and especially to be seen as defenders of the troops—in contrast with their image during Vietnam as the party of war protestors. For a brief time, in the spring of 2003, it seemed that their political bets had paid off. Then the insurgency sprouted in summer 2003, picking up momentum in the fall. By early 2004, just in time for primary season, Iraq began spinning out of control. The Democrats' Iraq dilemma had returned.

Howard Dean exemplified the quandary. He became the surprise early front-runner in the Democratic primaries in late 2003 and early 2004 by tapping into discontent with the war. A former governor of Vermont, he had an advantage that Clinton, Kerry, and John Edwards did not possess—he hadn't voted on the congressional war resolution. He made his opposition to the war clear before the invasion, and thus he had credibility on the issue. Through an innovative fundraising and communication apparatus, Dean racked up money and supporters. He favored a withdrawal of US troops from Iraq and their replacement with armed forces from the region. He defended the war in Afghanistan, and in fact called for more US troops there—but in 2004, the war that mattered to voters was Iraq. Dean's candidacy raised the specter of the Democrats nominating an "antiwar" candidate to run against Bush.

That prospect filled the party's power brokers with dread. Like George McGovern, Dean was not the choice of the party establishment, and his opposition to the war in Iraq spoke more to the passions of grassroots activists and the young than to mainstream Democrats. No wonder, then, that the Democratic Leadership Council attacked Dean as representing the "McGovern-Mondale wing" of the Democratic Party, characterized, the DLC said, by "weakness abroad and elitist, interest-group liberalism at home."[16]

"Is Dean another McGovern?" asked Joan Vennochi in the title of a *Boston Globe* column.[17]

The Republicans were already shaping the race, as they had in 2002, along national-security lines. The 2004 election would be a choice between "victory in Iraq or insecurity in America.... As long as George W. Bush is president, the front lines of the War on Terror will be Baghdad and Kandahar, not Boston and Kansas City," said Bush campaign chief Ken Mehlman. "When liberty's survival is threatened by terrorists in Iraq and elsewhere, our leading critics offer weakness and vacillation. Instead of support, they cut and run."[18]

The Democratic mainstream was relieved when Dean faltered and more-centrist Democrats like John Kerry and John Edwards moved to the fore. It would eventually be Kerry—a supporter of the 2002 Iraq resolution—who sewed up the nomination in 2004.

By this point, George W. Bush's sky-high approval numbers were a distant memory. But whatever voters had thought of the president, they knew where he stood. With Kerry, it was never quite as clear. In the tense climate of 2004, Kerry's image as a "man of nuance"[19] turned off many American voters. They saw it as trying to have it both ways. He could never quite explain, for example, whether he felt that his vote for authorizing the war had been a mistake.

Nothing exemplified Kerry's conflicted positions more than his vote on an $87 billion appropriations bill for Iraq in October 2003. At the time, the war had already begun to take a turn for the worse, but Kerry had said a month earlier that however one felt about the war, voting against the appropriations was a vote against our troops. "I don't think any United States senator is going to abandon our troops and recklessly leave Iraq to whatever follows as a result of simply cutting and running," he said. He supported the $87 billion in supplemental funding—provided that the administration rescinded some of its tax cuts to pay for it. The administration refused, and the supplemental-funding bill, without the payment provisions, came up for a vote.

Kerry voted against it.

That would have been bad enough, but Kerry compounded it the following March during a campaign stop. When asked about his vote, he referred to the original version of the bill he had supported and said, "I actually did vote for the $87 billion before I voted against it."

The Republicans portrayed Kerry as unreliable on defense. "My friends," Vice President Dick Cheney began. "On vital matters of national security, Sen. Kerry offers a record of weakness and a strategy of retreat. President Bush offers a record of steady purpose and resolute action and a strategy for victory."[20]

The Bush campaign, like Nixon's 1972 effort, was tough and unrelenting—and it had to be, as the race was close, down to the final day. At every turn, Bush and his surrogates portrayed Kerry's approach to national security as out of step with a post-9/11 age. They said that this was especially true when it came to Kerry's understanding of the War on Terror and his suggestion, on more than one occasion, that it should never have been declared.

"We have to get back to the place we were, where terrorists are not the focus of our lives, but they're a nuisance," Kerry told the *New York Times Magazine* in an October 2004 profile.[21] One of Kerry's foreign policy advisors, Richard Holbrooke, said, "We're not in a war on terror in the literal sense."[22]

The Bush campaign pounced.

Responding to Holbrooke's suggestion that the "War on Terror" was really just a metaphor, like Lyndon Johnson's War on Poverty, the president said: "I've got news. Anyone who thinks we are fighting a metaphor does not understand the enemy we face and has no idea how to win the war and keep America secure."[23]

The campaign tried to reinforce the point with a political ad that reminded viewers old enough to remember of the 1984 "bear in the woods" spot by Ronald Reagan. The original ad had featured a voice-over saying that some people saw the bear and some didn't—metaphors for the Republicans who recognized the national-security challenges posed by the Soviet Union and the Democrats who did not. Now, in the Bush ad, wolves moved toward the camera as a voice-over told listeners that in the 1990s, Kerry had supported cuts to the intelligence budget "so deep they would have weakened America's defenses." And weakness, the ad reminded viewers, "attracts those who are waiting to do America harm."[24]

On election day, Bush won reelection narrowly. This time, he took a majority of the popular vote, though the race came down in the electoral college to the state of Ohio.

If Bush hadn't so successfully revived the Democrats' McGovern image among voters, it's doubtful that he would have beaten Kerry. The Nixonian categories on national defense framed his entire campaign. But those same categories would come back to haunt him when Iraq became an albatross around Republicans' necks.

✫ ✫ ✫ ✫ ✫

For a good while, the Bush administration made political hay out of Democratic divisions on Iraq—and Republicans compared the Democrats' interest in getting out of the war to their dovish tendencies during Nixon's time. "Our country is at war," a Republican National Committee ad intoned. "Our soldiers are watching and our enemies are too. Message to Democrats: Retreat and Defeat is not an option."[25] Or, as Republican House Speaker Dennis Hastert put it, speaking more bluntly: "The Democratic Party sides with those who wish to surrender."[26]

These attacks hit Democrats where they had been vulnerable since McGovern, but as the war wore on, the party's mainstream centrist candidates—Hillary Clinton, John Kerry, John Edwards—also faced increasing pressure from the party's antiwar Left. Slowly but surely, the Democrats became more aggressive in attacking the administration.

As Iraq continued to spiral downward in 2006, the worst year of the insurgency, Democratic withdrawal resolutions were put forward—one from Kerry and one from Senator Russ Feingold—calling for withdrawal by July 2007. Again, the GOP leaders used the Democratic efforts to portray them as unserious about national defense.

Voters had a choice, President Bush said, "between two parties with two different attitudes on this war on terror." Republicans, he said, understood the nature of the enemy and its desire to attack America again, but the Democrats "offer nothing but criticism and obstruction and endless second-guessing."[27]

By November 2006, though, defending the Iraq War had run its course. Voters still worried about Democrats on national security, but they would not reward Republicans with midterm victories. The Democrats won big, taking back both the Senate and the House of

Representatives. It was the beginning of more than a half decade in which the Democrats began to reverse their national-security disadvantage. For Democrats, Iraq had become Vietnam—and George W. Bush had become Richard Nixon.

Iraq as Vietnam, Bush as Nixon

"Iraq is George Bush's Vietnam," Senator Ted Kennedy said in a Washington speech. Later, in a television interview, the senator said, "We're facing a quagmire in Iraq, just as we faced in Vietnam.... We didn't understand what we were getting ourselves into in Vietnam. We didn't understand what we were doing in Iraq. We had misrepresentations about what we were able to do militarily in Vietnam. I think we are finding out that in Iraq as well."[28]

"Surely I am not the only one who hears echoes of Vietnam," said Virginia senator Robert Byrd in April 2004, after the United States had spent a gruesome month in Iraq, with the insurgents killing American contractors and hanging their lifeless bodies from bridges in Fallujah.[29] Byrd, who as a young senator had voted for the Tonkin Gulf Resolution in 1964 authorizing military action in Southeast Asia, noted this war's parallels: a distant foreign war, a muddled set of objectives and justifications, a downward spiral—and a persistent call for staying the course from military planners. April 2004 was a watershed month; the first revelations of the Abu Ghraib scandal also came out during this time. The mounting fiasco in Iraq clearly pushed the Democrats toward a more vocal opposition to the war—and pushed observers across the spectrum toward more Vietnam War analogies.

"Now we have Vietnam [in Iraq]," said retired army general William Nash. "You've got a sovereign government over there, a big embassy, and 140,000 U.S. soldiers. And our ability to influence political decisions is finite."[30]

"Some of the strategic mistakes are very similar," said United States Marine Corps general Anthony Zinni, and explained:

> First of all, in Vietnam we went in with a flawed strategy. Remember, the strategy was that we had to stop communism before the dominoes fell.... The second comparison is trying to draw the American people

into support of the war by cooking the books. We did it with the Gulf of Tonkin situation, where we were led to believe there was an attack on our destroyers while they were innocently in international waters, when they weren't.... And here we have had the case for WMD as an imminent threat for not using international authority to go in.[31]

The deteriorating war effort in Iraq presented Democrats with powerful political opportunities. First, it gave them leverage against Bush and the Republicans in the approaching 2006 midterm elections. Second, more broadly, the failing war gave new empowerment to Democratic doves, who had been sidelined in the run-up to the invasion—and, really, since the ascent of Bill Clinton. Now, facing a war with the potential to shape generational attitudes as Vietnam had, Democrats understood that Iraq gave them a chance not only for political victory but also for transformation of their party.

Though Iraq, as Vietnam had, became a theme for Democrats, it wasn't only Democrats who drew the analogy. Before the invasion, one of the biggest skeptics on the GOP side was US Representative and House Majority Leader Dick Armey. When it became clear that Bush planned to invade, Armey thought of Vietnam and how it had destroyed Lyndon Johnson. He told Bush: "Mr. President, if you go in there, you're likely to be stuck in a quagmire that will endanger your domestic agenda for the rest of your presidency."[32] As the insurgency worsened, Republican senator and later defense secretary (under Obama) Chuck Hagel compared Iraq with Vietnam, another futile war: "The longer we stay in Iraq," Hagel said, "the more similarities will start to develop, meaning essentially that we are getting more and more bogged down, taking more and more casualties, more and more heated dissension and debate in the United States."[33]

Still, Armey's and Hagel's voices were a minority among Republicans in the early stages. Even nominal non-Republicans, like the *New York Times*'s Tom Friedman, resisted making Vietnam-Iraq analogies for a time. Friedman was no fan of Bush, but he supported the invasion, and he was reluctant to see the war become a domestic political linchpin, which would make its successful prosecution nearly impossible. Still, by fall 2006, Friedman conceded that the parallel between the insurgency in Iraq and the Tet Offensive of 1968 had some merit. "The jihadists want to sow so much havoc that Bush supporters will be defeated in the midterms and the president will face a revolt from his own party, as well as from Democrats, if he does not begin a pullout from Iraq.... It would be depressing to see the jihadists influence our politics with a Tet-like media/war frenzy," he said.[34]

And that is precisely what happened. Not only did the war take on the feel of Vietnam in the late sixties and early seventies; its commander in chief also assumed a public image, at least among the opposition, as a man of unmitigated evil and treachery.

When he compared Iraq with Vietnam in 2004, Ted Kennedy completed the analogy by saying that George W. Bush had created "the largest credibility gap since Richard Nixon."[35] Indeed, as Bush's polls plummeted and commentators painted him as a failed president—the worst president ever, according to historian Sean Wilentz—he began to resemble that beleaguered, friendless man who had sat in the Oval Office a generation earlier. In a 2006 Associated Press poll, respondents were asked to rank public figures as "heroes" or "villains." Bush ranked as the top villain, with 25 percent of the vote, well ahead of Osama bin Laden.[36] "A lot of us used to say President Bush will look good and he'll be vindicated in the public eye," said former press spokesman Ari Fleischer. "But realistically speaking, I don't see a lot of the people who write history all of a sudden changing their mind about George W. Bush."[37]

The nature of the Iraq debacle—especially the issue of WMD—also began to heighten Bush's Nixonian profile. An iconic bumper sticker of the era was "Bush Lied, People Died," and books came out with titles like *The Lies of George W. Bush* and *Lies and the Lying Liars Who Tell Them.* Michael Moore built his 2004 blockbuster film, *Fahrenheit 911,* around themes involving Bush's dishonesty. Paul Krugman suggested that Iraq could be the worst lie in American history, making Bush, by extension, a greater villain than Nixon: "The public was told that Saddam posed an imminent threat. If that claim was fraudulent, the selling of the war is arguably the worst scandal in American political history—worse than Watergate, worse than Iran-contra."[38]

No wonder, then, that as Bush's second term wound down, calls for impeaching him were heard on the left. Some of it had gotten started even earlier. In spring 2004, Ralph Nader became the first to call for Bush's impeachment. Branding the president a "messianic militarist" in a speech at the Council on Foreign Relations, Nader said Bush should be impeached, as the Constitution permitted, for high crimes and mis-demeanors—in this case, for taking the nation into war in Iraq "based on false pretenses."[39] A year later, a poll by the conservative-leaning *Rasmussen Reports* found that 32 percent of respondents favored Bush's impeachment and removal from office.[40]

The following year, 2006, Congressman Keith Ellison of Minnesota called for "Watergate-style" hearings on the Bush administration's abuses, as he saw it, of its executive authority, especially as regarded Iraq. "I think that the indications are there have been impeachable offenses committed. But I think that the most important thing is to begin the investigative process, begin the inquiry into these things," he said.[41] Ellison's measure went nowhere, but it was part of an expanding context of condemnation of Bush as a lying, scheming president whose likes hadn't been seen since Nixon.

Even when Bush's time in office neared its end, the Left did not cease in its efforts to bring him down. After first trying to impeach Cheney, Congressman Dennis Kucinich of Ohio introduced thirty-five articles of impeachment against Bush in 2008. The core offense was, again, taking the country to war on false pretenses.[42] Kucinich's efforts never came to a House vote, however, since they were squelched by Nancy Pelosi and Steny Hoyer. They figured efforts were better spent at regaining the White House—which, with the Democrats' new star candidate, Barack Obama, now seemed within reach.

Obama the Candidate: Channeling Nixonian Centrism

Barack Obama and Richard Nixon have about as much in common as fire and ice, but as presidential candidates, they did make similar appeals to common dreams and aspirations during contentious times. In pledging to heal the nation's divisions—those caused not only by the war in Iraq but also more broadly by the ongoing Red-Blue divide—Obama positioned himself as a Nixonian uniter of the center. He got his start on those themes when he came to national prominence in 2004, at the Democratic National Convention, where he delivered an inspirational speech that stressed American unity.

When Obama came on the scene, the most contentious national issue was Iraq—just as, when Nixon resurfaced in 1968, the divisive issue was Vietnam. Obama had an ace up his sleeve that no other serious presidential contenders could boast: he had voted against the war, albeit symbolically, as an Illinois state senator. Thus Hillary Clinton, Joe Biden, and even John Kerry (who some thought might try again for the presidency in 2008) were stuck: Though they had all become critics of the war and of President Bush, they would not admit, at least in 2008, that their votes authorizing military force were mistaken. Their quandary made them look evasive and insincere—lambasting Bush and the war's progress but refusing to take responsibility for their own role in the disaster. Obama, by contrast, had a clear record of opposition to what he had called "a dumb war."

Obama launched his campaign with Iraq as the defining issue separating him from his rivals, especially Hillary Clinton, the front-runner and for many, the presumed nominee. Clinton was hobbled by her determination to stay the centrist course. She was late to recognize that the ground had shifted under the Democrats' feet by 2008, so that her support for the war resolution and her measured criticism of the war since were alienating the liberal activist base that supported Obama. She struggled to square her own centrist credentials—and her more hawkish national-security tendencies—with the need to reach out to the party's antiwar Left. It was a dilemma Obama did not face.

"Even at the time," Obama said of the decision to invade Iraq, "it was possible to make judgments that this would not work out well."[43] He was tireless in touting his judgment to oppose the war while also making clear that he was no George McGovern.

"I am running for President because it's time to turn the page on a failed ideology and a fundamentally flawed political strategy, so that we can make pragmatic judgments to keep our country safe," Obama said. "That's what I did when I stood up and opposed this war from the start, and said that we needed to finish the fight against al Qaeda.... And that's what I'll do as President of the United States."[44]

His formulations were pithy and effective.

"We continue to be in a war that should never have been authorized," he said. "I am proud of the fact that way back in 2002, I said that this war was a mistake."[45]

In a later foreign policy speech, he said: "The first thing we have to do is end this war. And the right person to end it is someone who had the judgment to oppose it from the beginning."[46]

Yet it is important to remember that Obama did not position himself as a standard Democratic "peace" candidate—far from it. Instead, he identified himself as a more restrained advocate of the national interest, one not opposed to all wars by any means; he said that he supported the war in Afghanistan, and he famously (and prophetically, it turned out) said in a presidential debate that he would unilaterally go into Pakistan to get Osama bin Laden if he thought the intelligence was good enough to warrant the move. Obama identified himself with nothing less than foreign policy realism—the approach so identified with Nixon and Henry Kissinger, and to some extent also with Bush's father. And Obama made this connection explicit.

"This is not an argument between Democrats and Republicans," he told David Brooks. "It's an argument between ideology and foreign policy realism. I have enormous sympathy for the foreign policy of George H. W. Bush. I don't have a lot of complaints about their handling of Desert Storm. I don't have a lot of complaints with their handling of the fall of the Berlin Wall."[47]

In 2008, candidate Obama performed something of a Nixonian feat—he ran simultaneously as an unsentimental, levelheaded foreign policy realist, one not afraid to confront America's adversaries, and also as the hope of the antiwar Democratic Left, citing his opposition to the war in Iraq as proof of his credentials. It was a skillful, winning performance, and it won some disgruntled Republicans and foreign policy advisors over to Obama's side in the campaign.

After forty years of dominance on the issue, the Republicans had lost their national-security advantage. Bush's 2007 surge had finally begun to turn things around in Iraq, but from a political standpoint, that was too late—the war in Iraq and all of its costs, human, financial, and political, dominated the 2008 presidential campaign. Most Americans now agreed that going into Iraq was a mistake; they wanted out; and most important of all, they blamed President Bush for it. Thus when John McCain, Obama's hawkish Republican opponent in the campaign, argued for staying the course in Iraq and following most of Bush's policies, Obama told voters that his contender would represent a third Bush term—something that American voters certainly didn't want.

When he entered the White House in 2009, Obama had a chance to build on the Democrats' new image on national security. He wound down the American troop presence in Iraq in 2011, and he began a scheduled withdrawal from Afghanistan. Conservative critics warned that both moves were hasty, and they criticized his posture of "leading from behind," suggesting that America was really losing ground internationally. But politically, getting out of Iraq and Afghanistan was a winner for Obama. Nothing bolstered his standing like the May 2011 killing of Osama bin Laden, in a commando raid ordered by Obama over the objections of some senior advisers. Taking place just months before the tenth anniversary of 9/11, the death of bin Laden set off national celebrations. It seemed that Obama's restrained style of national-security leadership was working. And he ran for reelection in part on his apparent successes as commander in chief.

"You know, in a world of new threats and new challenges, you can choose leadership that has been tested and proven," Obama said. "Four years ago I promised to end the war in Iraq. We did. I promised to refocus on the terrorists who actually attacked us on 9/11, and we have. We've blunted the Taliban's momentum in Afghanistan and in 2014, our longest war will be over. A new tower rises above the New York skyline, al-Qaida is on the path to defeat and Osama bin Laden is dead."[48]

That image was seriously undermined, though, by the attack on the American consulate in Benghazi, Libya, in September 2012—on September 11, in fact. The attack resulted in the death of the American ambassador to Libya, Christopher Stevens, and set off ongoing investigations about the administration's policy in Libya as well as its public explanations of the origins of the attacks, which it had at first attempted to blame on an anti-Islamic video. The assault was, in fact, a terrorist attack, and the administration's deceptions about who knew what, and when, aroused Nixonian questions.

Benghazi occurred just seven weeks before the November election, but it wasn't enough to erase Obama's lead over Mitt Romney. Obama prevailed on election day, winning 51 percent of the vote—he was the first Democratic president to win over 50 percent of the popular vote in two elections since Franklin Roosevelt. But his national-security advantage, and that of his party, soon came crashing down.

Not a Nixonian Realist: Obama Exposed

By midway through his second term, Obama was reeling under one international crisis after another, and resembling George W. Bush in the beleaguered state of his foreign policy. As Obama's own defense secretary, Chuck Hagel, put it in August 2014, the world was "exploding all over."[49] Consider the state of affairs when he spoke.

Americans were trying to come to terms with a world in which Vladimir Putin had illegally seized Crimea; in which twenty thousand Russian troops were massed on the border of Ukraine, ready to invade at a moment's notice; in which Iran moved ever closer to a nuclear capability, thanks to the Obama administration's excessive faith in negotiation and in the Tehran regime's good intentions; in which Iraq was collapsing, overrun by the brutal forces of Isis, or the Islamic State, eradicating all that American forces had achieved in the country; and in which another Israel-Palestine war threatened, with Israel increasingly being criticized in international opinion, even as the country took commonsense measures to defend itself from Hamas rocket attacks. Bloodletting in Syria continued, too, as over 170,000 lives had been lost in the war against Bashar al-Assad—a year after Obama had infamously backed off from his own "red line" in Syria. "The administration has no policy in Syria, has no strategy in Syria," Senator Bob Corker said in 2014.[50] Events since then have not invalidated that judgment.

Further, Obama offered no credible threat that would curtail the development of nuclear weapons in North Korea and Iran. China also continued to support the murderous regime in Pyongyang, which expanded its nuclear arsenal and threatened to provoke a nuclear arms race in East Asia.[51] And in US-China relations, on most substantive issues, Xi Jinping ran circles around Obama in the same way that Putin had done.

In most of these situations, moreover, Obama seemed either unconcerned or caught unawares. He foolishly dismissed Isis as a "JV team" just months before it conquered large swaths of Iraq. He seemed disinterested or timid when it came to Putin's provocations—and seemingly oblivious to any connection the Russian leader's aggression may have had to his decision to remove the missile defense shield from Eastern Europe.

President Obama's obviously sincere desire to spare American armed forces further involvement in world hot spots stems from a wise instinct—an instinct of skepticism and restraint—but it is too often employed as an absolute. In effect, our noninvolvement has real-world costs, often gruesome ones, for millions around the world who thought they might be able to look to America for help. In staying out and letting problem spots fester, Obama has also frittered away American power and prestige. His detachment is a curious legacy for a president who once sought to inspire. As Jennifer Rubin wrote, "Being the author of a 'you're on your own' foreign policy is nothing to brag about, from a geopolitical or moral perspective."[52]

Where the United States had been, for seventy years, the world's lead actor in protecting democratic governments, adjudicating disputes, and putting teeth into UN resolutions, Obama would walk us back into a narrower definition of American capabilities, interests, and options. He offers nothing to counter our allies' growing conviction that the United States is a paralyzed country that they cannot count on for support. "If not letting America have its own way is Mr. Obama's objective, he is an unparalleled foreign-policy success," wrote John Bolton.[53]

All of this stands in stark contrast to the engagement and conviction with which Nixon formulated and pursued his foreign policy. Derided at times as a cold-blooded realist, Nixon showed his willingness to take risks when he stood by Israel in the Yom Kippur War of 1973. His outreach to China, lamented by conservatives, gave him Cold War leverage with the Soviet Union and smoothed the way for America's exit from Vietnam. His détente with the Soviet Union positioned the United States as a buffer between the world's two great Communist powers, both lessening the risk to Americans of armed confrontation and keeping the Soviets and the Chinese from healing their breach. These policies, whatever flaws one may see in them, were consistently guided by Nixon's interpretation of the national interest.

It's hard to find that same focus in the record Obama has compiled. By contrast, what has become clear as Obama's presidency has unfolded is that he is not, as he claimed in 2008, a foreign policy "realist" along the lines of George H. W. Bush, for whom he professed admiration, let alone Richard Nixon and Henry Kissinger. He simply does not have a foreign policy vision that squares with such a characterization, principally because, I would argue, he is so deficient in understanding the national interest—the rallying point of true realists. This problem, in turn, stems, I believe, from factors ranging from his lack of conviction about American primacy in the world, to his preference for words over action, to his preference for domestic policy over international relations.

Some foreign policy analysts still insist that Obama is a realist. Writing in 2014 in *Politico*, Fred Kaplan argued that "the single word that best sums up his foreign policy is 'realist'—in some cases, as one former adviser told me, 'hard-nosed,' even 'cold' realist." He went on: "He has ended the regime-changing wars he inherited, and done much to avoid new ones. He rarely hectors foreign leaders about their internal affairs, at least in public. He suffers no ideological hang-ups about negotiating with dreadful rulers or sworn enemies, such as Iran, for the sake of national-security interests."[54]

What Kaplan's statement misses is a clear definition of the national interest. Perhaps he is right that Obama really did have the national interest in mind when he acquiesced to Vladimir Putin, and got steam-rolled by Xi Jinping; watched from the sidelines as Iran's 2009 democracy movement got snuffed out; and abandoned Iraq prematurely, in defiance of warnings about the rise of militant groups like the Islamic State. But if so, Obama's understanding of the national interest is deficient, to put it mildly. It's not clear to me how policies that seem unambiguously to diminish the power and influence of the United States can be regarded as being in the national interest.

I'm not one who views Obama as the reincarnation of George McGovern, at least where foreign policy is concerned. No president with his willingness to use drone strikes and send commandos in to kill Osama bin Laden deserves such a label. Rather, what I see in Obama's foreign policy—and again, looking at it through the lens of what Nixon did before him—is a fundamental lack of strategy, of principled definition of goals, and of determination on tactics and the means to achieve them. Instead, there is simply drift, and the drift is enabled, in my view, by the lack of conviction about certain fundamental American ideals. Thus Obama's "realist" label seems wholly unearned.

Former CIA director John McLaughlin had a related take, one that emphasizes the administration's fundamental lack of strategic clarity:

It's not clear to me whether what we're seeing is classic realism or improvisation that looks like realism.... I'd like more evidence of strategy, the true hallmark of classic realism in foreign policy. Without a strategic focus, what looks like realism can sometimes be little more than "muddling through"—that is, avoiding the worst outcomes, staying just ahead of calamity and worrying about what comes next when we have to. That does seem what America is doing in many parts of the world these days.[55]

Even liberals have grown disheartened with the president. "What's frustrating to me sometimes about Obama is that the world seems to disappoint him," said *New Yorker* editor David Remnick—an Obama biographer and admirer—on the MSNBC program *Morning Joe*.[56] And even Democrats worry about Obama's long-range defense budget, which would shrink the US army to its smallest size since before the Second World War.

Of course, most of Obama's critics remain on the right, but their views carry more weight now than they did in, say, 2012. John McCain, always a champion of a muscular American presence abroad, has been a fierce critic of Obama's foreign policy. Many centrist or independent voters would agree with his 2014 assessment of Obama in which he excoriated the president for his "lack of realism" in foreign affairs:

For five years, Americans have been told that "the tide of war is receding," that we can pull back from the world at little cost to our interests and values. This has fed a perception that the United States is weak, and to people like Mr. Putin, weakness is provocative. That is how Mr. Putin viewed the "reset" policy. United States missile defense plans were scaled back. Allies in Eastern Europe and Georgia were undercut. NATO enlargement was tabled. A new strategic arms reduction treaty required significant cuts by America, but not Russia. Mr. Putin gave little. Mr. Obama promised "more flexibility." Mr. Putin also saw a lack of resolve in President Obama's actions beyond Europe. In Afghanistan and Iraq, military decisions have appeared driven more by a desire to withdraw than to succeed. Defense budgets have been slashed based on hope, not strategy. Iran and China have bullied

America's allies at no discernible cost. Perhaps worst of all, Bashar al-Assad crossed President Obama's "red line" by using chemical weapons in Syria, and nothing happened to him.[57]

Building on that critique, Paul Ryan focused on Obama's failure to back up American commitments. "What I've seen is, in far too many cases, the president doesn't back up his words with actions," said Ryan in a speech at the Center for a New American Security in Washington. And he criticized the president for a pledge he made in the West Point speech to remove all US troops from Afghanistan by 2016. "In other words, we've told our enemies: 'Wait us out,'" Ryan said. "We should bring our troops home as soon as possible but not before we finish the job," he added.[58] And, like many conservatives, he blamed the dissolution of Iraq on the president's inattention and particularly on his failure to secure a status-of-forces agreement that would maintain a robust American troop presence in the country.

Allies have been critical as well. "If your image in the world is feebleness, it doesn't pay," said Israeli defense minister Moshe Yaalon. "I heard voices of disappointment in the region," he said. "I was in Singapore and heard disappointment about China getting stronger and the US getting weaker.... "Look what's happening in Ukraine, where the United States is demonstrating weakness, unfortunately."[59] Yaalon suggested that Israel could rely only on itself, not the United States, for its future security.

While Obama is principally responsible for the failure of his foreign policy, in another sense the problem is larger than his presidency: the Democratic foreign policy bench has become frighteningly thin. And this in its own way relates, again, back to Nixon, as you recall from my discussion in chapter 6 of how Nixon's foreign policy achievements created the conditions in which the GOP absorbed most of the Democratic hawks. (Those who didn't defect to the GOP, like Joe Lieberman, became isolated within the party, a caucus unto themselves.) In part, the Democrats' approach to foreign policy is so fraught because it is promulgated by lightweights—Obama, I would argue, is among them.

Consider Hagel's departure as defense secretary in 2014—he was already the third man to serve in that post under Obama, in itself a sign of discord. Not many qualified, impressive Democratic candidates stepped forward, because there simply aren't many.[60] Ashton Carter, who became Obama's nominee to replace Hagel, is an impressive figure, and he has done his best despite trying circumstances at the Pentagon. But the field was frighteningly thin to begin with; Hagel himself had been a Republican. In fact, the two-term Democratic presidents since Nixon, Clinton and Obama, had *three* moderate realist Republican defense secretaries: Bill Cohen under Clinton, and Robert Gates and Hagel under Obama. In a post-Nixon world, it's almost unthinkable that a GOP president would choose a Democrat for defense secretary.

The upshot is this: Under Obama, the Democrats have lost their short-lived advantage on national security and once again become suspect, in voters' minds, as the "weak on defense" party. An October 2014 Gallup poll showed the GOP holding a nineteen-point lead over Democrats on which party could better handle "the situation with Islamic militants in Iraq and Syria" and a thirteen-point lead on foreign affairs more generally.[61]

Hindsight allows us to see the continuum of first-term policies with second-term results, making clear that these outcomes are tied to Obama's foreign policy—not "bad luck" for a world spinning out of control. In 2016, then, Republicans will have an opening to reclaim their mantle as the national defense party—a scenario many would have found unbelievable just a few years ago. This will especially be the case for Republicans if they run against Hillary Clinton, Obama's secretary of state during his first term, when the wheels were set in motion for much of what has occurred since.

Everything Old Is New Again

Beyond foreign policy, the presidencies of George W. Bush and Barack Obama demonstrated the enduring power of the categories of polarization that Richard Nixon had first identified and exploited. Indeed, the polarization that characterized the country in the Bush and Obama years far exceeded, in purely partisan terms, that of the Nixon era. Consider the hardening of party identifications that has taken place during their presidencies.

A June 2014 Pew Center poll found that Americans hold staunchly liberal or conservative views in higher proportions today than they

did in Nixon's day. "Among those with a high level of political engagement—consistently voting in elections and following government and
politics carefully—nearly half say they would go so far as to describe
the other side as a threat to the country," wrote David Lauter in a report
on the Pew poll.[62]

Or consider a Gallup study that evaluated the most polarized years
in the electorate by measuring how the opposing party's voters viewed
the sitting president—that is, by gauging the difference in presidential
approval ratings between Democrats and Republicans. Of the ten years
with the most polarized results, nine are from the Bush or Obama
presidencies. "Bush accounts for the 2nd, 3rd, 4th, 7th and 10th most
polarizing years. President Obama accounts for the 1st, 5th, 6th and 8th
most polarizing years. (Bill Clinton's 1996 is the only pre-2001 year to
crack the top 10.)" Another Gallup chart showed the average party gap
in approval ratings for every president since Dwight Eisenhower. The
presidencies with the two biggest gaps? Bush and Obama.[63]

Both presidents not only presided over polarized electorates; they
pursued deeply polarizing policies. Some historians believe that the Iraq
War was even more divisive on partisan lines than the Vietnam War.[64]
Obama's Affordable Care Act is the most divisive piece of domestic legislation since the New Deal era—but unlike FDR's New Deal reforms,
it was passed without a single vote from the opposing party. Neither
Bush nor Obama showed the ability to negotiate a way back to a more
unifying, centrist—and Nixonian—approach. On the contrary, their
leadership only widened the national divide.

George W. Bush's goal seemed to be to recapture the leadership
mantle of Ronald Reagan—while rejecting the political example of
Nixon—and that of his own father, a Republican moderate. Bush ran as a
"uniter, not a divider," but he divided the country as few presidents have
ever done. Post 9/11, his stress on national security—it was the only thing
he stressed, really; his constant emphasis that America was on a "war
footing"; and his "with us or against us" approach were extraordinarily
divisive, domestically and internationally. In a way, these themes could
be thought of as Bush's version of Nixon's silent majority strategy in the
early 1970s: only those who didn't recognize the al-Qaeda threat could
fail to back the president. It was the same politics of division—but with
a crucial difference.

What Nixon did brilliantly that Bush couldn't do—except briefly after 9/11—was to bring Americans together around policies that were supported across the political spectrum. Even when Nixon was politically divisive, his policies enjoyed broad support—including his Vietnam policies, which reflected the public desire to get out of the war while also pursuing an honorable peace. Nixon was rewarded with an historic landslide in 1972. Contrast this with Bush, who barely won reelection in 2004 and presided over blowout congressional defeats in 2006 and 2008, as the country definitively rejected his policies.

It seemed, in 2008 at least, and for a time afterward, that Obama understood the brilliance of Nixon, most of all his insight that you can build a majority by rallying the American people around common hopes, dreams, and fears. Obama's appeal to a country beyond partisan lines was one that Nixon would have recognized. But as his term went on, Obama, like Bush, proved unworthy of Nixon's political inheritance. He lacked entirely the practical flexibility that Nixon showed, as well as the political skill to construct coalitions. These were skills mastered by Nixon's true political heir, Bill Clinton. The longer Obama stayed in the White House, the more it became apparent that he was ideologically rigid and strategically provincial. No one would ever have described Richard Nixon this way.

What the presidencies of Bush and Obama leave in their wake is a country facing enormous challenges—with a hollowed-out middle class, a deteriorating national defense, spiraling debt and deficits, and proliferating threats abroad. Republicans say that it's Obama's fault; Democrats say that it's Bush's. Who would have dreamed that America, desperate for leadership after two failed presidencies, would one day be nostalgic for an old campaign theme—"Richard Nixon: Now more than ever!"

THE
NIXON
LEGACY

CHAPTER 9

Watergate and the End of Bipartisan Politics

I think [Watergate] really just made people so cynical about politics and politicians. It just deepened the feeling that government is not to be trusted.

—ROBERT DALLEK[1]

The public was told that Saddam posed an imminent threat. If that claim was fraudulent, the selling of the war is arguably the worst scandal in American political history—worse than Watergate, worse than Iran-contra.

—PAUL KRUGMAN[2]

We've had three major scandals in the last 40 years. Scandals are a dime a dozen in this town—sexual, financial, and all the rest—three big ones involving the distortion and abuse of institutions: Watergate, Iran-Contra, and the IRS. The first two were ravenously covered by the media, they were Republican presidents' problems. [Obama's IRS scandal] is not being pursued and the president knows that.

—GEORGE WILL[3]

If you want to understand the polarization of today, the gridlock of today, the extreme partisanship that infects our politics today, you have to study Richard Nixon because that's at the root of all of it.

—CHUCK TODD[4]

Talk of impeachment is in the air," wrote Peter Baker in the *New York Times* in August 2014. "A handful of conservatives issue statements and sell T-shirts promoting impeachment their party leaders consider a fool's errand. Democrats beat the drums even louder, raising money by scaring supporters into taking it seriously."[5] Indeed, in summer 2014, several hardline conservative groups were arguing that President Obama should be impeached—and though no mainstream GOP leader had seconded that thought, Obama and the Democrats did their best to make it pay politically, using the threat of impeachment in their fundraising appeals.

"If history seems intent on repeating itself as farce," Baker continued, "the events of recent days have served as a reminder that 40 years after

President Richard Nixon resigned in the face of impending impeachment, the nation he left behind is still struggling to define the contours
of presidential power and the nature of political accountability."[6]

Although the Republicans didn't move to impeach President Obama,
as some impassioned representatives and Tea Party supporters had
wished, the talk of impeachment didn't start in 2014; indeed, nearly from
the beginning of his presidency, Obama was the subject of impeachment
rumors on the right. That it was never taken too seriously shouldn't
obscure how comfortable a portion of the GOP base felt with the concept—which, before Richard Nixon's presidency, was a tool regarded as
dire in the extreme.

Republicans haven't been alone in wanting to impeach the other
party. During President George W. Bush's presidency, as we have seen,
a number of Democrats put forward impeachment proposals against
him. They resented the president's policies in Iraq and elsewhere, but
they were also motivated by payback—because their own president, Bill
Clinton, really had been impeached, in 1998. Clinton went to trial in the
Senate and was acquitted.

In the forty years since Watergate, the most infamous scandal in
American history, impeachment—usually in word but, in Clinton's case,
also in deed—became a frequently voiced idea by the party out of the
White House.

"Now impeachment is tossed around as if it's just another part of the
process," said former defense secretary William Cohen. Cohen had been
a young Republican congressman on the House Judiciary Committee
in 1974 and voted to impeach his own president. "You're talking about
reversing election results.... It's pretty awesome power there. It should
be used only on great occasions."[7]

"We've gotten sloppy about this," commented Elizabeth Drew, who
covered Watergate. "Politicians for their own reasons—the Democrats
as well as Republicans—exploit the term 'impeachment,'" she said.
"Democrats are just as bad as Republicans about this. They're raising money off the impeachment term just like the Republicans. This
is disgusting. It's an awful serious thing to talk about impeaching a
president."[8]

As Drew, Cohen, and others have pointed out, throwing around loose
talk of impeachment has a politically corrosive impact on the electorate:

it deepens the partisan divide, exacerbating the ideological divisions that have rendered our government in Washington dysfunctional. That sense of a chasm between the parties—which I wrote about in my 2012 book, *Hopelessly Divided*—has important roots in the Watergate scandal and especially in what happened afterward. Ironically, Nixon's resignation has been regarded as a moment of bipartisan consensus: it was his own party, the Republicans, who pushed for his removal from office, not just the Democrats. But post-Watergate, any sense of partisan comity quickly eroded, only rarely to reappear.

Richard Nixon's "most durable legacy," wrote *Los Angeles Times* columnist Doyle McManus, "may be the heightened cynicism and partisanship that has infected both parties ever since [Watergate]."[9] I don't agree with McManus that this is Nixon's most vital presidential legacy; I favor the domestic and foreign policy achievements as his more enduring record. And I think one can condemn what went on during Watergate—as I certainly do—while also raising questions, as I'll do in this chapter, about whether Nixon's successors committed offenses that were, in substance at least, as bad or worse than his own.

But I do agree that in terms of Watergate itself, if not of Nixon, cynicism and partisanship are the most important legacies. The ugly affair was a death knell for bipartisanship in Washington and the clarion call for the scandal-driven politics of today.

Watergate in Retrospect

At this late date, forty-some years after the fact, and with movies and books enshrining Watergate so deeply in the American political imagination, I confess that it feels somewhat strange to summarize these events, as so many before me have already done. And yet, a generation of Americans has come to maturity knowing of Watergate only as a motif or image for political scandal. They inherited a political system far more partisan and polarized than the one their parents came up in, without really knowing why. So let me summarize the events and history of Watergate briefly—and then discuss what, to me and to many others, seems like the graver crime connected with it.

Watergate was, as the Nixon White House infamously attempted to describe it, a "third-rate burglary"[10]—in formulation, in tactics, in execution, and most of all in its political goals. During his first term in office, Nixon, increasingly concerned by the release of confidential information—some of it bearing on national security—organized a team, "the plumbers," to stop leaks. Insiders noted that after Daniel Ellsberg's publication of the *Pentagon Papers* in 1971, Nixon became determined to find out what his political adversaries knew.

On June 17, 1972, five burglars broke into the headquarters of the Democratic National Committee in the Watergate complex, perhaps seeking information on the Democratic campaign for president that was about to kick off (it was nearly time for the party conventions), though precisely what they were after has been disputed. They bungled the job and were arrested, and it was soon learned that they were working for the Committee to Reelect the President—with the ominous and memorable acronym, CREEP.

At first, it seemed that the scandal would not touch Nixon. But in spring 1973, during congressional hearings on the break-in, Alexander Butterfield, a White House deputy, revealed that a taping system had been installed in the Oval Office to record the president's conversations. Thus, finding out what the president knew about the break-in and what he had done about it would be easy: just listen to the tapes.

But Nixon refused to make the tapes available, citing executive privilege. As the months wore on, and more witnesses came before Congress, Nixon's protestations seemed increasingly suspicious. At Congress's urging, Attorney General Elliot Richardson had appointed a special prosecutor, Archibald Cox, to investigate any and all crimes committed in the affair. Richardson pledged to Congress that he would not dismiss the special prosecutor, no matter what he uncovered, except for "cause" (gross improprieties or malfeasance). Cox insisted that Nixon give him the tapes, issuing a subpoena for their release, but the president refused. Instead, he offered a review and summary of the tapes' contents. Cox rejected that proposal.

On Saturday, October 20, 1973, in the Saturday Night Massacre, Nixon ordered Richardson to fire Cox—though he would surely *not* be firing him for cause. Richardson refused and resigned. Nixon then ordered Richardson's deputy, William Ruckelshaus, to fire Cox. Ruckelshaus, too, refused and resigned. Finally, Nixon asked Solicitor General Robert Bork—now acting head of the Justice Department—to do the deed, and Bork complied. Nixon's act was widely seen as an abuse of presidential authority. Within days, majorities of Americans supported his impeachment.

From there, Watergate was a long death march for Nixon. His presidency, with its many achievements, slowly lost focus and direction as his energies were diverted to finding some way to end the Watergate crisis. Finally, in July 1974, when Nixon lost at the Supreme Court in his case over executive privilege, he was forced to release full transcripts of the tapes. They contained the famous "smoking gun" conversation, which revealed that Nixon had orchestrated, almost immediately after the break-in, the cover-up and obstruction of justice involving the investigation. Most notably, he had tried to use the CIA to impede the FBI's investigation.

On August 8, 1974, Nixon addressed the nation and announced that he no longer had enough support in Congress to forestall impeachment, and that he did not believe that he should spend his energies fighting further. "America needs a full-time president," he said. He would resign the presidency effective at noon the next day, August 9. He remains the only American president to resign the office.

Nixon's downfall remains an American epic of unique drama and cautionary power. But what few understand about the scandal, even today, is that part of the motivation for his "dirty tricks," break-ins, and plumbers was that the president knew that he had done something more serious than any of these activities—something that no less of an expert than Lyndon Baines Johnson considered to be "outright treason."

Strong documentary evidence suggests that in 1968, presidential candidate Nixon, through the intercession of Anna Chennault, a Republican activist with ties to the Saigon government, had taken covert steps to interfere with the Paris peace talks involving the Vietnam War. The goal was to prevent a peaceful resolution of the war before the election. In the final week of the campaign, President Johnson had initiated a bombing halt in an effort to bring the North Vietnamese to the peace table.

Working closely with John Mitchell, Chennault urged the South Vietnamese government of Nguyên Văn Thiêu to hold off on the peace overtures—advising it that the South could get better terms from a prospective Nixon administration. Johnson got wind of it and confronted Nixon, who denied having had anything to do with it. But FBI agents listened in on communications from the South Vietnamese embassy in Washington and heard Chennault telling the Vietnamese ambassador that her "boss" wanted the Saigon regime to "hold on, we're gonna win"—thereby suggesting that the Vietnamese government should wait until Nixon was in the White House to start peace negotiations. Tapes released in recent years capture Johnson, in a phone conversation with Everett Dirksen, calling Nixon's actions "treason."

Johnson gave the intelligence on Chennault and Nixon to his vice president, the man who was now the Democratic presidential nominee and Nixon's opponent in the 1968 election, Hubert Humphrey. But Humphrey refused to release it, infuriating his boss. LBJ aide Joe Califano wrote that the president thought Humphrey's refusal to let the public know was "the dumbest thing in the world not to do."[11]

The peace talks did break down—Thiêu pulled out of them—and candidate Nixon said to reporters, "In view of early reports this morning, prospects for peace are not as bright as they were even a few days ago."[12] A few weeks later, Nixon would go on to eke out a close win over Humphrey, Johnson's hand-picked successor.

And here is where the connection with Watergate comes in. As students of the scandal know, every bit as shocking as the 1972 Watergate break-in was another break-in Nixon had ordered but that hadn't taken place: in 1971, at the Brookings Institution. The president wanted to seize information he believed the think tank had in the fall of 1968—when Chennault was doing her work—concerning American diplomacy with North and South Vietnam. The White House tapes capture Nixon ordering the mission.

"I want it implemented on a thievery basis. Goddamn it, get in and get those files. Blow the safe and get it."[13]

What was he after? Nixon scholar Ken Hughes, author of the 2014 book *Chasing Shadows: The Nixon Tapes, the Chennault Affair, and the Origins of Watergate* believes that Nixon wanted to get the information out of Brookings—where he believed it was housed—so that the public could never learn of his 1968 intrigue. As George Will reminded us, "The Logan Act of 1799 makes it a crime for a private U.S. citizen, which Nixon then was, to interfere with U.S. government diplomatic negotiations."[14] Nixon ordered the 1971 Brookings break-in just days after the publication of *The Pentagon Papers*, whose secrets predated Nixon's administration, but which made clear the risks of secret information being revealed to the public.

Not everyone accepts the Chennault story. "I did not believe then and do not believe now" that Nixon would have orchestrated or even condoned such a back-channel mission, Pat Buchanan contended.[15] Nixon maintained his innocence for the rest of his days, while Chennault just as adamantly insisted on his involvement: "I couldn't do anything without instructions.... I was constantly in touch with Mitchell and Nixon."[16]

Hughes maintains, and his scholarship is persuasive, that the Chennault episode lay at the root of Nixon's obsession with secrecy and his eventual road to Watergate. If one accepts the Chennault narrative, it makes no real difference whether Nixon's efforts were instrumental in Thiêu's decision to back out of the talks (which the Vietnamese president may have done anyway). What matters is that Nixon, as a private citizen, was willing to interfere with peace talks to enhance his presidential chances. Set against that crime, the crimes of Watergate frankly pale by comparison. Perhaps, then, Nixon did get his comeuppance in being forced to resign the presidency—but not for the reasons most people assume.

Gerald Ford and the Pardon

Gerald Ford took office in circumstances no president had ever faced, but he had the goodwill of the American people. When he said, "Our long national nightmare is over,"[17] it resonated with Americans who wanted to focus less on punishing Nixon than on allowing the government to function again. To be sure, there were others who were more interested in what Nixon's fate would be. He had flown back from Washington on the helicopter to his home in San Clemente, California, but he still faced the real possibility of criminal charges.

All that changed on Sunday, September 8, 1974, when President Ford announced a "full, free and absolute pardon unto Richard Nixon for all offenses against the United States which he, Richard Nixon, committed or may have committed or taken part in during the period from January 20 through August 9, 1974." The pardon, Ford said, was necessary to allow the nation to move on. Nixon's predicament, he said, represented "an American tragedy in which we all have played a part. It could go on and on and on, or someone must write the end to it. I have concluded that only I can do that, and if I can, I must."[18] Ford believed that without the pardon, Nixon would certainly be indicted and, in high probability, convicted—but that that would only spark a long appeal process, dragging the country further into the Watergate morass. The pardon would free Nixon entirely of the threat of prosecution and prison and also allow the country to turn the page.

Today, Ford's pardon is widely regarded as the right decision—and he received a Profile in Courage Award from the Kennedy Center in 2001, when he was 88. In 1974, though, Ford's decision transformed him from a benign and popular caretaker president to one of the most suspected men in the country.

The reaction from the press and the public was overwhelmingly negative. Ford's approval rating plummeted from 71 percent to 49 percent in just days, a record decline. His press secretary, J. F. terHorst, resigned, expressing the views of many in his letter to the president:

> I cannot in good conscience support your decision to pardon former President Nixon even before he has been charged with the commission of any crime. As your spokesman, I do not know how I could credibly defend that action in the absence of a like decision to grant absolute pardon to the young men who evaded Vietnam military service as a matter of conscience and the absence of pardons for former aides and associates of Mr. Nixon who have been charged with crimes—and imprisoned—stemming from the same Watergate situation.[19]

Angry Americans deluged the White House with telegrams. A large crowd gathered within an hour outside Lafayette Park, across the street from the White House, to protest the pardon. Others called their congressional representatives and urged them to impeach Ford. The *New York Times*, which had cheered the arrival of the new president, now condemned him for short-circuiting the wheels of justice and putting the president above the law.

"Far from writing 'The End' on the tragedy of Watergate, President Ford's sweeping pardon of former President Nixon has only muddied further the ambiguities and uncertainties left in the wake of that whole lamentable episode," the *Times* editorialized. The article went on to say:

A more divisive and distasteful outcome could scarcely be imagined....
Though now protected in his person, Mr. Nixon's stewardship in the
office of President will be more open to controversy than ever before.
How are the citizens of today and the future generations to know,
beyond challenge, whether any or all of the criminal accusations
against the former President were justified, whether they could be
made to stick before a jury of citizens within the system of criminal
justice?[20]

The biggest source of discontent involved the widespread suspicion
that the pardon reflected a "deal" made between Nixon and Ford—
Nixon's abdication of office in exchange for Ford's indemnifying him
from any criminal prosecution. "The son of a bitch pardoned the son
of a bitch," Carl Bernstein told Bob Woodward over the phone when he
learned the news.[21] It seemed plausible to many that Nixon would only
have agreed to leave the White House under such a stipulation.

Yet, forty years on, the perspective of history shows clearly that
Ford was not only courageous to pardon Nixon but he was also right.
Certainly the new president wasn't gaining himself any political advantage: He may as well have been signing his death warrant for the 1976
election, which he would go on to lose, narrowly, to Jimmy Carter. But
history has disproved the accusations many leveled against him at the
time.

No evidence has ever surfaced to show that a "deal" was made
between Nixon and Ford. Moreover, contrary to the widespread charge
that the pardon was "letting Nixon off," the pardon came with an
implicit admission of guilt—after all, you don't get pardoned for things
you didn't do. Before agreeing to grant the pardon, Ford made sure that
his lawyers had in fact confirmed that accepting a pardon carried with
it "an imputation of guilt," and that when one accepts a pardon, he or
she also admits guilt, which they found in the precedent of a 1915 case,
Burdick v. *U.S.* Ford made sure that Nixon himself was aware of this
before the pardon was granted, and Nixon was.[22]

Another condemnation of the pardon involved the concern of the
New York Times and others that Nixon would be able to regain posses-
sion of his presidential records—and possibly destroy the evidence—
thus depriving history of ever getting the full picture of the Watergate

affair. "Without the firm seal of a conclusive judgment by constitutional instructions," the *Times* said, "the way will be open wide for a subsequent demagogic rewriting of history that could poison the political atmosphere for generations to come."[23] In fact, the pardon, as Ken Gormley and David Shribman wrote, was "inextricably tied to Ford's efforts to keep Nixon's White House papers and tapes in government custody. Without Ford's insistence, at least some of these historical documents likely would have gone up in a smoky bonfire in California. Ford made sure that White House records of official business and renderings of executive-branch conversations would be accessible too." Ford refused to allow thousands of boxes containing Nixon's presidential records to leave the White House. He got Nixon to agree to surrender custody of the materials at the same time that the pardon was negotiated.[24]

Within a decade after the pardon, 54 percent of Americans agreed that the decision was the right one. When Ford received his Kennedy Center honor, Ted Kennedy himself admitted that he was wrong to previously oppose the pardon, and that Ford had been right. It's likely that the political climate would have been even more divisive had Ford left Nixon unprotected from prosecution. It's easy to imagine a nation riven by the spectacle of the trial and likely conviction of a former president. As it was, the effects that followed in the wake of the Watergate scandal and Nixon's resignation would be felt for years and decades to come, changing our politics forever.

The Aftermath: The Watergate Babies and Jimmy Carter

The effect of Watergate on party politics was felt quickly: In the 1974 midterm elections, Democrats won forty-nine seats in the House, pushing their margin above two-thirds, and they picked up three Senate seats, bringing their advantage there to a commanding 61–38. Between picked-up seats and retirements, seventy-five new Democrats would enter Congress. They were different in crucial ways from their predecessors.

Many, if not most, Democrats owed their elections to the anti-Republican tide in the electorate sparked by Nixon and Watergate. The entering class, then, became known as the "Watergate Babies." The term was apt for its reference to youth, because the Watergate Babies were on average two decades younger than the previous party average; more than half were under forty.[25] They came from a different generation, with a different outlook: in short, they were the first wave of baby boomer electoral power.

"Clearly we don't think of ourselves as New Dealers at all, or proponents of the Great Society either," said Representative James Blanchard of Michigan.[26] "We are not a bunch of little Hubert Humphreys," Senator Gary Hart similarly commented.[27] "We were the children of Vietnam, not World War II," pointed out Congressman (and later Senator) Tim Wirth of Colorado. "We were products of television, not of print. We were products of computer politics, not courthouse politics. And we were reflections of JFK as president, not FDR."[28]

They were also the products of colleges and universities, not labor unions, and they tended to see old-time Democratic machine politics as corrupt and even evil—the kind of leadership they felt had lost its moral legitimacy in the wake of Vietnam and Watergate. Their insurgent outlook was distinctively left wing and very much in the temper of the times. Many had been former student activists. They came charging into Congress determined to transform it, eager to push the nation's political agenda leftward.

It didn't take long for the new mavericks to clash with the old-line Democratic Party guard, especially at the committee level. New rules mandated that committee leadership be elected by all members of the congressional caucus, not just the committee members; the young insurgents unceremoniously grilled the committee heads in closed-door hearings, which often grew contentious. One committee chairman sealed his fate by referring to the newbies as "boys and girls." Four prominent committee heads, all Southerners, were voted out, effectively ending the seniority system in what one newsweekly called "the biggest power shake-up in more than half a century."[29] The insurgent spirit and anti-authoritarianism of the new congressional Democrats was reminiscent of the 1972 convention in Miami.

The newbies also broke from their elders on the Cold War. Where the older generation of Democrats, even the liberals, had been more or less committed anti-Communists, the Watergate class downplayed and sometimes even dismissed the seriousness of the Soviet threat and the imperative of maintaining America's military strength. Their most dramatic demonstration of this new outlook came in their first year in office, 1975, when North Vietnam, breaking the terms of the 1973 ceasefire, invaded the South. Ford went to Congress asking for emergency funds of $300 million to bolster the Saigon government. But the overwhelmingly Democratic Congress, with its many new members, refused. The South Vietnamese were left to fend for themselves, and on April 30, 1975, Saigon fell to the North Vietnamese Communists, sealing the end of the Vietnam War. Forty years later, though the United States has restored diplomatic relations with Vietnam, the country remains Communist.

The Democrats' reflexive anti-anti-Communism showed up again early in 1976, when Congress voted 323–99 to reject Ford's request for covert military aid to anti-Communist forces in Angola, who were fighting Soviet and Cuban forces. Moreover, the Democrats passed the Clark Amendment, permanently barring aid to the National Union for the Total Independence of Angola, or UNITA, the anti-Soviet group in Angola. The even-tempered Ford could barely conceal his anger.

"The Congress has stated to the world that it will ignore a clear act of Soviet-Cuban expansion by brute military force into areas thousands of miles from either country," he said.[30] Henry Kissinger, who had stayed on as Ford's secretary of state, said that the congressional vote showed that "we are living in a nihilistic nightmare. It proves that Vietnam is not an aberration but our normal attitude."[31] Indeed: Angola, too, fell to the Communists. The country's civil war raged for decades.

But perhaps the Watergate Babies' most far-reaching impact came on US intelligence services. In December 1974, Seymour Hersh published an article in the *New York Times* chronicling the intelligence abuses of the Nixon administration, which included illegal wiretaps and espionage committed against American citizens, especially war protestors, administration critics, and other controversial figures. In response, Democratic senator Frank Church of Indiana set up a committee to study illegal intelligence-gathering practices. In the nation's angry and cynical post-Watergate mood, Church's timing couldn't have been better.

Church's hearings ripped the lid off the many secrets of the national-security state that had arisen since the end of the World War II and the dawn of the Cold War. Americans were shocked to learn that their government had ordered, and often carried out, assassinations of foreign leaders considered enemies of the United States. In other cases, the government, usually through the CIA—which Church dubbed "a rogue elephant"[32]—had engineered coups. And our intelligence agencies had routinely spied on and violated the privacy rights of American citizens, including opening their mail.

The reforms that arose out of the Church hearings are still with us today: especially in the establishment of the Federal Intelligence Surveillance Act (FISA) in 1978, which required that federal agencies get warrants before conducting domestic surveillance. The George W. Bush administration would make FISA a household word a generation later, when it bypassed the court to conduct domestic surveillance after 9/11. But more importantly, FISA effectively set up what came to be known as the "wall of separation," banning information sharing between intelligence and law enforcement agencies—that is, the CIA and the FBI. These restrictions were tightened further during the Clinton years.

Most Americans knew little or nothing about the wall until after 9/11, when it became apparent that the attacks could have been stopped had the nation's intelligence agencies been able to communicate with each other. The Army Intelligence and Special Operations Command (AISOC), for instance, knew the names and whereabouts of four of the eventual 9/11 hijackers—including ringleader Mohammed Atta—in 1999. But because of the FISA wall—a wall built by the Church Committee, a direct outgrowth of Watergate—AISOC could not share this information with the FBI.[33]

Three years after the attacks, Attorney General John Ashcroft testified before the 9/11 Commission. His statement offered eloquent proof of the damage that "the wall" had done to American intelligence-gathering and law enforcement:

> In the days before September 11, the wall specifically impeded the investigation into Zacarias Moussaoui, Khalid al-Midhar and Nawaf al-Hazmi. After the FBI arrested Moussaoui, agents became suspicious of his interest in commercial aircraft and sought approval for a criminal warrant to search his computer. The warrant was rejected because FBI officials feared breaching the wall. When the CIA finally told the FBI that al-Midhar and al-Hazmi were in the country in late August, agents in New York searched for the suspects. But because of

the wall, FBI headquarters refused to allow criminal investigators who knew the most about the most recent al Qaeda attack to join the hunt for the suspected terrorists. At that time, a frustrated FBI investigator wrote headquarters, quote, "Whatever has happened to this—someday someone will die—and wall or not—the public will not understand why we were not more effective and throwing every resource we had at certain problems."[34]

Though the ramifications of some of their policy choices proved far-reaching, as we have seen, the Watergate Babies never regained the heady momentum of their early years. Soon enough, during the Carter presidency, they would be on the defensive, and after 1980, a more conservative tide would dominate. But the Watergate Babies marked a generational shift in the Democratic Party. George McGovern may have been beaten in 1972 for the presidency, but the party was, nonetheless, moving in the direction of the coalition he had built: younger; more liberal, even leftist, than centrist; and more diverse—with women, blacks, and Hispanics increasing in numbers in the coming years. These trends ensured that, despite the relatively centrist presidency of Bill Clinton in the 1990s, the Democratic Party at the national level has moved, for the most part, steadily leftward since Nixon.

Perhaps the Democratic Party would have changed in these ways even without Watergate. Certainly the trends were already in place, with the rise of a new generation, the decline of organized labor, and the impact of the antiwar and civil rights movements. But Watergate unquestionably provided enormous momentum for a generation of young progressives who would transform the Democratic Party.[35]

Campaign Finance Reform

Another major effect of Watergate was the flurry of new laws passed to reform the nation's campaign finance system. Unfortunately, however, just as the Church-era reforms wound up hampering intelligence gathering, the ultimate effect of the campaign finance reforms was to *raise* the cost of campaigns, allowing big-money groups to dominate campaign funding and ensuring that, a generation later, our political system is more awash in money than ever before.

In the aftermath of Watergate, calls for reform were everywhere. The Watergate scandal had revealed, among other things, that the Nixon White House had benefited from a slush fund from undeclared donors and had sold ambassadorships in exchange for large campaign donations. Perhaps most notoriously, in exchange for a $2 million donation from the Associated Milk Producers Incorporated (AMPI), the Nixon administration agreed to boost subsidies to the milk lobby by $100 million, which led to a significant price spike for consumers buying milk. (On the White House tapes, some of Nixon's men are heard laughing among themselves, saying that they had better go out and stock up on milk before the price goes up.) "It was a simple trade," said Richard Reeves, author of *Richard Nixon: Alone in the White House.* "Nixon got $2 million for charging American consumers $100 million."[36]

All of this whetted the appetite for more comprehensive measures to control how money flowed in the political system. As it happened, a Nixon-era law, the Federal Elections Campaigns Act, had been passed in 1971. FECA imposed individual spending limits and disclosure requirements on candidates running for federal offices, as well as on parties and political action committees, or PACs. But FECA had clearly been inadequate to prevent the Watergate financial abuses.

So in 1974, after Nixon had left office, Congress passed several amendments to the law. The most important steps were those establishing strict financial limits and disclosure requirements for donations to campaigns, setting up the Federal Election Commission (FEC) as a campaign watchdog, and instituting public financing of presidential elections—in which the nominees of the major parties would receive public funding up to a certain limit, as long as they did not go outside the financing system and seek additional private donations. The amendments placed strict spending limits on House, Senate, and presidential candidates: $25,000 for House campaigns; $35,000 for Senate campaigns; and $50,000 for presidential campaigns.[37] And the new amendments limited independent expenditures—that is, how much individuals or groups could give to campaigns—to $1,000 per candidate.[38] The disclosure requirements ensured that candidates would have to submit quarterly reports, which would be made publicly available, on their spending and contributions; likewise, any donor giving more than $100 to a candidate had to submit his or her name and contact information to the FEC. These all sounded like sensible measures, but they would play out in ways hard to foresee in 1974.

Candidates, lobbyists, wealthy individuals, and the parties themselves evolved evermore-ingenious paths around the rules. Seeking alternative means of funneling campaign money to candidates, political players soon found their silver bullet: so-called independent expenditures, campaign spending by third parties not coordinated with the campaigns.

They were helped by a landmark Supreme Court decision, *Buckley v. Valeo*, in 1976, which struck down many of the key provisions of the 1974 FECA amendments: the limits to what candidates could spend on their own campaigns (with the exception of presidential candidates accepting public funding) and the expenditure limits for third-party donors. Wealthy donors could only contribute so much to a candidate directly, the court maintained, but if they wanted to spend unlimited amounts in setting up their own organization to, say, run ads for that candidate—or against the opposing candidate—they were free to do so, so long as they were not formally coordinating their efforts with the candidate or the campaign. To deny these donors the right to spend money for these purposes, the court held, represented an unconstitutional denial of free speech. In essence, the court was agreeing to limits on contributions (what you can give directly to a campaign) while barring limits on *expenditures* (what you can spend on politics, broadly defined). The decision paved the way for the campaign finance Wild West that soon developed.

After the Buckley decision, another funding source came to dominate campaign spending: soft money, or contributions not specifically designated for federal campaigns and that could thus be disbursed by party committees however they wished. Soft money was the fuel behind the soon-famous "issue ads," which highlighted divisive issues and used them to attack candidates—without technically being ads for the candidate's opponent. Such ads came to define political campaigns, especially at the House and Senate level.

The effects can be seen by looking at some numbers over the years. In 1974, House candidates spent, on average, $53,384 on their primary- and general-election campaigns, while Senate candidates spent $437,482; by 2010, those totals were $1,130,559 and $6,340,912—increases far outstripping inflation. Adjusting for inflation, House candidates have recently been spending, on average, 4.78 times as much as their 1974 predecessors, while Senate candidates are laying out 3.28 times as much.[39]

Outside groups, like PACs, have followed the same trajectory. In 2010, the Supreme Court's even-more-influential decision in *Citizens United v. Federal Election Commission* raised the ante further, effectively creating Super PACs—and making the already-money-saturated American system into what I have called, in an earlier book, an "American casino."[40]

Campaign finance, national-security policy, and the leftward shift of the Democratic Party: all are substantive developments rooted crucially in the traumas and consequences of Watergate. But beyond these issues, the scandal had even more overarching effects on the character of our politics.

Watergate and the Politics of Scandal

Perhaps more than any other effect, Watergate created a new politics of scandal. Today, we are accustomed to a partisan political atmosphere infected with the most outrageous assertions being made on both sides—with the one-sided content and perspective offered by the competing political news channels Fox and MSNBC, and with how no sitting president any longer seems to be able to complete his term without the hovering threat, whether serious or specious, of impeachment. Of course, Watergate did not create this climate on its own: the scandal followed the winding down of the most divisive war in American history. But Watergate was the climactic blow to American innocence in the wake of the Vietnam tragedy. Its power over our political imaginations is memorialized by the fact that the suffix, and Watergate synonym, *-gate* is now attached to nearly every remotely serious political scandal or controversy: "Contra-gate," "Lewinsky-gate," "Iraq-gate," "IRS-gate," and "Benghazi-gate."

"Any politician who can be 'gated' is put on the defensive and is in part, presumed guilty," wrote political scientist Michael Genovese.[41]

It has gotten to the point where Americans expect political scandals, especially from the other side of the aisle. When the opposing party sits in the White House, that president becomes the embodiment of corruption, incompetence, dishonesty, and sometimes outright evil. Sooner or later, that president—whether Ronald Reagan or Bill Clinton, George W. Bush or Barack Obama—will hear the calls for impeachment. And by now, this culture of political character assassination has become a self-renewing cycle.

Many saw, for example, payback for Nixon's demise in the GOP's campaign, a generation later, to impeach Bill Clinton. Did that even up the score? Not at all. And George W. Bush didn't get impeached, but he faced everything else—accusations of outright lying about national-security matters; of cooking intelligence; of having received advance notice of the 9/11 attacks (or, conversely, of being so clueless that he left the country defenseless against them); and of serially violating the Constitution. A documentary filmmaker even fantasized about Bush's assassination. Obama was barely in office before the calls went up that he was a radical socialist and that his health care plan was an unconstitutional power grab. In time, calls went up for his impeachment as well.

This intense reaction to opposing-party presidents, I believe, reflects the ideological polarization of the parties—in itself a legacy of Watergate. But it is also a consequence of how after Watergate, as Genovese wrote, "we began to stress the character of candidates over their competence as leaders. The search for the pure, replaced the search for the capable. Personal virtue rose as the hunt for competence declined."[42] And perhaps the leading institutional symptom of this malady was the Office of the Independent Counsel, which quickly became a kind of political star chamber.

The Independent Counsel

The independent counsel, originally known (more aptly, as it would turn out) as the "special prosecutor," was a direct outgrowth of Watergate. Created in 1978 in response to the calls for reform in the aftermath of Nixon's resignation, the independent counsel would have an effect its creators never intended: it cast the shadow of impeachment over most of Nixon's successors.

The Democrat-led Congress, trying to prevent another Saturday Night Massacre, passed the Ethics in Government Act in 1978. Its intention was to create an office that would be autonomous in investigating wrongdoing by high federal officials, with an unlimited budget and no deadline pressure. The president would not be able to fire the special prosecutor; only the attorney general would have this authority, for "good cause." Thus, so it was believed in 1978, the special prosecutor would be impartial. But while the office was created to be above politics, it proved to be more political than anything else. Some began calling the office the "fourth branch of the American government."

Perhaps the best characterization of the law was that of Elliot Richardson, who said that it should have been called the "no ethics in government act,"[43] because, post-Watergate, the clear assumption was that no one in government was trustworthy. As it turned out, the special prosecutor's office, like all government creations, needed to justify its existence. This meant that it would always be on the lookout for targets, as opposed to being an available tool, ready when something truly serious needed looking into. And whatever party held the lever to the office through Congress would try to use it for political gain.[44]

Nothing brought home the office's abuses more than the two most famous, or infamous, special prosecutors: Lawrence Walsh and Kenneth Starr.

In November 1986, Attorney General Edwin Meese met the press with stunning news: the Reagan administration had been trading arms with the Iranian mullahs in exchange for Iranian influence in securing the release of American hostages in Lebanon. Apparently, the trades had worked, at least to some degree, as several hostages had come home, but the arms sales, conducted in secret, stunned Congress and the American public. The Reagan administration had essentially paid bribes to a regime that had a prominent place on the State Department's list of state sponsors of terrorism.

The news grew surreal a week later, when another report revealed that the administration had not only traded weapons for hostages but had also used some of the funds from the arms deals to funnel resources and assistance to the Nicaraguan Contras, the anti-Communist rebels fighting the Soviet-backed Ortega regime. At the time, the Congressional Boland Amendment had outlawed aid to the Contras. Now, a full-blown scandal was at hand, one serious enough to wound or maybe even bring down President Reagan, if he was aware of what had been going on. Meese said he hadn't been.

"How can so much of this go on and the president not know it?" asked the furious ABC news anchor Sam Donaldson at the Meese briefing. "He is the president of the United States. Why doesn't he know?"

"Because somebody didn't tell him, that's why," Meese said, satisfying no one.[45]

To determine whether this was really true, and to get to the root of the illegalities and players at the root of the affair, an independent counsel was named in December 1986: Lawrence Walsh, a Republican who had had a career of great distinction. Walsh had been a federal judge, had practiced law on Wall Street, and had been the next in command at the Justice Department in the Eisenhower administration. He was nearly seventy-five when he accepted the independent counsel's job.

Despite his age, Walsh stayed on the Iran-Contra case for an amazing six years, not closing his investigation until 1993, the first year of Bill Clinton's presidency, after running up a federal tab of $47 million. For all of his efforts, he secured just one conviction and jail term, for a CIA operative. His other two big convictions, for National Security Advisor John Poindexter and NSA operative Oliver North, were overturned on appeal. At that point, it would have been reasonable for Walsh to close his investigation, which Republicans now considered a witch hunt. But it dragged on for years more.

Those Republicans still willing to give Walsh the benefit of the doubt lost all faith in his integrity on the evening of October 31, 1992, the Friday before the presidential election. In what should have been called the "Halloween massacre," Walsh announced his indictment of former defense secretary Caspar Weinberger in the Iran-Contra affair. It was a blatantly political move: polls showed Governor Bill Clinton of Arkansas closing in on President Bush, who had been facing an uphill battle all year long. The election was four days away. With fresh reminders of Iran-Contra and his own murky role in the affair, Bush saw his support plunge more than 10 percent. By election morning, his defeat seemed a foregone conclusion. Clinton won the election handily.

"They skirted the law, some of them broke the law, and almost all of them tried to cover up the president's willful activities," Walsh wrote in his report.[46] Certainly there were valid grounds for these conclusions, and no one knew more about the matter than Lawrence Walsh. But his indictment of Weinberger could easily have waited a week. Walsh's attempt to influence a presidential election and his unwillingness to close his investigation in a timely fashion undermined his credibility.

Walsh's efforts were defended by most Democrats, however, who had little reason to fear the independent counsel statute—until five years later, when Bill Clinton found himself mired in the Monica Lewinsky mess.

Kenneth Starr, a former appeals court judge and solicitor general for President George H. W. Bush, was originally appointed as independent counsel to investigate the Clintons' Whitewater real estate deals—"Whitewatergate," some Republicans called it—and the suicide death of White House deputy counsel Vince Foster. Due to the broad discretion of the independent counsel's statute, Starr gained authority to expand his investigation almost without limit. He looked into matters including the firing of White House Travel Office employees, the abuse of FBI files, Paula Jones's sexual harassment suit against the president, and the alleged perjury and obstruction of justice committed by the president in covering up his extramarital affair with Monica Lewinsky—in which he tried to compel Secret Service employees to tell what they knew about the affair.

Starr was acting, as Walsh had before him, more as a prosecutor than as a "counsel." Starr's efforts reached their nadir with the publication of the salacious *Starr Report*, which alleged that Clinton had indeed committed perjury and obstruction of justice by giving misleading or false statements in his sworn deposition. The counsel thus concluded that Clinton had committed impeachable offenses, though impeachment itself was for the House of Representatives to pursue. Polls showed that a solid majority of Americans, regardless of their views on Clinton, disagreed with impeaching him. Starr's investigation, which ran seven years and cost taxpayers $70 million, made clear once and for all that the independent counsel law had failed. In late 1999—less than a year after Clinton was acquitted in his Senate trial—Congress mercifully let the law expire.

"I think what Watergate did in part was to put people into the disposition of criminalization of political differences," said Michael Barone. "The independent counsel law was an institutional form of that... trying to decapitate effective people in the opposite party's administration. That has become a mode of thought that we see. We have Democratic

Congressmen who urged the impeachment of George W. Bush now decrying Republican attempts or talk to impeach President Barack Obama."[47]

In short, the independent counsel statute wound up solving none of the problems it had been created to address and mostly creating new ones. "The special prosecutor is a Watergate invention," said Boston College Law School Associate Dean George Brown. "But the issue of how exactly you prosecute politicians is still with us."[48]

Americans across the political spectrum slowly learned that not every political scandal was "Nixonian," or "equal to or worse than Watergate," as so many of them were often described. On the other hand, since Watergate, some presidential scandals *have* risen to that level—and some may even be worse. As I see it, three in particular stand on par with Watergate: the Iran-Contra scandal, the missing WMD in Iraq, and the Obama administration's abuse of the IRS.

Worse than Watergate?

"This presidency is over," said Charles Krauthammer in late 1986, referring to that of Ronald Reagan. "1987 will be a Watergate year, and the following, an election year."[49]

By then, the contours of the Iran-Contra scandal were already known: Senior Reagan administration officials, in defiance of an embargo on arms sales to Iran, secretly organized arms sales to Tehran in exchange for Iranian assistance in securing the release of seven American hostages held in Lebanon—and they diverted funds from these illegal arms sales to assist the anti-Communist Contras in Nicaragua. Reagan considered the Contras "the moral equal of our Founding Fathers,"[50] and he used the broad but imperative language common to modern presidents, in the words of his national security adviser, to keep "body and soul together."[51] At the time, funding for the Contras was prohibited by the congressional passage of the Boland Amendment.

The administration's plan relied on Israel to ship weapons to Iran; the United States would then replace the weapons Israel shipped and receive payment from the Iranians via the Israelis. In return, the Iranians promised to work to achieve the release of the hostages. The diversion of funds to the Contras, meanwhile, was the brainchild of Lieutenant

Colonel Oliver "Ollie" North, then a National Security Council staffer, who arranged for the funds transfer with the blessing of National Security Adviser John Poindexter. Both assumed that they were serving Reagan's will, if only implicitly.

Thus Iran-Contra, as the scandal soon came to be called—though some called it "Contra-gate" or "Iran-gate," making the obvious connection—focused, as Watergate had, on what Reagan himself had known of these activities, and when he had known it. Reagan admitted that he had endorsed the plan to sell arms to Iran to free the hostages, which he insisted was not an "arms for hostages" deal, though everyone knew that it was. Reagan claimed to know nothing about the subsequent diversion of funds to the Contras. During 1986 and 1987, the Iran-Contra scandal led many to suspect that yet another president—who, like Nixon, had won his reelection in an historic landslide—might face impeachment.

"It was more than enough to raise dread echoes of the word so often tossed around in hyperbole, so rarely in earnest: Watergate," wrote George Church in *Time* magazine.

> The parallels might be exaggerated—this scandal, after all, was announced by the Administration rather than forced out by the courts—but they were there just the same. Once again there were rumors of documents being destroyed (by North and Poindexter). Once again the White House was resisting demands for a special prosecutor (now called independent counsel) put forth by Congressmen who did not trust the Administration to investigate itself. Once again congressional hearings were getting ready to launch upon their unknown and potentially damaging course. Worst of all, there was a revival, before last Tuesday's press briefing was over, of the quietly poisonous question so well remembered from 1973: "What did the President know and when did he know it?"[52]

In the end, the Tower Commission, appointed by the president, blamed Reagan's hands-off management style for allowing the operation to develop without his knowledge but found no evidence that he had known about it. This conclusion was almost as unsettling as if the president *had* known: It disturbed many that Reagan was so removed from crucial operations in his White House that something of this magnitude had occurred right under his nose. What was worse, some asked, a criminal president or one perhaps approaching senility?

In the end, fourteen administration officials were indicted and eleven were convicted in the Iran-Contra affair, though most of these convictions were nullified on appeal or by pardons from Reagan's successor, George H. W. Bush. The question today is, was Iran-Contra worse than Watergate? In my view, you can make a good case for it.

Consider the law breaking involved in Iran-Contra and the significance of these laws. The arms sales to Iran, a state sponsor of terrorism, violated the Arms Export Control Act. Reagan was required by law to notify Congress that he was making such a sale (illegal as it was)—but he notified no one. And, of course, the diversion of funds to the Contras violated the Boland Amendment banning financial aid to the Contras. Iran-Contra represented a circumvention of the congressional role in foreign policy. It represented unilateral executive power—what came to be known among conservatives as the "unitary executive"—in defiance of the checks and balances set up by the Constitution.

Yet Ronald Reagan's popularity and rising historical standing has relegated Iran-Contra to a blot on an otherwise-successful presidency. Iran-Contra does not cast the same shadow on his political legacy as Watergate does for Nixon.

The controversies surrounding the administration of George W. Bush are much fresher in American memory—none more than the issue of the missing WMD, the primary rationale for his fateful decision to launch a preemptive war against Iraq and Saddam Hussein in 2003. Most readers won't need much of a recap on how that decision turned out: over four thousand American troops dead, tens of thousands of casualties, and more than $1 trillion in costs. Throw in the turmoil that has gripped Iraq ever since, with the rise of ISIS and the return of sectarian bloodshed, and you have what many consider the worst foreign policy blunder in American history.

It was, as even its supporters admitted, a war of choice, undertaken to remove what the president called "an imminent threat" to the safety of the United States. It was a choice whose devastating, indeed generational, consequences continue to play out.

But making bad decisions, however costly, is not in itself a "scandal." The scandal element of the Iraq War is not that it proved wrongheaded or unwinnable, but that the justification for launching the war in the first place—Saddam Hussein's WMD—proved invalid. And that the administration, which tried without much success to disguise its eagerness for war, knowingly—at least this is the accusation—used half-baked if not fraudulent intelligence to make its case for war.

"Anyone who talks about an 'intelligence failure' is missing the point," wrote Paul Krugman early on, in summer 2003, when questions about the war's necessity were just beginning to trouble Americans. "The problem lay not with intelligence professionals, but with the Bush and Blair administrations. They wanted a war, so they demanded reports supporting their case, while dismissing contrary evidence."[53] Lest anyone think that this complaint comes just from liberals, consider the words of Max Hastings, the eminent (and conservative) British historian. In 2003, Hastings wrote of Tony Blair, in words that could apply equally to Bush: "The prime minister committed British troops and sacrificed British lives on the basis of a deceit, and it stinks."[54]

The Bush administration and its political supporters tried for over a year after the invasion to claim that the WMD would yet be found. Paul Wolfowitz, one of the war's intellectual architects, alleged, along with others, that Iraq had probably had time to move its stockpiles out of the country, perhaps to Syria. Others seconded that view or alternative versions of it. In the meantime, however, the Iraq Survey Group—organized by the CIA and Pentagon—made a systematic search of postwar Iraq and found nothing. It was true, as conservatives were quick to point out, that as the ISG's leader, David Kay, reported, Saddam may have had the production capacity to reconstitute his chemical and biological programs if international economic sanctions had been lifted. Kay also believed, as did Wolfowitz, that Saddam may have moved some of his WMD into Syria.

But Kay's successor at the ISG, Charles Duelfer, found no evidence for this claim. And the group's final report, published at the end of September 2004, declared that Iraq had destroyed its chemical, biological, and nuclear stockpiles in the 1990s. In 2013, in an article in *Foreign Policy*, Duelfer argued that Bush himself had not deceived the American people; rather, the president was poorly served by bad intelligence. "The intelligence wasn't cooked or slanted to make policymakers happy," Duelfer wrote. "It was just wrong. That made Bush mistaken—but it doesn't make him a liar."[55]

Many disagree with Duelfer's claim that the intelligence was free from political influence. "At the time there were a lot of concerns that [intelligence] was being politicized by certain individuals within the administration that wanted to get that intelligence base that would justify going forward with the war," said John Brennan, then deputy CIA director and later CIA director under President Obama. "Some of the neocons...were determined to make sure that the intelligence was going to support the ultimate decision."[56]

That same sense was shared in Britain, as revealed in the infamous "Downing Street Memo," released in 2005. The memo contains the notes to a July 2002 meeting between Richard Dearlove, head of MI6, the British intelligence agency, and Prime Minister Blair. The memo referred to war as "inevitable," and went on to say that "Bush wanted to remove Saddam, through military action, justified by the conjunction of terrorism and WMD. But the intelligence and facts were being fixed around the policy." And it continued: "The case was thin. Saddam was not threatening his neighbours and his WMD capability was less than that of Libya, North Korea or Iran."[57]

In February 2003, the Bush administration sent Secretary of State Colin Powell to the UN to make the case for an invasion and demonstrate that Saddam had reconstituted his WMD programs. Powell displayed dramatic overhead photos that showed, he claimed, that Saddam had constructed a number of mobile chemical-weapons laboratories. He dramatically held up a vial of anthrax. His bravura performance built the momentum for war. Yet he eventually discovered that the intelligence was faulty at best, fraudulent at worst. He later called his presentation a permanent blot on his record.

"There were some people in the intelligence community who knew at that time that some of these sources were not good, and shouldn't be relied upon, and they didn't speak up," he said in 2005. "That devastated me."[58]

Powell seemed to have doubts early on. In the months before the war, he had asked his chief of staff, Lawrence Wilkerson: "I wonder what'll happen when we put 500,000 troops into Iraq and comb the country from one end to the other and find nothing?"[59]

Although I often disagree with Paul Krugman, it's difficult for me to dispute his 2003 assessment that we looked at previously: "The public was told that Saddam posed an imminent threat. If that claim was fraudulent, the selling of the war is arguably the worst scandal in American political history—worse than Watergate, worse than Iran-contra."[60] Indeed, our entry into the war in Iraq, on the basis of intelligence claims that seem, at best, specious, may belong in a category of its own. (In 2014, the *New York Times* reported that between 2004 and 2011, American troops had "secretly reported finding roughly 5,000 chemical warheads, shells or aviation bombs." Conservative defenders of Bush touted the news, but all of the weapons were made before 1991, and were "filthy, rusty or corroded, a large fraction of them could not be readily identified as chemical weapons at all.[61]")

As for the Obama administration's IRS scandal, the full significance is not yet clear—in good part because, unlike the Republican scandals I just described, the mainstream media shows little interest in pursuing it. This is scandalous in itself, and bears out long-running critiques of the established media by conservatives, who note how curiously uncurious reporters become when the abuser of power is a Democratic president. In the IRS case, there is an unambiguous abuse of power. The only question that remains to be answered is how culpable the president himself is for it.

The case grew out of abuses in the IRS's office in Ohio, always the epicenter of presidential elections, where the agency selected certain political groups applying for nonprofit status for close scrutiny. The IRS is supposed to vet tax-exempt claims closely. What set off alarms was that the agency did so in a targeted fashion, based on the groups' names or political goals. In particular, they went after groups with "Tea Party" in their names. And in 2012, the agency adjusted its criteria further, telling its employees to be on the lookout for groups referring to the Bill of Rights or the Constitution and for "political action type organizations involved in limiting-expanding government."[62] (The agency did look into some left-wing groups as well, but not with nearly the same intensity and interest.)

The public first learned of the scandal when the IRS's director of tax-exempt organizations, Lois Lerner, fessed up to it at a bar association meeting. By revealing what the IRS had done preemptively, Lerner clearly hoped to get ahead of the story and control the narrative. She then immediately clarified that she herself had done nothing wrong, and took the Fifth Amendment.[63] From there, things got murky.

When the revelations led to congressional hearings and then subpoenas, the IRS claimed, amazingly, to have lost the thousands of relevant e-mails that Lerner and others had sent in reference to the conservative-group targeting. The agency had suffered a "hard-drive crash," director John Koskinen told an incredulous House committee, and the e-mails could not be recovered. Listening to this dog-ate-my-homework story was too much for Trey Gowdy, who ripped into Koskinen at a congressional hearing. Here was Koskinen, who ran the most powerful and most feared of all government agencies short of the FBI, an agency that told Americans to hold onto every scrap of paper pertaining to their finances for seven years, lest they face threat of audit, and now, charged with systematic abuse of political groups, it was claiming that it had lost all its records? Koskinen had little retort but a smirk and indignation at having his integrity questioned. But Gowdy's outrage was shared by millions of Americans, who have found themselves in the crosshairs of an agency that often seems out of control and ruthless.

It's worth noting that the crimes at the center of today's IRS scandal would have been considered impeachable in 1974—the second count in the bill of impeachment against Nixon cited his use of the IRS against his political enemies. In the Obama IRS scandal, we await further information tying the president more directly to the agency's behavior—or exonerating him of the blame. But at minimum, it represents government power run amok, in a different way than Watergate did.

"The Watergate break-in was the professionals of the party in power going after the party professionals of the party out of power," wrote Daniel Henninger in the *Wall Street Journal*. "The IRS scandal is the party in power going after the most average Americans imaginable."[64]

And in fact, the core of the Watergate scandal was the Nixon team's attempt to outrun government attempts—by the FBI and the Justice Department—to investigate what had happened. In the IRS scandal, one of the government's fundamental agencies, with enormous size and discretionary powers, abused the rights of ordinary American citizens. No less a Nixon expert than Pat Buchanan saw the IRS scandal outstripping Watergate.

"It is worse than what Nixon allegedly did," Buchanan said on *The McLaughlin Group*.

> Somebody said they are out to harass people by having audits of them and this was an article of impeachment against Nixon. This screams for an independent prosecutor to investigate this.... It's a violation of their constitutional rights and the person responsible has taken the Fifth Amendment. You think the Nixon White House or any other Republican administration would get away with that? Everybody would be screaming for an independent counsel if only to go after the folks at the IRS.[65]

Some believe that, at least thematically, President Obama helped set the IRS abuses in motion with his public statements condemning small political groups. In his 2010 State of the Union address, with Supreme Court justices seated just feet away, Obama lambasted the court's *Citizens United* decision, which eased campaign finance rules and paved the way for what have come to be known as Super PACs. A few months later, in a radio address, Obama warned of "shadowy groups with harmless sounding names" who threatened the American democratic system.[66] Democratic senators publicly urged the IRS to investigate Tea Party and other nonprofit conservative groups.

What were Lois Lerner and her colleagues doing, after all, but investigating groups with "harmless sounding names"? As for being "shadowy," as Daniel Henninger pointed out in the *Wall Street Journal*, most of these groups did indeed operate in the shadows, in small towns all around the United States, far from the centers of government and media power: in places like Franklin, Tennessee; Livonia, Michigan; Lucas, Texas; Middletown, Delaware; Fishersville, Virginia; Jackson, New Jersey; Redding, California; Chandler, Arizona; and many other places.[67]

I'm gravely concerned that the American media is so uninterested in investigating the Obama administration's IRS scandal. At minimum, we have a massively powerful federal agency declaring war against Americans of a certain political persuasion. That alone is worthy of an investigation on the level of Watergate, regardless of what remains to be discovered about any direct presidential role in the scandal.

The Watergate Legacy: Partisanship, Polarization, and Loss of Trust

In the mid-1980s, more than a decade after Watergate, C. L. Sulzberger, a Paris-based, onetime *New York Times* foreign correspondent and nephew of the paper's former publisher, came back to the United States for a visit. Taking in the political climate, Sulzberger was stunned to discover that the bitterness Watergate had fostered remained very much alive. The anger, he said, "was astonishingly personal," and he compared it with the "kind of personal hatred that survivors of Hitler and Stalin in Germany and Russia felt toward their persecutors." Reflecting on the source of this hatred, he wrote: "I cannot explain this extraordinarily venomous sentiment, this blind rage that focused its attention entirely on one man and displayed not the faintest sign of forgiveness."[68]

That atmosphere of the offspring of Watergate described by Sulzberger predominates today: in polarized political parties, partisan media, cynical and distrustful voters. For years now, Americans have been telling pollsters that they dislike both parties, and that both parties are too ideological—unwilling to compromise and make commonsense agreements in the national interest. Congress today has the lowest approval ratings in its history. Demonization of political opponents, relentless personal attacks, and an insatiable hunger for scandal characterize Republican and Democratic Party politics today, especially during election cycles. Finding cooperation across the aisle is exceedingly rare, as was illustrated again in September 2014, when President Obama went to war—without Congressional authorization—against ISIS, in both Iraq and Syria. Obama didn't ask for permission and Congress didn't insist on it. The legislators were more interested in their reelection campaigns. If the president's war worked out, it would be all to the good; if it didn't, they wouldn't have to answer for their votes authorizing it.

The country has no leaders.

"When I was elected as a Republican to Congress in 1966 and assigned to the House Judiciary Committee, I was impressed at how nonpartisan it was," wrote Thomas F. Railsback, a Republican who helped draft the bills of impeachment against President Nixon and became one of six Republicans on the committee to vote for impeachment. "Seldom was a bill passed out of committee without bipartisan support. The House at that time did not get a lot of publicity. After the Watergate break-in, the revelation of the White House tapes and the impeachment inquiry before the House Judiciary, that was to change."[69] Railsback said that back then, many members had friends on both sides of the aisle; even the impeachment vote was bipartisan. But the post-Watergate elections of November 1974, he believed, ushered in the new breed of hyperpartisan politician. "The climate today in Congress appears even more fractured," he wrote.[70]

Watergate owes some of its power to coming on the heels of the Vietnam War. "It was a part of a one-two punch," Robert Thompson of Syracuse University wrote of the scandal, "the other being the loss of the Vietnam War—that delivered the current sense of cynicism about government. When the smoke cleared in the Watergate scandal, we had been blatantly lied to by our highest officials. That changed us."[71]

Other factors contributed to Americans' loss of trust in the government—the Cold War's end, money in politics, redistricting, changing demographics—but Watergate was the turning point. Americans have never regarded their government with the same degree of confidence and trust since. "There's a difference between skepticism," the *Chicago Tribune* editorialized on Watergate's fortieth anniversary, "which is healthy, and cynicism, which corrodes."[72] My 2013 book, *The End of Authority*, looked at how this breakdown of trust has corroded not just the American political system but governments around the world. The wreckage is pervasive.

In the United States, these twin effects—increased partisanship and loss of public trust—are self-reinforcing. The political and ideological divisions that Watergate exposed and exacerbated changed both parties forever. The more partisan it grew, the more disillusioned the American electorate became with our political institutions. The souring public mood, in turn, motivated both parties to put forth increasingly partisan candidates. On goes the cycle, with the nation's most pressing problems left unaddressed, and the American people telling pollsters that they don't expect their children to live as well as they have. That's another way of saying that people have lost their faith in the American dream.

All this may sound like a lot of baggage to be hanging on one political scandal. To be sure, as I've tried to suggest here, Watergate arose out of a context of other events and factors. But if there is one political event in the last half century most responsible for the state of our politics today, Watergate is surely it.

CHAPTER 10

Nixon's Final Comeback
The Postpresidency

Now Richard Nixon's name will live in obloquy, at least pending some distant work of revisionists which challenges the imagination.

—*ARKANSAS GAZETTE*, AUGUST 1974[1]

I don't know what the future brings, but whatever it brings, I'll still be fighting.

—RICHARD NIXON, *FROST/NIXON: THE COMPLETE INTERVIEWS*[2]

I believe that in Reagan's second term the voice was the voice of Reagan but the hands were the hands of Nixon.

—ARNOLD BEICHMAN[3]

There he was, back on the front page, making policy. God, what a comeback. Who'd have believed it possible?

—STEPHEN AMBROSE[4]

He was stretched out flat on his back," Gerald Ford remembered. "There were tubes in his nose and mouth, and wires led from his arms, chest and legs to machines with orange lights that blinked on and off. His face was ashen, and I thought I had never seen anyone closer to death."[5] It was October 1974, and Ford, who had become president two months earlier on Richard Nixon's resignation, was visiting the former president in Long Beach Memorial Hospital. Nixon had suffered another severe episode of phlebitis, a malady that plagued him over the years, and he had never been in such severe medical straits. His left leg was enlarged, he had a blood clot and large hematomas, consistent with Grey Turner's sign, which can predict acute pancreatitis.

It was hard to miss the symbolism of Ford's visit: the new president sitting at the bedside of the disgraced former president, who now lay possibly near death. Nixon's condition, it must have seemed to his many opponents and critics, was a metaphor for the damage he had wrought upon the country as well as his own moral ruin. Even if he survived his medical ordeal, he would surely never a play a role in national affairs again.

That Nixon was a broken man was the predominant consensus, both before and after his near-miss hospital stay, from which he did eventually recover. From the moment the helicopter lifted Nixon above the White House lawn for his flight to exile in San Clemente, California, on August 9, 1974, it seemed clear that Nixon's political legacy would be one of disgrace.

"There is reason to hope that, in more than the personal sense, the age of Nixon has ended," wrote Anthony Lewis of the *New York Times*.[6] "Less than two years after standing on a political pinnacle few men have ever attained, the almost undisputed leadership of the most powerful country on earth, he has sunk into an abysm of disgrace as deep as the peak was high," editorialized the *Baltimore Sun*.[7] "Now Richard Nixon's name will live in obloquy, at least pending some distant work of revisionists which challenges the imagination," wrote the *Arkansas Gazette*.[8]

Yet Nixon never saw things that way. Certainly, he was in despair; he had become the first president ever to resign the office, and his legal status—in the month before Gerald Ford's pardon—was precarious. He had expended considerable sums of money on legal defense. But from the earliest days of his exile in San Clemente, Nixon did not act like a man who felt he had no role in the world. On the contrary: He told a waiting crowd at El Toro Marine Base, where he landed when he arrived from Washington, that he had no plans for a quiet and uneventful retirement. Just words, many surely thought. But consider what happened the next day.

Nixon had retained a staff of nearly two dozen assistants and secretaries and called them together for a 7:30 a.m. meeting—for which he had to wake some of them. Dressed in a suit and tie despite the summer heat, he was irked when he saw that some of the attendees were wearing Bermuda shorts. He wasted no time getting down to business.

"I called you here to discuss an important topic," he said. "And that is, what are we going to do about the economy in the coming year?"[9]

Nixon's drive, self-discipline, and determination to win redemption would not allow him to go quietly into retirement. Over the next two decades, Nixon would use his genius in foreign affairs to forge a role as an elder statesman—a public intellectual and both a domestic and foreign affairs advisor. Nixon at times pushed too hard; until the 1990s, he was at times rebuffed by presidents wary of being associated with him, especially presidents from his own party. But he pushed on, in the process becoming the true creator of the modern postpresidency—for which credit more commonly goes to Jimmy Carter. But Carter's post-presidency was based largely on humanitarian and charitable efforts; he fashioned himself a global problem solver and do-gooder. By contrast, Nixon's post–White House career, rather than being above politics, was steeped in politics—it was essentially a shadow presidency, mostly devoted to American foreign policy. He put forward a vision of foreign policy realism, "hard" détente, and a rational approach to dealing with the Russians and Chinese.

And he would exert important, if subtle, influence on the foreign policy of both Ronald Reagan and George H. W. Bush. Nixon's foreign policy realism, which he put forth regularly in books throughout the 1980s, stood as a counterpoint to Reagan's views. In Reagan's first term, he felt pressure from the Nixon example to move closer to the center in his policy and stance toward the Soviet Union; in Reagan's second term, as the president embraced Mikhail Gorbachev, the Nixon model served as a skeptical corrective, warning the administration not to go too far, too fast. Conversely, the lessons learned from Nixon stiffened Reagan's successor, George Bush, to be more hawkish. Herein lay the true triumph seen in Nixon's postpresidency: not just the fact that, after rising from his hospital bed, he was able to achieve a dramatic turnaround in the eyes of both the public and the political elite but also, more substantively, that he continued to have a say in the great matters of state and continued to shape events. The capstone, of course, was his relationship with Bill Clinton during his final years and Clinton's powerful tribute to Nixon at his funeral.

His postpresidency, then, was nothing less than Nixon's final comeback. Like his other reinventions, it represented a profound act of will and determination.

Postresignation Despair

It would be difficult to overstate the dire predicament Nixon faced in late 1974.

For starters, there was the matter of his legal status and the effect the events had on his health. The stress of Watergate and his resignation, the suspense of waiting to see what President Ford would do on the pardon question, and other legal stresses—he was hit with more than sixty lawsuits after leaving office—caused Nixon's health to decline. Sometime between August and September 1974, David Eisenhower reportedly phoned Ford and told him that if a decision on the pardon did not come soon, Nixon "might go off the deep end."[10] Finally, Ford got word to Nixon's people that he would issue a full pardon if the former president understood that his acceptance was an acknowledgement of guilt and agreed not to hold on to his presidential papers and tapes. Though Nixon publicly expressed gratitude for the pardon, in private he was angry: He believed that Lyndon Johnson and John Kennedy had done far-worse things in office. But he agreed to the pardon's terms; he issued a statement in which he did not concede criminality but did say that he had failed to deal properly with Watergate, and that his failures had left him with "a burden that I shall bear every day of life that is left to me."[11] And he signed an agreement with the government to share custody of his presidential materials.

Still, squaring away the issue of releasing the presidential materials and gaining Ford's pardon did little for Nixon's overall well-being. For one thing, the public strongly disapproved of the pardon. For another, Nixon was mentally and physically breaking down. One of his aides, Benton Becker, visited him after the pardon and was appalled by his condition. Meeting with President Ford afterward, Becker told the president that he wondered whether Nixon would still be around by the time of the next election.

"Well," Ford said, "1976 is a long time away."

"I don't mean 1976," said Becker. "I mean 1974."[12]

By October 1974, Nixon's condition was reported as critical after a flare-up of his phlebitis. At one point, Nixon told friends later, he had slipped into a state of near shock, and then felt a slap and heard voices saying, "Richard pull yourself back."[13] Later that month, he was listed as critical for a few days. When his condition stabilized, Ford made his visit to see him in the hospital. Meanwhile, due to his condition, Nixon was exempted from testifying in the trials of his former aides.[14]

Adding to these woes were Nixon's financial troubles. His legal bills—topping perhaps $750,000, including half-a-million dollars in back taxes and mortgage payments—clouded his future. His phlebitis-induced hospital stay also added to the financial hit—it cost him $23,000, because he had not purchased health insurance after leaving office. (The health plan that Teddy Kennedy had helped to kill would have come in handy.) At one point, Nixon's bank account totaled about $500.[15] And given his state of disrepute, he had no sure way to generate additional income.

And it wasn't as if his departure from office had silenced the voices of his critics and political foes. On the contrary, they seemed more emboldened than ever; with Nixon stripped of any power to make their lives difficult, they said whatever they pleased about him in the media, and the Nixon name was one of the nation's most despised—at least, to hear the mainstream media tell it. Certainly Nixon received few visitors from official Washington life. The first round of Watergate books, including Bob Woodward and Carl Bernstein's *All the President's Men*, began appearing, most portraying Nixon as immoral, scheming, and vengeful, a wholly unfit man to wield the powers of the nation's highest office. Nixon probably didn't read them, but he could not ignore them; he even blamed Woodward and Bernstein's follow-up book, *The Final Days*, for causing his wife Pat's first stroke. As the exiled president, he was trying, he said later, to "shut myself off from the past."[16] Another close associate said: "He was really a beaten man."[17]

But Nixon was never beaten: not in 1952, not in 1960, not in 1962, and not now. He refused to consider that the rest of his life would be spent away from any kind of political role, even though he knew he would never again hold office. In 1975, he visited with Senator Barry Goldwater—the conservative stalwart who had been one of the key Republicans to tell him that he had to go—and told him that, somewhere down the road, he wanted to become a Republican spokesman on important international issues. Somewhat to Goldwater's astonishment, Nixon even suggested that he should be made ambassador to China. After a flabbergasted Goldwater relayed this conversation to the press, an infuriated Nixon denied that he had made any such suggestion.[18]

Clearly, the road back would be long and slow. From August 1974 until early 1977, Nixon lived mostly out of the public eye, staying close to San Clemente and emerging only rarely, when he took long, solitary walks on the beach. The *New York Times*, never known for its sympathy, described him as "a frail and lonely recluse clinging to a hope of salvaging his reputation and, some persons say, on returning some day to

politics." The *Times* portrait went on: "The desire for political rehabilitation and acceptance, his acquaintances say, appears to be the subject
most constantly on Mr. Nixon's mind. His moods, they say, shift suddenly, from buoyant confidence to spells of withdrawn, almost sullen
reflection interspersed with bursts of angry impatience over the rate of
his physical recovery and the state of his finances."[19]

The major exception to Nixon's quiet life in the first few years
after his resignation was his February 1976 trip to China to visit with
Chairman Mao. It was Nixon's first trip abroad since leaving office—and
not surprisingly, he chose the site of his greatest political triumph. He
spent several hours with Mao and other Chinese leaders and addressed
an audience of several hundred in the Great Hall of the People. If Nixon
hoped that the trip would begin his public rehabilitation, he was wrong,
at least in the eyes of the press. Many in the mainstream media condemned him for trying to recapture past glories, an effort they found
unseemly, if not even illegal.

David Broder, normally a reserved, inside-the-beltway commentator, could barely restrain his contempt for Nixon's gesture. He savaged
Nixon for his "utter shamelessness" and condemned his need "to salvage
for himself whatever scrap of significance he can find in the shambles
of his life."[20]

Barry Goldwater, too, weighed in. The Arizona senator suggested
that Nixon be charged with violating the Logan Act, which bans private
citizens from negotiating with foreign countries (and which Nixon may
have already violated in 1968, with his efforts to stall the Vietnam peace
talks). "If he wants to do this country a favor," Goldwater said of Nixon's
China trip, "he might stay over there."[21]

Broder and Goldwater weren't the only ones disgusted by Nixon's
trip, for which the former president had brought along more than twenty
journalists—ensuring plenty of coverage. Nixon hadn't cleared the trip
with the White House, and his return to China occurred just as Ford
was battling for his political life in the New Hampshire primary against
his insurgent challenger, Ronald Reagan. Ford's men were livid.

Ford eked out a win in New Hampshire over Reagan, 51 percent to 49
percent, but the president and his aides considered that the publicity of
Nixon's trip had not served him well. "I presume there will be evidence
that it probably hurt," Ford said in a postprimary interview.[22] He was
probably right: in early 1976, Nixon's popularity remained low, and his

association with Ford—cemented by the pardon—was already a huge obstacle for the president to overcome, without voters having to read about Nixon hobnobbing with Mao in Beijing.[23] The Nixon connection was particularly poisonous when Ford was trying to beat back Reagan's challenge, since Reagan was the champion of the party's insurgent conservative movement, which had never trusted Nixon.

Ford just barely got past Reagan for the GOP nomination, and he still faced a steep uphill climb against Jimmy Carter in the fall. Nixon understood that he could damage Ford's chances by coming out too publicly for him, so he kept his distance. From San Clemente, he watched as Ford lost one of the closest presidential elections in history.

Whether it was the return of the Democrats to the White House that motivated him—because he could no longer politically damage a Republican presidential occupant—or that he simply had decided that it was time, Nixon, starting in 1977, became much more visible. Criticism, like that which had greeted his China trip, would not deter him. Had it ever?

Nixon and David Frost

The real start of Nixon's postpresidency came in 1977, when he agreed to an exclusive series of television interviews with the British journalist David Frost, who had interviewed him during the 1968 presidential campaign. Though Nixon had already signed a multi-million-dollar deal to author his memoirs, which he was then writing, he needed cash badly at this time, and the Frost interviews would pay him $600,000 and perhaps, when all was said and done, close to $1 million. Those figures prompted harsh criticism that Nixon was profiting from his crimes. The memoir deal met with similar outrage. But the anger was soon obscured by the interest millions of Americans had in hearing from Nixon in a one-on-one format for the first time since his resignation.

The interviews, which, in unedited form, stretched over twenty-eight hours, were conducted over twelve days in March 1977 and broadcast in four ninety-minute segments in May. The major broadcast networks, leery of purchasing the programs and being accused of "checkbook journalism"—let alone giving Nixon a platform—passed on the program, and Frost ended up producing them independently at his own expense. But he syndicated the show through a network of 155 local stations, and his gamble paid off. The Nixon interviews with Frost were the most watched news interviews in television history, with an audience for the peak installment equaling that of America's number one-rated sitcom at that time, *Happy Days*.[24] Segments were devoted to foreign and domestic policy as well as to "Nixon the man," but the installment most Americans would remember concerned Watergate.

In those segments, viewers finally had their chance, through Frost's interrogation, to hear Nixon confront the facts of Watergate and own up—or not—to his role in it. In the climactic discussion of the series, Frost and Nixon engaged in a tense duel over the former president's culpability for the misdeeds in Watergate. Nixon would never grant Frost's argument that he had in fact obstructed justice. But once Frost dropped this line of questioning and asked Nixon if he would not say something to the American people about his role and his responsibility in the scandal, Nixon obliged.

> "I let down my friends," he began.
>
> I let down the country, I let down our system of government and the dreams of all those young people that ought to get into government but will think it is all too corrupt and the rest.... Yep, I let the American people down. And I have to carry that burden with me for the rest of my life. My political life is over. I will never yet, and never again, have an opportunity to serve in any official position. Maybe I can give a little advice from time to time.[25]

For the most part, critics in the media and elsewhere were tough on Nixon. "To say that mistakes were made is not enough," former Watergate special prosecutor Leon Jaworski wrote in *Newsweek*. "To deny impeachable acts and criminal wrongdoing is untruthful."[26] The magazine itself was no gentler, blasting Nixon for being "careless of the record, heedless of the proper limits of power, unable to plead guilty to anything much worse than 'screwing up' and coming no closer in history to that final absolution in history he seeks."[27] Allowing that Nixon's remorse was "far from feigned," and that he "even seems at last to realize that his agony was caused by his own failings," *Time* suggested Nixon could probably not have gone any further. "This, perhaps, is as much as he ever can or will feel about his role in those years that were as much an ordeal for the country as for him. It may not be quite enough to alter Richard Nixon's place in history."[28]

The reaction of the American public was more mixed. To be sure, few Americans were swayed in their overall views of Watergate or of Nixon's role in it. A Gallup survey conducted after the Frost programs showed Americans still largely convinced that Nixon was covering up information (69 percent), that he had obstructed justice and perhaps committed other crimes (72 percent), and that he should have no future role in a public capacity (75 percent). But 44 percent of viewers felt more sympathetic to Nixon than they had before the broadcasts, and only 20 percent felt less so.[29]

If the public was relatively split and Nixon's most devout critics saw the 1977 programs as a grab for money and sympathy, Nixon loyalists were moved by his intellectual depth and seriousness about politics, history, life, and death. What the Frost programs signaled above all was Nixon's readiness to be seen again and to resume, in some fashion, a public role. As he told Frost near the end of their historic discussions: "I don't know what the future brings, but whatever it brings, I'll still be fighting."[30]

The Long Road Back

In May 1978, Nixon published *RN: The Memoirs of Richard Nixon*, a 1,184-page memoir covering everything from the day of his birth to the day he left Washington as a disgraced ex-president. The book, wrote *Time*, though it broke no new ground and offered Nixon's same basic account of the Watergate affair, was nevertheless a "valuable contribution to the history of his times."[31] Grosset & Dunlop, the book's publisher, called *RN* Nixon's "message not only to us here and now, but down through the ages."[32] Certainly anyone interested in American political history or foreign affairs would consult the book.

The book kicked up protest campaigns to persuade bookstores not to carry it, and at first, these efforts seemed to have the desired effect: "Sales of Richard Nixon's memoirs are sluggish," reported the AP, citing book chains that were not selling out their supplies and bookstore operators who said they wouldn't put the book in their store windows because it wouldn't help sales. Other book outlets starting marking down the $19.95 cover price on their copies.[33]

Yet the early reports proved inaccurate. By June, the book was on bestseller lists, and some book dealers were selling out of it. Tellingly, the book was most popular in the West and Midwest and least popular in Washington, Boston, and New York. All told, the memoir may have sold more than 330,000 copies—making it the best-selling presidential memoir in history, up to that point.[34] Unequivocally, *RN* restored Nixon's financial fortunes. And it made his increased presence in American life, both in word and deed, more accepted. As for restoring his reputation, that judgment remained, as it always would remain, up to individual Americans. Still, the memoirs were a heady experience for Nixon, and they foreshadowed more successes, more normalization.

Nixon closed out 1978 with a visit to Britain's Oxford Union. Protestors came out in full force, but Nixon's speech was generally well received—even the *New York Times* conceded that he had gotten "a warm, at times almost rapturous reception."[35] His interview on a French television station also went over well. Ninety percent of call-ins to the program praised Nixon or asked friendly questions. Clearly moved by the response, Nixon told the interviewer: "So long as I have a breath in my body, I am going to talk about the great issues that affect the world. I am not going to keep my mouth shut. I am going to speak out for peace and freedom."[36]

"It is too bad," wrote an American journalist to his editor back home, "that he can't run for president of France. He would win hands down."[37]

All of this was prior to January 1979, when Nixon returned for the first time to the White House itself. The occasion was a state dinner thrown by the Carter administration for Chinese Deputy Prime Minister Teng Hsiao-p'ing. It turned out that Teng asked if he could see Nixon, so Carter's hand was forced. The invitation was a clear reflection of Nixon's continuing warm relations with the Chinese establishment—as opposed to being the result of a new enthusiasm on the part of the American public or the political class.

The disgraced former president was, in fact, "being invited to grace the symbol that he disgraced," said Senator Lowell P. Weicker Jr., a liberal Republican from Connecticut and former key member of the Senate Watergate Committee.[38] His sentiments were echoed by Republican congressman John Anderson of Illinois, who would run for president as an independent in 1980. "I do not feel, given the circumstances in which he left office, that it is appropriate for him to attend state functions of this kind," he said.[39] Anderson had called on Nixon to resign in May 1974. "It's one thing for him to live out his life as a private citizen. It's another thing for him to take steps to rehabilitate himself as a credible voice in connection with public affairs and public policy."[40]

But Carter defended the invitation, noting that "one of the major achievements of President Nixon was to open up an avenue of communication and consultation and negotiation with the Chinese, which resulted ultimately in normal relationships."[41]

In response to the invitation, Nixon played things low key as he had in the past. He expressed gratitude to the president for inviting him and eagerness to meet Teng, whom he had not met on previous visits to China, but said he would have no official comments on other matters. Nixon did meet with Carter in the White House family quarters briefly, and he was allowed to come down the Grand Stairway in a procession including Vice President Walter Mondale, House Speaker Tip O'Neill, and their wives.

In 1979, the Nixons moved to New York. He began hosting stag dinners with journalists, politicians, and intellectuals at his apartment and discussing, as always, foreign policy. Guests included *New York Times* publisher Arthur Sulzberger, ABC News president Roone Arledge, anchorman David Brinkley, and many others.[42] In 1980, *New York* magazine put Nixon on its cover with the title, "Nixon's New Life in New York."[43]

As the 1980 election approached, Nixon spoke out forcefully for Ronald Reagan, whom he had once regarded with thinly veiled condescension. His first published piece (other than his adaptation of his memoirs) since his resignation was a letter in the *New York Times* in support of Reagan's candidacy.[44] In the fall of 1980, in another sign of his growing acceptance, Nixon spent a week as a *Today Show* guest, answering questions on the presidential campaign from Theodore Wright.[45]

The year 1980 also saw the publication of Nixon's second postpresidential book, *The Real War*. Written in the context of the shah of Iran's overthrow and the Soviet invasion of Afghanistan, the book attacked

Carter-era foreign policy. The *New York Times* characterized the publication as an "exhortation to face up to the conflict and fight—without the
use of arms, if possible but without shying away from force if necessary."
Nixon took tough positions in the book, sometimes sounding more
like Reagan. Though he mentioned Carter sparingly, the writing clearly
reflected Nixon's displeasure with the Carter foreign policy, which he
regarded as weak and wrongheaded. In language that sounded quite
combative from the architect of détente, Nixon wrote of the relationship
between the United States and the Soviets:

> It may seem melodramatic to treat the twin poles of human experi-
> ence as represented by the United States and the Soviet Union as the
> equivalent of Good and Evil, Light and Darkness, God and the Devil;
> yet if we allow ourselves to think of them that way, even hypotheti-
> cally, it can clarify our perspective on the world struggle.... The United
> States represents hope, freedom, security, and peace. The Soviet Union
> stands for fear, tyranny, aggression, and war. If these are not poles of
> good and evil in human affairs, then the concepts of good and evil
> have no meaning.[46]

The Real War became an international bestseller, and though critical
of the book, the *New York Times* acquired serialization rights, which gave
Nixon's argument wide distribution.[47]

In 1982, Nixon moved to Saddle River, New Jersey, where he held
foreign policy salons and received a stream of visitors. Saddle River
became, in particular, a place of pilgrimage for GOP presidential candidates. Nixon had labored long and hard to rebuild his reputation, and
his efforts were bearing fruit during the time he lived here, though his
place in history remained shadowed by Watergate. Nixon, however, was
more interested in the present and future, especially as regarded foreign
policy. And he sought to use his influence constructively for the benefit
of Ronald Reagan, whose policies he largely supported, but whose skills
at diplomacy, he felt, were lacking.

By 1984, with another presidential campaign looming, Reagan's hardline anti-Communism had made nerves jittery in the United States and
the West. Even as polls showed that a majority of Americans agreed with
Reagan's general views on the Soviets, many feared that his aggressive

policies could lead to war. Nixon's next postpresidency book, *Real Peace*, came out at the height of these tensions, and it received warm reviews—the best he had gotten as an author. Nixon's tough but measured take in the book—in which he stressed using the full range of tools, from economic power to diplomacy to military deterrence, with an emphasis on resuscitating "hard-headed détente"—found sympathetic ears.

His criticisms of Reagan were only implied but all the more meaningful considering that he supported the president's defense buildup. What he objected to, as he carefully put it, was Reagan's disinterest in an improved US-Soviet relationship. To Nixon's mind, the massive American military buildup made an improved relationship between the countries *more* achievable, not less: he did not see having a large military capability merely as an end in itself but also as a means of achieving more concrete goals. As the *New York Review of Books*—not exactly a Nixon organ—put it: "At a time when [the U.S.-Soviet] relationship is worse than it has been in a generation, the renewed advocacy of détente by one of the shrewdest Presidents in foreign affairs in the century merits our attention."[48]

Others wished Nixon had drawn the contrast more sharply. As a *Washington Post* review of the book complained, Nixon

> directly criticizes Jimmy Carter for conducting "détente without deterrence." But only indirectly does he criticize Ronald Reagan for what might be called deterrence without détente. Herein lies the book's principal defect. Ever the Option B man, Nixon has got the substance right. But he is soft on Reagan, only gently disapproving, even though it is Reagan who, by virtue of being in power, now carries the burden of American policy. It is Reagan who is challenging Nixon's legacy.... Nixon should be taking Reagan on.[49]

Real Peace even won praise from George McGovern, Nixon's vanquished foe from 1972. "He has a better feel for détente between the two superpowers than any president since Roosevelt," McGovern said of Nixon.[50]

Nixon's book had come out a few weeks before the death of Yuri Andropov in January 1984—a time in which the Cold War was at its coldest since the early sixties. The harrowing made-for-TV film about nuclear annihilation, *The Day After,* had broadcast a few months earlier. In *Newsweek,* Jonathan Alter wrote that Nixon's expertise of a decade earlier was sorely missed. "Nixon," Alter wrote,

> *he* would know how to approach the Russians. Then the familiar profile appeared on television, and there was the former president discoursing on U.S.-Soviet relations and the importance of the Soviet President's funeral. In fact, Nixon won't be part of the official American delegation. But the speculation that he might, and TV coverage of his opinion on the matter, were two more indications that nearly 10 years after leaving the White House in disgrace, Richard Nixon is well on his way back to respectability.[51]

The Shadow President of the Reagan Years

Nixon's star was clearly in ascent. In May 1984, he gave a speech—and received a standing ovation—at, of all places, the American Society of Newspaper Editors. Given Nixon's famously hostile relationship with the media, such a reception couldn't have been more surprising or symbolic of his rehabilitation. Confirming his new standing was the laudatory write-up of the speech in the *Washington Post* by Mary McGrory, a long-time Nixon critic. McGrory, in fact, had made it onto Nixon's "Enemies List" for her "daily hate Nixon articles." Now, she sang a different tune, not only praising Nixon's informed, nuanced foreign policy presentation but contrasting it with what she saw as the crude and overly confrontational approach of President Reagan.

"This was a Nixon his old adversaries in the press had never seen," McGrory wrote of Nixon's talk. "He was serene, rational, calm, logical. He made eminently sensible remarks about U.S. foreign policy. During the question period he unfurled a positively brilliant scenario of the Democratic presidential race. It was a Nixon without sneers or smears." In listening to Nixon speak, McGrory said she thought that Republicans "now may be gripped by regret. By contrast with President Reagan, Nixon is a tower of intellect and enlightenment, particularly with regard to the Soviets and the need to get along with them." She said the once-disgraced ex-president "showed the dazzled editors the intelligence for the job he was forced out of. It was only character that was wanting."[52]

The raves for Nixon's presentation were even more striking considering that, in substance, he largely supported the Reagan foreign policies. He backed Reagan's defense spending and military buildup, stressing that it was vital for the United States to reach parity with the Soviets on having land-based nuclear missiles. He also backed the administration's support of José Napoleon Duarte's right-wing government in El Salvador as a bulwark against Communist aggression. A Soviet victory there, Nixon wrote, would give Moscow a missile site "eight minutes from Washington."[53] But it was the context Nixon was able to provide for these policies, and the depth to which he was able to engage them and their ramifications, that made these positions more persuasive to this audience.

In retrospect, it shouldn't be surprising that Nixon's reputation rebounded so strongly during the Reagan years. For one thing, Reagan's staunch conservatism shed new light on Nixon's essential moderation, especially domestically. In the Reagan era, where domestic social welfare policies were under attack, liberals looked to the Nixon policies with new appreciation. And black entrepreneurs and businesspeople, angered by Reagan's disinterest in maintaining the minority-business programs that Nixon had started, invited the former president to speak at their events.[54]

But the most compelling comparison came on foreign policy: In the eighties, Cold War tensions ran especially high, and even many Republicans worried that Reagan was pushing too hard and provoking the Soviets. During his first term, Reagan made Democrats and Republicans crave Nixon's sophisticated diplomacy and the days of détente.

Perhaps that was why Representative Morris Udall told an audience that Nixon was probably "one of the two or three people on this planet who could lead the way to reduction of the arms race." Suddenly realizing what he was saying, the representative joked: "I'll probably wash my mouth out with soap." Nixon couldn't resist sending Udall, who had been one of his former critics, a letter a week later, writing, "While I probably ought to send you a cake of soap," I appreciated your generous remarks."[55] Senator Mark Hatfield was another former Nixon foe—he, too, had held a spot on the "Enemies List"—who had developed an appreciation for the former president's wisdom. Hatfield invited Nixon to speak to a small group of senators and other officials.

"We had not heard such a profound overview of the world in years," he said.[56]

In August 1984—in the midst of an unfolding presidential campaign—came the tenth anniversary of Nixon's resignation. The *New York Times* marked the occasion with an article by Jonathan Herbers titled "After Decade, Nixon Is Gaining Favor." Herbers wrote: "A decade later he has emerged at 71 years of age as an elder statesman, commentator on foreign and domestic affairs, adviser to world leaders, a multimillionaire and a successful author and lecturer honored by audiences at home and abroad."[57]

Yet Herbers also noted the fault lines: not just among Nixon's detractors and most Democrats but also among conservatives in the Republican Party, now in the ascendancy with Reagan in the White House. The conservatives did not consider Nixon one of them; they never had. Richard Viguerie, the pioneering conservative fundraiser, saw Nixon as a custodian to Lyndon Johnson's Great Society policies and accused him of making "sweetheart deals" with the Soviet Union. Viguerie and other conservatives lamented Nixon's reemergence. So, too, for more narrowly political reasons, did mainstream Republicans, whatever their private views. They were relieved when Nixon stayed away from the GOP National Convention that summer in Dallas.

Nixon's resurgence, it should be said, made its deepest inroads with the political class and, to some extent, with the media—not necessarily with the American people. His return to stature was not primarily a popular phenomenon. It was more a reflection of the respect he was held in by those whose opinion he valued most. Though he cared what the American people thought of him, his driving ambition was to reassume a prominent place among those who were engaged in the great affairs of the world.

In 1982, Robert Kaiser pointed to "a Washington Post-ABC poll, in which, asked which of the last nine presidents had 'set the lowest moral standards,' 53 percent of respondents picked Nixon. Lyndon Johnson came in second with 8 percent. So, clearly, Nixon was far from a beloved figure by average Americans. But as Kaiser also accurately assessed, Nixon wasn't interested in winning back mass popular support. He was playing to the establishment, and to history."[58]

Indeed, as Stephen Ambrose wrote, "He did not want forgiveness, nor sympathy, nor understanding; he wanted respect. Slowly, over the decade and a half following his resignation, he earned that respect the hard way, Nixon's way."[59]

In May 1986, Nixon graced the cover of *Newsweek* with the headline "He's Back: The Rehabilitation of Richard Nixon." Though the article was reasonably balanced and noted Nixon's unique—and for many, still notorious—status, its predominant theme was a recognition of all that he had accomplished since resigning in 1974. Nixon had to be gratified when he read the magazine's litany:

> It's hard to say what finally signifies redemption for a disgraced president, the first ever to resign the office: Is it writing an article on summitry for *Foreign Affairs*, and having Ronald Reagan telephone for advice? Is it appearing on Rolling Stone's list of "Who's Hot: The New Stars in Your Future"? Is it getting a standing ovation from the American Newspaper Publishers Association, or being asked to arbitrate a labor dispute that threatened to disrupt the World Series, or being besieged by autograph seekers on a casual Burger King pit stop in New Jersey? Richard Milhous Nixon has done all those things and more in recent months; at 73, he is well launched in yet another new life, this time as the presiding sage of Saddle River, N.J.[60]

All of this was gratifying to Nixon, but his deepest ambitions remained not popular acceptance but playing a role and making a difference in the nation's foreign policy. Two months after Ronald Reagan began his second term in office, Mikhail Gorbachev was selected as the new general secretary of the Communist Party in Moscow. Unlike recent Soviet leaders, Gorbachev was young—just fifty-four—and reform-minded. He quickly set the Soviet Union on an ambitious project called perestroika (restructuring), which would seek to make the Soviet system more efficient and competitive. New ways and habits would need to be learned, especially glasnost (openness) as well as a new frankness about shortcomings and the need for change.

Gorbachev's arrival heralded a new chapter in the Cold War. After a tentative first meeting in late 1985, he and Reagan began forging a productive working relationship, and serious progress toward arms control now became a real possibility—especially since the Soviet Union simply could not financially afford the arms race any longer, at least at the levels it had reached. When Reagan and Gorbachev met in Reykjavik in 1986, they came within a whisker of a sweeping arms control deal that would have eliminated all new strategic missiles and even contemplated the possibility of eliminating nuclear weapons altogether. But the deal fell through when Gorbachev insisted that the United States confine the Strategic Defense Initiative (SDI), the missile-defense system often mocked as "Star Wars," to the laboratory. The failure to secure an agreement disappointed the US president, but a year later in Washington, he and Gorbachev would sign the historic treaty eliminating intermediate-range nuclear and conventional ballistic missiles. Clearly, Ronald Reagan had come a long way from the days when politicians in both parties worried that he might provoke a nuclear conflict.

Reagan's evolution met with celebration among moderates, but conservatives, for whom he had been a beacon of strength, felt disillusioned and even betrayed. Columnists like George Will felt that the president had fallen for a romantic image of Gorbachev and the hopes of being remembered in history as a peacemaker. For these conservatives, Reagan's move toward Gorbachev was uncomfortably reminiscent of the president whose détente policies they had so opposed: Richard Nixon. And Reagan didn't allay their concerns when he admitted, "I have frequently talked to President Nixon. He had great experience and is most knowledgeable on international affairs."[61]

Had Nixon influenced Reagan with his arguments and example? Arnold Beichman, a preeminent conservative scholar and anti-Communist, thought so. In 1989, just after Reagan left office, he wrote in *Commentary*:

> For some months now I have been trying to figure out where and how President Reagan's leap of faith in Mikhail Gorbachev started. After careful study of Nixon's latest book of foreign-policy prescriptions plus his earlier post-presidential writings, I believe that in Reagan's second term the voice was the voice of Reagan but the hands were the hands of Nixon.... [I]t is no mean achievement to have served as the

President's President, to have transformed a conservative Reagan into
a detentist Reagan.[62]

But in fact, in the waning years of Reagan's second term, Nixon's
deep-seated realism began to push his opinion in the other direction:
Although he was pleased that Reagan had made progress with the
Soviets, Nixon worried that the president might be placing too much
faith in Gorbachev. The Soviet leader, Nixon sensed, was not as different from his predecessors as Reagan and Secretary of State George
Shultz believed. And here, ironically, Nixon's skepticism was more in
line with that of the conservatives, whom he often opposed and who
opposed him.

In 1987, Nixon was invited to meet secretly with Reagan in the
White House. The president had been stung by articles written by
Nixon and Henry Kissinger suggesting that he was being duped by
Gorbachev, and he wanted to reach some accord with Nixon on Soviet
policy. In the meeting, Nixon urged Reagan to be more hawkish with
Gorbachev, and he warned him against making any agreements that
would remove missiles from Western Europe. Reagan felt Gorbachev
was sincere in wanting to wind down the arms race, but Nixon was not
persuaded. Gorbachev, he told the president, "could not have gotten his
present position or have retained it unless he wanted to be in a position
to neutralize Europe or dominate it by either conventional or nuclear
blackmail."[63] The two presidents did not agree. Later that year, Nixon
warned Reagan in a letter: "Just remember, Rome was not built in a day
and it takes more than three days to civilize Moscow."[64]

Hindsight now allows us to see where, in some areas, Nixon's views
did not pan out. Reagan and Shultz, wrote James Mann, "intuited more
quickly what [Gorbachev's] leadership of the Soviet Union might mean
for American foreign policy."[65]

But the broader point is this: The Reagan-Nixon relationship contained an ongoing tension—between Reagan's conservative idealism and
Nixon's realism. In Reagan's first term, his conservative idealism took
the form of a more confrontational attitude toward the Soviets; Nixon
was there to caution him about the costs of such a policy. In Reagan's
second term, his conservative idealism took the form of conciliation,
improved relations, and historical agreements; Nixon was there to

caution about the dangers of letting down our guard and adopting an overly credulous attitude toward a Soviet leader.

In the end, Nixon came to respect Reagan, but he also felt that the fortieth president was given too much credit for the American victory in the Cold War. As he told Monica Crowley:

> You know, as much as I think Reagan absolutely did right on the arms buildup, I cannot stomach those who go overboard on it and say that was the only thing responsible for the collapse of communism. We, of course, were going after the Russians that way years before. We fought for the bombers and all the rest. I'm not trying to minimize Reagan, but he was only part of what brought down communism. Communism would have collapsed by its own weight anyway. The Reagan buildup probably accelerated the process because the Russians were forced to match us. But I think credit belongs to *all* of the Cold War presidents, from Truman to Bush.[66]

Indeed, if there is an unsung hero in the fall of the Soviet Union, it's Nixon.

The Final Push

It would once have been difficult to imagine a dedication ceremony for a Nixon Presidential Library. But in 1990, a swelling crowd including prominent figures like Bob Hope, Gene Autry, and Billy Graham were on hand, and more than a thousand reporters came out to Yorba Linda to attend the dedication. Former presidents Ford and Reagan made the trip, along with the current president, George H. W. Bush. Only Jimmy Carter, pleading a previous commitment, was absent.[67]

The media sounded the now-familiar themes of Nixon's rehabilitation and reinvention; his comeback from political purgatory left many amazed. On *Nightline*, Barbara Walters hosted a segment entitled, "The Resurrection of Richard Nixon," in which she interviewed historians Stanley Kutler and Stephen Ambrose. "Have we finally reached a point where we can take a full and honest measure of the man?" she asked.[68]

Nixon himself kept providing new standards and offering new material by which others could take that "honest measure." In 1992, he published what some considered his best book, *Seize the Moment*, a work more heavily concerned with contemporary affairs than his previous titles had been. In *Foreign Affairs*, William G. Hyland praised the former president for addressing the crucial foreign policy issues of the day and formulating clear positions on them. In a prescient observation in the book, Nixon criticized American policy makers for failing to distinguish allies from adversaries in the Middle East—an old problem, to be sure, and one that would continue to wreak havoc in years to come.

Another striking aspect of *Seize the Moment* was that Nixon's criticisms were leveled, implicitly at least, at Republican administrations—by 1992, the year the book came out, the GOP had controlled the White House for twelve years. In earlier books, Nixon had subtly and indirectly criticized Reagan's foreign policies; now, more directly, he took on President George H. W. Bush. He felt that Bush did not appreciate his advice. Nixon, much as he would later threaten to do with Clinton, also exerted his power by releasing semicritical op-eds in major newspapers. "If he cultivated Nixon," Crowley wrote, "Bush would get valuable advice and prominent ally; if he ignored him, he would face a troublesome adversary. Nixon knew his power and he never failed to use it."[69]

In 1989, Bush's first year in office, Nixon supported the president's response to the Chinese crackdown against prodemocracy protestors in Tiananmen Square. Bush resisted pressure from the Right and the Left to take a harder line and impose economic sanctions, choosing less stringent measures and preserving his options. A harsher American response, Nixon warned, could drive Beijing back into constructive relations with Moscow and threaten the balance of power. He applauded Bush's caution.

Nixon regarded George Bush as a good man who didn't measure up to his moment in history. He had disdain for James Baker, Bush's secretary of state, whom he saw as a shrewd businessman and political pro, not as a statesman. Baker, in turn, resented Nixon for his propensity for going over his head to give advice directly to Bush.[70] Nixon often told Monica Crowley, his assistant later in his career, that the Bush administration had no one that was in Henry Kissinger's league. "Bush should listen to Kissinger," Nixon said. "After all, he knows more about the Middle East in his sleep than most of these other clowns running around Bush will ever know."[71]

In 1990, when Saddam Hussein invaded Kuwait, Nixon watched from the sidelines as Bush and Baker worked to assemble an international coalition to force the Iraqi dictator to withdraw. Nixon was frustrated by the pace of Bush's preparations. Showing again that he treated each situation as it came, and was not bound to ideological ways of looking at the world, Nixon was a pure hawk on what became known as the Gulf War. His criticism of Bush, which he made in private, concerned what he felt was excessive caution and indecision as well as putting too much credence in the hopes of a diplomatic solution—especially in tandem with the Soviet Union.

Nixon wrote to Brent Scowcroft, Bush's national security adviser, that diplomacy was not a realistic expectation, and that once American forces were fully arrayed in the Gulf, the president should give Saddam one final ultimatum and then go in. He was frustrated with what he saw as the administration's passivity.[72] "What are we going to do," he asked Monica Crowley, "debate Hussein until he leaves Kuwait?"[73] Even as the American buildup proceeded, Bush and Baker strenuously pursued diplomacy, which Nixon felt, past a certain point, was a waste of time and politically damaging.

Nixon believed fervently that the United States was right to wage war in the Gulf. As he wrote in a *New York Times* op-ed: "If Saddam Hussein gains in any way from his aggression, despite our unprecedented commitment of economic, diplomatic and military power, other aggressors will be encouraged to wage war against their neighbors and peace will be in jeopardy everywhere in the world. That is why our commitment in the gulf is a highly moral enterprise."[74]

On January 16, 1991, Scowcroft called Nixon to inform him that Bush had given the order to commence the air war over Baghdad and elsewhere in Iraq. Nixon was pleased, but watching Bush's address to the nation, he felt that the president stressed the United Nations' role too much. "No one should have the idea that after this war the UN will suddenly be this great body for world leadership," he told Crowley. "Every parliament stinks, and the UN is the most uncontrollable, unfair parliament of all."[75] Then, in late February, Bush himself called Nixon to inform him about the start of the ground war in Iraq. Nixon was pleased and once again somewhat surprised by Bush's backbone; he had worried that Baker's obsessions with a diplomatic solution, especially one forged with the Soviets, would prevail. But Bush stood firm.

Nixon's hawkish counsel likely helped the president find his footing. He gave Bush full credit for his leadership in the war a year later, when speaking of the president, who was then engaged in a tough and ultimately unsuccessful reelection campaign, Nixon told Larry King: "As he demonstrated so eloquently by his actions during the Persian Gulf War, he's a strong leader; he believes in freedom, he believes in democracy and he believes in doing what is necessary to deter and punish aggression. So that tells me he's a man of principal [*sic*]."[76]

But Nixon was also deeply frustrated by the Bush administration, and what vexed him most was its failure, as he saw it, to seize an historic moment—when, after the Soviet Union's fall, a renewed Western push for democracy was possible. "Bush and Baker suffered from a great lack of creativity in foreign policy," Nixon told Crowley. "It was a damn shame that they were in charge at the end of the Cold War."[77] He was convinced that Bush and Baker, like Reagan and Shultz before them, put too much faith in Mikhail Gorbachev and failed to see the dangers of so fully embracing the Soviet leader.

Counter to all the triumphalism of the early nineties that followed the fall of the Berlin Wall and the eventual dissolution of the Soviet Union, Nixon felt that the United States was squandering a golden opportunity. He circulated a memo entitled "How to Lose the Cold War," in which he accused Bush of "failing to seize the moment to shape the history of the next half-century."[78] Most presciently, Nixon stressed the importance of supporting the Democratic movements in Russia before they were crushed by more autocratic forces. If that happened, he warned, the United States would live to regret its inaction as new Russian despots came to the fore. In words that read starkly now, Nixon all but predicted the rise of Vladimir Putin:

If Yeltsin fails, the prospects for the next 50 years will turn grim. The Russian people will not turn back to Communism. *But a new, more dangerous despotism based on Russian nationalism will take power.... If a new despotism prevails, everything gained in the great peaceful revolution of 1991 will be lost.* War could break out in the former Soviet Union as

the new despots use force to restore the "historical borders" of Russia.[79]
(Emphasis added.)

Following the 1992 election, Nixon began to conduct the most
rewarding of his postpresidential relationships—with Bill Clinton, who
had defeated Bush in the election. The Clinton-Nixon relationship, as
I described in chapter 7, would not have developed as it did if the new
president hadn't gone out of his way to cultivate Nixon. It was a remarkable and surprising relationship, and had Nixon's health held out beyond
1994, it would have been fascinating to see what directions it might have
taken. Certainly the world did not lack for challenges during the Clinton
years, even if a booming domestic economy kept many Americans'
minds off these troubles.

Without question, it was Bill Clinton who did more than any other
president to bring Nixon back into the fold. It's easy to forget that when
Clinton took office in 1993, Nixon still stood outside the accepted circle
of presidential politics. Gerald Ford, Jimmy Carter, Ronald Reagan, and
George H. W. Bush had all kept him at arm's length, at best. As I argue
in chapter 7, Clinton's relationship with Nixon, as well as his absorp-
tion of Nixon's political lessons, make him Nixon's true heir. Though
Nixon had criticisms of Clinton and did not relate to him in a cultural
sense—he was, after all, a womanizing, draft-dodging baby boomer, in
Nixon's view—he admired Clinton's political instincts.

Thus it was fitting to hear Clinton's words in his eulogy for Nixon
in April 1994: "May the day of judging President Nixon on anything less
than his entire life and career come to a close."[80] Over four thousand
people, packing the grounds of Nixon's boyhood home, now the site
of the Nixon Presidential Library, heard Clinton memorialize a world
leader who had seen the highest of highs and lowest of lows during his
long career, but who never lost sight of the broader picture of the world
and America's place in it.

World leaders came from dozens of nations to attend the funeral,
and the congressional delegation numbered over one hundred. Even
Spiro Agnew, Nixon's former vice president, who had resigned in disgrace and held a grudge against Nixon ever since, made an appearance.

Henry Kissinger, who had collaborated with Nixon in world-changing events and vied with him for who deserved more credit, paid tribute

to the former president: "Nixon's greatest accomplishment was as much moral as political: to lead from strength at a moment of apparent weakness; to husband the nation's resilience and thus to lay the basis for victory in the Cold War."[81]

And Senate Minority Leader Bob Dole, who had had a fractious relationship with Nixon, could barely suppress his tears as he honored the man he believed to be America's central postwar figure: "Strong, brave, unafraid of controversy, unyielding in his convictions, living every day of his life to the hilt, the largest figure of our time whose influence will be timeless—that was Richard Nixon."[82]

As Crowley herself put Nixon's later admiration, reflecting a few years afterward: "The wheel of history had turned; time had changed perceptions. Nixon was too large a figure, too complex and too great an influence on the twentieth century to remain a persona frozen in 1974."[83]

Redemption and Legacy

Not surprisingly, how one regards Nixon's postpresidency depends crucially on how one regards Nixon himself. While a longtime critic like Carl Bernstein could acknowledge that Nixon had "come back from the dead,"[84] he didn't say it approvingly, and he still found most everything that Nixon said or did in his retirement objectionable. Even by the time of Nixon's death, Watergate defined his image in the public mind. A 2002 Gallup poll found that 54 percent of people still disapproved of his performance as president. In a 2006 Quinnipiac poll asking respondents to list the worst president in American history, Nixon came in second— topped only by then-president George W. Bush. It seems unlikely that Watergate and Nixon will ever be delinked.

Yet the Watergate scar is clearly not the full measure of Nixon—or must not be—for those who wish to reckon with our history honestly. Throughout this book, I have tried to set forth the foundational influence Nixon had on the world, through his foreign policy, as well as on American politics, in ways that remain enduring today. (And, of course, given the stature of the United States, to shape and influence American politics is unavoidably to shape and influence the world.) Nixon's impact extended as well to the years of his postpresidency, as

I have emphasized here. The evidence is clear that, as the years passed, his counsel was increasingly sought within Republican circles, and that Republican presidents were influenced by his views. That Bill Clinton, a child of the 1960s, came to Nixon for advice repeatedly only emphasizes how valued his insights came to be. And moreover, the arguments he made in his ten postpresidential books—especially about international affairs, and particularly on post-Soviet Russia—have turned out to be, like his foreign policy, farsighted and even prophetic.

"There are generally two models for the modern ex-POTUS," wrote Christopher Beam for *Slate* in 2009. "The fade into relative obscurity favored by Gerald Ford and Ronald Reagan; and the activist, globe-trotting, elder statesman model as practiced by Jimmy Carter and Bill Clinton."[85] Indeed, most Americans are familiar with the high-profile postpresidencies of Carter and Clinton. Carter has forged a postpresidency unlike any that previously existed. His establishment of the Carter Center in Atlanta to advance human rights and promote conflict resolution was a grand gesture, one reflecting the huge ambitions that he had once had for his presidency. His work for Habitat for Humanity, efforts to monitor elections in troubled regions, and general energy in pursuing a vigorous and useful life are certainly admirable. But his international outreach efforts were sometimes painfully naïve and caused headaches for his successors, whose wishes he rarely consulted. In particular, Carter's harsh, intemperate attacks on Israel, which he has compared with an apartheid regime, have infuriated conservatives and defenders of the Jewish State. Yet Carter won the Nobel Peace Prize in 2002.

Clinton, too, has blazed a formidable path. His Clinton Foundation and Clinton Global Initiative have raised impressive sums for HIV/AIDS programs, the battle against climate change, public health programs, and combating poverty. And Clinton remains a Democratic Party star, with his two-term presidency widely regarded as a success.

And yet the Carter and Clinton examples are not the only models for an active postpresidency, as suggested by Beam. Somehow the journalist overlooked the Nixonian model, which closely resembles one from antiquity with which Nixon would have been familiar: that of the retired sage, available to dispense statesman-like advice. To be sure, Nixon's unique circumstances in part dictated his options; he wouldn't have been able to globe-trot the world as a philanthropist or gadfly even if he had wanted to. But he never would have wanted to, any more than he would have sought a life of golf and poolside crossword puzzles. As he told David Frost:

> The unhappiest people in the world are those in the watering places, the international watering places, like the south coast of France and Newport and Palm Springs and Palm Beach...going to parties every night, playing golf every afternoon, then bridge. Drinking too much. Talking too much. Thinking too little. Retired. No purpose.... [T]hey don't know life. Because what makes life mean something is purpose. A goal. The battle. The struggle. Even if you don't win.[86]

What Nixon aspired to was a life of intellectual and political engagement. His effort to establish himself as America's foreign policy sage bore considerable fruit. His aim, as Burton Kaufman summarized it, was "to put Watergate behind him to gain the respect of the very groups he had always regarded as his enemies; to become once more a person of influence nationally and globally; and most important, to establish what he still believed was his rightful place as the nation's best post-World War II president and one of the nation's great presidents."[87] The judgment as to whether these things took place, of course, will depend on who renders it. But clearly Nixon remade himself, post-Watergate, in an extraordinary way.

Jonathan Aitken, a conservative former parliamentarian in Britain who interviewed Nixon and authored a biography on him, tells of watching Nixon during his 1978 Oxford University visit. The place was rowdy with students protesting his visit and firing hostile questions at him. Aitken was struck by the hardy way Nixon stood up to the response.

"Yeah, I screwed up," Nixon told one student. "You're right. And I paid the price. Mea culpa. But let's get on. You'll be here in the year 2000 and we'll see how I'm regarded then."

Aitken also remembered a talk Nixon gave to a group of conservatives at his home on the day in 1978 that Karol Wojtyla of Warsaw was elected Pope John Paul II. The then-editor of the *Times* of London,

William Rees-Mogg, asked Nixon if the choice would be significant in ways political as well as religious.

"You bet!" Nixon replied. "A Polish Pope could be the spark to set alight a fire in Eastern Europe that will destroy Communism."[88]

It was that kind of insight and sharp analysis—the kind that a decade and a half later had Nixon warning of a new Russian despotism in the post-Soviet era—that made the man so difficult to dismiss, even for his detractors. If his Watergate legacy furnished the ultimate negative model for politicians, his postpresidency provided a more positive standard for them to follow: "You're never beaten until you quit," as he liked to say. "By his resilience," Aitken wrote, "he rebuilt much of his own reputation in his own lifetime. A hundred years on from his birth, his legacy looks solid and the memories of his character flaws are fading. On the stock exchange of history, shares in Nixon are a good buy."[89]

Nixon in 2016

America is in trouble today not because her people have failed but because her leaders have failed. And what America needs are leaders to match the greatness of the people.

—RICHARD NIXON, 1968[1]

When I was an undergraduate in the spring of 1972, I took a course with then–Harvard professor and future ambassador to India, UN ambassador, and US senator from New York, Daniel Patrick Moynihan, who had just left the Nixon administration. Along with other wise advice, Professor Moynihan implored us not to have a monolithic and narrow view of politics. Speaking to those of us who might be inclined to join the antiwar or other protest movements—which were still going at the time, though they were beginning to wane—he told us to understand what we were protesting about and what we wanted before taking action. And then he surprised us by encouraging us—and particularly me—to study the record and accomplishments of Richard Nixon. See if you don't agree, he said, that Nixon is one of the most successful presidents in pushing a fundamental overhaul of domestic policy along with an articulation of a realistic foreign policy—not only to extricate us from Vietnam but also to put us in a preeminent position vis-à-vis the Russians. You need to appreciate Nixon.

Forty-three years after the fact, I'm doing what Moynihan—my former teacher, friend, and later client—entreated me to do. I think Pat was right. I've examined Nixon's achievements as he suggested, and I'm arguing that he was the preeminent political leader and president of the postwar era, with influence and importance that are still felt today. The exploration has been as fascinating and rewarding as Pat promised.

The mistake people make with Nixon is in assuming that he wasn't a good president because of his failures as a person, especially because of his involvement in Watergate. Much of the recent writing about him has focused on Watergate and his crimes. I don't dismiss these incidents, not for one second. But to focus solely on Nixon's misdeeds is, in my judgment, myopic and misses the larger point about his strategic vision domestically and internationally.

I recognize that many people across the political spectrum view Nixon with abhorrence.

I understand how they feel; I blanched, too, when reading and hearing the White House tapes, and when reviewing again the web of conspiracy and criminality that eventually engulfed his presidency. But we might consider, by way of comparison, the example of Lyndon Johnson: even though Johnson sat in the Oval Office and used crude terms in talking about blacks with Senator Richard Russell, he is still remembered as a civil rights hero. Nixon's civil rights achievements are remarkable, too. Bottom line: From 1969 to 1974, Nixon had a profound impact on American social, economic, and foreign policy, as well as a transformative impact on our politics. Terrible as it was, Watergate cannot negate all that.

What I've tried to do with this book is something radically different than other Nixon critics have done. I haven't sought to parse Watergate, Nixon's personality, the "Enemies List," or do a psychiatric profile of the guy. I have looked instead at the policy outputs, the political impact, and the long-term impact of his presidency. In my view, Nixon's foreign policy was among the most successful of our time, his domestic policy was transformational, and his impact on both the Right and the Left was as substantial as anybody's—in fact, greater than anybody's. Put another way, he got as much done to advance conservative principles as Ronald Reagan, and he did as much for the Left as any president, including Barack Obama. I urge readers to take an objective look at his record. In a time when we have a president, Obama, whose skills as a world leader are degraded and dismissed, Nixon's leadership should be seen in a more favorable light.

As this book goes to press, the 2016 presidential campaign is getting into full swing. It promises to be a hard-fought race, and will certainly be much closer than 2008 and maybe even 2012. As in all presidential contests, the winning candidate will be the one who does a better job of convincing Americans that he or she can lead them to a promising future. In my view, that candidate will need to do what all winning candidates have done since 1968: adapt the Nixon template to present-day conditions and issues.

That will mean, speaking generally, that the winner will be the candidate who appeals across a broad range of crucial issues, highlighting how the other side is simply not up to the challenge. What are some of these issues? Immigration, for one: A Nixonesque winning candidate would likely push a tough immigration reform program that would have a pathway to citizenship but that prioritizes border security first. He or she would be a tough-minded reformer of our education system, pushing school choice and charter schools, dealing with the testing challenges, and taking on the teachers' unions.

A Nixon-like candidate in 2016 would have something to say about American competitiveness more broadly—not just in terms of education but as far as our business environment and our suffocating regulatory and tax structures. Where Nixon was a presidential visionary on the environment, his 2016 successor will need to be a visionary on energy issues. He or she will need to articulate how the United States can maximize our remarkable boon of shale gas reserves while also honoring environmental and ecological concerns.

Above all, on foreign policy, a Nixonesque candidate would hold President Obama accountable for his failures and reconnect voters with the role of American power in the world. Ronald Reagan called America "a shining city upon a hill"; Nixon didn't use such exalted language, but he believed in America as the crucial actor in the world, and he would argue today that we need to reclaim that mantle. You can bet that, as the president who negotiated détente with the Soviet Union but then stood up to the Russians in the Yom Kippur War of 1973, Nixon would take a different approach to the Ukraine crisis than Obama has done.

As I write this in late 2015, the campaign is still taking shape on the Republican side, with many candidates currently vying for the nomination. By contrast, on the Democratic side, barring some unforeseen disaster, the party shows every sign of having settled on its nominee: Hillary Clinton. What would Nixon say about Hillary and the various Republican contenders—and what advice might he give them? How would he see the essentials of the 2016 showdown?

He would probably say, for starters, that Hillary needs to be nimble in dealing with her ongoing e-mail scandal—but that she might be through the worst of it. He might also conclude, having watched her showdown with Republicans on the Benghazi committee, that she is fortunate in her enemies. The Democrats of his time knew how to nail someone to the wall, he would say; he had experienced that firsthand. The Republicans we've got today, he'd sigh, can't talk and tie their shoes at the same time.

Hillary is well-positioned, he'd go on, but she still hasn't been road tested, and she continues to struggle with how to distance herself from President Obama. Nixon would remember well the trouble he had in 1960, when President Eisenhower, asked about a major idea Nixon had contributed as his vice president, told reporters to "give me a week. I may think of one."[2] Now the shoe is on the other foot: Nixon would be trying to figure out what Hillary has accomplished. But rather than extrapolating—and if I may be allowed some poetic license—let me try to tune him in:

Hillary, look: You've got to get away from Obama and that record. You need your own identity. He's kept you hamstrung, and you've shown discipline in not criticizing him overtly. You broke away a few times, as when you reversed yourself on the Trans-Pacific Partnership, and before that, when you said that you would handle Ukraine differently, or that "Don't do stupid stuff" is not a foreign policy—I could almost imagine Kissinger saying that! But you need a platform of your own that distinguishes you, and you need to do it without incurring his wrath. You don't want a sitting president angry at you, to say nothing of the party dissension that would cause.

Most of all, you need an economic and social philosophy that deals with the problem that, while the Left wants to take on inequality, the rest of the country wants to create some goddamn jobs. I think you've got to recapture that voice you had at the end of the 2008 primaries: a sense of urgency, confidence, and leadership—with some defiance thrown in! That's when you became a candidate that people could relate to, and gave them a sense that you represent the best of America, rather than a sense of drift and whining and anger, which we have seen in your career at other points. Americans love a fighter.

That's how I won.

Look, I'm not a Democrat—you don't need me to tell you that. But I know your position. They're trying to do to you what they did to me: slander you, make you out to be something you're not. I get that. Bill can be useful to you, of course, on fundraising and speaking at big rallies and events—but not all the time. Your problem with him isn't the one that you think: It's really a question of how you can use him to validate your candidacy instead of detract from it. I had the same issue with Eisenhower in 1960; we didn't have it worked out. You need a two-step, a way to use Bill while also minimizing him, just as you need to use Obama while distancing yourself from him. You've heard of triangulation? Your husband didn't invent it, but he can tell you who did.

I won't wish you good luck, but I will wish you well.

We can imagine Nixon then turning to the Republicans. He would begin by stressing how, given that the Democrats have won the popular vote in five of the last six elections, the GOP must hold the conservative base but also expand it—as he once did. He'd say that they need to win Florida and Ohio, and also take a few Midwestern states, to ensure a victory. They need a progrowth, positive agenda emphasizing the future, talking about the kind of nation we can be—not the kind of nation we are. But to hear it directly from him:

Having lived in Saddle Brook, I've watched Chris Christie—and he isn't ready for the national stage. He's better suited to his home state of New Jersey. And he won't win over the conservative base. Rand Paul was interesting on paper, but given our challenges with ISIS and al-Qaeda, his isolationist foreign policy just isn't viable. He is channeling Robert Taft! That didn't work the first time. The smartest Republican out there, in terms of ideas, is Ted Cruz; ideas matter to him, and I respect that. I enjoy listening to him in the debates. But he's too far to the right. He has consistently supported shutting down the government. The Republicans can't nominate someone like that. Too divisive. Marco Rubio is a tremendous talent, politically speaking—that kind of ease on the campaign trail and in debates comes to very few of us. But he's a boy wonder. Do we want another of those, after

Obama? Still, Rubio is a strong contender, and I think he can finesse the conservative-centrist divide within the party.

Of course, the Republican race has been turned upside down by the "outsider" trend. We've seen trends like this before, but maybe nothing like it for several generations. Republican voters have a real fascination this cycle with the nonpolitician, most of all—and it's that fascination that explains Donald Trump and Ben Carson, too, even though they express very different moods and have different styles. Carson is a terrific person—a great American, you might say. But he's not presidential material.

Trump is something else. He is the living expression of the silent majority, circa 2016. You don't think there's anger and frustration out there? Just look at the crowds the man draws. This mood has been building for years. Anyone looking at the 2010 and 2012 primaries, just as I observed in the underlying trends in 1964, could have seen this in the cards. Still, I have to hand it to the Donald—we didn't have someone like him back in the days before reality TV. I wouldn't bet on him to win the nomination, but my goodness—he's a political force. He has upended our politics. If you don't believe me, ask Jeb Bush! He was the pick of the conventional-wisdom crowd. We saw how that worked out, didn't we?

But there is a lesson in Bush's flameout—and it's not just that Americans didn't want another Bush, though that's probably true. Jeb somehow missed how restive and angry the Republican Party is in 2015—just as it was in 1968, when I was running. Back then, it wasn't just the Goldwater wing but those concerned about race, values, and crime—the silent majority, again. Today, it's economic angst, anxiety about America's role in the world, lack of control of our borders, and a sense that everything is falling apart. Jeb tacked left when he should have tacked right. Failing to read the public mood is fatal for any political leader.

Whoever wins the Republican nomination, they'll have to remember that—and, if I may be allowed, I'd advise them to brush up on their Nixon. What does that mean? It means, among other things, honoring the complexity of politics and human nature—and making it work for you. Despite what the Left has said about me, I was really a moderate Republican. I accepted the New Deal, and all these years later, people with any fairness can see that I was a much more progressive president than many who have come after me. Even Obama said that he's not as liberal as I was—and he's right!

Yet my rhetoric was conservative, and that wasn't just political positioning. Those were my values at the end of the day. I was a conservative in the small-*c* sense—I never had a liberal bone in my body—even if some of my policies were expansive on the government side. I saw that they would shore up social cohesion, and that's a conservative goal. I built my Southern strategy and my silent majority.

So, Marco, or Ted, or Donald, or Ben—hell, I'll even throw Christie in there: Good luck to you. You've first got to lock up the conservative base, but it's not just a matter of mouthing conservative pieties; you need to offer something substantive. Right now, there is a lot of anger in the country, and you, the Republicans, have to find a way to channel it positively; that's what the silent majority was all about. You have to give people reason to believe again. You need to reclaim some of Reagan's vision and appeal in 1980. You have to prove yourselves as conservatives while also reaching out to moderates—in short, you have to unify your party, and then you have to go on from there and unify the country. Sure, it's difficult, but for God's sake, it's been done before. I'm counting on one of you to do it. And you know why?

Because Hillary is vulnerable. Anyone can see that. You need to make the case that she represents failed policies of the past and the presidency of her husband that remains mired in controversy, and that you have the ideas and the leadership for America's future. You need to represent what I represented: a practical, tough-minded candidate for a country that desperately needs smart leadership. You need to tap into the frustration many have in this country about the way things are going—yet to do it in a way that somehow is inspiring, that fires up every Republican, yet also wins over uncommitted voters.

In other words, men, you need to thread the needle. I know about that. I made a political career doing it. If you can do it, too, you'll win in 2016.

I should tell you, though, that the Clintons have always been gracious to me, and if I'm wrong and a Republican doesn't win, I expect to be in the front row at Hillary's inaugural—in spirit only, of course. But I trust that none of you will hold that against me.

☆ ☆ ☆ ☆ ☆

And anyone who doubts that Richard Nixon will preside—in spirit only, to be sure—over the 2016 presidential campaign, and over the 2017 inauguration, and much of what then follows, simply hasn't been paying attention to politics in the United States. The helicopter that bore Nixon away in August 1974 took him out of the White House, but not out of the game. He shadows America still.

Notes

Introduction: Walking in Nixon's Shadow

1 Bob Dole, quoted in "Senator Bob Dole's Comments at President Nixon's Funeral," CNN Web site, June 17, 1997, http://www.cnn.com/ALLPOLITICS/1997/gen/resources/watergate/dole.speech.html.

2 John Dean, quoted in Scott Porch, "What the Archives Say about Nixon," *Daily Beast*, August 8, 2014, http://www.thedailybeast.com/articles/2014/08/08/what-the-archives-say-about-nixon.html.

3 Peter Roff, "The Never-Ending Nixon Wars: The 37th President May Never Be Fully Understood," *U.S. News & World Report*, October 28, 2014, http://www.usnews.com/opinion/blogs/peter-roff/2014/10/28/john-dean-and-roger-stone-continue-the-nixon-wars.

4 Richard Cohen, "Richard Nixon's Lasting Damage to the GOP," *Washington Post*, August 4, 2014, http://www.washingtonpost.com/opinions/richard-cohen-richard-nixons-lasting-damage-to-the-gop/2014/08/04/c28d552e-1c0c-11e4-ae54-0cfe1f974f8a_story.html.

5 Anthony Lewis, "Vietnam Delenda Est," *New York Times*, December 23, 1972.

6 Robert Dallek, "Legacy Tarnished by His Own Words: In 'The Nixon Defense,' John W. Dean Returns to Watergate," *New York Times*, July 27, 2014, http://www.nytimes.com/2014/07/28/books/in-the-nixon-defense-john-w-dean-returns-to-watergate.html.

7 Frank Mankiewicz, quoted in Jennifer C. Kerr, "Frank Mankiewicz, Aide to Robert Kennedy, Dies at 90," *PBS Newshour* Web site, October 24, 2014, http://www.pbs.org/newshour/rundown/frank-mankiewicz/.

8 Patrick J. Buchanan, "Nixon and Kennedy: The Myths and Reality," *American Conservative*, November 19, 2013, http://www.theamericanconservative.com/nixon-and-kennedy-the-myths-and-reality/.

9 Richard Nixon, quoted in Edwin Warner, "Richard Nixon: An American Disraeli?," *Time*, November 27, 1972, http://content.time.com/time/subscriber/printout/0,8816,944518,00.html.

10 Richard Nixon, quoted in Alan Axelrod, *The Real History of the Cold War: A New Look at the Past* (New York: Sterling, 2009), 366.

11 Warner, "An American Disraeli?"

12 Sam Tanenhaus, "Original Sin: Why the GOP Is and Will Continue to be the Party of White People," *New Republic*, February 10, 2013, http://www.newrepublic.com/article/112365/why-republicans-are-party-white-people.

13 Richard Nixon, quoted in William Costello, *The Facts about Nixon: An Authorized Biography* (New York: Viking, 1960), 4.

14 Patrick Buchanan, quoted in Richard Reeves, *President Nixon: Alone in the White House* (New York: Simon & Schuster, 2001), 295.

15 William Rusher, quoted in "Rusher, William Allen," Sarah Katherine Mergel, American National Biography Online, October 2014, http://www.anb.org/articles/16/16-03915.html.

16 David U. Himmelstein and Steffie Woolhandler, "I Am Not a Health Reform," *New York Times*, December 15, 2007, http://www.nytimes.com/2007/12/15/opinion/15woolhandler.html.

17 Robert Gottlieb, *Forcing the Spring: The Transformation of the American Environmental Movement* (Washington, DC: Island, 2005), 152–53.

18 Robert Mason, *Richard Nixon and the Quest for a New Majority* (Chapel Hill: University of North Carolina Press, 2004), 144.

19 Steven F. Hayward, *The Age of Reagan: The Fall of the Old Liberal Order; 1964–1980* (New York: Random House), 220.

20 Adlai Stevenson, quoted in Rick Perlstein, *Nixonland: The Rise of a President and the Fracturing of America* (New York: Simon & Schuster, 2009), 6–8.

21 Richard Nixon, "Address Accepting the Presidential Nomination at the Republican National Convention in Miami Beach, Florida," Gerhard Peters and John T. Woolley, eds., American Presidency Project, (speech, Miami Beach, August 8, 1968), http://www.presidency.ucsb.edu/ws/?pid=25968.

22 Perlstein, *Nixonland*, 234.

23 James Reston, quoted in Dennis Wainstock, *Election Year 1968: The Turning Point* (New York: Enigma Books, 2012), 174.

24 "1968: NIXON VS. HUMPHREY VS. WALLACE," Museum of the Moving Image: Living Room Candidate, Presidential Campaign Commercials 1952–2012, http://www.livingroomcandidate.org/commercials/1968/crime.

25 Timothy Crouse, *The Boys on the Bus* (New York: Ballantine Books, 1972), 260.

SECTION I
THE NIXON RECORD

Chapter 1: The Domestic Policy Pragmatist

1 Joan Hoff, *Nixon Reconsidered* (New York: Basic Books, 1994), 113–14.

2 Daniel Patrick Moynihan, quoted in Joseph J. Sabia, "Why Richard Nixon Deserves to be Remembered along with 'Brown,'" History News Network, May 5, 2004, http://hnn.us/article/5331.

3 Hoff, *Nixon Reconsidered*, 8.

4 Richard Nixon, quoted in Michael Genovese, *The Nixon Presidency* (New York: Greenwood, 1990), 74.

5 Joseph J. Sabia, "Richard Nixon: Racial Healer," FrontPageMagazine.com, May 24, 2004, http://archive.frontpagemag.com/readArticle.aspx?ARTID=12915.

6 Daniel Patrick Moynihan, quoted in Sabia, "Nixon Deserves to be Remembered."

7 Matthew J. Lindstrom and Zachary A. Smith, *The National Environmental Policy Act: Judicial Misconstruction, Legislative Indifference, and Executive Neglect* (College Station: Texas A&M University Press, 2001), 4.

8 John Mitchell, quoted in "John N. Mitchell Dies at 75; Major Figure in Watergate," *New York Times*, November 10, 1988, http://www.nytimes.

com/1988/11/10/obituaries/john-n-mitchell-dies-at-75-major-figure-in-watergate. html?pagewanted=print.

9 "John N. Mitchell," WikiQuote, November 12, 2013, http://en.wikiquote.org/ wiki/John_N._Mitchell.

10 Daniel Patrick Moynihan, quoted in Michael A. Genovese, "Richard M. Nixon and the Politicization of Justice," in *Watergate and Afterward: The Legacy of Richard M. Nixon*, ed. Leon Friedman and William F. Levantrosser (Westport, CT: Greenwood, 1992), 70.

11 Richard Nixon, quoted in Stephen Smith and Kate Ellis, "Campaign '68: Nixon," American Public Media: *American RadioWorks* Web site, 2015, http:// americanradioworks.publicradio.org/features/campaign68/b3.html.

12 David Frum, *How We Got Here: The 70's, the Decade That Brought You Modern Life—for Better or Worse* (New York: Basic Books, 2000), 258.

13 Robert Reinhold, "20 Years of School Integration Won Much, but Much Is Undone; Floodgates Opened," *New York Times*, May 12, 1974, http://query .nytimes.com/mem/archive/pdf?res=9905EED6103BE53ABC4A52DFB366838F6 69EDE.

14 Samantha Meinke, "Milliken v. Bradley: The Northern Battle for Desegregation," *Michigan Bar Journal* 90, no. 9 (September 2011): 20–22.

15 Sabia, "Racial Healer."

16 Ray Price, quoted in Sabia, "Nixon Deserves to be Remembered."

17 George P. Shultz, "How a Republican Desegregated the South's Schools," *New York Times*, January 8, 2003, http://www.nytimes.com/2003/01/08/opinion/how-a-republican-desegregated-the-south-s-schools.html?pagewanted=all&src=pm.

18 Richard Nixon, quoted in Ibid.

19 Quoted in Sabia, "Racial Healer."

20 Shultz, "A Republican Desegregated the South's Schools."

21 Daniel Patrick Moynihan, quoted in Sabia, "Nixon Deserves to be Remembered."

22 Tom Wicker, quoted in Shultz, "A Republican Desegregated the South's Schools."

23 *Fortune* magazine, quoted in Douglas E. Schoen, "Richard Nixon—the Last Great Liberal," Fox News Web site, January 9, 2013, http://www.foxnews.com/ opinion/2013/01/09/richard-nixon-last-great-liberal.html.

24 "5 Things to Know about Affirmative Action," Alicia Stewart, CNN: In America Web site, October 10, 2012, http://inamerica.blogs.cnn.com/2012/10/10/5-things-to-know-about-affirmative-action/.

25 Arthur Fletcher, quoted in "Affirmative Action," *An Assessment into President Richard Nixon's Domestic Policies*, http://nixonwebsite.weebly.com/civil-rights. html.

26 Ray Price, quoted in Dean J. Kotlowski, *Nixon's Civil Rights: Politics, Principle, and Policy* (Cambridge, MA: Harvard University Press, 2002), 128.

27 Graham T. Molitor, quoted in Robert E. Weems, *Business in Black and White: American Presidents and Black Entrepreneurs in the Twentieth Century* (New York: New York University Press, 2009), 122.

28 Jeffrey A. Raffel, *Historical Dictionary of School Segregation and Desegregation: The American Experience* (Westport, CT: Greenwood, 1998), 185–86.

29 Patrick J. Buchanan, "The Neocons and Nixon's Southern Strategy," Patrick

J. Buchanan Web site, December 30, 2002, http://buchanan.org/blog/pjb-the-neocons-and-nixons-southern-strategy-512.

30 Ibid.

31 Daniel Patrick Moynihan, *Daniel Patrick Moynihan: A Portrait in Letters of an American Visionary*, ed. Steven R. Weisman (New York: PublicAffairs, 2010), 201.

32 Richard Nixon, quoted in Nina Totenberg, "Tape Reveals Nixon's Views on Abortion," NPR Web site, June 23, 2009, http://www.npr.org/templates/story/story.php?storyId=105832640.

33 Allen Barra, "Female Athletes, Thank Nixon," *New York Times*, June 16, 2012, http://www.nytimes.com/2012/06/17/opinion/sunday/female-athletes-thank-nixon.html?_r=0.

34 Ibid.

35 Hoff, *Nixon Reconsidered*, 106.

36 Ibid.

37 Ibid., 113.

38 Richard Nixon, quoted in "The Seventh Crisis of Richard Nixon," *Time*, April 20, 1970, http://content.time.com/time/subscriber/article/0,33009,944009,00.html.

39 Richard Nixon, quoted in "Nixon's Court: Its Making and Its Meaning," *Time*, November 1, 1971, http://content.time.com/time/subscriber/article/0,33009,905464-2,00.html.

40 Bob Woodward and Scott Armstrong, *The Brethren: Inside the Supreme Court* (New York: Simon & Schuster, 1979), 221.

41 John Ehrlichman, quoted in John Cloud, "William Rehnquist: 1924–2005," *Time*, September 4, 2005, http://content.time.com/time/nation/article/0,8599,1101296,00.html.

42 Richard Nixon, "Special Message to the Congress Recommending a Program to End Hunger in Africa" (letter, Washington, DC, May 6, 1969), American Presidency Project, http://www.presidency.ucsb.edu/ws/?pid=2038.

43 Richard Nixon, quoted in Mike Alberti and Kevin C. Brown, "Guaranteed Income's Moment in the Sun," *Remapping Debate*, April 24, 2013, http://www.remappingdebate.org/sites/default/files/Guaranteed%20income%E2%80%99s%20moment%20in%20the%20sun_0.pdf, 5.

44 Alberti and Brown, "Guaranteed Income."

45 Hoff, *Nixon Reconsidered*, 128.

46 Ibid., 132.

47 James Reston, "President Nixon, Poverty and Peace," *New York Times*, August 10, 1969.

48 Richard Nixon, "Annual Message to the Congress on the State of the Union" (speech, Washington, DC, January 22, 1971), Gerhard Peters and John T. Woolley, eds., American Presidency Project, http://www.presidency.ucsb.edu/ws/?pid=3110.

49 Hoff, *Nixon Reconsidered*, 134.

50 Richard Nixon, quoted in Ibid., 119.

51 Joan Hoff, "Nixon Had Some Successes, before His Disgrace," *New York Times*, June 13, 2012, http://www.nytimes.com/roomfordebate/2012/06/13/did-any-good-come-of-watergate/nixon-had-some-successes-before-his-disgrace.

52 Nixon, "Annual Message to the Congress."

53 Richard Nixon, "Address on the State of the Union Delivered before a Joint Session of Congress" (speech, Washington, DC, January 30, 1974), American Presidency Project, http://www.presidency.ucsb.edu/ws/?pid=4327.

54 Ibid.

55 Ray Price, quoted in Kevin G. Hall, "Democrats' Health Plans Echo Nixon's Failed GOP Proposal," McClatchyDC, November 28, 2007, http://www.mcclatchydc.com/2007/11/28/22163/democrats-health-plans-echo-nixons.html#storylink=cpy.

56 Price, quoted in Ibid.

57 Richard Nixon, quoted in Ibid.

58 Herbert Stein, quoted in Friedman and Levantrosser, *Watergate and Afterward.*

59 William E. Leuchtenburg, *The American President: From Teddy Roosevelt to Bill Clinton* (New York: Oxford University Press, 2015), 495.

60 "Economic Stabilization Act of 1970 (Public Law 92-210)," in *Code of Federal Regulations of the United States of America* (Washington, DC: US Government Printing Office, 1974).

61 Jack Lewis, "The Birth of EPA," *EPA Journal* (November 1985), United States Environmental Protection Agency, http://www2.epa.gov/aboutepa/birth-epa.

62 Ibid.

63 Ibid.

64 Gaylord Nelson, "Earth Day '70: What It Meant," *EPA Journal* (April 1980), United States Environmental Protection Agency, http://www2.epa.gov/aboutepa/earth-day-70-what-it-meant.

65 Quoted in Hoff, *Nixon Reconsidered*, 21.

66 Richard Nixon, quoted in Elizabeth Drew, "Nostalgia for Nixon?," *Washington Post*, June 9, 2007, http://www.washingtonpost.com/wp-dyn/content/article/2007/06/08/AR2007060802260.htm.

67 Lewis, "Birth of EPA."

68 Richard Nixon, quoted in Scott Carlson, "The EPA's Best Intentions," Richard Nixon Historical Research Center, November 15, 2013, http://blog.nixonfoundation.org/2013/11/epas-best-intentions/.

69 Richard Nixon Foundation, *Richard Nixon and the Rise of the Environment*, YouTube, uploaded April 22, 2010, https://www.youtube.com/watch?v=27U9K46pbm4.

70 Ibid.

71 James F. Ryan, "The Nixon Legacy," *Today's Chemist at Work* 11, no. 7 (July 2002): 9; Glen Sussman, "The Environment as an Important Public Policy Issue," *Quest* 9, no. 2 (2006), http://ww2.odu.edu/ao/instadv/quest/Environment.html.

72 Tom Wicker, *One of Us: Richard Nixon and the American Dream* (New York: Random House, 1991), 518.

73 Ryan, "Nixon Legacy."

74 James Inhofe and David Vitter, quoted in Jillian Rayfield, "'Ridiculous Pseudo-Science Garbage': Meet the GOP's Environment Leaders!," Alternet, July 27, 2013, http://www.alternet.org/tea-party-and-right/ridiculous-pseudo-science-garbage-meet-gops-environment-leaders.

75 Richard M. Nixon, quoted in *The Nixon Tapes: 1973*, ed. and ann. Douglas Brinkley and Luke Nichter (New York: Houghton Mifflin Harcourt, 2015), 26.

76 Martin Anderson, quoted in Bernard Rostker, *I Want You! The Evolution of the All-Volunteer Force* (Santa Monica, CA: RAND, 2006), 33–34.

77 William Westmoreland and Milton Friedman, quoted in Charles Brunie, "Milton and Me," *New York Sun*, April 20, 2007, http://www.nysun.com/opinion/milton-and-me/52905/.

78 "All-Volunteer Military Was a Highlight of Nixon's Presidency," *New York Times*, May 1, 1994, http://www.nytimes.com/1994/05/01/opinion/l-all-volunteer-military-was-a-highlight-of-nixon-s-presidency-954225.html.

Chapter 2: The Foreign Policy Visionary

1   Henry Kissinger, *On China* (New York: Penguin Books, 2011), 273.

2   Orville Schell, "Nixon's Balancing Act," *Washington Post*, February 25, 2007, http://www.washingtonpost.com/wp-dyn/content/article/2007/02/22/AR2007022201570.html.

3   Richard Nixon and Nikita Khrushchev, quoted in William Safire, "The Cold War's Hot Kitchen," *New York Times*, July 23, 2009, http://www.nytimes.com/2009/07/24/opinion/24safire.html?pagewanted=print.

4   Richard Nixon and Nikita Khrushchev, quoted in "Better to See Once," Time, August 3, 1959, http://content.time.com/time/subscriber/printout/0,8816,825793,00.html.

5   Ibid.

6   Richard Nixon, "Address to the Nation on the War in Vietnam" (speech, Washington, DC, November 3, 1969), Gerhard Peters and John T. Woolley, eds., American Presidency Project, http://www.presidency.ucsb.edu/ws/?pid=2303.

7   Richard Nixon, quoted in Iwan Morgan, *Nixon* (London: Arnold, 2002), 115.

8   Richard Nixon, "Statement on the Death of Four Students at Kent State University, Kent, Ohio" (statement, Washington, DC, May 4, 1970), Gerhard Peters and John T. Woolley, eds., American Presidency Project, http://www.presidency.ucsb.edu/ws/?pid=2492.

9   Richard Nixon, "Address to the Nation on Vietnam."

10 Ibid.

11 Miller Center for Public Affairs, "Richard Nixon: Foreign Affairs," University of Virginia: Miller Center, 2015, http://millercenter.org/president/nixon/essays/biography/5.

12 Richard Nixon, quoted in Nancy Gibbs and Michael Duffy, *The Presidents Club: Inside the World's Most Exclusive Fraternity* (New York: Simon & Schuster, 2012), 285.

13 Richard Nixon, "Address to the Nation Announcing Conclusion of an Agreement on Ending the War and Restoring Peace in Vietnam" (speech, Washington, DC, January 23, 1973), Gerhard Peters and John T. Woolley, eds., American Presidency Project, http://www.presidency.ucsb.edu/ws/?pid=3808.

14 Larry Berman, *No Peace, No Honor: Nixon, Kissinger, and Betrayal in Vietnam* (New York: Free Press, 2001), 8.

15 Richard Nixon, quoted in Berman, *No Peace, No Honor*, 7.

16 Andrew Osborn and Peter Foster, "USSR Planned Nuclear Attack on China in 1969," *Telegraph*, May 13, 2010, http://www.telegraph.co.uk/news/worldnews/asia/china/7720461/USSR-planned-nuclear-attack-on-China-in-1969.html.

17 Richard Nixon, quoted in Kissinger, *On China*, 218.

18 Henry Kissinger, quoted in Reeves, *Alone in the White House*, 283.

19 Richard Nixon, quoted in Leonard Garment, *Crazy Rhythm: From Brooklyn and Jazz to Nixon's White House, Watergate, and Beyond* (Cambridge, MA: Da Capo, 1997), 86.

20 Richard M. Nixon, "Asia after Viet Nam," *Foreign Affairs*, October 1967, http://www.foreignaffairs.com/articles/23927/richard-m-nixon/asia-after-viet-nam.

21 Robert G. Sutter, *U.S.-Chinese Relations: Perilous Past, Pragmatic Present* (Lanham, MD: Rowman & Littlefield, 2010), 72.

22 Joseph Luns, quoted in "Nixon's Coup: To Peking for Peace," *Time*, July 26, 1971, http://content.time.com/time/magazine/article/0,9171,877008,00.html.

23 Seymour Topping, "Journey for Peace," *New York Times*, July 16, 1971.

24 Perlstein, *Nixonland*.

25 Ministry of Foreign Affairs of the People's Republic of China, "Nixon's China's Visit and 'Sino-U.S. Joint Communiqué,'" http://www.fmprc.gov.cn/mfa_eng/ziliao_665539/3602_665543/3604_665547/t18006.shtml.

26 Quoted in Perlstein, *Nixonland*.

27 Jerome A. Cohen, "The Shanghai Communique Forty Years Later: A Job Well Done," *South China Morning Post*, February 22, 2012, http://www.cfr.org/china/shanghai-communique-forty-years-later-job-well-done/p27611.

28 James Mann, *About Face: A History of America's Curious Relationship with China, from Nixon to Clinton* (New York: Vintage, 1998), 16.

29 Ibid.

30 Richard Nixon, "Toasts of the President and Chairman Chang Ch'un-ch'iao at a Banquet in Shanghai" (speech, Shanghai, February 27, 1972), Gerhard Peters and John T. Woolley, eds., American Presidency Project, http://www.presidency.ucsb.edu/ws/?pid=3755.

31 Stephen E. Ambrose, *Nixon Volume II: The Triumph of a Politician, 1962–1972* (New York: Simon & Schuster, 1987).

32 Stephen E. Ambrose, quoted in Michael Kort, *The Columbia Guide to the Cold War* (New York: Columbia University Press, 1998), 66.

33 Richard Nixon, quoted in James E. Goodby, *At the Borderline of Armageddon: How American Presidents Managed the Atom Bomb* (New York: Rowman & Littlefield, 2006), 93.

34 Ambrose, quoted in Kort, *Columbia Guide*.

35 Richard Nixon, "Radio and Television Address to the People of the Soviet Union" (speech, Moscow, May 28, 1972), in *Public Papers of the Presidents of the United States: Richard Nixon* (Washington, DC: Office of the Federal Register, National Archives and Records Service, 1972), 176.

36 Ibid.

37 Fredrik Logevall and Andrew Preston, *Nixon in the World: American Foreign Relations, 1969–1977* (Oxford, UK: Oxford University Press, 2008), 26.

38 Warren I. Cohen, "Chinese Lessons: Nixon, Mao, and the Course of
    U.S.-Chinese Relations," *Foreign Affairs*, March/April 2007, http://www.
    foreignaffairs.com/articles/62462/warren-i-cohen/chinese-lessons-nixon-mao-
    and-the-course-of-u-s-chinese-relations.
39 Robert Kaplan, "The Realist Creed," Real Clear World, November 20, 2014,
    http://www.realclearworld.com/articles/2014/11/20/the_realist_creed_110813.
    html.
40 Henry Kissinger, quoted in Walter Isaacson, *Kissinger: A Biography* (New York:
    Simon & Schuster, 1992), 336.
41 Richard Nixon, quoted in Jason Maoz, "Thirty-Six Years Ago Today,
    Richard Nixon Saved Israel—But Got No Credit," *Commentary*, October
    6, 2009, https://www.commentarymagazine.com/culture-civilization/
    history/web-exclusive-thirty-six-years-ago-today-richard-nixon-saved-
    israel%E2%80%94but-got-no-credit/.
42 Golda Meir, quoted in Richard Nixon Foundation, "The Yom Kippur War: 40
    Years of Survival," October 7, 2013, http://nixonfoundation.org/news-details.
    php?id=28.
43 Stephen Ambrose, quoted in Ibid.

SECTION II
THE NIXON INFLUENCE

Chapter 3: Nixonizing the Republicans; Part One:
The Southern Strategy and the Silent Majority

1 Kevin Phillips, quoted in Sabia, "Nixon Deserves to be Remembered."
2 Spiro Agnew, quoted in David Paul Kuhn, *The Neglected Voter: White Men and
   the Democratic Dilemma* (New York: Palgrave MacMillan, 2007), 59.
3 Matthew D. Lassiter, "Who Speaks for the Silent Majority?," *New York Times*,
   November 2, 2011, http://www.nytimes.com/2011/11/03/opinion/populism-and-
   the-silent-majority.html.
4 Quoted in Jackie Calmes, "Democrats Try Wooing Ones Who Got Away: White
   Men," *New York Times*, March 2, 2014, http://www.nytimes.com/2014/03/03/us/
   politics/democrats-try-wooing-ones-who-got-away-white-men.html.
5 Frank Houston, quoted in Ibid.
6 Spiro Agnew, quoted in Arthur Schlesinger Jr., "The Amazing Success Story
   of 'Spiro *Who*?,'" *New York Times*, July 26, 1970, https://www.nytimes.com/
   books/00/11/26/specials/schlesinger-spiro.html.
7 "Presidential Elections Data," Gerhard Peters and John T. Woolley, eds.,
   American Presidency Project, 2015, http://www.presidency.ucsb.edu/elections.
   php.
8 Steve Kornacki, "The 'Southern Strategy,' Fulfilled," *Salon*, February 3, 2011,
   http://www.salon.com/2011/02/03/reagan_southern_strategy/.
9 "Election of 1964," Gerhard Peters and John T. Woolley, eds., American
   Presidency Project, 2015, http://www.presidency.ucsb.edu/showelection.
   php?year=1964.

10 Ted van Dyk, "How the Election 1968 Reshaped the Democratic Party," *Wall Street Journal*, August 23, 2008, http://online.wsj.com/news/articles/SB121944770970665183.

11 Ibid.

12 US Census Bureau, "South Region—Race and Hispanic Origin: 1790 to 1990," table 4, http://www.census.gov/population/www/documentation/twps0056/tab04.pdf.

13 "Age-Specific Net Migration Estimates for US Counties, 1950–2010," Richelle Winkler, Kenneth M. Johnson, Cheng Cheng, Jim Beaudoin, Paul R. Voss, and Katherine J. Curtis, University of Wisconsin-Madison, 2013, http://netmigration.wisc.edu/.

14 "Wofford, Thomas Albert, (1908–1978)," Biographical Directory of the United States Congress: 1774–Present, http://bioguide.congress.gov/scripts/biodisplay.pl?index=W000666.

15 Patrick L. Cox and Michael Phillips, *The House Will Come to Order: How the Texas Speaker Became a Power in State and National Politics* (Austin: University of Texas Press, 2011), 101.

16 David S. Broder, "Jesse Helms, White Racist," *Washington Post*, July 7, 2008, http://www.washingtonpost.com/wp-dyn/content/article/2008/07/06/AR2008070602321.html.

17 "10 Senators Who Switched Parties: J. Strom Thurmond," Real Clear Politics, March 29, 2013, http://www.realclearpolitics.com/lists/senators-who-switched-parties/j-strom-thurmond.html.

18 Harold Paulk Henderson, "Howard Hollis 'Bo' Callaway (b. 1927)," *New Georgia Encyclopedia*, August 6, 2013, http://www.georgiaencyclopedia.org/articles/government-politics/howard-hollis-bo-callaway-b-1927.

19 Richard Nixon, quoted in Perlstein, *Nixonland*, 88.

20 NIXON VS. HUMPHREY VS. WALLACE, Museum of Moving Image.

21 Kevin Phillips, quoted in James Boyd, "Nixon's Southern Strategy: 'It's All in the Charts,'" *New York Times*, May 17, 1970, http://www.nytimes.com/packages/html/books/phillips-southern.pdf.

22 Lee Atwater, quoted in Rick Perlstein, "Lee Atwater's Infamous 1981 Interview on the Southern Strategy," *Nation*, November 13, 2012, http://www.thenation.com/article/170841/exclusive-lee-atwaters-infamous-1981-interview-southern-strategy.

23 Patrick J. Buchanan, *The Greatest Comeback: How Richard Nixon Rose from Defeat to Create the New Majority* (New York: Random House, 2014), 71–72.

24 Ibid., 78–79.

25 Hoff, *Nixon Reconsidered*, 78.

26 David Frost, *Frost/Nixon* (New York: Harper Collins, 2007), 192–93.

27 Van Dyk, "Election 1968."

28 "Election of 1968," Gerhard Peters and John T. Woolley, eds., American Presidency Project, http://www.presidency.ucsb.edu/showelection.php?year=1968.

29 Ibid.

30 "Independent Ads: The National Security Political Action Committee 'Willie Horton,'" Inside Politics, 2002, http://www.insidepolitics.org/ps111/independentads.html.

31 Lee Atwater, quoted in Lawrence Freedman, "Reagan's Southern Strategy Gave Rise to the Tea Party," *Salon,* October 27, 2013, http://www.salon.com/2013/10/27/reagans_southern_strategy_gave_rise_to_the_tea_party/.

32 "Up from the Southern Strategy," *New York Times,* December 29, 2002, http://www.nytimes.com/2002/12/29/opinion/up-from-the-southern-strategy.html.

33 Richard Nixon, quoted in Perlstein, *Nixonland,* 31.

34 Richard M. Nixon, "'Checkers Speech' (speech, Los Angeles, September 23, 1952)," University of Virginia: Miller Center, http://millercenter.org/president/nixon/speeches/speech-4638.

35 Ibid.

36 "Man and Woman of the Year: The Middle Americans," *Time,* January 5, 1970, University of Colorado, http://www.colorado.edu/AmStudies/lewis/film/middle.htm.

37 Nixon, "Address Accepting the Presidential Nomination."

38 "Man and Woman of the Year," *Time.*

39 Richard Nixon, quoted in Liz Sidoti, "Reaching for the Middle, Pulled to Edges," Associated Press, March 18, 2013, http://bigstory.ap.org/article/column-reaching-middle-pulled-edges.

40 Perlstein, *Nixonland,* 277.

41 Lassiter, "Who Speaks for the Silent Majority?"

42 Ibid.

43 Nixon, "Address to the Nation on the War in Vietnam."

44 "Nixon's 'Silent Majority' Speech" (speech, November 3, 1969), George Mason University: Roy Rosenzweig Center for History and New Media, http://chnm.gmu.edu/hardhats/silent.html.

45 "November 15, 1969," DemocraticUnderground.com, November 15, 2006 http://www.democraticunderground.com/discuss/duboard.php?az=view_all&address=364x2721543.

46 Spiro Agnew, quoted in Mason, *Quest for a New Majority,* 99.

47 Spiro Theodore Agnew, "Spiro Theodore Agnew: Television News Coverage" (speech, Des Moines, November 13, 1969), American Rhetoric, http://www.americanrhetoric.com/speeches/spiroagnewtvnewscoverage.htm.

48 Kevin Phillips, quoted in Boyd, "Nixon's Southern Strategy."

49 Pat Nixon, quoted in Gloria Steinem, "In Your Heart You Know He's Nixon," *New York,* October 28, 1968, http://nymag.com/news/politics/45934/.

50 Ibid.

51 Richard Nixon, "Remarks on Accepting the Presidential Nomination of the Republican National Convention" (speech, Miami Beach, August 23, 1972), Gerhard Peters and John T. Woolley, eds., American Presidency Project, http://www.presidency.ucsb.edu/ws/?pid=3537.

52 Kevin Phillips, quoted in Geoffrey Kabaservice, *Rule and Ruin: The Downfall of Moderation and the Destruction of the Republican Party, from Eisenhower to the Tea Party* (New York: Oxford University Press: 2012), 274.

53 Patrick Buchanan, quoted in Sam Tanenhaus, "How Republicans Got That Way," *New York Review of Books,* May 24, 2012, http://www.nybooks.com/articles/archives/2012/may/24/how-republicans-got-way/?pagination=false.

54 "Ronald Reagan Quotes," goodreads Web site, 2015, https://www.goodreads.com/author/quotes/3543.Ronald_Reagan.

55 Ronald Reagan, "First Inaugural Address (January 20, 1981)," University of Virginia: Miller Center, http://millercenter.org/president/reagan/speeches/speech-3407.

56 Bill Clinton, quoted in Stephen A. Smith, ed., *Preface to the Presidency: Selected Speeches of Bill Clinton 1974–1992* (Fayetteville: University of Arkansas Press, 1996), 89.

57 Barack Obama, quoted in Matt Bai, "Working for the Working-Class Vote," *New York Times Magazine*, October 15, 2008, http://www.nytimes.com/2008/10/19/magazine/19obama-t.html?pagewanted=all.

58 Barack Obama, quoted in William Safire, "Catchwords of this Year's Campaign," *New York Times*, October 2, 2008, http://www.nytimes.com/2008/11/02/opinion/02iht-edsafire.1.17444370.html.

59 Ibid.

60 Sarah Palin, quoted in Jane Mayer, "The Mousy Majority," *New Yorker*, August 29, 2012, http://www.newyorker.com/online/blogs/newsdesk/2012/08/ann-romneys-bid-for-women-at-the-rnc.html.

61 Christopher Taylor, "Sarah Palin's 'Real Americans,'" *Washington Examiner*, May 31, 2011, http://washingtonexaminer.com/sarah-palins-real-americans/article/145801.

62 Sarah Palin, quoted in Sam Stein, "Palin Explains What Parts of Country Not 'Pro-Americans,'" *Huffington Post*, May 25, 2011, http://www.huffingtonpost.com/2008/10/17/palin-clarifies-what-part_n_135641.html.

63 Richard Nixon, quoted in "Nixon: Program Transcript," PBS Web site: *American Experience*, 1990, http://www.pbs.org/wgbh/americanexperience/features/transcript/nixon-transcript/.

64 Mitt Romney, quoted in David Corn, "Secret Video: Romney Tells Millionaire Donors What He Really Thinks of Obama Voters," *Mother Jones*, September 17, 2012, http://www.motherjones.com/politics/2012/09/secret-video-romney-private-fundraiser.

65 Buchanan, *Greatest Comeback*, 293.

66 Ibid., 329–30.

67 Sean Theriault, "Party Polarization in the US Congress: Member Replacement and Member Adaptation," *Party Politics* 12, no. 4 (2006): 483–503.

68 Zack C. Smith, "Newt Gingrich's Nixon Connection," *Politico*, January 19, 2012, http://www.politico.com/news/stories/0112/71684_Page2.html.

69 Jon Meacham, "Why Newt Is like Nixon," *Time*, January 23, 2012, http://ideas.time.com/2012/01/23/why-newt-is-like-nixon/?xid=huffpo-direct.

Chapter 4: Nixonizing the Democrats; Part One: Stealing the Domestic Center from Liberals

1 Richard Nixon, quoted in Peter Passell and Leonard Ross, "Daniel Moynihan and President-Elect Nixon: How Charity Didn't Begin at Home," *New York Times*, January 14, 2013, http://www.nytimes.com/books/98/10/04/specials/moynihan-income.html.

2 Melvin Small, ed., *A Companion to Richard M. Nixon* (Malden, MA: Wiley-Blackwell, 2011).

3 John Mitchell, quoted in Frederick F. Siegel, *Troubled Journey: From Pearl Harbor to Ronald Reagan* (New York: Hill and Wang, 1984), 229.

4 John Mitchell, quoted in William Safire, "Watch What We Do," *New York Times*, November 14, 1988, http://www.nytimes.com/1988/11/14/opinion/essay-watch-what-we-do.html.

5 Hoff, *Nixon Reconsidered*, 49.

6 Barack Obama and Bill O'Reilly, quoted in *Obama: "In a Lot of Ways, Richard Nixon Was More Liberal than I Was,"* Real Clear Politics, February 3, 2014, http://www.realclearpolitics.com/video/2014/02/03/obama_in_a_lot_of_ways_richard_nixon_was_more_liberal_than_i_was.html.

7 Sidney Blumenthal, "Ghost in the Machine," *New Yorker*, October 2, 1995, http://www.newyorker.com/magazine/1995/10/02/ghost-in-the-machine.

8 Sam Tanenhaus, *The Death of Conservatism* (New York: Random House, 2009), 71.

9 Quoted in William F. Buckley Jr., "Moynihan at the ADA," *Sarasota Herald*, September 27, 1967, http://news.google.com/newspapers?nid=1774&dat=196709 27&id=BD0gAAAAIBAJ&sjid=_WUEAAAAIBAJ&pg=7322,6243341.

10 Daniel Patrick Moynihan, quoted in Buckley, "Moynihan at the ADA."

11 Daniel P. Moynihan, "Myths and Demands of Liberal Politics: MOYNIHAN'S POLITICS OF STABILITY," *Harvard Crimson*, September 30, 1967, http://www.thecrimson.com/article/1967/9/30/myths-and-demands-of-liberal-politics/.

12 Steven Weisman, "How to Govern a Divided Country," *New York*, September 19, 2010, http://nymag.com/news/politics/68317/.

13 Moynihan, *A Portrait in Letters*, 162.

14 Warner, "An American Disraeli?"

15 Richard Nixon, quoted in Passell and Ross, "Daniel Moynihan and President-Elect Nixon."

16 Richard Nixon, quoted in Warner, "An American Disraeli?"

17 Richard Nixon, quoted in John Bew, "Rethinking Nixon: Forty Years after Watergate, Can the 37th President Be Rehabilitated?," *New Statesman*, September 18, 2014, http://www.newstatesman.com/politics/2014/09/rethinking-nixon-forty-years-after-watergate-can-37th-president-be-rehabilitated.

18 David E. Rosenbaum, "Senate Rights Bloc May Founder on School Busing Issue," *New York Times*, January 23, 1972, http://query.nytimes.com/mem/archive/pdf?res=9500E4D7173AE73ABC4B51DFB7668389669EDE.

19 Ibid.

20 William F. Ryan, quoted in "Anti-Busing Move Assailed in House; Liberals Angry, but Eastland Bids Nixon Go Further," *New York Times*, March 21, 1972, http://query.nytimes.com/mem/archive/pdf?res=9B06E6DB173FE53ABC4951DFB5668389669EDE.

21 James C. Corman, quoted in Ibid.

22 Ted Kennedy, quoted in Ibid.

23 Shirley Chisholm, quoted in "Nixon's Plan for Quality Education, No More Busing," *Afro American*, March 25, 1972, http://news.google.com/newspapers?nid=2211&dat=19720325&id=EicmAAAAIBAJ&sjid=J_4FAAAAIBAJ&pg=595,1737031.

24 Jesse Jackson, quoted in Tom Wicker, "They're Feeding 50 Million Hungry

Jim Crow," *Miami News*, March 25, 1972, http://news.google.com/newspape
rs?nid=2206&dat=19720324&id=g-5WAAAAIBAJ&sjid=bUINAAAAIBAJ&
pg=4876,1628999.

25 "Anti-Busing Move Assailed," *New York Times.*
26 "A Jarring Message from George," *Time,* March 27, 1972, http://cgi.cnn.com/
ALLPOLITICS/1996/analysis/back.time/9603/27/."
27 Edmund S. Muskie, quoted in "How the Candidates Stand on Busing," *Life,*
March 3, 1972, 31.
28 George McGovern, quoted in "Anti-Busing Move Assailed," *New York Times.*
29 George McGovern, quoted in "How the Candidates Stand," *Life.*
30 John Ehrlichman, quoted in Hugh Davis Graham, *Collision Course: The Strange
Convergence of Affirmative Action and Immigration Policy in America* (Oxford,
UK: Oxford University Press, 2003), 71.
31 George Meany, quoted in Graham, *Collision Course,* 72.
32 Daniel Patrick Moynihan, quoted in Passell and Ross, "Daniel Moynihan and
President-Elect Nixon."
33 Passell and Ross, "Daniel Moynihan and President-Elect Nixon."
34 William F. Ryan, quoted in Alberti and Brown, "Guaranteed Income."
35 Walter Mondale, quoted in Stephen M. Gillon, *The Democrats' Dilemma: Walter
Mondale and the Liberal Legacy* (New York: Columbia University Press, 1992),
130.
36 Frank Stricker, *Why America Lost the War on Poverty: And How to Win It* (Chapel
Hill: University of North Carolina Press, 2007), 242.
37 James Welsh, "Welfare Reform: Born, Aug. 8, 1969; Died, Oct. 4, 1972–; A Sad
Case Study of the American Political Process," *New York Times,* January 7, 1973,
http://query.nytimes.com/gst/abstract.html?res=9F01E3DB133DEF32A25754C0A
9679C946290D6CF.
38 John McCain, quoted in Marc J. Selverstone, *A Companion to John Kennedy*
(Malden, MA: Wiley-Blackwell, 2014).
39 Robert Reich, "Nixon Proposed Today's Affordable Care Act," *Salon,* October
29, 2013, http://www.salon.com/2013/10/29/nixon_proposed_todays_
affordable_care_act_partner/.
40 Teddy Kennedy, quoted in *National Health Insurance Debate under Nixon,*
YouTube, 1:40, uploaded November 5, 2007, https://www.youtube.com/
watch?v=iGKkPEvD2OM.
41 *National Health Insurance Debate,* YouTube.
42 Steven Pearlstein, "Kennedy Saw Health-Care Reform Fail in the '70s; Today's
Lawmakers Don't Have To," *Washington Post,* August 28, 2009, http://www.
washingtonpost.com/wp-dyn/content/article/2009/08/27/AR2009082703919.
html.
43 Andrew Biemiller, Omar Burleson, and Donald Clancy, quoted in Rick Mayes,
Universal Coverage: The Elusive Quest for National Health Insurance (Ann Arbor:
University of Michigan Press, 2001), 92–93.
44 *Washington Post,* quoted in Mayes, *Universal Coverage,* 93.
45 Pearlstein, "Kennedy Saw Health-Care Reform Fail."
46 Nixon, "Annual Message to the Congress."
47 Ibid.

THE NIXON EFFECT

THE NIXON EFFECT

48 Richard Nixon, quoted in Drew, "Nostalgia for Nixon?"

49 Drew, "Nostalgia for Nixon?"

50 Mike Kiernan, "Nixon, Humphrey, and McGovern: Environmental Issues in Politics," *Mother Earth News* (July/August 1972), http://www.motherearthnews.com/nature-and-environment/environmental-issue-politics-zmaz72jaztak.aspx?PageId=1.

51 Richard Nixon, "Special Message to the Congress on Draft Reform" (letter, Washington, DC, April 23, 1970), Gerhard Peters and John T. Woolley, eds., American Presidency Project, http://www.presidency.ucsb.edu/ws/?pid=2483.

52 L. Sandy Maisel and Mark D. Brewer, *Parties and Elections in America: The Electoral Process* (Lanham, MD: Rowman & Littlefield, 2009), 275.

53 Rich Yeselson, "George McGovern: America's Critic and Champion," *American Prospect*, October 22, 2012, http://prospect.org/article/george-mcgovern-americas-critic-and-champion.

54 Ibid.

55 Joyce Milton, quoted in Hayward, *Age of Reagan*, 355.

56 Democratic Party Platform, 1972, quoted in Hayward, *Age of Reagan*, 355.

57 Hayward, Age of Reagan, quoted in Steven Hayward, "George McGovern, RIP," *Powerline*, October 21, 2012, http://www.powerlineblog.com/archives/2012/10/george-mcgovern-rip.php.

58 David E. Rosenbaum, "George McGovern Dies at 90, a Liberal Trounced but Never Silenced," *New York Times*, October 21, 2012, http://www.nytimes.com/2012/10/22/us/politics/george-mcgovern-a-democratic-presidential-nominee-and-liberal-stalwart-dies-at-90.html?_r=0.

59 Hayward, "George McGovern, RIP."

60 Hayward, *Age of Reagan*, 355.

61 James O'Hara, quoted in Paul F. Boller Jr., *Presidential Campaigns: From George Washington to George W. Bush* (Oxford, UK: Oxford University Press, 2004), 335.

62 Richard Nixon, quoted in Conrad Black, *Richard M. Nixon: A Life in Full* (New York: PublicAffairs, 2008), 828.

63 Theodore White, quoted in Rosenbaum, "George McGovern Dies at 90."

64 George Meany, quoted in Yeselson, "George McGovern."

65 John Connally, quoted in "Connally Sets Up Panel of Democrats for Nixon," *New York Times*, August 10, 1972, http://timesmachine.nytimes.com/timesmachine/1972/08/10/79473046.html?pageNumber=24.

66 Timothy Noah, "'Acid, Amnesty, and Abortion': The Unlikely Source of a Legendary Smear," *New Republic*, October 22, 2012, http://www.newrepublic.com/article/108977/acid-amnesty-and-abortion-unlikely-source-legendary-smear.

67 Richard Nixon, quoted in Gladwin Hill, "Nixon Denounces Press as Biased," *New York Times*, November 8, 1962, http://timesmachine.nytimes.com/timesmachine/1962/11/08/86996940.html.

68 Yeselson, "George McGovern."

69 Michael Barone, "From McGovern to Obama," American Enterprise Institute, October 22, 2012, http://www.aei.org/publication/from-mcgovern-to-obama/.

70 Peter Grier, "Election Results 2012: Who Won It for Obama?," *Christian Science Monitor*, November 7, 2012, http://www.csmonitor.com/USA/DC-Decoder/Decoder-Buzz/2012/1107/Election-results-2012-Who-won-it-for-Obama-video.

71 Ross Douthat, "Republicans, White Voters, and Racial Polarization," *New York Times*, August 6, 2013, http://douthat.blogs.nytimes.com/2013/08/06/republicans-white-voters-and-racial-polarization/.

72 Ibid.

Chapter 5: Nixonizing the Republicans; Part Two: The Conservative Revolt

1 John Ashbrook, quoted in Charles A. Moser, "Promise and Hope: The Ashbrook Presidential Campaign of 1972," Ashbrook Center, http://ashbrook.org/about/john-ashbrook/promise-and-hope/.

2 Richard Nixon, quoted in Rick Perlstein, "'I Didn't Like Nixon until Watergate': The Conservative Movement Now," *Huffington Post*, May, 11, 2011, http://www.huffingtonpost.com/rick-perlstein/i-didnt-like-nixon-until-_b_11735.html?view=print.

3 Quoted in Moser, "Promise and Hope."

4 Quoted in Ibid.

5 Ibid.

6 Ibid.

7 Lee Edwards, *The Conservative Revolution: The Movement That Remade America* (New York: Simon & Schuster, 1999), 161.

8 Richard Nixon, quoted in Ibid.

9 Ibid.

10 Nicole Hemmer, "Richard Nixon's Model Campaign," *New York Times*, May 10, 2012, http://campaignstops.blogs.nytimes.com/2012/05/10/richard-nixons-model-campaign/.

11 Ronald Reagan, "A Time for Choosing" (speech, Los Angeles, October 27, 1964), Ronald Reagan Presidential Foundation & Library, http://www.reaganfoundation.org/tgcdetail.aspx?p=TG0923RRS&lm=reagan&args_a=cms&args_b=1&argsb=N&tx=1736.

12 Frank Meyer, quoted in Hayward, *Age of Reagan*, 208.

13 Edwards, *Conservative Revolution*, 163.

14 Ibid.

15 *Human Events*, quoted in Sara Diamond, *Roads to Dominion: Right-Wing Movements and Political Power in the United States* (New York: Guilford, 1995), 113.

16 *National Review*, quoted in Ibid. 114.

17 Edwards, *Conservative Revolution*.

18 American Conservative Union, quoted in Diamond, *Roads to Dominion*, 115.

19 L. Brent Bozell, quoted in Donald T. Critchlow, *The Conservative Ascendancy: How the GOP Right Made Political History* (Cambridge, MA: Harvard University Press, 2007), 90.

20 Richard Nixon, quoted in John Fund, "Nixon at 100: Was He 'America's Last Liberal'?," *National Review*, January 11, 2013, http://www.nationalreview.com/node/337447/print.

21 H. R. Haldeman, *The Haldeman Diaries: Inside the Nixon White House* (New York: Putnam, 1994), 31.

22 Ibid., 117–18.

23 Richard Nixon, quoted in Roger Lowenstein, "The Nixon Shock," *Bloomberg Businessweek,* August 4, 2011, http://www.businessweek.com/printer/articles/870-the-nixon-shock.

24 Leuchtenburg, *The American President,* 495

25 Herbert Stein, quoted in Yergin and Stanislaw, *Commanding Heights,* 61.

26 Ibid., 62.

27 Richard Nixon, quoted in Ibid., 63.

28 *New York Times,* quoted in Lowenstein, "The Nixon Shock."

29 Ibid.

30 Nancy L. Cohen, "Why America Never Had Universal Child Care," *New Republic,* April 24, 2013, http://www.newrepublic.com/article/113009/child-care-america-was-very-close-universal-day-care.

31 John Ashbrook, quoted in Moser, "Promise and Hope."

32 James J. Kilpatrick, quoted in Donald T. Critchlow and Nancy MacLean, *Debating the American Conservative Movement: 1945 to the Present* (New York: Rowman & Littlefield, 2009), 155.

33 Richard Nixon, quoted in Ibid.

34 Richard Nixon, "Veto of the Economic Opportunity Amendments of 1971," Gerhard Peters and John T. Woolley, eds., American Presidency Project, December 9, 1971, http://www.presidency.ucsb.edu/ws/?pid=3251.

35 James Buckley, quoted in Cohen, "Why America Never Had Universal Child Care."

36 Kimberly J. Morgan, "A Child of the Sixties: The Great Society, the New Right, and the Politics of Federal Child Care," *Journal of Policy History* 13, no. 2 (2001): 235–36.

37 Walter Mondale, quoted in Gail Collins, "The State of the 4-Year-Olds," *New York Times,* February 13, 2013, http://www.nytimes.com/2013/02/14/opinion/collins-the-state-of-the-4-year-olds.html?_r=0.

38 Richard Nixon, "Remarks to the Nation Announcing Acceptance of an Invitation to Visit the People's Republic of China," (televised broadcast, Burbank, CA, July 15, 1971), Gerhard Peters and John T. Woolley, eds., American Presidency Project, http://www.presidency.ucsb.edu/ws/?pid=3079.

39 Ibid.

40 Mike Mansfield and Gerald Ford, quoted in Carroll Kilpatrick, "President Agrees to Visit China," *Washington Post,* July 16, 1971, http://www.washingtonpost.com/wp-srv/inatl/longterm/flash/july/china71.htm.

41 William Rusher, quoted in Julian E. Zelize, *Arsenal of Democracy: The Politics of National Security—from World War II to the War on Terrorism* (New York: Basic Books, 2010), 241.

42 William Loeb, quoted in Walt Hintzen, "The Right Wing v. Nixon," *Time,* August 16, 1971, http://content.time.com/time/magazine/article/0,9171,877188,00.html.

43 Edwards, *Conservative Revolution,* 169.

44 Water H. Judd, quoted in Ibid., 169.

45 Ibid., 169.

46 Ibid., 170.

47 Diamond, *Roads to Dominion,* 116.

48 William F. Buckley Jr., "Say It Isn't So, Mr. President," *New York Times Magazine*, August 1, 1971, http://timesmachine.nytimes.com/timesmachine/1971/08/01/issue.html.
49 William F. Buckley Jr., quoted in Ibid.
50 James Buckley, quoted in Buckley, "Say It Isn't So."
51 Edwards, *Conservative Revolution*.
52 Hintzen, "The Right Wing."
53 Walt Hintzen, quoted in Robert Walters, "Anti-Nixon Conservatives Stirring," *Spokesman-Review*, November 10, 1971.
54 Edwards, *Conservative Revolution*.
55 John Ashbrook, quoted in Jack Rosenthal, "Ashbrook, Nixon's Rival on the Right, Finding Florida Campaign Trail Rough," *New York Times*, February 15, 1972.
56 Diamond, *Roads to Dominion*, 116.
57 Richard A. Viguerie, quoted in Edwards, *Conservative Revolution*, 173.
58 John Ashbrook, quoted in Moser, "Promise and Hope."
59 Kabaservice, *Rule and Ruin*, 331.
60 Zelize, *Arsenal of Democracy*.
61 Edwards, *Conservative Revolution*.
62 "The 1964 Republican Campaign," PBS Web site: *American Experience,* http://www.pbs.org/wgbh/americanexperience/features/general-article/rockefellers-campaign/.
63 Paul Weyrich, quoted in Critchlow, *Conservative Ascendancy*, 128.
64 Kabaservice, *Rule and Ruin*, 334.
65 "The Equal Rights Amendment: Unfinished Business for the Constitution," Equal Rights Amendment, http://www.equalrightsamendment.org/.
66 Phyllis Shlafly, quoted in "The Equal Rights Amendment Falters and Phyllis Schlafly Is the Iron Fist behind the Slowdown," *People* 3, no. 16 (April 28, 1975), http://www.people.com/people/archive/article/0,,20065183,00.html.
67 Betty Ford, quoted in Critchlow, *Conservative Ascendancy*, 139.
68 Critchlow, *Conservative Ascendancy*, 140.
69 Ibid., 142.
70 John Chamberlain, quoted in Ibid., 166.
71 Mickey Edwards, quoted in Ibid., 145.
72 Gerald Ford, quoted in Kabaservice, *Rule and Ruin*, 346.
73 Ronald Reagan, quoted in Rupert Colley, "Ronald Reagan and the Cold War: A Summary," History in an Hour, February 6, 2011, http://www.historyinanhour.com/2011/02/06/ronald-reagan-cold-war/.
74 Kabaservice, *Rule and Ruin*, 348.
75 Ibid.
76 Critchlow, *Conservative Ascendancy*, 165.
77 Howard Jarvis, quoted in Daniel A. Smith, *Tax Crusaders and the Politics of Direct Democracy* (New York: Routledge, 1998), 28.
78 Howard Jarvis, quoted in Ibid., 25.
79 Howard Jarvis, "Sound and Fury over Taxes: Howard Jarvis and the Voters Send a Message: 'We're Mad as Hell!,'" *Time*, June 19, 1978, http://content.time.com/time/magazine/article/0,9171,919742,00.html.

80 Quoted in "The Message of the Off-Year Elections: In a Quirky Mood, Worried about Money, Voters Turn Conservative," *Time*, November 20, 1978, http://content.time.com/time/magazine/article/0,9171,948300,00.html.

81 Ibid.

82 Ronald Reagan, "Acceptance Speech at the 1980 Republican Convention" (speech, Republican National Convention, Detroit, July 17, 1980), National Center for Public Policy Research, http://www.nationalcenter.org/ReaganConvention1980.html.

83 George J. Church, "Reagan Coast to Coast," *Time*, November 17, 1980, http://content.time.com/time/subscriber/printout/0,8816,950482,00.html.

Chapter 6: Nixonizing the Democrats; Part Two: Vietnam, McGovern, and the End of National-Security Liberalism

1 "Democratic Party Platform of 1972," American Presidency Project, John Woolley and Gerard Peters, eds., July 10, 1972, http://www.presidency.ucsb.edu/ws/?pid=29605.

2 Nixon, "Address to the Nation on the War in Vietnam."

3 Daniel Patrick Moynihan, quoted in Charles Horner, "A Born Controversialist," *Wall Street Journal*, October 9, 2010, http://www.wsj.com/articles/SB10001424052748703735804575535263041283030.

4 Jeane Kirkpatrick, "Dictatorships and Double Standards," *Commentary*, November 1, 1979, http://www.commentarymagazine.com/article/dictatorships-double-standards.

5 Madeline Albright, "Interview by Matt Lauer," *Today Show*, February 19, 1998.

6 "Vietnam War: Allied Troop Levels 1960–73," American War Library, December 6, 2008, http://www.americanwarlibrary.com/vietnam/vwatl.htm.

7 "The Tet Offensive," U.S.history.org, 2015, http://www.ushistory.org/us/55c.asp.

8 Quoted in Joshua Muravchik, "'Scoop' Jackson at One Hundred," *Commentary*, July 1, 2012, http://www.commentarymagazine.com/article/scoop-jackson-at-one-hundred/.

9 Perlstein, *Nixonland*, 218.

10 Ronald Radosh, *Divided They Fell: The Demise of the Democratic Party, 1964–1996* (New York: Free Press, 1996), 61–63.

11 Ibid., 64–65.

12 Ibid., 105.

13 "The Divisions in the Democratic Party," Lanny Davis, *ABC News* Web site, August 9, 2006, http://abcnews.go.com/Politics/story?id=2291284.

14 Richard Nixon, quoted in *Nixon Campaign Ad—Vietnam (1968)*, YouTube Video, 1:00, uploaded January 7, 2011, https://www.youtube.com/watch?v=W3KoYveOmiQ.

15 Nixon, "Address to the Nation on the War in Vietnam."

16 Robert Mann, *A Grand Delusion: America's Descent into Vietnam* (New York: Basic Books, 2001), 665.

17 George McGovern, quoted in Robert Sam Anson, *McGovern: A Biography* (New York: Holt, Rinehart and Winston, 1972), 174–78.

18 George McGovern, quoted in Chris Hedges, "McGovern: He Never Sold His Soul," truthdig, October 21, 2012, http://www.truthdig.com/report/item/mcgovern_he_never_sold_his_soul_20121021.

19 George McGovern, quoted in Michael S. Sherry, *In the Shadow of War: The United States since the 1930s* (New Haven: Yale University Press, 1995), 320.

20 Radosh, *Divided They Fell*, 177–78.

21 Spencer C. Tucker, ed., *The Encyclopedia of the Vietnam War: A Political, Social, and Military History* (Oxford: Oxford University Press, 2011), 336–37.

22 Henry Kissinger, *Ending the Vietnam War: A History of America's Involvement in and Extrication from the Vietnam War* (New York: Simon & Schuster, 2003), 591.

23 Quoted in Muravchik, "'Scoop' Jackson at One Hundred."

24 George McGovern, quoted in Anne-Marie Brady, *Making the Foreign Serve China: Managing Foreigners in the People's Republic* (Oxford, UK: Rowman & Littlefield, 2003), 178.

25 Ibid.

26 Mao Zedong, quoted in Ibid., 178–79.

27 George McGovern, quoted in Thomas Dye and Harmon Zeigler, *The Irony of Democracy: An Uncommon Introduction to American Politics* (Boston: Wadsworth, 2009), 66.

28 "Republican Party Platform of 1972," August 21, 1972, Gerhard Peters and John T. Woolley, eds., American Presidency Project, August 21, 1972, http://www.presidency.ucsb.edu/ws/?pid=25842.

29 Nixon, "Address to the Nation on the War in Vietnam."

30 Spiro Agnew, quoted in Bruce Biossat, "Agnew's Switch: Attacks McGovern," *Times-News*, October 12, 1972, http://news.google.com/newspapers?nid=1665&dat=19721012&id=uFtPAAAAIBAJ&sjid=WiQEAAAAIBAJ&pg=6865,3983368.

31 Nixon, "Address to the Nation on the War in Vietnam."

32 Biossat, "Agnew's Switch."

33 *McGovern Defense (Nixon, 1972)*, Museum of the Moving Image: Living Room Candidate, Presidential Campaign Commercials 1952–2012, 1:00, 2012, http://www.livingroomcandidate.org/commercials/1972/mcgovern-defense.

34 John Connally, quoted in "Connally Sees More Democrats Supporting Nixon," *New York Times*, September 1, 1972, http://query.nytimes.com/mem/archive/pdf?res=990DE2D8123AE73ABC4951DFBF668389669EDE.

35 John Connally, quoted in Eileen Shanahan, "Connally to Work to Re-Elect Nixon," *New York Times*, July 15, 1972, http://query.nytimes.com/mem/archive/pdf?res=9901E0D91F3EE63BBC4D52DFB1668389669EDE/.

36 John Connally, quoted in "Connally Sees More Democrats Supporting Nixon," *New York Times*.

37 James T. Wooten, "Nixon Democrats Striving to Exploit Split in Party," *New York Times*, August 31, 1972, http://query.nytimes.com/mem/archive/pdf?res=9504E6D81330E73BBC4950DFBE668389669EDE.

38 Richard Nixon, quoted in Bruce Miroff, *The Liberals' Moment: The McGovern Insurgency and the Identity Crisis of the Democratic Party* (Lawrence: University Press of Kansas, 2007), 232.

39 Theodore White, quoted in Rosenbaum, "George McGovern Dies at 90."

40 Theodore White, quoted in George Packer, "The Republicans' 1972," *New Yorker,* January 30, 2012, http://www.newyorker.com/online/blogs/comment/2012/01/the-republicans-1972.html.

41 Jeffrey Bloodworth, *Losing the Center: The Decline of American Liberalism, 1968–1992* (Lexington: University Press of Kentucky, 2013), 108.

42 Ibid., 111.

43 Quoted in Radosh, *Divided They Fell,* 158.

44 Bloodworth, *Losing the Center,* 113.

45 Daniel P. Moynihan, "The United States in Opposition," *Commentary,* March 1, 1975, http://www.commentarymagazine.com/article/the-united-states-in-opposition/.

46 Ibid.

47 Daniel Patrick Moynihan, quoted in "Daniel Patrick Moynihan," *Daily Telegraph,* March 28, 2003, http://www.telegraph.co.uk/news/obituaries/1425828/Daniel-Patrick-Moynihan.html.

48 United Nations, "United Nations General Assembly Resolution 3379," November 10, 1975.

49 Daniel Patrick Moynihan, quoted in "Moynihan's Moment: The Historic 1975 U.N. Speech in Response to 'Zionism is Racism,'" *UN Watch* blog, December 30, 2012, http://blog.unwatch.org/index.php/2012/12/30/moynihans-moment-the-historic-1975-u-n-speech-in-response-to-zionism-is-racism/.

50 William F. Buckley Jr., "A Personal Memoir," *National Review,* April 1, 2003, http://www.nationalreview.com/article/206405/moynihan-william-f-buckley-jr.

51 "GIVING THEM HELL AT THE U.N." *Time,* January 26, 1976, cover.

52 Moynihan, quoted in Horner, "A Born Controversialist."

53 Ronald D. Elving, "Rebels of '94 and 'Watergate Babies' Similar in Class Size, Sense of Zeal," CNN Web site, January 26, 1998, http://www.cnn.com/ALLPOLITICS/1998/01/26/cq/elving.html.

54 Richard Armitage, quoted in Lauren Zanolli, "What Happened When Democrats in Congress Cut Off Funding for the Vietnam War?," History News Network, April 7, 2013, http://hnn.us/article/31400.

55 Bloodworth, *Losing the Center,* 149–50.

56 Patrick Caddell, quoted in "Complete Program Transcript," PBS Web site: *American Experience,* http://www.pbs.org/wgbh/americanexperience/features/transcript/carter-transcript/.

57 Jimmy Carter, quoted in Ibid.

58 George McGovern, quoted in Muravchik, "'Scoop' Jackson at One Hundred."

59 Bloodworth, *Losing the Center,* 150–51.

60 Ibid.

61 Jimmy Carter, "University of Notre Dame—Address at Commencement Exercises at the University" (speech, South Bend, IN, May 22, 1972), Gerhard Peters and John T. Woolley, eds., American Presidency Project, http://www.presidency.ucsb.edu/ws/?pid=7552.

62 Jimmy Carter, quoted in Betty Glad, "The Real Jimmy Carter," *Foreign Policy,* January 21, 2010, http://www.foreignpolicy.com/articles/2010/01/21/the_real_jimmy_carter.

63 Jeane Kirkpatrick, quoted in Marjorie Hunter, "United Nations Jeanne Jordan Kirkpatrick; Carter Policy Called Unclear Effort to Reclaim Party Doctorate on Peronist Movement," *New York Times*, December 23, 1980, http://query.nytimes. com/mem/archive/pdf?res=9C03E7D6143AE732A25750C2A9649D94619FD6CF.

64 Jeane Kirkpatrick, quoted in Murray Friedman, *The Neoconservative Revolution: Jewish Intellectuals and the Shaping of Public Policy* (Cambridge, UK: Cambridge University Press, 2005), 150.

65 Kirkpatrick, "Dictatorships and Double Standards."

66 Hunter, "United Nations Jeanne Jordan Kirkpatrick."

67 Jeane Kirkpatrick, quoted in Bloodworth, *Losing the Center*, 153–54.

68 Ibid., 154.

69 Ronald Reagan, quoted in "Presidential Debate in Cleveland" (presidential debate, Cleveland, October 28, 1980), American Presidency Project, http://www. presidency.ucsb.edu/ws/index.php?pid=29408.

70 "1980 Presidential Debates," CNN Time Web site: All Politics, 1996, http://www. cnn.com/ALLPOLITICS/1996/debates/history/1980/index.shtml.

71 Critchlow, *Conservative Ascendancy*, 179–80.

72 Ronald W. Reagan, "Address to Members of the British Parliament" (speech, London, June 8, 1982), Ronald Reagan Presidential Museum & Library, http:// www.reagan.utexas.edu/archives/speeches/1982/60882a.htm.

73 Ibid.

74 Muravchik, "'Scoop' Jackson at One Hundred."

75 Jeane Kirkpatrick, "1984 Jeane Kirkpatrick" (speech to Republican National Convention, Dallas, August 20, 1984), CNN Time: All Politics, http://www.cnn. com/ALLPOLITICS/1996/conventions/san.diego/facts/GOP.speeches.past/84. kirkpatrick.shtml.

76 Philip Lentz, "Defense Workers Jeer Dukakis," *Chicago Tribune*, September 13, 1988, http://articles.chicagotribune.com/1988-09-13/news/8801290879_1_anti-dukakis-michael-dukakis-foreign-policy.

77 Josh King, "Dukakis and the Tank," *Politico*, November 17, 2013, http://www. politico.com/magazine/story/2013/11/dukakis-and-the-tank-99119_Page4. html#ixzz35s38JtQo.

78 Ibid.

Chapter 7: Triangulation Redux:
How Bill Clinton Became a Nixon Heir

1 Richard Nixon, quoted in Roger Stone, "Nixon on Clinton," *New York Times*, April 28, 1994, http://www.nytimes.com/1994/04/28/opinion/nixon-on-clinton. html.

2 Bill Clinton, quoted in Dana Davidsen, "Bill Clinton: Nixon a 'Communist' Compared to Modern GOP," CNN Web site: *political ticker . . .* blog, May 14, 2014, http://politicalticker.blogs.cnn.com/2014/05/14/bill-clinton-nixon-a-communist-compared-to-modern-gop/.

3 Bill Clinton, quoted in "A President's Learning Curve," *Newsweek*, July 30, 2000, http://www.newsweek.com/presidents-learning-curve-161551.

4 Bill Clinton, "Remarks at the Funeral Service for President Richard Nixon in Yorba Linda, California," Gerhard Peters and John T. Woolley, eds., American Presidency Project, April 27, 1994, http://www.presidency.ucsb.edu/ws/?pid=50052.

5 Ibid.

6 R. W. Apple Jr., "For Clinton and Nixon, a Rarified Bond," *New York Times*, April 25, 1994, http://www.nytimes.com/1994/04/25/us/for-clinton-and-nixon-a-rarefied-bond.html.

7 Bill Clinton, *My Life* (New York: Knopf, 2004), 437.

8 Richard Nixon, quoted in Stone, "Nixon on Clinton."

9 Diane Hollern Harvey, "The Public's View of Clinton," in *The Postmodern Presidency: Bill Clinton's Legacy in US Politics*, ed. Steven E. Schier (Pittsburgh: University of Pittsburgh Press, 2000), 141.

10 David Gergen, *Eyewitness to Power: The Essence of Leadership, Nixon to Clinton* (New York: Simon & Schuster, 2001), 86.

11 William Schneider, "Of Resentment & Empathy: Mr. Nixon, Meet Mr. Clinton," *Los Angeles Times*, May 1, 1994, http://articles.latimes.com/1994-05-01/opinion/op-52447_1_dick-nixon.

12 Ibid.

13 Lassiter, "Who Speaks for the Silent Majority?"

14 Bill Clinton, quoted in Matthew D. Lassiter, *The Silent Majority: Suburban Politics in the Sunbelt South* (Princeton, NJ: Princeton University Press, 2006), 320.

15 William J. Clinton, "The President's Radio Address" (speech, Washington, DC, September 4, 1993), Gerhard Peters and John T. Woolley, eds., American Presidency Project, http://www.presidency.ucsb.edu/ws/index.php?pid=47027.

16 Richard Nixon, "Address to the Nation."

17 Richard Nixon, quoted in Schier, *Postmodern Presidency*, 175.

18 Bill Clinton, quoted in John J. Pitney Jr., "Clinton and the Republican Party," in Ibid., 175.

19 Bill Clinton, quoted in Ibid., 175.

20 Bill Clinton, quoted in Doyle McManus, "Clinton Takes a Veiled Swipe at Dole on Militias," *Los Angeles Times,* June 2, 1995, http://articles.latimes.com/1995-06-02/news/mn-8602_1_militia-movement.

21 Richard Nixon, quoted in Pitney, "Clinton and the Republican Party," 174.

22 Ibid.

23 Ibid., 174.

24 Ibid., 174.

25 John Ehrlichman, quoted in Ibid., 174.

26 Bill Clinton, "Address before a Joint Session of the Congress on the State of the Union," (State of the Union speech, Washington, DC, January 23, 1996), Gerhard Peters and John T. Woolley, eds., American Presidency Project, http://www.presidency.ucsb.edu/ws/?pid=53091.

27 Ron Haskins, "Interview: Welfare Reform, 10 Years Later," Brookings Institute, August 24, 2006, http://www.brookings.edu/research/interviews/2006/08/24welfare-haskins.

28 Bruce Reed, quoted in R. Kent Weaver, *Ending Welfare as We Know It* (Washington, DC: Brookings Institution Press, 2000), 128.

29 Clinton, "Address before a Joint Session of Congress."

30 Bill Clinton, quoted in Barbara Vobejda, "Clinton Signs Welfare Bill amid Division," *Washington Post,* August 23, 1996, http://www.washingtonpost.com/wp-srv/politics/special/welfare/stories/wf082396.htm.

31 Ted Kennedy, quoted in Peter Edelman, "The Worst Thing Bill Clinton Has Done," *Atlantic,* March 1, 1997, https://www.theatlantic.com/past/docs/issues/97mar/edelman/edelman.htm.

32 Vobejda, "Clinton Signs Welfare Bill."

33 Bill Clinton, "How We Ended Welfare, Together," *New York Times,* August 22, 2006, http://www.nytimes.com/2006/08/22/opinion/22clinton.html?pagewanted=print.

34 Bill Clinton, quoted in "Clinton Campaigns for Weapons Ban in Letter to Hunters," *New York Times,* May 1, 1994, http://www.nytimes.com/1994/05/01/us/clinton-campaigns-for-weapons-ban-in-letter-to-hunters.html.

35 Justice Department, quoted in "Violent Crime Control and Law Enforcement Act of 1994," National Criminal Justice Reference Service, October 24, 1994, https://www.ncjrs.gov/txtfiles/billfs.txt.

36 Clifton Curry, "The Federal Crime Bill: What Will It Mean for California?," Legislative Analyst's Office, September 27, 1994, http://www.lao.ca.gov/1994/pb092794.html.

37 Bill Clinton, "Remarks on the Signing of NAFTA (December 8, 1993)" (speech, Washington, DC), University of Virginia: Miller Center, http://millercenter.org/president/speeches/speech-3927.

38 David Bonior, quoted in James Gerstenzag and Michael Ross, "House Passes NAFTA, 234–200: Clinton Hails Vote as Decision 'Not to Retreat': Congress: Sometimes Bitter Debate over the Trade Pact Reflects Hard-Fought Battle among Divided Democrats. Rapid Approval Is Expected in the Senate," *Los Angeles Times,* November 18, 1993, http://articles.latimes.com/1993-11-18/news/mn-58150_1_trade-pact.

39 Richard Gephardt, quoted in Gilbert A. Lewthwaite, "Gephardt Declares against NAFTA: Democrat Cites Threat to U.S. Jobs," *Baltimore Sun,* September 22, 1993, http://articles.baltimoresun.com/1993-09-22/news/1993265014_1_gephardt-nafta-treaty.

40 Newt Gingrich, quoted in Kenneth J. Cooper, "House Approves US-Canada-Mexico Trade Pact on 234 to 200 Vote, Giving Clinton Big Victory," *Washington Post,* November 18, 1993, http://www.washingtonpost.com/wpsrv/politics/special/trade/stories/tr111893.htm.

41 William Clinton, in William Clinton, George Bush, Jimmy Carter, Gerald Ford, and Al Gore, "Remarks by President Clinton, President Bush, President Carter, President Ford, and Vice President Gore in Signing of NAFTA Side Agreements" (speech, Washington, DC, September 14, 1993), in Natalie Goldstein, *Globalization and Free Trade* (New York: Infobase Publishing, 2009).

42 Jim Goldgeier and Derek Chollet, "The (Bill) Clinton Legacy," *Huffington Post,* May 25, 2011, http://www.huffingtonpost.com/jim-goldgeier-and-derek-chollet/the-bill-clinton-legacy_b_106089.html.

43 William Clinton, quoted in Eyder Peralta, "New Documents Provide Insight into Relationship of Presidents Clinton, Nixon," NPR Web site, February

14, 2013, http://www.npr.org/blogs/thetwoway/2013/02/14/172007758/new-documents-provide-insight-into-relationship-of-presidents-clinton-nixon.

44 Bill Clinton, quoted in "Clinton: 'The President Is Relevant,'" *Time*, April 18, 1995, http://content.time.com/time/nation/article/0,8599,3632,00.html.

45 Michael Waldman, quoted in Steven M. Gillon, *The Pact: Bill Clinton, Newt Gingrich, and the Rivalry That Defined a Generation* (New York: Oxford University Press, 2008), 145.

46 William Clinton, quoted in Sidney Blumenthal, *The Clinton Wars* (New York: Farrar, Straus and Giroux, 2003), 132.

47 Clinton, *My Life*, 654.

48 Ibid.

49 Newt Gingrich, quoted in Keith Lee Rupp, "Government Shutdown Déjà Vu," *U.S. News & World Report*, October 2, 2013, http://www.usnews.com/opinion/blogs/keith-rupp/2013/10/02/house-republicans-forgot-the-lessons-of-the-clinton-shutdowns.

50 *New York Daily News*, quoted in Linda Killian, "Why Newt Gingrich Will Never Be President," *Atlantic*, November 16, 2011, http://www.theatlantic.com/politics/archive/2011/11/why-newt-gingrich-will-never-be-president/248456/.

51 Bill Clinton, quoted in "What Clinton Said," *Washington Post,* January 17, 1998, http://www.washingtonpost.com/wp-srv/politics/special/clinton/stories/whatclintonsaid.htm#Arafat.

52 Richard Nixon, quoted in "'I Am Not a Crook': How a Phrase Got a Life of Its Own," NPR Web site, November 17, 2013, http://www.npr.org/templates/story/story.php?storyId=245830047.

53 Bill Clinton, quoted in "What Clinton Said," *Washington Post*.

54 Lydia Saad, "Bush Presidency Closes with 34% Approval and 61% Disapproval," Gallup, January 14, 2009, http://www.gallup.com/poll/113770/Bush-Presidency-Closes-34-Approval-61-Disapproval.aspx.

55 Richard Nixon, quoted in David Cross, "Nixon and Clinton Sitting in a Tree…," Following the Presidents, February 22, 2013, http://followingthepresidents.com/2013/02/22/nixon-and-clinton-sitting-in-a-tree/.

56 Richard Nixon, quoted in Monica Crowley, *Nixon off the Record: His Candid Commentary on People and Politics* (New York: Random House, 1996), 61.

57 Richard Nixon, quoted in Ibid., 68–69.

58 Richard Nixon, quoted in Marvin Kalb, *The Nixon Memo: Political Respectability, Russia, and the Press* (Chicago: University of Chicago Press, 1994), 145.

59 Richard Nixon, quoted in Crowley, *Nixon off the Record*, 167–68.

60 Richard Nixon, quoted in Monica Crowley, *Nixon in Winter: The Final Revelations about Diplomacy, Watergate, and Life out of the Arena* (New York: Random House, 1998), 128.

61 Richard Nixon, quoted in Ibid., 129.

62 Richard Nixon, quoted in Ibid., 129.

63 Stone, "Nixon on Clinton."

64 John M. Broeder, "Clinton, Nixon Join on Yeltsin Wavelength; Presidency: The Baby Boomer and the Ex-President He Once Opposed Find Common Ground on the Question of Aid to Russia," *Los Angeles Times*, March 10, 1993, http://articles.latimes.com/1993-03-10/news/mn-1053_1_common-ground.

65 Apple, "A Rarified Bond."
66 Richard Nixon, quoted in Ibid.
67 Bill Clinton, quoted in Ibid.
68 Bill Clinton, quoted in Ibid.
69 Stone, "Nixon on Clinton."
70 Crowley, *Nixon off the Record*, 219–20.
71 David Brinkley, quoted in Jan Crawford, "Letters Reveal Friendship between Presidents Clinton and Nixon," CBS News Web site, February 14, 2013, http://www.cbsnews.com/news/letters-reveal-friendship-between-presidents-clinton-and-nixon/.
72 Bill Clinton, quoted in Apple, "A Rarified Bond."
73 Bill Clinton, quoted in Associated Press, "Richard Nixon's Quiet Foreign Policy Advice to Bill Clinton Revealed in Newly Declassified Documents," *Daily News*, February 14, 2013, http://www.nydailynews.com/news/politics/nixon-foreign-policy-advice-bill-clinton-revealed-article-1.1264304.
74 Apple, "A Rarified Bond."
75 David Gergen, quoted in Kalb, *The Nixon Memo*, 185.
76 Gergen, *Eyewitness to Power*, 86.

Chapter 8: They Didn't Listen to Nixon: Foreign Policy and Polarization under Bush and Obama

1 George W. Bush, "President Bush's Second Inaugural Address," NPR Web site, January 20, 2005, http://www.npr.org/templates/story/story.php?storyId=4460172.
2 Brent Scowcroft, quoted in Jeffrey Goldberg, "Breaking Ranks," *New Yorker*, October 31, 2005, http://www.newyorker.com/magazine/2005/10/31/breaking-ranks.
3 Roger Cohen, "Ambivalence about America," *New York Times*, August 18, 2014, http://mobile.nytimes.com/2014/08/19/opinion/roger-cohen-ambivalence-about-america.html?ref=todayspaper&_r=0&referrer=.
4 "Presidential Approval Ratings—George W. Bush," Gallup, January 11, 2009, http://www.gallup.com/poll/116500/presidential-approval-ratings-george-bush.aspx.
5 William Kristol and Robert Kagan, quoted in Francis Fukuyama, "After Neoconservatism," *New York Times*, February 19, 2006, http://www.nytimes.com/2006/02/19/magazine/neo.html?pagewanted=all&_r=1&.
6 Francis Fukuyama, quoted in Isaac Chotiner, "The Neo-Neo-Conservative," *Washington Monthly*, May 2006, http://www.washingtonmonthly.com/features/2006/0605.chotiner.html.
7 Colin Powell, quoted in "Ideas and Consequences," *Atlantic*, October 1, 2007, http://www.theatlantic.com/magazine/archive/2007/10/ideas-and-consequences/306193/.
8 Brent Scowcroft, quoted in Glenn Kessler, "Scowcroft Is Critical of Bush," *Washington Post*, October 16, 2004, http://www.washingtonpost.com/wp-dyn/articles/A36644-2004Oct15.html.
9 Scowcroft, quoted in Goldberg, "Breaking Ranks."

10 Michael Isikoff and David Corn, *Hubris: The Inside Story of Spin, Scandal, and the Selling of the Iraq War* (New York: Crown, 2006), 22–23.

11 Karl Rove, quoted in Thomas B. Edsall, "GOP Touts War as Campaign Issue," *Washington Post*, January 19, 2002, http://www.washingtonpost.com/wp-dyn/content/article/2007/08/13/AR2007081300840.html.

12 Saxby Chambliss campaign ad, quoted in Andy Barr, "Cleland Ad Causes Trouble for Chambliss," *Politico*, November 12, 2008, http://www.politico.com/news/stories/1108/15561.html.

13 Isikoff and Corn, *Hubris*, 148–49.

14 Hillary Clinton, "Floor Speech of Senator Hillary Rodham Clinton on S. J. Res. 45, A Resolution to Authorize the Use of United States Armed Forces against Iraq" (speech, Washington, DC, October 10, 2002), Democratic Underground, http://www.democraticunderground.com/discuss/duboard.php?az=view_all&address=132x4020176.

15 Peter Zimmerman, quoted in Isikoff and Corn, *Hubris*, 137–38.

16 Democratic Leadership Council, quoted in Ibid.

17 Joan Vennochi, "Is Dean Another McGovern?," *Boston Globe*, November 18, 2003, http://www.boston.com/news/globe/editorial_opinion/oped/articles/2003/11/18/is_dean_another_mcgovern/.

18 Ken Mehlman, quoted in Michael Finnegan, "Bush Campaign Chief Calls Democrats Weak on Security," *Los Angeles Times*, November 23, 2003, http://articles.latimes.com/2003/nov/23/nation/na-security23.

19 Jonah Goldberg, "John Kerry, International Man of Nuance," Townhall, September 10, 2004, http://townhall.com/columnists/jonahgoldberg/2004/09/10/john_kerry,_international_man_of_nuance/page/full.

20 Dick Cheney, quoted in Laura McCallum, "Cheney Hammers on National Security Issues in Rosemount; Ventura Endorses Kerry," Minnesota Public Radio Web site, October 22, 2004, http://news.minnesota.publicradio.org/features/2004/10/22_mccalluml_cheney/.

21 John Kerry, quoted in Matt Bai, "Kerry's Undeclared War," *New York Times Magazine*, October 10, 2004, http://www.nytimes.com/2004/10/10/magazine/kerrys-undeclared-war.html.

22 Richard Holbrooke, quoted in Ibid.

23 George W. Bush, quoted in Richard W. Stevenson, "Bush Attacks Kerry as Weak on Security," *New York Times*, October 23, 2004, http://www.nytimes.com/2004/10/23/politics/campaign/23bush.html.

24 Ibid.

25 Republican National Committee ad, quoted in E. J. Dionne Jr., "Beyond the War Spin," *Washington Post*, December 13, 2005, http://www.washingtonpost.com/wp-dyn/content/article/2005/12/12/AR2005121201264.html.

26 Dennis Hastert, quoted in Ibid.

27 George Bush, quoted in Michael A. Fletcher, "Bush Attacks 'Party of Cut and Run,'" *Washington Post*, September 29, 2006, http://www.washingtonpost.com/wp-dyn/content/article/2006/09/28/AR2006092801844.htm.

28 Ted Kennedy, quoted in Robert K. Brigham, "Iraq vs. Vietnam," *Vassar, the Alumnae/i Quarterly* 102, no. 4 (2006), http://vq.vassar.edu/issues/2006/04/features/iraq-vs-vietnam.html.

29 Robert Byrd, quoted in Susan Page, "Is Iraq Becoming Another Vietnam?," *USA Today*, April 13, 2004, http://usatoday30.usatoday.com/news/world/iraq/2004-04-13-vietnam-iraq-cover_x.htm.

30 William Nash, quoted in Jonathan Rauch, "Iraq Is No Vietnam. But Vietnam Holds Lessons for Iraq," *National Journal* 36, September 11, 2004, 2710–11.

31 Anthony Zinni, quoted in "U.S. Is Committing Same Mistakes in Iraq as in Vietnam, Says General," *New Perspectives Quarterly* 31, no. 2, May 18, 2004, http://www.digitalnpq.org/global_services/global%20viewpoint/05-18-04.html.

32 Dick Armey, quoted in Isikoff and Corn, *Hubris*, 24.

33 Chuck Hagel, quoted in "Hagel: Iraq Growing More like Vietnam," CNN Web site: Politics, August 18, 2005, http://www.cnn.com/2005/POLITICS/08/18/hagel.iraq/.

34 Thomas L. Friedman, "Barney and Baghdad," *New York Times*, October 18, 2006, http://www.nytimes.com/2006/10/18/opinion/18friedman.html.

35 Ted Kennedy, quoted in "Kennedy Slams Bush Credibility Gap," compiled by Heather Riley, CNN.com, April 6, 2004, http://www.cnn.com/2004/ALLPOLITICS/04/06/tue.hot/.

36 Darlene Superville, "Bush Tops Hero and Villain Lists of 2006," *Seattle Times*, December 29, 2006, http://www.seattletimes.com/nation-world/bush-tops-hero-and-villain-lists-of-2006/.

37 Ari Fleischer, quoted in Taegan Goddard, "Was George W. Bush the Worst President Ever?," the *Week*, April 24, 2013, http://theweek.com/article/index/243205/was-george-w-bush-the-worst-president-ever#axzz351JBkXIJ.

38 Paul Krugman, "Standard Operating Procedure," *New York Times*, June 3, 2003, http://www.nytimes.com/2003/06/03/opinion/standard-operating-procedure.html.

39 Ralph Nader, quoted in Thomas J. Lueck, "Nader Calls for Impeachment of Bush over the War in Iraq," *New York Times*, May 25, 2004, http://www.nytimes.com/2004/05/25/us/nader-calls-for-impeachment-of-bush-over-the-war-in-iraq.html.

40 "32% Favor Bush Impeachment," *Rasmussen Reports*, December 15, 2005, http://legacy.rasmussenreports.com/2005/Impeachment.htm.

41 Keith Ellison, quoted in Mike Mulcahy, "Ellison Compares Bush to Nixon," Minnesota Public Radio blog, August 9, 2006, http://blogs.mprnews.org/capitol-view/2006/08/mprs_tim_pugmir/.

42 Ben Pershing, "Kucinich Forces Vote on Bush's Impeachment," *Washington Post*, June 11, 2008, http://www.washingtonpost.com/wp-dyn/content/article/2008/06/10/AR2008061003087.html.

43 Barack Obama, quoted in John Whitesides, "Obama Says He Opposed Iraq War from Start," *Reuters*, February 12, 2007, http://www.reuters.com/article/2007/02/12/us-usa-politics-obama-idUSN0923153320070212.

44 Barack Obama, "Obama's Speech on Iraq, March 2008" (speech, Fayetteville, NC, March 19, 2008), Council on Foreign Relations, http://www.cfr.org/elections/obamas-speech-iraq-march-2008/p15761.

45 Barack Obama, quoted in Jeff Zeleny, "As Candidate, Obama Carves Antiwar Stance," *New York Times*, February 26, 2007, http://www.nytimes.com/2007/02/26/us/politics/26obama.html?pagewanted=all.

46 Barack Obama, "Barack Obama's Foreign Policy Speech" (speech, Chicago, October 2, 2007), Council on Foreign Relations, http://www.cfr.org/elections/barack-obamas-foreign-policy-speech/p14356.

47 Barack Obama, quoted in David Brooks, "Obama Admires Bush," *New York Times,* May 16, 2008, http://www.nytimes.com/2008/05/16/opinion/16brooks.html.

48 Barack Obama, quoted in "Transcript: President Obama's Convention Speech," NPR Web site, September 6, 2008, http://www.npr.org/2012/09/06/160713941/transcript-president-obamas-convention-speech.

49 Chuck Hagel, quoted in Jeryl Bier, "Defense Secretary: 'The World Is Exploding All Over,'" *Weekly Standard* blog, August 13, 2014, http://www.weeklystandard.com/blogs/defense-secretary-world-exploding-all-over_802893.html.

50 Bob Corker, quoted in Mark Landler, "Obama to Detail a Broader Foreign Policy Agenda," *New York Times,* May 24, 2014, http://www.nytimes.com/2014/05/25/world/obama-to-detail-a-broader-foreign-policy-agenda.html.

51 Andrew Brown, "North Korea Holds Key to a China Nightmare," *Wall Street Journal,* May 6, 2014, http://online.wsj.com/news/articles/SB10001424052702304831304579544771916974110.

52 Jennifer Rubin, quoted in Ibid.

53 John Bolton, "Doubling Down on a Muddled Foreign Policy," *Wall Street Journal,* May 28, 2014, http://online.wsj.com/articles/john-bolton-doubling-down-on-a-muddled-foreign-policy-1401317355.

54 Fred Kaplan, "The Realist: Barack Obama's a Cold Warrior Indeed," *Politico,* February 27, 2014, http://www.politico.com/magazine/story/2014/02/barack-obama-realist-foreign-policy-103861.html#ixzz3LMB7x1kF.

55 John McLaughlin, quoted in "The Steel in Barack Obama's Spine," *Politico,* March 3, 2014, http://www.politico.com/magazine/story/2014/03/obama-russia-ukraine-foreign-policy-test-104211.

56 David Remnick, quoted in Evan McMurry, "*New Yorker*'s Remnick on Obama: 'The World Seems to Disappoint Him,'" *Mediaite,* May 6, 2014, http://www.mediaite.com/tv/new-yorkers-remnick-on-obama-the-world-seems-to-disappoint-him/.

57 John McCain, "Obama Has Made America Look Weak," *New York Times,* March 14, 2014, http://www.nytimes.com/2014/03/15/opinion/mccain-a-return-to-us-realism.html.

58 Paul Ryan, quoted in Martin Matishak, "Ryan: Obama Foreign Policy 'Weak, Indecisive,'" the *Hill,* June 11, 2014, http://thehill.com/policy/defense/208984-ryan-obama-foreign-policy-weak-indecisive.

59 Moshe Yaalon, quoted in Jack Moore, "Israel Defence Minister Moshe Yaalon Slams Barack Obama's 'Weak and Feeble' Foreign Policy," *International Business Times,* March 18, 2014, http://www.ibtimes.co.uk/israel-defence-minister-moshe-yaalon-slams-barack-obamas-weak-feeble-foreign-policy-1440714.

60 Julie Hirschfeld Davis, "Top Candidates to Succeed Hagel Are Longtime National Security Specialists," *New York Times,* November 24, 2014, http://www.nytimes.com/2014/11/25/us/politics/2-former-defense-department-insiders-are-contenders-to-succeed-hagel.html.

61 Andrew Dugan, "U.S. Voters Give GOP Edge vs. Dems on Handling Top

Issues," Gallup, October 13, 2014, http://www.gallup.com/poll/178268/voters-give-gop-edge-handling-top-issues.aspx.

62 David Lauter, "Americans Increasingly See Opposing Party as 'Threat' to Nation," *Los Angeles Times*, June 12, 2014, http://www.latimes.com/nation/politics/politicsnow/la-pn-partisan-polarization-20140611-story.html.

63 Chris Cillizza, "What George W. Bush Meant for Politics," *Washington Post*, April 25, 2013, http://www.washingtonpost.com/blogs/the-fix/wp/2013/04/25/what-george-w-bush-meant-for-politics/.

64 Robin Toner and Jim Rutenberg, "Partisan Divide on Iraq Exceeds Split on Vietnam," *New York Times*, July 30, 2006, http://www.nytimes.com/2006/07/30/washington/30war.html?ex=1156305600&en=2c8785b10c8ad115&ei=5070.

SECTION III
THE NIXON LEGACY

Chapter 9: Watergate and the End of Bipartisan Politics

1 Richard Dallek, quoted in Gerald F. Seib, "Why Watergate Lives On 40 Years after Nixon Resignation," *Wall Street Journal*, August 4, 2014, http://online.wsj.com/articles/why-watergate-lives-on-40-years-after-nixon-resignation-1407167209.

2 Krugman, "Standard Operating Procedure."

3 George Will, quoted in Keith Koffler, "George Will Compares IRS Scandal to Watergate, Iran Contra," *White House Dossier*, February 4, 2014, http://www.whitehousedossier.com/2014/02/04/george-compares-irs-scandal-watergate-iran-contra/.

4 Chuck Todd, *U.S. Politics Today Is "Still Bearing the Scars of Watergate,"* NBC News video, August 8, 2014, http://www.nbcnews.com/nightly-news/forty-years-after-watergate-nixons-unlikely-staying-power-n176506.

5 Peter Baker, "40 Years Later, Still Trying to Define Presidential Power," *New York Times*, August 3, 2014, http://www.nytimes.com/2014/08/04/us/richard-nixons-tenure-and-downfall-are-reassessed.html.

6 Ibid.

7 William Cohen, quoted in Seib, "Why Watergate Lives On."

8 Elizabeth Drew, quoted in Baker, "40 Years Later."

9 Doyle McManus, "What's the Secret of Nixon's Unpopularity?," *Los Angeles Times*, October 30, 2015, http://www.latimes.com/opinion/op-ed/la-oe-mcmanus-column-nixon-resignation-tapes-20140809-column.html.

10 "'A Third-Rate Burglary Attempt,'" Ron Zeigler, quoted in "A Watergate Glossary: The Names, Dates and Quotations That Defined a Scandal," CNN Time, http://www.cnn.com/ALLPOLITICS/1997/gen/resources/watergate/glossary.alt.html.

11 Joe Califano, quoted in Jules Witcover, "Did Nixon Commit Treason?," *Baltimore Sun*, August 18, 2014, http://www.baltimoresun.com/news/opinion/oped/bs-ed-witcover-0819-20140818,0,4976192,print.story.

12 Richard Nixon, quoted in Ibid.

13 Richard Nixon, quoted in George F. Will, "Richard Nixon's Long Shadow," *Washington Post,* August 6, 2014, http://www.washingtonpost.com/opinions/ george-f-will-nixons-long-shadow/2014/08/06/fad8c00c-1ccb-11e4-ae54-ocfe1f974f8a_story.html.

14 Ibid.

15 Buchanan, *Greatest Comeback,* 357.

16 Anna Chennault, quoted in Witcover, "Did Nixon Commit Treason?"

17 Gerald Ford, "Gerald R. Ford's Remarks upon Taking the Oath of Office as President," (speech, Washington, DC, August 9, 1974), Gerald R. Ford Presidential Library & Museum, http://www.fordlibrarymuseum.gov/library/ speeches/740001.asp.

18 Gerald Ford, "Remarks on Signing a Proclamation Granting a Pardon to Richard Nixon" (speech, Washington, DC, September 8, 1974), Gerhard Peters and John T. Woolley, eds., American Presidency Project, http://www. presidency.ucsb.edu/ws/?pid=4695.

19 J. F. terHorst, quoted in Bruce Weber, "J. F. terHorst, Ford Press Secretary, Dies at 87," *New York Times,* April 1, 2010, http://www.nytimes.com/2010/04/02/ us/02terhorst.html?_r=0.

20 "Pardon for What?," *New York Times,* September 10, 1974.

21 Carl Bernstein, quoted in Rick Perlstein, "Watergate's Most Lasting Sin: Gerald Ford, Richard Nixon, and the Pardon that Made Us All Cynics," *Salon,* September 8, 2014, http://www.salon.com/2014/09/08/watergates_most_ lasting_sin_gerald_ford_richard_nixon_and_the_pardon_that_made_ us_all_cynics/.

22 Ken Gormley and David Shribman, "The Nixon Pardon at 40: Ford Looks Better than Ever," *Wall Street Journal,* September 5, 2014, http://online.wsj.com/ articles/ken-gormley-and-david-shribman-the-nixon-pardon-at-40-ford-looks-better-than-ever-1409955912?mod=WSJ_hps_sections_opinion.

23 "Pardon for What?," *New York Times.*

24 Gormley and Shribman, "The Nixon Pardon at 40."

25 Ronald D. Elving, "Rebels of '94."

26 James Blanchard, quoted in David W. Rohde, *Parties and Leaders in the Postreform House* (Chicago: University of Chicago Press, 1991), 48.

27 Gary Hart, quoted in Rick Perlstein, "America's Forgotten Liberal," *New York Times,* May 26, 2011, http://www.nytimes.com/2011/05/27/opinion/27Perlstein. html.

28 Tim Wirth, quoted in Ron Elving, "Congressman's Exit Closes the Book on 'Watergate Babies,'" NPR blog, January 31, 2014, http://www.npr.org/blogs/ itsallpolitics/2014/01/30/269003155/congressmans-exit-closes-book-on-watergate-babies.

29 *US News & World Report,* quoted in Julian E. Zelizer, *On Capitol Hill: The Struggle to Reform Congress and Its Consequences, 1948–2000* (New York: Cambridge University Press, 2004), 168.

30 Gerald Ford, quoted in "Ford Rebuffed on Angola Aid," *Rome News-Tribune,* January 28, 1976, http://news.google.com/newspapers?nid=348&dat=19760128&i d=5wUvAAAAIBAJ&sjid=QTMDAAAAIBAJ&pg=6252,3399729.

31 Henry Kissinger, quoted in Julian E. Zelizer, "How Congress Got Us Out of Vietnam," *American Prospect*, February 19, 2007, http://prospect.org/article/how-congress-got-us-out-vietnam.

32 Frank Church, quoted in Chris Mooney, "Back to Church," *American Prospect*, December 19, 2001, http://prospect.org/article/back-church.

33 "The Wall of Separation between Law-Enforcement and Intelligence," DicoverTheNetworks.org, http://www.discoverthenetworks.org/viewSubCategory.asp?id=182.

34 John Ashcroft, quoted in Ibid.

35 Ron Elving, "Congressman's Exit."

36 Richard Reeves, quoted in Peter Overby, "Illegal during Watergate, Unlimited Campaign Donations Now Fair Game," NPR Web site, November 16, 2011, http://www.npr.org/blogs/itsallpolitics/2011/11/16/142314581/illegal-during-watergate-unlimited-campaign-contributions-now-fair-game.

37 Mark Stencel, "The Reforms," *Washington Post*, June 13, 1997, http://www.washingtonpost.com/wp-srv/national/longterm/watergate/legacy.htm.

38 Ibid.

39 Victoria A. Farrar-Myers, "The Ripple Effect of Scandal and Reform: The Historical Impact of Watergate Era Finance Regulation and Its Progeny," in *Watergate Remembered: The Legacy for American Politics*, ed. Michael A. Genovese and Iwan Morgan (New York: Palgrave MacMillan, 2012), 136.

40 Doug Schoen, *American Casino: The Rigged Game That's Killing Democracy* (New York: Velocity, 2012).

41 Michael A. Genovese, "The Long Legacy of Watergate," in Genovese and Morgan, *Watergate Remembered*, 186.

42 Ibid., 185.

43 Elliot Richardson, quoted in Genovese and Morgan, *Watergate Remembered*, 76.

44 Clodagh Harrington, "Watergate and Scandal Politics," in Genovese and Morgan, *Watergate Remembered*, 76.

45 Sam Donaldson and Edwin Meese, quoted in Richard C. Thornton, *The Reagan Revolution IV: From Victory to the New World Order* (Arlington: Djt Analytics, 2013), 500.

46 Lawrence Walsh, quoted in Julie Novkov, *The Supreme Court and the Presidency: Struggles for Supremacy* (Los Angeles: SAGE Reference, 2013), 70.

47 Michael Barone, quoted in American Enterprise Institute, *Watergate Revisited*.

48 George Brown, quoted in Sean Smith, "Watergate's Legacy," *Boston College Chronicle*, May 8, 1997, http://www.bc.edu/bc_org/rvp/pubaf/chronicle/v5/My8/watergate.html.

49 Charles Krauthammer, quoted in *Ronald Reagan Documentary*, 4:15:14.

50 Ronald Reagan, "Remarks at the Annual Dinner of the Conservative Political Action Conference" (speech, Washington, DC, March 1, 1985), Gerhard Peters and John T. Woolley, eds., American Presidency Project, http://www.presidency.ucsb.edu/ws/?pid=38274.

51 Ronald Reagan, quoted in "THE IRAN-CONTRA REPORT [key sections]," Gerhard Peters and John T. Woolley, eds., American Presidency Project, November 18, 1987, http://www.presidency.ucsb.edu/PS157/assignment%20files%20public/congressional%20report%20key%20sections.htm.

52 George J. Church, "Who Was Betrayed?," *Time*, December 8, 1986, http://content.time.com/time/subscriber/article/0,33009,963029,00.html.
53 Krugman, "Standard Operating Procedure."
54 Max Hastings, quoted in Ibid.
55 Charles Duelfer, "No Books Were Cooked," *Foreign Policy*, March 18, 2013, http://www.foreignpolicy.com/articles/2013/03/18/no_books_were_cooked_bush_iraq_wmd_intelligence.
56 John Brennan, quoted in "Interview: John Brennan," *Frontline*, June 20, 2006, http://www.pbs.org/wgbh/pages/frontline/darkside/interviews/brennan.html.
57 "Downing Street Memo," quoted in Walter Pincus, "British Intelligence Warned of War," *Washington Post*, May 13, 2005, http://www.washingtonpost.com/wp-dyn/content/article/2005/05/12/AR2005051201857.html.
58 Colin Powell, quoted in Steven R. Weisman, "Powell Calls His U.N. Speech a Lasting Blot on His Record," *New York Times*, September 9, 2005, http://www.nytimes.com/2005/09/09/politics/09powell.html.
59 Colin Powell, quoted in David Corn, "'Hubris': New Documentary Reexamines the Iraq War 'Hoax,'" *Mother Jones*, February 16, 2013, http://www.motherjones.com/politics/2013/02/hubris-rachel-maddow-documentary-iraq-war-david-corn.
60 Krugman, "Standard Operating Procedure."
61 C. J. Chivers, "The Secret Casualties of Iraq's Abandoned Chemical Weapons," *New York Times*, October 14, 2014, http://www.nytimes.com/interactive/2014/10/14/world/middleeast/us-casualties-of-iraq-chemical-weapons.html?smid=tw-nytimesworld.
62 "Lawyer Confirms She Asked Planted Question That Broke Open IRS Scandal," Fox News Web site, May 18, 2013, http://www.foxnews.com/politics/2013/05/18/lawyer-confirms-asked-planted-question-that-broke-open-irs-scandal/.
63 Ibid.
64 Daniel Henninger, "The High Price of Obama Fatigue," *Wall Street Journal*, June 19, 2014, http://www.wsj.com/articles/the-high-price-of-obama-fatigue-1403139022.
65 Pat Buchanan, quoted in Jeff Poor, "Pat Buchanan: Obama's IRS Scandal Worse than Nixon," Breitbart, June 28, 2014, http://www.breitbart.com/Breitbart-TV/2014/06/28/Pat-Buchanan-Obamas-IRS-Scandal-Worse-than-Nixon.
66 Barack Obama, "Weekly Address: President Obama Challenges Politicians Benefiting from Citizens United Ruling to Defend Corporate Influence in Our Elections," White House Web site (weekly address, Washington, DC, August 21, 2010), President Barack Obama Web site, https://www.whitehouse.gov/the-press-office/2010/08/21/weekly-address-president-obama-challenges-politicians-benefiting-citizen.
67 Henninger, "Obama Fatigue."
68 C. L. Sulzberger, quoted in Jeffrey Frank, "Nixon's Nightmare—and Ours—Forty Years Ago," *New Yorker*, July 30, 2014, http://www.newyorker.com/news/daily-comment/nixons-nightmare-forty-years-ago.
69 Thomas F. Railsback, "House Handled Trauma with Bipartisanship, Now Lost," *New York Times*, June 14, 2012, http://www.nytimes.com/roomfordebate/2012/06/13/did-any-good-come-of-watergate/house-handled-trauma-with-bipartisanship-now-lost.

70 Ibid.

71 Robert Thompson, quoted in Daniel P. Finney, "Watergate Scandal Changed the Political Landscape Forever," *USA Today,* June 16, 2012, http://usatoday30. usatoday.com/news/nation/story/2012-06-16/watergate-scandal-changed-political-landscape/55639974/1.

72 "The Damaging Legacy of Nixon and Watergate," *Chicago Tribune,* August 7, 2014, http://www.chicagotribune.com/news/opinion/editorials/ct-edit-nixon-watergate-resign-0807-jm-20140807-story.html.

Chapter 10: Nixon's Final Comeback: The Postpresidency

1 *Arkansas Gazette,* quoted in Anna Quindlen, "Public & Private; Living Will," *New York Times,* April 27, 1994, http://www.nytimes.com/1994/04/27/opinion/public-private-living-will.html.

2 Richard Nixon, quoted in *Frost/Nixon: The Complete Interviews,* interview by David Frost, directed by Jørn Winther, aired May 1977 (Los Angeles: Liberation Entertainment, 2008), DVD.

3 Arnold Beichman, "Richard Nixon," *Commentary,* March 1, 1989, http://www.commentarymagazine.com/article/richard-nixon/.

4 Stephen Ambrose, quoted in Broder, "Clinton, Nixon Join on Yeltsin Wavelength."

5 Gerald R. Ford, *A Time to Heal: The Autobiography of Gerald R. Ford* (New York: Harper & Row, 1979), 299.

6 Anthony Lewis, "The Age of Nixon," *New York Times,* August 10, 1974.

7 *Baltimore Sun,* quoted in "Editorials on Nixon," *New York Times,* August 10, 1974.

8 *Arkansas Gazette,* quoted in Quindlen, "Public & Private."

9 Richard Nixon, quoted in Burton I. Kaufman, *The Post-Presidency from Washington to Clinton* (Lawrence: University of Kansas Press, 2012), 402.

10 David Eisenhower, quoted in Ibid., 404.

11 Richard Nixon, quoted in Ibid., 405.

12 Gerald Ford and Benton Becker, quoted in Andrew Downer Crain, *The Ford Presidency: A History* (Jefferson, NC: McFarland, 2009), 60.

13 Richard Nixon, quoted in Larry Martz, Thomas M. DeFrank, and Howard Fineman, "The Road Back," *Newsweek,* May 19, 1986.

14 Kaufman, *Post-Presidency,* 407.

15 Ibid., 410.

16 Richard Nixon, quoted in Martz, DeFrank, and Fineman, "The Road Back."

17 Quoted in Ibid.

18 Kaufman, *Post-Presidency,* 408.

19 Everett R. Holles, "Nixon Losing Transitional Staff; Lonely, Ill, He Looks to New Role," *New York Times,* February 9, 1975, http://query.nytimes.com/gst/abstract.html?res=9400EFD81731E034BC4153DFB466838E669EDE.

20 David Broder, quoted in David Greenberg, *Nixon's Shadow: The History of an Image* (New York: Norton, 2003), 284.

21 Barry Goldwater, quoted in Kaufman, *Post-Presidency,* 409.

22 "Ford View of Vote: Nixon Trip to China 'Probably Harmful,'" *New York Times,*

February 27, 1976, http://query.nytimes.com/gst/abstract.html?res=9C00E1DA11
3CE334BC4F51DFB466838D669EDE.

23 James Naughton, "Nixon Trip Revives Issue Vexing to Ford in Primary," *New York Times*, February 21, 1976, http://query.nytimes.com/gst/abstract.html?res=
9E06E2D8173BE334BC4951DFB466838D669EDE.

24 David M. Alpern, "Watching Nixon," *Newsweek*, May 16, 1977.

25 Richard Nixon, quoted in "'I Have Impeached Myself,'" *Guardian,* September 7, 2007, http://www.theguardian.com/theguardian/2007/sep/07/greatinterviews1.

26 Leon Jaworski, quoted in Alpern, "Watching Nixon."

27 *Newsweek*, quoted in David Greenberg, "Richard Nixon Is Still Dead," *Slate*, August 10, 1999, http://www.slate.com/articles/news_and_politics/hey_
wait_a_minute/1999/08/richard_nixon_is_still_dead.single.html.

28 "Nixon Talks," *Time*, May 9, 1977, http://content.time.com/time/magazine/article/0,9171,947900,00.html.

29 Kaufman, *Post-Presidency*, 409.

30 Richard Nixon, quoted in Frost, *Frost/Nixon: The Complete Interviews*.

31 "Nixon's Memoirs: I Was Selfish," *Time*, May 8, 1978, http://content.time.com/time/magazine/article/0,9171,919598,00.html.

32 Grosset & Dunlop, quoted in Ibid.

33 "Early Reports Show Sales of Nixon Book Are Sluggish," *Wilmington Star-News,* May 14, 1978, http://news.google.com/newspapers?nid=1454&dat=19780513&id=
070sAAAAIBAJ&sjid=PBMEAAAAIBAJ&pg=6499,2679778.

34 Kaufman, *Post-Presidency*, 415.

35 Roy Reed, "Welcome for Nixon at Oxford Is Warm," *New York Times*, December 1, 1978, http://query.nytimes.com/gst/abstract.html?res=9906E5D91130E632A257
52C0A9649D946990D6CF.

36 Richard Nixon, quoted in Ibid.

37 Quoted in Kaufman, *Post-Presidency*, 418.

38 Lowell Weicker, quoted in Martin Tolchin, "Nixon's Invitation Reactions Mixed," *New York Times*, January 17, 1979, retrieved from Google News, https://news.google.com/newspapers?nid=1356&dat=19790117&id=Yp5PAAAAIBAJ&sjid=wQUEAAAAIBAJ&pg=6990,4620982&hl=en.

39 John Anderson, quoted in "An 'Appropriate' Complaint," *Washington Post*, July 31, 1979, http://www.washingtonpost.com/archive/politics/1979/07/31/an-appropriate-complaint/49395a06-fa6f-4bce-ab4a-184a25027ef6/.

40 John Anderson, quoted in Tolchin, "Nixon's Invitation Reactions Mixed."

41 Jimmy Carter, quoted in Martin Tolchin, "Nixon, at Teng's Dinner, Said to Plan a China Trip; Meeting with Carter," *New York Times*, January 30, 1979, http://query.nytimes.com/gst/abstract.html?res=990CE6D81639E732A25753C3A9679C
946890D6CF.

42 Greenberg, *Nixon's Shadow*, 286.

43 "Nixon's New Life in New York," *New York*, June 9, 1980.

44 Black, *A Life in Full*, 1027.

45 Kaufman, *Post-Presidency*, 421.

46 Richard Nixon, quoted in Ralph Summy, Michael E. Salla, and David Lange, eds., *Why the Cold War Ended: A Range of Interpretations* (Westport, CT: Greenwood, 1995), 124.

47 Kaufman, *Post-Presidency*, 416.

48 *New York Review of Books*, quoted in Robert Tucker, "Nixon's Nip at Reagan," *New York Times*, January 29, 1986, http://www.nytimes.com/books/98/06/14/specials/nixon-real.html.

49 Stephen Rosenfeld, "Richard Nixon: Saving the World," *Washington Post*, January 22, 1984.

50 George McGovern, quoted in Jonathan Alter and John J. Lindsay, "Nixon: The Long Climb Back," *Newsweek*, February 20, 1984.

51 Ibid.

52 Mary McGrory, "Deft Nixon Performance Shows Intelligence Was Never the Issue," *Washington Post*, May 10, 1984.

53 Richard Nixon, quoted in Jonathan Friendly, "Nixon Wins Applause from Newspaper Editors," *New York Times*, May 10, 1984, http://www.nytimes.com/1984/05/10/us/nixon-wins-applause-from-newspaper-editors.html.

54 Howard Fineman, "Nixon: the Comeback Kid," *New York Times*, October 18, 1985.

55 Morris Udall and Richard Nixon, quoted in David M. Alpern and John J. Lindsay, "Nixon in Prime Time," *Newsweek*, April 16, 1984.

56 Mark Hatfield, quoted in Ibid.

57 John Herbers, "After Decade, Nixon Is Gaining Favor," *New York Times*, August 5, 1984, http://www.nytimes.com/1984/08/05/us/after-decade-nixon-is-gaining-favor.html?pagewanted=all.

58 Robert G. Kaiser, "Comeback; What Power Does He Hold over Us?," *Washington Post*, August 5, 1984.

59 Stephen Ambrose, quoted in Sidney Blumenthal, "The Prime Republican," *New York Times*, November 24, 1991, http://www.nytimes.com/books/98/11/22/specials/ambrose-nixon3.html.

60 *Newsweek*, quoted in Martz, DeFrank, and Fineman, "The Road Back."

61 Ronald Reagan, quoted in "Reagan, Nixon Conferred on Summit Talks," *Los Angeles Times*, September 16, 1985, http://articles.latimes.com/1985-09-16/news/mn-21950_1_summit-meeting.

62 Beichman, "Richard Nixon."

63 Ronald Reagan, quoted in "Dick & Ronnie & God & Gorby," *Vanity Fair*, February 2009, http://www.vanityfair.com/politics/features/2009/02/reagan-excerpt200902.

64 Richard Nixon, quoted in Ibid.

65 James Mann, quoted in Ibid.

66 Richard Nixon, quoted in Crowley, *Nixon off the Record*, 24.

67 Kaufman, *Post-Presidency*, 402.

68 Barbara Walters, "The Resurrection of Richard Nixon," *Nightline*, July 19, 1990.

69 Crowley, *Nixon off the Record*, 56.

70 Ibid., 231.

71 Richard Nixon, quoted in Ibid., 230.

72 Crowley, *Nixon in Winter*, 224.

73 Richard Nixon, quoted in Ibid., 224.

74 Richard Nixon, "Why?," *New York Times*, January 6, 1991, http://www.nytimes.com/ref/opinion/150pclassic.html?_r=0.

75 Richard Nixon, quoted in Crowley, *Nixon in Winter*, 235.

76 Richard Nixon, quoted in "Encore Presentation: Interview with Richard Nixon," CNN Web site, http://transcripts.cnn.com/TRANSCRIPTS/0506/05/lkl.01.html.

77 Richard Nixon, quoted in Crowley, *Nixon in Winter*, 174.

78 Richard Nixon, quoted in Martin Walker, "Elder Statesmen Gain Wealth of Experience," *Guardian*, March 16, 1992.

79 Ibid.

80 Clinton, "Funeral Service for President Richard Nixon."

81 Henry A. Kissinger, "Eulogy for Richard M. Nixon," Henry A. Kissinger Web site, April 27, 1994, http://www.henryakissinger.com/eulogies/042794.html.

82 Dole, quoted in "Senator Bob Dole's Comments."

83 Crowley, *Nixon off the Record*, 219–20.

84 Carl Bernstein, quoted in "Bernstein on Nixon: He Came Back from the Dead," UPI, July 23, 1986, http://www.upi.com/Archives/1980-1989/text/1986/07/23/Bernstein-on-Nixon-He-came-back-from-the-dead/9032522475200/.

85 Christopher Beam, "Mr. Ex-President," *Slate*, January 15, 2009, http://www.slate.com/articles/news_and_politics/politics/2009/01/mr_expresident.html.

86 Richard Nixon, quoted in Stephen E. Ambrose, "Why We Should Rue the Day Richard Nixon Resigned the Presidency," *Los Angeles Times*, November 24, 1991, http://articles.latimes.com/1991-11-24/opinion/op-94_1_day-richard-nixon.

87 Kaufman, *Post-Presidency*, 429.

88 Richard Nixon, quoted in Jonathan Aitken, "Richard Nixon's Dark Side Has Obscured His Greatness," *Telegraph*, January 4, 2013, http://www.telegraph.co.uk/news/worldnews/us-politics/9780832/Richard-Nixons-dark-side-has-obscured-his-greatness.html.

89 Ibid.

Afterword: Nixon in 2016

1 Richard Nixon, "Address Accepting the Presidential Nomination at the Republican National Convention in Miami Beach, Florida" (speech, Miami Beach, August 8, 1968), Gerhard Peters and John T. Woolley, eds., American Presidency Project, http://www.presidency.ucsb.edu/ws/?pid=25968.

2 Dwight D. Eisenhower, "The President's News Conference" (news conference, Washington, DC, August 24, 1960), Gerhard Peters and John T. Woolley, eds., American Presidency Project, http://www.presidency.ucsb.edu/ws/?pid=11915.

Index